Nineteenth-Century Major Lives and Letters

Series Editor: Marilyn Gaull

This series presents original biographical, critical, and scholarly studies of literary works and public figures in Great Britain, North America, and continental Europe during the nineteenth century. The volumes in *Nineteenth-Century Major Lives and Letters* evoke the energies, achievements, contributions, cultural traditions, and individuals who reflected and generated them during the Romantic and Victorian period. The topics: critical, textual, and historical scholarship, literary and book history, biography, cultural and comparative studies, critical theory, art, architecture, science, politics, religion, music, language, philosophy, aesthetics, law, publication, translation, domestic and public life, popular culture, and anything that influenced, impinges upon, expresses or contributes to an understanding of the authors, works, and events of the nineteenth century. The authors consist of political figures, artists, scientists, and cultural icons including William Blake, Thomas Hardy, Charles Darwin, William Wordsworth, William Butler Yeats, Samuel Taylor, and their contemporaries.

The series editor is Marilyn Gaull, PhD (Indiana University), FEA. She has taught at William and Mary, Temple University, New York University, and is Research Professor at the Editorial Institute at Boston University. She is the founder and editor of *The Wordsworth Circle* and the author of *English Romanticism: The Human Context*, and editions, essays, and reviews in journals. She lectures internationally on British Romanticism, folklore, and narrative theory, intellectual history, publishing procedures, and history of science.

PUBLISHED BY PALGRAVE:

Shelley's German Afterlives, by Susanne Schmid
Coleridge, the Bible, and Religion, by Jeffrey W. Barbeau
Romantic Literature, Race, and Colonial Encounter, by Peter J. Kitson
Byron, edited by Cheryl A. Wilson
Romantic Migrations, by Michael Wiley
The Long and Winding Road from Blake to the Beatles, by Matthew Schneider
British Periodicals and Romantic Identity, by Mark Schoenfield
Women Writers and Nineteenth-Century Medievalism, by Clare Broome Saunders
British Victorian Women's Periodicals, by Kathryn Ledbetter
Romantic Diasporas, by Toby R. Benis
Romantic Literary Families, by Scott Krawczyk
Victorian Christmas in Print, by Tara Moore
Culinary Aesthetics and Practices in Nineteenth-Century American Literature, edited by Monika Elbert and Marie Drews
Reading Popular Culture in Victorian Print, by Alberto Gabriele
Romanticism and the Object, edited by Larry H. Peer
Poetics en passant, by Anne Jamison
From Song to Print, by Terence Hoagwood
Gothic Romanticism, by Tom Duggett
Victorian Medicine and Social Reform, by Louise Penner
Populism, Gender, and Sympathy in the Romantic Novel, by James P. Carson
Byron and the Rhetoric of Italian Nationalism, by Arnold A. Schmidt
Poetry and Public Discourse in Nineteenth-Century America, by Shira Wolosky
The Discourses of Food in Nineteenth-Century British Fiction, by Annette Cozzi
Romanticism and Pleasure, edited by Thomas H. Schmid and Michelle Faubert

Royal Romances, by Kristin Flieger Samuelian
Trauma, Transcendence, and Trust, by Thomas J. Brennan, S.J.
The Business of Literary Circles in Nineteenth-Century America, by David Dowling
Popular Medievalism in Romantic-Era Britain, by Clare A. Simmons

FORTHCOMING TITLES:

Beyond Romantic Ecocriticism, by Ashton Nichols
The Poetry of Mary Robinson, by Daniel Robinson
Romanticism and the City, by Larry H. Peer
Coleridge and the Daemonic Imagination, by Gregory Leadbetter
Romantic Dharma, by Mark Lussier
Regions of Sara Coleridge's Thought, by Peter Swaab

THE BUSINESS OF LITERARY CIRCLES IN NINETEENTH-CENTURY AMERICA

David Dowling

THE BUSINESS OF LITERARY CIRCLES IN NINETEENTH-CENTURY AMERICA
Copyright © David Dowling, 2011.

All rights reserved.

First published in 2011 by
PALGRAVE MACMILLAN®
in the United States—a division of St. Martin's Press LLC,
175 Fifth Avenue, New York, NY 10010.

Where this book is distributed in the UK, Europe and the rest of the world, this is by Palgrave Macmillan, a division of Macmillan Publishers Limited, registered in England, company number 785998, of Houndmills, Basingstoke, Hampshire RG21 6XS.

Palgrave Macmillan is the global academic imprint of the above companies and has companies and representatives throughout the world.

Palgrave® and Macmillan® are registered trademarks in the United States, the United Kingdom, Europe and other countries.

ISBN: 978-0-230-11046-5

Library of Congress Cataloging-in-Publication Data

Dowling, David Oakey, 1967–
    The business of literary circles in nineteenth-century America / David Dowling.
      p. cm.
    ISBN 978-0-230-11046-5
     1. American literature—19th century—History and criticism. 2. Authorship—Social aspects—United States—History—19th century. 3. Authorship—Economic aspects—United States—History—19th century. 4. Authors and publishers—United States—History—19th century. 5. Authors, American—19th century—Economic conditions. 6. Literature and society—United States—History—19th century. I. Title.

PS201.D688 2011
810.9′003—dc22   2010030068

A catalogue record of the book is available from the British Library.

Design by Newgen Imaging Systems (P) Ltd., Chennai, India.

First edition: February 2011

10 9 8 7 6 5 4 3 2 1

Printed in the United States of America.

Contents

Acknowledgments vii

Introduction 1

1 "As Merchants on the 'Change": The Economy of Literary Circles, 1807–1864 15

Part I Literary New Yorkers

2 "An Instinct for Gold": Irving's Knickerbockers 33

3 Staff Bonds: Bonner's *New York Ledger* 61

Part II New England Circles

4 "The Section to Which We Belong": Emerson's Transcendentalists 91

5 Boston and Beyond: Elizabeth Peabody's Promotional Practice 117

Part III Political Economy: North and South

6 Print Warriors: Garrison's Abolitionists 147

7 Proslavery and the Pen: Fitzhugh's Apologists 173

Conclusion: The Boston Bellamy Club, Rand's Objectivists, and Iowa Writers' Workshop 203

Notes 229

Index 289

Acknowledgments

My most immediate debts for this book are to the New York Public Library's Isaac Gewirtz and his helpful staff at the Henry W. and Albert A. Berg Collection of English and American Literature. The staff embraced the spirit of my research on the New England Circles and offered imaginative suggestions for making full use of the archive. Thomas Lannon of NYPL's Manuscripts and Archives Division furnished me with the very best of the library's holdings on Washington Irving's circle and the Robert Bonner Papers, treasure troves that included correspondence, business documents, love letters, and high stakes financial transactions. The Bonner Papers constitute a meticulous record of the literary business of the *New York Ledger* staff, and I am deeply grateful for the expert organization of this vast and revealing material. The concluding chapter of this book owes much to University Archivist, David McCartney, and Curator of Rare Books, David Schoonover in Special Collections at the University of Iowa Library. I particularly benefitted from rich conversations with David McCartney who generously shared his thorough and nuanced knowledge of the history of the Iowa Writers' Workshop and the legacy of Paul Engle, the director who brought this fledgling program into the limelight of the postwar literary market. David McCartney made navigating thirty-five boxes of virtually every known document associated with Engle's life not only manageable, but truly a pleasurable and exciting journey into the literary business of the world's most powerful writing program. Another source of insight for this book was Iowa colleague and fellow literary market scholar, Loren Glass. Our discussions on the ideological and financial significance of the literary intermediary were invaluable. Among other Iowa colleagues, Kathleen Diffley was always encouraging—my emphasis on nineteenth-century periodicals in this book owes much to her—along with Priya Kumar and Phil Round, whose collegiality continues to be a source of inspiration. I would like to thank the Department of English at the University of Iowa for endorsing this book and providing funds in support of the research undertaken. Iowa English is a prestigious literary circle unto itself that I am privileged to be a part of. Beyond these immediate debts I owe thanks to literary theorist David Simpson, who a long time ago in a graduate seminar in the shadows of the Colorado Front Range exhorted his listeners, myself among them, to never fear "thinking big." The expansive vision of this book traces back to his inspiring words.

Finally, Brigitte Shull, my editor, believed in this book unwaveringly from our first contact; her professionalism, trust, and total commitment have meant the world to me. My wife, Caroline Tolbert, and children, Jacqueline, Eveline, and Edward enabled me to realize the dream of this ambitious literary history with their love and support; their vitality is the light behind the words in the work.

INTRODUCTION

At one point in J.D. Salinger's *The Catcher in the Rye* (1949), narrator Holden Caulfield fixes his standard for judging literary quality. A novel passes his test if, upon finish reading it, he is overcome with the urge to have an intimate conversation with the author. "What really knocks me out is a book that, when you're all done reading it, you wish the author that wrote it was a terrific friend of yours and you could call him up on the phone whenever you felt like it," the disaffected youth says, sadly realizing that this "doesn't happen much, though."[1] Professional authors, Holden laments, are rarely accessible on such a personal level given the highly mediated modern literary marketplace, and its careful packaging of writers into brand names and their works into literary products.[2] Even if Holden had broken through his paralyzing self-consciousness to "call old Thomas Hardy up" (although the author had already been dead for twenty years), the gauze of fame and commercial culture's rituals of isolated consumption would have conspired to separate these like-minded literary souls from one another.[3] A century earlier, John S. Hart's *The Female Prose Writers of America* (1852) measured the worth of its authors by virtually the same standard, noting that "It seems to be an instinctive desire of the human heart, on becoming acquainted with any work of genius, to know something of its author," not out of "mere idle curiosity," but an acute response, like Holden's, to "the unmistakable impress of personal sympathy" on every page.[4] Such a desire for the embodied author is an admirable instinct that pays "homage," according to Hart, to "whatever is right and good" in their work and, given the inaccessibility of the literary celebrity, has encouraged readers to seek out biographies and one another's company as outlets for their passion.[5] The history of literary circles, the subject of this book, tells the story of such compassionate reaching out among authors who were first mutually admiring readers.

The warmth and excitement drawing authors and readers together, fueled as much by enterprise as imagination, has been obscured by two common critical stigmas associated with the concept of coterie authorship. Coteries are often linked to an overly particular, even antidemocratic sense of audience isolated from, and presumably sneering disdainfully at, a mass readership; likewise, coterie studies are assumed to indulge narrow fanatic biographical fascination. Although the major literary circles of the nineteenth-century United States may have shown signs of such self-serving insularity, they were nonetheless commercially engaged, and profoundly interested in gaining a broader audience, creatures of market culture talking back to their economic condition as much as they were actively seeking out ways to change it in order to realize a profit. Coteries, however apparently private, were thus public affairs, themselves mechanisms of literary production crucially linked to the publishing industry, often bearing a protocorporate demeanor and function, in which authors wrote to and for each other as much as they did for a mass public audience. Lytle Shaw, in a comment on twentieth-century New York poetry circles, argues that "by dramatizing both characters and cultural references operating, frequently, below 'public' radar"—as seen in such insider references as Thoreau's anonymous attack of Emerson's style of hospitality in the "Conclusion" of *Walden*, or the veiled dialogue and inside jokes between Hawthorne and Melville[6] in *Moby-Dick* (1851)—authors "could enter into a paradoxically public social discourse from a position often misunderstood as private."[7]

This book explores the commercial dimensions of that private/public social discourse, especially the economies of collaboration (for both social and economic capital building, which I discuss later) animating each literary circle's method of promoting the individual authors' careers in the free market. Like companies that were openly striving to differentiate themselves from others in the market, coteries, I argue, made every effort to assemble a unique collective identity to distinguish themselves from, and often in direct opposition to, others in the literary market. This did not prevent collaboration across coteries, but indeed encouraged it, as those who sought out publishing connections and literary innovations outside their circle, such as Emerson's efforts to draw Carlyle into the Transcendentalist circle, stood to profit handsomely, both in a literary sense of cross-fertilizing ideas, and a purely financial one. Of course, authors were not employees of their coteries, but nonetheless stood to benefit directly from their association with the circle much in the way workers enjoy privilege and status based on affiliation with powerful and prestigious companies. Ambitious authors impressed their individual stamp on that group identity, just as any key figure in a corporation would, to distinguish themselves from competitors writing in similar genres outside of the coterie.

This book deals with the inner workings of six of America's most important nineteenth-century circles, and how they helped build their writers' careers through counsel and collaboration within their ranks, as well as promote and publicize those careers in broader markets for literature. "Coterie," according to Shaw's formulation that frames my study, "in these models of association, is as much an idea about the social possibilities of affinity as it is a concrete sociological fact."[8] I extend this view to seek out the various models of coterie as reflecting ideas about social and commercial possibility within the capitalist context of the antebellum market revolution. Facing the impending threat of a potentially ruthless and dehumanizing capitalist ethos, coteries formed and functioned according to the principles they espoused about one of the most pressing concerns of the day—how economic changes were altering the ethical fabric of daily life—in some cases launching socialistic alternatives in the form of collectivist ideals about cooperative living, in obvious circles like the Transcendentalist, but also in such unlikely places as the benevolent paternalism of the proslavery Southern authors.[9] Coteries thus became both marketing vehicles and clearing houses for market critiques, often exposing the limitations of individualism and corrosive symptoms of the surging entrepreneurial economy while also championing the admirable qualities of the business world, which even a skeptic like Thoreau found irresistibly "alert, adventurous, unwearied."[10]

America's most distinctive literary circles transacted business in informal, yet ritualized and codified, methods of building social capital involving sharing both financial resources and professional support through guidance, inspiration, and collaboration. This book picks up where the other "circle books" have left off by bridging the aesthetic and personal dynamics of those groups to their engagement with the broader market for literature.[11] How did they promote themselves? Were there internal rivalries that had financial results? Was the tenor of each coterie communal or competitive? What were the political and aesthetic ramifications of the organizational model—from elite salon to gritty social reform think tank to commune—toward which each circle aspired? Were the social dynamics effectively or ineffectively tied to the market to bring the group notoriety, fame, and fortune? What moves—key executive business decisions with economic consequences—were vital to the coterie's survival or demise, and what ethos drove that business practice? What was the correlation between the shape of the individual author's career and that of their coterie's lifespan or history? Were authors who pushed the ideological boundaries of each circle, as Cornelius Matthews had done for Young America and Henry Thoreau for the Transcendentalists, just as vital to the status of their coteries as their ostensible figureheads and leaders? How was the coterie used as a method of political entrenchment as ideological chasms widened especially for the South? This book elaborates on my concern for patronage (begun in *Capital Letters: Authorship in the Antebellum Literary Market* [2009], and continued into other research on literary partnerships of the era), an underappreciated category in American literature, as a crucial mitigating factor of literary collaboration. It is largely underdiscussed because of the persistence of the myth of the autonomous romantic author, a notion dispelled by theorists, but whose alternative of self-promotion through the intermediary channels of the literary marketplace is rarely pursued at a thorough level except by a few, Cindy Weinstein and Leon Jackson among the most noteworthy. Trish Loughran's *The Republic in Print* (2007) posits that many local reading publics were plural, fragmented, scattered, and diffuse with uneven and sporadic distribution patterns, exposing the lack of a singular reading "public" handed down from triumphalist histories that have characterized knowledge of nation-building works like *Common Sense* as virtually universal.[12] By focusing on literary circles from an economic perspective, I extend this current research on the literary market into new territory on the social history of authorship. My aim is to expose how those circles were a curious mix of self-promotional free market capitalism and collaborative mutual aid with a socialistic bent borne out not only in their business practice, but also as major rhetorical topes that informed their writings. This introduction provides an overview of such complex, often paradoxical, positions literary coteries took with respect to the market, beginning with a socialized perspective on authorship through literary coterie formation and function as a locus of intermediary activity mitigating the process of literary production and reception.

A flurry of literary associations of creative writers, philosophers, and reformers from New York to Concord and south to New Orleans gathered during the formative stages of the commercialization of literature in America from 1807 through the Civil War as much out of a desire to forge sympathetic literary interests into personalized intimate bonds as to gain the professional advantages that accrue from the free exchange of trade secrets. Groups ranged from what Hawthorne called the "knot of dreamers" at Brook Farm, an early 1840s experiment in agrarian communal living by mainly philosophers, poets, and artists according to the principles of radical French socialist thinker Charles Fourier, to the close-knit serial fiction writing staff of America's best selling weekly magazine, the *New York Ledger*.[13] An improbable profession in the first half of the nineteenth-century United States, authorship was a tremendous risk if undertaken in the market alone and thus, like the Brook Farmers, writers "sought [their] profit by mutual aid."[14] It was thus no accident that intellectual coteries of all sorts suddenly emerged at this time, ranging from those codified in constitutional, legalistic language with bylaws and amendments, such as Brook Farm's sixteen "Articles of Agreement" (complete with a preamble, "We the undersigned do unite in a voluntary Association"), to informal literary circles and clubs, some new and others derivative of older groups.[15]

The antebellum market revolution that transformed literature into a trade not only encouraged the formation of such associations, but also gave rise to evermore specialization and its attendant credentialing, both formal and otherwise, heralding an era characterized by newly minted fields of intellectual expertise amid the burgeoning subdivisions of classified skills across the professions in the broader market. These networks gravitated together in such a way that anticipated labor unions' protection of individuals from financial vulnerability amid intensifying market competition by vesting them with special authority through the group's identity.[16] The belief took hold that cooperative effort held the potential to be more productive and efficient than individual ventures, articulating a faith in the efficacy of common enterprise. Angelina Grimke, the women's suffrage advocate from South Carolina, saw the power of associationism, proclaiming, "all Nature reads us an instructive lesson on the power of combination. In every object we behold we see the beauty of utility of this all pervading principle."[17] Holding such high currency in the culture as an approach to the spread of the professions that warned of the limitations of individualism as much as touting the utility and beauty of collectivism, the cultural condition abetted the formation of literary circles. Like other trade organizations, literary circles were not only protective or defensive measures against an increasingly hostile economic climate, but also constituted a way of establishing a literary brand name and thus became a potent means of marketing and promotion. The larger movement toward professionalism and specialization of which literary coterie formation was a part may have begun as a "withdrawal from an 'open' marketplace of services and ideas," as Melville scholar John Evelev asserts, "but was designed inevitably to return to that marketplace from a new position of authority."[18]

This book explores each circle's efforts to establish that new authority and promote it in the publishing industry through both the literature itself and its unique method of engaging the literary market.

The explosion of professional societies in antebellum America was part of a broader "wave of association" that included reading groups, book clubs, and conversation circles, consisting of both professionals and dilettantes for whom literature was not necessarily the primary vocation or means of financial support.[19] However avocational or part-time writing may have been for the vast majority of authors during the antebellum era—Emerson and Irving, for example, would respectively come to authorship from the ministry and the law—the desire to publish and become commercially engaged with the literary market still profoundly shaped their writings and dealings within their respective circles. The association movement appealed to Nathaniel Hawthorne, as he would join the ranks of Brook Farm; it also captured the imaginations of Herman Melville and Mark Twain, who would immortalize the ritual of the binding oath, a kind of solidarity against the world, on both the quarter deck of the *Pequod* in *Moby-Dick* and in the exchange of blood for eternal brotherhood between Huck Finn and Tom Sawyer. The irony Miles Coverdale, Hawthorne's professional poet and narrator of *The Blithedale Romance* (1852), finds irreconcilable and damningly hypocritical to their mission is their interest in at once separating from "the weary treadmill of the established system" within its "greedy, struggling, self-seeking world" and seeking "the possibility of getting the advantage over the outside barbarians in their own field of labor."[20] Instead of seeing these contradictions as irreconcilable, I find the formation of coteries based on "familial love" replacing "pride and selfish competition," the capital building within the literary coteries, not so much at odds with, but a natural extension of, the group's desire to do competition in the larger marketplace. Indeed, one gesture of precisely that "familial love" for the close friends within the literary circle was to advance successfully and profitably its name in the marketplace, thereby amassing sufficient capital to perpetuate its mission and enjoy "the privilege of going on," as nineteenth-century American author Lucy Larcom described it.[21] Brook Farm's endurance depended less on the fortitude of its philosophical principle than it did on its capacity to profit from its farming; finances would also cut short the best aesthetic intentions of many group artistic enterprises throughout the nineteenth century. All literary circles discussed in this book, even the most seemingly anticommercial of them, sought out audiences, and interfaced with the bourgeoning publishing network at the time, engaging its proliferating legions of intermediaries, and their diverse functions as agents, editors, publishers, and promoters to serve the professionalization of authorship.[22]

Enter the Intermediary

Retrieving authorship from the isolated romantic artist figure, the solitary creative sufferings made famous by Byron and by Goethe's young Werther, and placing it in a social context answers to Holden's anguish at being caught in a kind of middleground between product and producer, a predicament reflective of the increasing isolation of readers from writers brought upon by the privately consumed literary product that ironically inspires human connection without embodying it.[23] Those intermediaries would become the core of so many of the longest lasting and successful literary circles of the nineteenth century. Publishers, not writers, would provide the glue that held together Young America, and the *New York Ledger* circle, for example. In other cases, authors would play the role of primary financial underwriter and promoter, as in the case of Emerson. Editor/publishers like Bonner and Duyckinck linked themselves as much to the business world as to the literary, making their life's work the promotion of their writers in such a fully dedicated way that they certainly lived "for" literature as much as they lived "off of" it. Duyckinck's massive *Cyclopedia of American Literature* (1855), a two-volume tome over a thousand pages, was his love letter to the profession, a chronicling of the authors of his time commonly underestimated in terms of its inclusiveness of the commercial.[24]

A major contention of this book is that such literary intermediaries who profoundly shaped the fate of a work in the market were often members of, or closely connected to, its author's own literary circle, making the process of marketing success follow an associational chain in which, in Pierre Bourdieu's words, "personal judgments...are always collective judgments in the sense of position-takings referring to other position-takings through the intermediary of the objective relations between the positions of their authors within the field."[25] Such intermediaries mitigated the production and destruction of fame as Leon Jackson has beautifully described in his tracing of the rise and fall of Thomas Carlyle within the transcendental circle. Emerson's aggressive, even manic, circulation of *Sartor Resartus* fanned the flames of Carlyle's fame, transforming him into an honored and emulated charter member of the Concord clique with a celerity matched only by the haste with which the Scot's racist comments on the eve of the Civil War abruptly turned him out in the cold.[26] Carlyle's drastic decline in status and effective expulsion from the Transcendentalist circle illustrates precisely how "the degree of recognition and consecration" might depend on the way in which "the entire structure of the field interposes itself between producers and their work."[27]

In Hart we see literary biography in an unlikely cluster of female writers, yet one that also indulges and realizes, however manufactured to meet the expectations of conventional antebellum gender ideology, the potential for the author in association. Collective biography, the main project of this book, has been defined as a form of prosopography by Lawrence Stone in 1971 as "the investigation of the common background characteristics of a group of actors in history by means of a collective study of their lives."[28] Holden's example points to a process that had begun in America over a century earlier, in which readers formed groups and associations based on mutual interests as readily as writers. Similarly, authors who may have appeared to toil in isolation were thoroughly socialized by the mid-twentieth century into an increasingly corporate literary market mitigated by a wide array of diverse and thriving literary coteries. The origins of those literary circles, the most recognizable coteries of nineteenth-century America, and a few others either lost to history, or whose group status is often overlooked, like Robert Bonner's *New York Ledger* authors, share space in this book because of their unique socioliterary attitudes toward this key phase in the development of capitalism.

As the clustering or listing of authors for the purposes of commemoration or group biography, prosopography brings a decidedly socialized perspective on authorship, an inclination visible in the yearning for a humanized author behind the literary commodity. Viewing authors in groups, especially as members of the circles in which they moved, dismantles the myth of writing as a solitary feverish race devoid of camaraderie or aid in a free market that pitted authors against each other. Yet prosopography, as Alison Booth has noted in her unearthing of nineteenth-century women's group biographies, is subject to the fabrication of a unified character and group identity where there was none, a kind of misleading "Who Is Not Who," like any narrative, that will never finally fix and define its subject "through the published equivalents of the team photo."[29] On the one hand, a circle like the Transcendentalists was really no circle at all, no coherent identity of like-minded authors, but rather one that united to differ. But on the other, its members clearly clung to their contacts, poured over each other's writings, and tracked one another's progress, reflecting the importance of the literary circle, if not as bearing a singular recognizable face, as a locus of social activity for the promotion of individual authors in print culture.

The history of American literary circles exposes the networks through which authors moved, and how each writer's currency as they circulated throughout the literary market was largely attributable to their coterie affiliation. As the market revolution transformed authorship into a competitive industry in the early nineteenth-century in the United States,[30] writers gravitated toward each other for support in response to "the values of economy" that would otherwise promote their individualistic pursuit of their trade, the kind of individualism Bourdieu defines as "a self-fulfilling prophecy which tends to destroy the philosophical foundations of...collective responsibility (toward industrial accidents, sickness or poverty) which has been a fundamental achievement of social thought."[31] Bourdieu's comments on the present day are applicable to the antebellum U.S. literary market transformation and authors' responses toward collectivization: "The reign of 'commerce' and the 'commercial' bears down more strongly every day on literature, particularly through the concentration of publishing, which is more and more subject to the constraints of immediate profit," he writes, lamenting, not unlike Melville's excoriation of his own literary circle in *Pierre* (1852) in the chapter, "Young America in Literature." Bourdieu goes further, asserting that the profit motive's pervasiveness meant literature "has been handed over to the most opportunistic servants of the publishers—or of their accomplices, with favor traded to favor."[32] However vitriolic this view of the injustices of literary business practice is, the effects are not always crippling, but rather, have inspired cohesiveness, collectivization, and thus cross-fertilizing creativity not only for survival in the market, but also as a method of reimagining how one might engage it, and succeed in it professionally.

THE BUSINESS OF LITERARY CIRCLES

A sense of family drove coterie formation, as it often articulated the defense of a way of life, a battle for legitimacy of the code of ethics governing that lifestyle and attitude toward the world, whether flip and noncommittal like the Knickerbockers, earnestly nationalistic like Young America, staunchly nonconformist like the Transcendentalists, purportedly paternalistic and nurturing like Fitzhugh's Southern Clan, or militant in its egalitarianism like Garrison's abolitionists to the North. These circles reconceived the notion of authorship through a group identity they were proud to represent in their own works, in some cases competing for a leadership role of the coterie by establishing one of its signature voices. We often hear of Hemingway and the Lost Generation, or Ginsberg and the Beat Generation, for example. But careers ebbed and flowed depending on the kind of relationships developed within the literary circles, the collaborations, the key moments of advocacy, so crucial to authorial progress. During the life-span of the coteries I investigate, each member's career was in flux, rising and falling with respect to those of their colleagues, some responding to inspiring works of their cohort, others turning away from its aesthetic or political patterns of growth. Thoreau would find profound inspiration for *A Week on the Concord and Merrimack Rivers*, for example, in Fuller's *A Summer on the Lakes*, while Melville would deviate from the strident nationalism of Young America throughout the 1850s. Irving's cluster of bachelors would spin off a dizzying array of *The Sketch Book* variations, proving their admiration for him though such literary emulation. On the other hand, it was clear that some coteries functioned on the knowledge that certain genres or styles were not to be meddled with since other members had taken those reigns; Thoreau's early tutelage under Emerson had him mimicking the Concord bard's writing as well as his hairstyle and dress, until growing into his own authorial identity, urged in part by Emerson's fruitless attempts at nurturing him into a poet, an affair so protracted and torturous that Emerson ultimately ordered the young Thoreau to burn all his verses. Thoreau would never seriously write poetry again, nor would any other Transcendentalist for that matter.

The organizing principle behind the chapters in this book is that internal relationships among authors impacted the external linking opportunities they sought in the broader market. The six literary coteries I discuss, and their various branches, divide this book into three sections by region. Part I provides an economic history of coterie formation and the role of the literary intermediary in its first chapter and then focuses on the New York scene in the second, which traces the Knickerbocker circle from its origins with the Lads of Kilkenny, especially Washington and William Irving and James Kirk Paulding, the founders of *Salmagundi*, to its later generation of Young America. I have chosen to discuss another New York group of writers not commonly observed as a whole, for they were mainly considered a cluster of employees for Robert Bonner's *New York Ledger*. The core of his staff, however, shared long careers with Bonner, and operated under similar conditions, publishing writings that often inspired and responded to each other. The *Ledger* circle shows how an ostensibly commercial enterprise like a popular weekly magazine took up many of the same concerns about money, particularly by way of critiques of various consumer and business practices and their attendant ethos, as their more literary counterparts at Duyckinck's salon at 20 Clinton Place. I argue that these coteries were not as internally, nor as externally, divided and hostile as Perry Miller and others have maintained (making Melville's branch of Young America arch enemies of the Irvingesque sentimentalists of Gaylord Taylor's Knickerbockers), but instead tended to circulate freely among each other with productive results. Part I, therefore, illustrates how a commercial circle like Bonner's mixed staff of men and women could share similar concerns for market developments as the seemingly alien knot of mostly bachelor authors of the literary Knickerbockers; the high-low art division, as a result, appears to be an artificial construct in this light, as both coteries tended to build social, cultural, and economic capital based on the same methods.

The Concord circles led by Ralph Waldo Emerson and Elizabeth Peabody make up Part II, which takes up this celebrated circle in two chapters to establish its complex and wide-reaching network. Emerson was the financial underwriter of much of the Transcendentalist enterprise operating out of Concord. Elizabeth Peabody's work as a promoter of young Transcendental talent, however, has been overlooked, as histories (until recently with Megan Marshall's *Peabody Sisters* [2005]) tend to focus instead on Hawthorne's exploits. Instead, I treat Hawthorne and his sister-in-law as the power center for promoting literary prestige beyond Concord and throughout associations they influenced. Peabody's leadership and promotional style will emerge differently from Emerson's, reflecting her unique outlook on the market revolution in contrast to Emerson's own market sensibility developed by way of his prodigious professional experience.

Part III casts the concept of the literary coterie in relatively new light, exploring the pre–Civil War propaganda machines from the North and South, specifically focusing on their use of the market as their ideological terrain for moral higher ground. Fitzhugh and the South would notoriously launch quasisocialist rants against the north, as well as carefully crafted sentimental tales of slavery's benevolent paternalism in directly response to Stowe's *Uncle Tom's Cabin*. Garrison at the North self-consciously crafted himself into a "figure of speech," as R. Jackson Wilson has it, a public persona shaping the identity of his circle's fierce abolitionist identity, to spur on his legions and strengthen his own propaganda machine, ironically, also basing its claims in economic terms sympathizing with the plight of oppressed labor, only directing it at the political depravity of Southern slavery.[33]

The concluding chapter bridges into the present by way of Gilded Age socialist Edward Bellamy's circle, hardcore capitalist Ayn Rand's Objectivist following, and Paul Engle's postwar Iowa Writers' Workshop. I have chosen these circles, rather than the more visible ones of Howells and the *Atlantic* circle that built literary realism after the Civil War, and the Beat Generation of the mid-twentieth century so inextricably bound to the counterculture and later protest movements of the 1960s, because of their economic significance. Bellamy and Rand's capacity to generate best-selling fiction out of economic philosophies diametrically opposed to each other sets into relief a sense of the diversity of positions on the market and their expressions within the social dynamic of their coteries. Bellamy advocates for a literary marketplace with no intermediaries, urging that "the people are solely the judges,"[34] and thus condemns factors that predetermine reception, like the manipulative use of sentiment in popular fiction Henry James complained of as a gross "meddling between the supply and demand of a commodity."[35] Worried that coteries would lead to internal and exclusive cliques complete with their own in-jokes and nomenclature, Bellamy wanted a literature for the people, and thus fully intelligible by the people. The resistance, therefore, is to a snobbish use of self-referential particularity that becomes clubbish or territorial, compartmentalizing and clustering the author as a reified object unproblematically into one coterie or another.[36]

Current research on literary coteries describes small intimate circles of known readers opposite the broader mass public in keeping with the notion "associated most frequently with British Renaissance writers and Anglo-American modernists, [that] the coterie author is one who self-consciously produces work for a small and selective audience," as Matthew Giordano notes in a study assessing Melville's narrowing of audience for his poetry as his career progressed.[37] Instead of coteries, per se, I employ the broader term, circles, that suggests engagement with the wider market of social capital building through bonding that might lead to bridging and thus increased profit potential. As such, I focus on the sociology of literary business at the level of the coterie in this book as transforming in function toward a more commercially sensitive responsiveness to the demands of the market than in the prior historical period of the early republic or another national context, as in the French salon system, in which artists and authors would visit weekly at the home of a wealthy aristocratic lady to discuss social, scientific, and aesthetic issues, providing a base for authors. The American system was instead a hybrid of privilege and professional exchange in which the informal friendship could easily be used as the social lubricant for the dissemination of one's work.

The prior generation of the 1790s, particularly the New York Friendly Club, had already shifted toward a more commercial orientation than its prior incarnation before the Revolutionary War. David S. Shields' *Civil Tongues and Polite Letters in British America* (1997) helps explain how the commercialization of clubs grew out of the earlier "anthology" and "friendly" societies. He notes that after 1776, such "discursive institutions nurtured by belles letters [that] had survived the revolution" were forced to justify themselves according to the "republican critique," which found such gatherings frivolous vestiges of aristocracy and thus unproductive for nation-building in the spirit of democracy. Shields argues that such groups shut down because "the competitive ethos of the marketplace could not be escaped in a commercial setting."[38] Instead, as Stephen Shapiro argues in *The Culture and Commerce of the Early American Novel: Reading the Atlantic World-System* (2008), there was a distinct shift from the early gentrified clubs and those of the late eighteenth century. Shields effectively describes how "the ersatz gentry clubs fell away" but falsely assumes that they did not survive or adapt to the new increasingly commercial environment as Shapiro does. Indeed, the persistence of the New York Friendly Club well after the revolution into the increasingly commercial era of the 1790s anticipates the Knickerbockers of the early 1800s I discuss. Both groups signal precisely the shift Shapiro identifies in these clubs that adapted themselves to the competitive ethos of the marketplace rooted in an inescapable commercial setting because "its members were products and participants in the world of extramural commerce." This explains why the original Knickerbockers were ideally positioned to transform literature into a profession precisely when "clubbable discourse managed to survive only insofar as it became more formerly commercialized with links with bookstores" and, I would add, the lucrative periodical market, as the emergence of the *Knickerbocker Magazine*, and the appearance of Irving's associates in Bonner's *Ledger* attest.[39] Catherine Kaplan has also argued in *Men of Letters in the Early Republic: Cultivating Forms of Citizenship* (2008) that the Friendly Club represented a distinct move away from the earlier supposition that citizenship was essentially political to embrace a new conception of the realm of public men outside of politics. Combined with Shapiro's insight about club culture's adaptation to the commercial world, Kaplan's proof that new support for the civic significance of the literary life signals that the culture was primed for the professionalization of authorship.[40]

Hence an antimaterialistic bent in the literature could be wedded to the free market in fruitful ways, producing a kind of innovative critical capitalism that might nurture authors within a group identity and promote them under their name, not unlike how a family rears a child. "Capitalism requires love," as Deidre N. McCloskey writes in *The Bourgeois Virtues* (2006), reclaiming the more salvageable remnants of a middle-class ideology that has been thoroughly attacked and discarded for the greater part of the past millennium.[41] Assaults on coteries, however, are not habitually pitched at the bourgeoisie, but rather at the elites. At a closer look, most coteries were anything but financially secure, and as such, relied on a wide variety of mechanisms of promotion, brokering, and bartering, by which to sustain themselves, as the historical overview in the next chapter shows.

CHAPTER 1

"AS MERCHANTS ON THE 'CHANGE": THE ECONOMY OF LITERARY CIRCLES, 1807–1864

Why did Melville cling so tightly to his Knickerbocker roots and remain lifelong friends with Young America's central coordinator, Evert Duyckinck, even decades after publicly assaulting him in the pages of *Pierre*, his most bizarre and angry fictional fulmination against the literary market? Why would Thoreau, long after his personal falling out with Emerson, persistently identify himself as a Transcendentalist? One of the premises of this book is to revise the notion that these groups were factionalized and shared little, if any, common ground, which is a method of understanding antebellum U.S. literary coteries handed down by Perry Miller's *The Raven and the Whale* (1956). Although some loose definitions of "Knickerbocker" describe New York writers in general, I use the term specifically as it applies to Irving's original Lads of Kilkenny and its growth into later generations such as the Bread and Cheese Club, which scattered and coalesced into Evert Duyckinck's Young America. All these groups consciously acknowledged their legacy in Irving. The two major Knickerbocker circles were more cohesive and collaborative than Miller and others after him, such as Andrew Delbanco and Edward Widmer, have posited partially in pursuit of a more captivating historical narrative yarn. Delbanco characterizes Young America as opinionated confrontational, even crude, quintessential New Yorkers embodying a democratic and politically engaged "scrappy, streetfighter style" opposite the Whiggish "soft focus" Knickerbocker circle of sentimentalists "nostalgic for a bygone era when people knew to which class they belonged, [who] described a softer, gentler world that existed, of course, mainly in their imaginations, and who wrote with fairy tale charm."[1] The Knickerbockers, according to this definition, were effete snobs, more jingle writers than poets producing such plums as John Howard Payne's laughably saccharine sentimental pap, "Woodman Spare that Tree!" ("Touch not a single bough! / In my youth it sheltered me /And I'll protect it now").[2] But the Knickerbockers were not afraid of the dark, as much of N.P. Willis's poetry illustrates, especially his moody and melancholy ruminations on the ravages of fame on private life such as the one in his 1848 narrative poem, "The Wife's Appeal." Further, Miller's *Raven and the Whale*, while a defining and pioneering literary historical narrative of New York literary circles nonetheless would make it appear that the only categories of authorship at the time might be defined by these two circles, which he forces into opposite camps thus obscuring their considerable overlap and mutual exchange of literary ideas and business leads, which were often one and the same.

The tendency to limit discussion to the Knickerbockers and Young America leaves out a wide range of orientations toward the literary vocation beyond these two camps. A relocated Transcendentalist like Margaret Fuller, for example, was the colleague of pulpy urban sensationalist George Foster, as their radically diverse authorial identities were housed under the single roof of Horace Greeley's *Tribune*. My aim in Part I (the following two chapters) is to show how New York could have accommodated such dissimilar groups, who nonetheless made contact through gatherings such as Anne Lynch's parties that played host to some of the broadest cross-sections of literati in the city's history. At such parties, authors appeared not as solo entrepreneurs, but as coterie affiliates out to connect with members of distant literary circles, in part, through the novelty of their circle's distinction.

Authors from different literary circles did not want to alienate each other; on the contrary, most were in dialogue with each other the way competing companies with similar products and overlapping consumers often straddle the line between collaboration and competition, colored by mutual respect, as between literary teams in the race for readers. An immediate exception would be Robert Bonner's advertising tactics and stentorian displays of economic dominance over rival magazines—blacking out on one occasion a full edition of a competing periodical by purchasing all its advertising space and firing canons on another in a chest-thumping celebration for achieving the widest circulation in the nation—at the far extreme end of the continuum of hostile opposition. Even the war of words over slavery was fought out in the rhetorical debate over the morality, or lack thereof, in Northern versus Southern markets, both decrying savage avarice as the root of their opponent's evil. Antimarket rhetorical tropes often shared essentials of form and function across literary circles with slight variations made to seem larger than they were, a common tactic of commercial advertising designed to establish product differentiation. Authors across the coteries banded together as renegade romantics, yet carefully displaying their unique posture toward the market, deliberately rebelling against the perceived lifestyle of steady labor and material reward for a free-spirited claim on the liberated artist's life.

Social and Economic Capital

Guests at the Lynch soirees represented virtually all classifications of authorship at the time, of varying degrees of professionalism, popular appeal, and literary prestige. They were not so much a marketplace for the wealthy and politically powerful to survey and select artistic talent whom they would like to patronize, as in the European salons, but rather, a place for the free exchange of ideas and interests among authors and artists of all stripes. A key difference from many European salons at which conversation was constrained by the interests, particularly the political views, of the patrons present, lay in the free nature of the gatherings. Catharine Maria Sedgwick observed that "Not in the world, with the exception of the United States, could a beautiful young woman take the responsibility unmatronized of such a 'reception,'" notable for its unpretentious air.[3] Its economic dimension, I would add to Sedgwick's astute observation, was pure Americana, for this was a marketplace of ideas featuring literary capitalism on a playing field that never was level, but always steeped in cross-currents of commercial and artistic prestige, in place of old world patronage. Guests knew this to be an opportunity to elevate their craft and thus raise the value of their works by accessing a rare intersection of the literary and art markets, and their attendant economies of exchange that always already was driven by status, both literary and commercial. Emma Embury, and the Cary sisters, as John Evelev reports, were hosts to such parties like the one at Lynch's on Valentine's Day in 1848 whose guest list represented a mix of editors like John Inman, members of the Young America circle, Evert Duyckinck and Cornelius Mathews, Knickerbockers William Cullen Bryant and Fitz-Greene Halleck, and even popular women novelists and reform writers Grace Greenwood, Caroline Kirkland, and Catharine Maria Sedgwick, and Lydia Maria Child.[4]

This crowd was far more diverse than the deceptive group portrait of the all-male authorial fraternity depicted in the 1864 painting, *Washington Irving and His Friends at Sunnyside*, which attempts to canonize New Englanders Emerson and Hawthorne harmoniously with Knickerbockers Irving, Cooper, Paulding, Halleck, and Simms. History suggests, however, that the social matrices of the antebellum literary market were never so homogenous or harmonious. Gatherings like Lynch's were ideal opportunities to build social, and eventually economic, capital through the free interchange of ideas for their writing as well as contacts for its publication and promotion.

It is important to consider that Margaret Fuller, though now a part of the New York scene as a writer for Greeley's *Tribune*, had her roots in Transcendentalism and that Child, by the time of Lynch's 1848 gathering, would have moved on by then from her former Garrison circle to edit the *National Anti-Slavery Standard*, and even was becoming increasingly estranged from the Transcendentalists. Lynch achieved insider status through her highly regarded 1841 miscellany, *The Rhode Island Book*, and later through her poetic contributions to *The Gift* (1845). Lynch had capitalized on her friendship with the influential Fanny Kemble to conscript the famed Asher B. Durand to illustrate her 1848 collection of poems, a work that reflects her considerable connections in literature, theater, and art.[5] As her network grew, her home increasingly became a place where "men and women of genius here meet, very much as merchants meet on 'Change, without ceremony, and for the exchange of thought...without eating or drinking, nothing in the shape of material refreshment being ever offered," a detail signaling professional collaboration, as captured in the analogy of the meetings to the New York Stock Exchange, instead of conventional entertainment of house guests.[6] Lynch's home became a place to do literary business across coteries, an informal opportunity for social capital building and exchange of information functioning, although on a larger more inclusive scale, in the manner of Bush (Emerson's Concord residence) as the epicenter for transcendental business, of Duyckinck's drawing room at 20 Clinton Place as the liar of Young America, and of the war room of Garrison's *The Liberator* on Boston's Park Church Street. A veritable "who's who" of the literary marketplace, Lynch's parlor became something of a bibliophile's dream to meet the artists and authors personally, realizing Holden's urge (and Salinger's by extension) for an embodied author behind his favorite books a century later.

It should be clear from the example of Lynch's gatherings that though individual coteries may have formed their own internal audiences and written for others (often the de facto leader) in their direct circle as exampled by Thoreau reading his manuscript of *A Week on the Concord and Merrimack Rivers* to Emerson from the cabin at Walden Pond, or E.D.E.N. Southworth immortalizing her editor, Robert Bonner, as the self-made Ishmael Worth in her serial fiction, they nonetheless hoped to engage those in other coteries. Reaching out to other circles, therefore, also brought with it an opportunity to promote works to a wider audience, making coterie culture not just an insulated cocoon for the like-minded, but, like Lynch's parties, a place where ideas are tried out on each other with an eye for its reception by the broader public. Herein the significance of "these weekly *reunions*," pointed toward a wider readership among even the most seemingly detached, romantic, and commercially disinclined literary circles. New York City profiler George Foster used such reunions as an occasion to brag about the wealth of Gotham's intellectual talent, noting that "during the Winter season there are three or four every week among the different literary coteries, [and] are a peculiarity of New York society, which has not been imitated elsewhere to any considerable extent, simply because the materials are wanting."[7] Indeed, such meetings likely would have occurred in other regions with more talent available, but what Foster's obvious barb at Boston hides is precisely how truly cosmopolitan the transcendental circle would become as it attracted Carlyle from overseas, and regularly initiated and utilized Boston and New York contacts. Indeed, Emerson himself would send Thoreau off to New York to stay with his brother while searching for publishers for his writings, an attempt that narrowly missed landing him precisely the sort of established and significant professional position that Margaret Fuller had with Horace Greeley's *Tribune*. Even the origin of the Transcendental Club speaks to the external outreach of the circle, as it originally began as a meeting with young rebellious and free thinking Unitarian minister Frederic Henry Hedge who visited from Bangor, Maine, for unfettered discourse with Emerson, George Ripley, and Emerson's cousin, George Putnam. They had originally called themselves "Hedge's Club," for the Maine resident's visits provided them with the occasion for their meetings, which grew into the "Transcendental Club" that directly shaped the daring and groundbreaking *Nature* (1836) by Emerson. Barbara Packer reminds us that this publication, along with the formation of the Transcendental Club, suggests that the Concord movement was "not an affair of isolated selves writing in lonely integrity, like Thoreau and Walden Pond. But Transcendentalism was also very much a coterie affair, and the strong emotions it evoked from its participants show how much fire lay beneath the native frost of the New England character."[8] And that coterie's fire, I argue, spread from Bangor to Boston, and from New York to Europe. This book describes how the coteries worked internally as well as how they reached outside of themselves to draw others in to disseminate their own influence to the mass readership.

Linked to regional authorial identity, coterie identity directly shaped an author's reputation in the market. The coterie name alone represented a form of symbolic capital by which the author might be associated with the prestige of the circle, and as cultural capital, reflected in the specialized knowledge and skill one was assumed to possess as a member of that group. Both symbolic and cultural capital were generated, as my case studies show, by the author's own career-building relationships, forms of bonding to create social capital, within the group, designed to sustain a professional career with monetary rewards, or economic capital. In his widely influential study of the erosion of associations and increasing withdrawal from civic life from 1960 to 2000, sociologist Robert D. Putnam has established that the most financially successful professionals are adept at not only building social capital within their own networks, but also actively forging bonds with outside groups.[9] Such social bridging is helpful in explaining the dynamic that animated cross-coterie parties like Anne Lynch's in which bridging, or linking, social capital networks are "outward looking and encompass people across diverse social cleavages," as David Halpern describes in his update of Putnam's theory.[10] Most coteries did not share the same position with other circles in the hierarchy of economic power or literary prestige given divergences in specialization encouraged by the market, so bridging often occurred on unequal footing, in which case the establishment of contacts could be thought of as "a vertical bridge across asymmetrical power and resources."[11] My concern is for the way in which the coterie name became a commodity itself circulating in the marketplace, crucially encoding the significance of literary works and their attendant authors' reputations as they circulated through myriad economies of exchange, in which authors "bought, sold, begged, borrowed, bartered, and gave away what they wrote," in Leon Jackson's words.[12] Writers like Melville and Thoreau continued to bear their old coterie's moniker out of both a desire for market significance when their careers were evaporating and a sense of lifelong pride in, and even indebtedness toward, the permanent kindred bond forged from their authorial births. Indeed, well after they had outgrown or diverged from their literary principles and thus had been placed outside its network of financial support, Melville and Thoreau treasured their rights to their respective coveted authorial surnames of Knickerbocker and Transcendentalist.

Even when aesthetic visions grew apart, affiliation remained strong to the origins of the author's vocation, as the family that spawned the writer. Irving's own use of nicknames for the Lads of Kilkenny reflects an amiable affection, a brotherly bond functioning as a kind of surrogate family. Theirs was a bachelor's haven that would become known for its sophomoric exploits (lively games of leap-frog on the lawn to the astonished glares of disapproving onlookers at such wasted talent), which would lead Irving to wonder decades later in a letter to Kemble, "Who would have thought that we should ever have lived to be two such respectable old gentlemen?"[13] Indeed, they paid each other's bills, lent each other lavish sums, gave each other ripe leads with publishers, pulled strings to place manuscripts, and, of course, challenged and inspired each another to reach new heights in their writings. Such relationships fit the mold of what Cindy Weinstein's *Family, Kinship, and Sympathy* (2004) identifies in a preponderance of antebellum novels featuring protagonists plagued by malicious biological family members who are replaced by more sympathetic nonrelatives; I would add that such protagonists, as in the case of Fanny Fern's *Ruth Hall* (1855), are often supported particularly by unrelated business agents in the literary market better than their own blood relatives.[14] Henry Brevoort, for example, was a far more earnest and ardent promoter of Irving's career than his own brother. Evert Duyckinck, likewise, was better than Melville's brother Allan in placing his work and establishing his career. Emerson proved a more favorable patron to Thoreau than his own parents in terms of providing financial support for his vocation. Weinstein's sense that fiction constantly replaces biological family members with market figures and business associates extends, according to my findings, to careers catalyzed by these coteries. As a surrogate family unit, the coteries' social dynamic plays variations on the keynote so pervasive in the culture of the domestic ideal of the close-knit family of separate individuals with the collective goal of supporting mutual growth, complete with elder leaders and sapling neophytes, sage mentors and budding protégés. In the Knickerbockers' case, as in many other all male coteries, the bachelor appeared to flout the family structure, but in fact replaced it with a fraternal order of sorts. I look at groups that challenge traditional notions of coteries, both commercially and politically through the *New York Ledger* staff writers that included Fanny Fern and E.D.E.N. Southworth, and through the most potent proslavery periodical of the antebellum South, and thus George Fitzhugh's favorite mouthpiece, *DeBow's Review*. Even after the Civil War, we find a Fitzhugh who barely recants his views, and remains staunchly loyal to his Southern roots and distinction as a rare species of the nineteenth century—a Confederate intellectual.

My considerations of such kinship in coterie identification "leads back to the question of the economic and social conditions of the gradual constitution of an artistic field capable of grounding belief in the quasi-magical powers attributed to the artist," because coteries functioned as much like small businesses as family units.[15] Those economic and social conditions that gave rise to the magical power attributed to the artist were indeed part and parcel of the veneer of power, and even mysticism, attached to coterie identity. Hawthorne was well aware of the connection between families and businesses, as he begins *The House of the Seven Gables* (1851) with the once proud Hepzibah now tending shop out of a portion of her transformed Pyncheon estate. Dickens would also bring the family and business into singular focus in *Dombey and Son* (1848). For as much as Hepzibah shrinks from the glare of consumer inspection, Dombey desperately seeks public approval and financial success to stop at nothing less than a grandiose vision of global dominance supplanting what should be paternalistic love for his new son. Victorian culture worried this question of filial love and fiscal business, often dramatizing the debilitating effects of their separation. But as long as the artist remained exalted and elevated, she could stand out in the market and attract similar affection from her coterie kin for her singular powers of imagination. As Marx tells us, products sell in the free market because of the human character attributed to them, lending them such quasi-magical powers as Bourdieu identifies in the artist. Circles bore such power: to be a Knickerbocker was to be a dreaming bachelor, inclined to wistfully drift into the recesses of the past; to be a *Ledger* writer was to be a popular storyteller of exciting and sentimental yarns as escapist as they were socially efficacious; to be a Transcendentalist was to promote with zeal nonconformist individualism as a kind of new religion of the self rooted in and reflected through nature; to be a Garrisonian abolitionist was to assault slavery with righteous democratic flourishes, and to be a Fitzhugh proslavery pundit was to return those blows with quasi-socialistic benevolent paternalism under the mantle of medieval aristocratic and chivalric gallantry. Sympathetic, humanistic yearnings—driven as much by aesthetic sensibility as by deeply felt understandings of social justice— were essential to the circles' more humanized and lasting reformulation of market value and exchange than the one that barters and trades in Wall Street's world of commodities. Literature was not literature unless it bore a critical distance from the market. Yet literary circles, as this book shows, were necessarily commercial in their anticommericalism, as economic success was not just a barrier, but an inspiration for their objectives, whether financial as in Bonner's *Ledger* staff, or political, as in Garrison and Fitzhugh's armies of writers, or aesthetic and ethical as in the Transcendentalists.

Marketing Circles, Circles Marketing

Literary coteries, dating from Irving's earliest Knickerbockers and their multiple branches, formed around convergent aesthetic tastes as much as they shared social and political sensibilities. Yet the underdiscussed thread that unites the literary circles of this book—the Knickerbockers, Robert Bonner's *New York Ledger* staff, the Transcendentalists, the Peabody/Hawthorne circle, William Lloyd Garrison's abolitionists, and George Fitzhugh's proslavery pundits—is the set of economic motives behind authorial associations. Writers, particularly those with reform agendas, such as the Transcendentalists, formed groups out of resistance to capitalism, often made explicit in their writings. Yet they also gathered resources and combined strengths to enter the free market under a group moniker that could simultaneously command attention and financial investment in its literary stock, as well as offer, through association with its affiliates, a humanizing and fulfilling way of engaging in professional enterprise. What is the work of writing, if not work, like the sort that had taken over nineteenth-century America, prompting both Henry David Thoreau and Alexis De Tocqueville to voice earnest alarm and even protest against the anxiety concomitant to such "perpetual striving" and incessant and obsessive toil taking over the country?[16] "The mass of men lead lives of quiet desperation," Thoreau observes, wondering "Where is the division of labor to end?"[17] Not only was intellectual work hardly considered labor in the new Republic, according to Nicholas K. Brommell's groundbreaking study of conceptions of labor in the antebellum United States, it also bore with it a decidedly social bent, a collaborative inclination that gave the impression that its workshops and factories were domesticated bastions of luxury, insulated from the mean streets of the market.[18] Nothing could be further from the truth, of course, as coteries and their manipulation of the publishing industry for the aid of their own writers, and the promotion of their group as a brand name were paramount to their existence. Publication, or any attempt thereof, is integral to my understanding of the economies of exchange, both monetary and otherwise, in place for circulating and expanding authors' writings and reputations as they intersected with the network of intermediaries in publishing industry. The literary circles that form my subject range in function from political war rooms of the North and South, to protocorporate entrepreneurial promotional machines for the advancement of their young talent into the market, to communal aesthetic bonding far removed from the market—an escapist image with considerable commercial clout at the time—group versions of the consultation between antebellum American romantics captured in *Kindred Spirits*, Asher B. Durand's 1849 ethereal painting of William Cullen Bryant and Thomas Cole (their topic is anything but financial) utterly swallowed by sylvan sensuality miles from the sight or sound of a machine.

The market conditions demanded awareness of the increasingly commercial nature of authorship; obliviousness to the social and economic nature of authorship, as scholars have fully demonstrated, was virtually unheard of, and if encountered, was usually a carefully crafted pose.[19] The ironies imbedded in the situation were especially acute, given that "literary activities were generally classed by New Yorkers as constituting an avocation, rather than a profession, and seldom as a means of earning one's livelihood," as John Paul Pritchard notes in his early history of criticism in antebellum New York.[20] The Knickerbocker school projected the anticommercial, sauntering bachelor image, making the untethered free agent lifestyle so appealing in the early decades of the century that it became an iconic staple of the culture by the time Donald Grant Mitchell ("Ik Marvel"), N.P. Willis, and George W. Curtis would enter the scene in the 1840s. The male sentimentalist exuded a carefully crafted rearguard indifference to the frenetic scramble for capital about him, offering a kind of escapist fantasy from the strictures, and anxieties over commercial, industrial, and technological innovations hurtling the nation toward the future of what Thoreau called "this nervous, bustling nineteenth century."[21]

Various articulations of antimaterialism would become the driving forces behind the formation of the ethos of not only the Knickerbocker and Transcendentalist circles, but less obviously among the most commercially aggressive of groups such as Bonner's *Ledger* staff, whose writers, like Anne Stephens, would pen cautionary tales about the dangers of being duped by false displays of material wealth, as E.D.E.N. Southworth would spin fables of love and money, like *The Lost Heiress*. Much of what we see, however, in coteries like the Knickerbockers and Transcendentalists is the promotion of a lifestyle that presumes that "economic power is first and foremost a power to keep economic necessity at arms length," as Pierre Bourdieu writes on the aristocracy of culture.[22] Much of the promotional power of these two circles depended upon their images not as literary products, per se, as did Bonner's *Ledger* staff, or political points of view, as in Garrison and Fitzhugh's propagandists, but in a stylized, bohemian, way of living. It is not by mistake, for example, that Washington Irving's long absence from America was because he had spent so much time in France following his successful foray into the English literary market, cementing his reputation, and thus gaining him entrance into the birthplace of bohemia, an environment that could not have been more suitable to the wandering bachelor persona of Irving's pen name and narrator, Geoffrey Crayon. Indeed, "making the art of living one of the fine arts means predisposing it to enter into literature [so that] the literary personage is not simply a fact of literature," because fiction writers "contribute greatly to the public recognition of this new social entity—especially by inventing and spreading the very notion of bohemia," as Bourdieu observes.[23]

It is my contention that coteries reimagined how a market might be entered to refigure the notion of the literary "product" through the group image and lifestyle thereof, as in the style of an artist's life, the pastime of living, in Thoreau's sense, a Concord saunterer whose wandering took him into nature rather than the urban centers and salon culture, the way Irving and his Geoffrey Crayon persona did. The collective identities of all coteries discussed in this book, for that matter, were self-consciously crafted as societies of artists marked not just by their alternative lifestyles that they endorsed and defended, sometimes taking on extreme political stridency in the case of Fitzhugh's proslavery writers in the South, nonetheless selling a Southern aristocratic quasisocialistic benevolent paternalism smacking of classical antiquity, and shamelessly appropriating codes of chivalry gleaned from so many Sir Walter Scott *Waverly* novels directly in tune with their nostalgia for the Scottish ancestry. Coteries also innovated the market in their own unique ways for rewards either in financial returns or at least social recognition for challenging conventional middle-class cultural codes of behavior. Literary circles not only established unique forms of artistic lifestyles they used to shape their works and promote themselves in the market, they also created their own economies of exchange internally. The most primary function of that internal economy of exchange relates directly to the most essential process of literary production involved in finding and honing materials, in using the circle as a testing and training ground to develop aesthetic technique, and sharpen social critiques that would go directly into their work, much of it openly collaborative in nature. The next function of the coterie is to provide a group name preparing the individual author's entry into the market, an association that reaches well beyond conventional categories of genre distinction. Defying the coterie rarely worked in the best professional interest of antebellum authors, while joining forces with it to defy the broader evils of marauding, cutthroat capitalism promised to pay handsome dividends.

Defying Market Culture

Literature indeed has its contentious edge; as Ishmael Reed has said, "writing is fighting," and so it was for every one of these groups, engaged as they were in some sort of ideological battle.[24] Even the seemingly harmless and innocuous wandering bachelors battled old world snobbery mocking American aspirations for literary relevance in the face of Byron and Scott. Like many late Victorian British women writers, American authors rooted in coterie culture of the antebellum era found "collaborative life and work functioned as a site of resistance...[through which] their lives and texts redraw the boundaries of ideologies that they all seem to find troubling: Cartesian definitions of subjectivity and solitary notions of creativity; industrial capitalism and alienated labor; and patriarchy and heterosexism."[25] Collaboration, I would add to this fine insight by book historian Jill Ehnenn, began from the most basic shared economic values through which they redrew the boundaries of such troubling ideologies. Indeed, shared attitudes toward money gelled groups, who were then challenged to replicate those views in the operation of their own dealings within the coterie itself.

Adopting a unique method of defying injustice in the market, reflective of deeper humanistic resistance and skepticism toward divided labor and industrialization, was essential to both the survival of individual literary careers in the new competitive publishing world, and for finding a distinct charisma individuals were incapable of forming on their own. Irving's mates would swagger onto the scene with just as much romantic studied indifference and calculated noncommittal affectations, the true origin, if there were any, of "cool," apologies to James Dean and Marlon Brando (of *The Wild One*), to create a new American Byron. Indeed, John W.M. Hallock's recent biography, *American Byron: Homosexuality and the Fall of Fitz-Greene Halleck* (2000), has positioned the poet and wit Knickerbocker loyalist in precisely this measure, noting his prominence as one of the most important American poets in the United States, thanks in part to his central role in the Bread and Cheese Club from 1824 to 1830 that included James K. Paulding, Gulian C. Verplank, Richard H. Dana, William Cullen Bryant, and James Fenimore Cooper, to bring light to his alarmingly abrupt rejection from the literary canon over the course of the next fifty years.

Halleck's fall from literary renown is telling of the political workings of the mechanism that produced, and destroyed, fame in the American culture. From within his coterie, his reputation flourished; posthumously, the association with these groups faded along with the luster of his poetic legacy. Defiance had longer commercial endurance if expressed from within the context of an established coterie, which provided a more stable base from which to hurl assaults at conventional business mores. Melville's *Pierre* (1852) is a sterling example of a lone wolf's cry of rebellion with no coterie to fall back on to support his bizarre enraged work as an ingenious send-up of the literary marketplace, mainly because so much of that novel eviscerated his old mates of Young America, not the least of which was Evert Duyckinck. Thus the disintegration of Melville's career began from the date of that novel's publication. With its strength in numbers, Flaubert's bohemian cohort contrastingly spewed venom with great confidence toward all facets of market exchange in shrill and reckless protests to make even the most stalwart American antimaterialists like Emerson blush. Flaubert would declare independence from market conditions in a formulation that positions writing as totally beyond market value: the notion of "priceless" art is clear in his insistence that "a work of art (worthy of that name and conscientiously done) is beyond appraisal, has no commercial value, cannot be paid for," protesting that the replacement of the patronage system with a free market competitive orientation toward authorship, one in which the writer "no longer receives a pension from the great," cannot be assumed to make him "very much freer and nobler," but rather, "the equal of a grocer."[26] He goes on in this 1867 letter to say, "nobody is rich enough to pay us...I don't see what relation there is between a five-franc coin and an idea."[27] The corresponding notion of such a flamboyant inversion of conventional economy in America could be found in Thoreau (of French ancestry) who would brag in *Walden* about how little he produced to make his living and how many days and hours he gladly spent at the pond, time hardly wasted, but of invaluable spiritual sustenance to him. The formulation of lost money, or at least surplus capital, equating to gained Transcendental wisdom, as also in Flaubert's sense, means that "the artist cannot triumph on the symbolic terrain except by losing on the economic terrain (at least in the short run), and vice versa (at least in the long run)," as Bourdieu affirms.[28]

Thoreau and Melville's audacity can be accountable, in part, to the fact that unlike E.D.E.N. Southworth in the early stages of her career, neither were writing hungry, but had Emerson's fortune and Judge Lemuel Shaw's dowry (Melville's dedication of *Typee* [1846] to Shaw speaks volumes of his gratuity to the judge's fortune that afforded him the privilege to write it) respectively underwriting their schemes. This did not mean they willfully renounced popular forms in their writings, their full engagement of which David S. Reynolds and Sheila Post have demonstrated, but certainly had more financial backing upon which to challenge the status quo.[29] Such fortunes "spare 'pure' writers the compromises to which an absence of income exposes them," in Bourdieu's assessment, as such compromises include time and conformity to conventional exposition of subject matter.[30] (A sterling twentieth-century example of freedom from such compromise is in the privileged career of Virginia Woolf, whose ownership and control of her own means of literary publication enabled her radical experiments in fiction that the mainstream market may not have tolerated). My approach to understanding the function of works as diverse as *Walden* and Southworth's *The Lost Heiress* in this book builds upon Bourdieu's axiom that the more commercial a work is, the more it responds to preexisting forms and preexisting consumer demand. Radical commercial innovation, I suggest, often operating with solid financial backing from Robert Bonner's high salaries to the Boston blue bloods' bankrolling of Garrison's abolitionist propaganda mill, was essential to the success of each coterie. This meant literary circles responded to dominant ideological structures that proved popular and pervasive in the culture by profoundly innovating and revising, rather than wholly rejecting or bluntly replicating, antimarket tropes bearing on sympathy and the importance of the domestic sphere. Such innovation is visible in the irony underlying seemingly less commercial works posing as "pure art," whose reliance on "symbolic capital, a kind of 'economic' capital denied but recognized, and hence legitimate" is actually "a veritable credit, and capable of assuring, under certain conditions and in the long term, 'economic' profits."[31]

American literary circles invented themselves precisely to gain a position in the literary market—in a commercialized book trade that dictated relevance—and also accommodate for the entrenched notion that literature could not by nature join forces with the market and remain literature. That paradoxical tension, I argue, was not crippling, so much as it was inspirational, drawing as it did on the prominent debates in contemporary discourse over capital—hard versus paper currency, the transformation of gender roles under the sea change brought by the market revolution, vocational versus personal ethics, the exploitation of cheap labor, growing class inequality and poverty acutely visible in urbanization, the transformation of the yeoman farmer into stock broker of nature's harvest—with fresh insight. The market was a lightning rod of political controversy in Jacksonian America. Whigs shrunk from what they frequently misrepresented as shrill and sweeping protest by Democrats against all things connected with the free market, "DOWN WITH THE BANKS! DOWN WITH THE MANUFACTORIES! DOWN WITH THE CORPORATIONS! DOWN WITH THE CAPITALISTS!" as Calvin Colton lampooned the fashionability of strident antimaterialism.[32]

A coterie's position on the market became a kind of trademark of its ideological stance and aesthetic sensibility, a moral passport to its audience's hearts, and thus their wallets. How business was done within each literary circle, as it worked to publish its writings, did not always correlate with the image, usually bearing on a complex paradoxical tension between antimaterialism and Franklinesque work ethic. Rather than seeking out discrepancies between the external image and internal business practice of each coterie, I discover what in their formula was commercially, and presumably also ideologically (if the example of Stowe's *Uncle Tom's Cabin* status as best selling novel of the entire nineteenth century and major catalyst for the Civil War is any indication), successful. Finding an audience through an attitude, often struck as a kind of theatrical perfomative pose, toward market conditions, was thus essential to establishing a sort of meta-genre for the author's works, an additional associational tag beyond the writer's designation within the ranks of other novelists, travel writers, philosophers, or poets of radically diverse political and social leanings. So, as the market was flush with nonfictional forms of travel writing, which spawned the literary sketch and much of the Transcendental writings, a writer like Margaret Fuller could assume that her association with the Concord circle (and its attendant aversion to avarice) and her work as first editor of *The Dial* would distinguish *A Summer on the Lakes* (1843) from other travel writers crowding the bookseller's shelves. A bonafide Lad of Kilkenny like James K. Paulding could bank on consumers' knowledge of his affiliation with the famous group, and let much of his career ride on that distinction, linked as it was to the defining economics of the detached disaffiliated, and both financially and ideologically un-invested, roaming bachelor.

Such careers reprised the coterie's signature themes for extended success beyond the circle's heyday, problematizing Bourdieu's claim that "adjustment to demand is never a result of a *conscious transaction* between producers and consumers, and still less of a deliberate search for adjustment, except perhaps in the case of the most heteronomous enterprises of cultural production (which, for this very reason, are correctly called 'commercial')," since finding an "audience which understands and appreciates it is almost always the effect of a *coincidence*."[33] Instead, in a case like Paulding's, it is clear that his success was both coincidental in the good fortune of being a part of the original Knickerbockers, and also very much a conscious transaction to perpetuate the success established by the group's renown. Such a conscious transaction is always already engaged in "the meaningful politics of print," as posited by Meredith McGill, in which the author's market engagement does not function to eclipse, but rather exposes "the republican understanding of print as public property sustain[ing] the culture of reprinting and involv[ing] publishers in the era's defining controversies over the nature and course of economic development."[34] Business, therefore, *is* the literature, as authors' attitudes toward the free market determine how the writing becomes the selling, and thus the key to political change. Indeed, the inclusion of Northern and Southern literary circles, Part III of this book, opposed over slavery is intended to highlight precisely the connection between promotion, advertisement, and dissemination of propaganda in the literary marketplace as the key to political change, such that "the politics of culture is played out at the level of form and format as well as in explicit themes of literary texts."[35] McGill's sense that authors were more proactive rather than reactive to shaping politics is evident in the impulse to form alliances through literary groups in the first place, according to the democratic principle of power en mass, bearing its noblest articulation through consensual deliberation, and its most brutal expression through the frenzy of the runaway mob. McGill's contention that all authorial subjectivity should not be seen as the territory upon which economic forces are played out—since Dickens's texts, for example, become a means for articulating economic positions in the culture—informs my sense of the work of literary coteries and their texts as offering the public a vocabulary through which to re-conceive of and thus shape economic ethical behavior in the form on unwritten etiquette at the very least, and codified law, at the most.[36] The next chapter examines how the Knickerbockers of New York politically positioned themselves, and how their economies of exchange amassed social and economic capital to develop America's first recognizable literary coterie into a wildly popular sensation in the literary market. It begins with Irving, but as we will discover, he was hardly operating alone.

Part I

Literary New Yorkers

Chapter 2

"An Instinct for Gold": Irving's Knickerbockers

In 1854, the Knickerbocker founding father Washington Irving received a set of galley proofs of his biographical portrait from his friend and admirer Evert Duyckinck, the ambassador of Young America, New York's newest incarnation of Irving's circle. Aware that Irving's renown had become by this time legendary in the United States, Duyckinck took care to allow the famous author the final say on his portrait before going to press with the *Cyclopedia of American Literature*, which would appear in 1855. The gesture was more than editorial; it was a ceremonial act of deference toward the original Knickerbocker from the chief intermediary of its kindred coterie, which had been flourishing under the energy and connections of Duyckinck since the 1840s. Before cementing this image of Irving for posterity in an official documentary portrait bearing the authority of common historical knowledge for what was to be the most comprehensive literary encyclopedia of American authors ever assembled at the time, Duyckinck did the courtesy of allowing the elder Irving to alter the entry under the guise of a routine checking for factual and grammatical accuracy.

Irving, whose notorious obsession with his public image nearly reached Whitmanian proportions, was more than happy to oblige Duyckinck. The entry remained virtually untouched by Irving's pen with one exception, in which a flurry of markings on one particular passage led the author to compose it from scratch on a separate sheet. The passage in question was of particular interest to Irving because it explained the move to England that had prompted him to write *The*

Sketch Book (1819) in the wake of the War of 1812, during which he wrote profiles of American generals for *Analectic Magazine*.[1] Irving reordered the sequence of events so that his sojourns through the English countryside would appear to have been completed *prior* to "the commercial revulsions" that threw him "upon his resources as an author."[2] In his version, he first finds himself and his family in dire financial need, and next "repairs to London for his excursions and his observations on rural life and manners," which provided materials for his book.[3] Crucially, Irving's version erased any implication that his sojourn was undertaken in the spirit of research by a professional author, hungry for materials to feed his commercial literary project. Instead, Irving insisted that those observations of the quiet country should resonate with those of his politically disinterested, economically solvent, wandering bachelor narrator, Geoffrey Crayon. For at stake was not only his own reputation, but also the public perception of the collective Knickerbocker mystique upon which so many New York literary careers depended.

Sorting out Irving's motives for the revision of his *Cyclopedia* entry illuminates the intermediary work (in this case, Duyckinck's) necessary for the maintenance of the original Knickerbocker image, rooted in the bachelor aesthetic as established in *Salmagundi; or the Whim-Whams of Opinions of Launcelot Langstaff and Others* (1807). This chapter demonstrates that as the Knickerbocker image grew and changed over time, its authors, who wrote from 1807 to 1837 (and later developed into Young America, 1837–55[4]), persistently drew upon, with varying success, the most commercially potent elements of its original blueprint. The Knickerbocker affiliation not only determined subjects and styles, but also functioned as a passport validating circulation throughout the ever-expanding antebellum publishing world. Irving was acutely aware of his name's value as a commodity in the literary market and generously used it for the promotion of his coterie mates. He was so ingenious at finessing the new literary market that fellow Knickerbocker James Fenimore Cooper exclaimed, "What an instinct that man has for gold!"[5] One researcher a century later labeled Irving's elaborate brokerage of authorial careers "Washington Irving's Literary Pimpery."[6] That image was at odds with the authorial persona he crafted for the public, which reflected a bachelor's carefree lifestyle oblivious to the anxieties of capital. Irving's promotion of the Knickerbocker identity distinctly distances authorship from aggressive capitalism in the grubby and vulgar market, while also carefully manipulating that very image to maximize commercial profit. Irving aimed to preserve his image as an amateur traveling bachelor who made casual narrative and visual sketches of his impressions of his travels, forming the defining features of the mythology of autonomous authorship at the very foundation of the Knickerbocker coterie's mystique.[7] This carefree, individualistic bachelor lifestyle, which began with the Lads of Kilkenny, masked the building of a concerted protocorporate literary empire from the social matrix of America's first professional literary circle.[8]

Irving's management of his public persona pointedly illustrates his willful suppression of his commercially inclined authorial identity, a stance traceable from the very beginnings of the Knickerbocker coterie, underscored by Duyckinck's inclusion in the *Cyclopedia* of a key passage to that effect from the 1834 Paris edition of *Salmagundi*. Significantly, Duyckinck had chosen to reprint that passage in his entry on James Kirk Paulding in the *Cyclopedia*. Paulding contributed to the periodical essays of *Salmagundi*, which ran twenty numbers from 24 January 1807 to 25 January 1808, along with Irving and his brother William, seventeen years his senior. In an association with the coterie that he would struggle to capitalize upon his entire career, Paulding's original connection with Irving was through his marriage to William's sister, which gained him admission into "a knot of young men of similar stamp," as Duyckinck writes, "who were members of the Calliopean Society, one of the first purely literary institutions established in the city."[9] According to Duyckinck, this early society was "the first" of its kind, and its authority derived from its specialization in "purely" literary subjects.

Interestingly, Duyckinck's promotion of Paulding's specialized literary authority through his membership in this circle carefully abridges the commercial angling concomitant to such specialization in the context of the transformation of authorship into a trade. Indeed, the story of *Salmagundi*'s publication, like that of *The Sketch Book*, functions in this brief biography as the story of Paulding's rise to literary success. Regardless of his relation by marriage to Irving's family, Paulding's place in Irving lore is not as brother-in-law, but as the coterie's chief authorial image of the economically disinterested roving bachelor so prominently displayed in his entry. The Knickerbocker charm remains intact in the humorous sketch and fable (masquerading as prefatory publication history) Irving added to the 1834 French edition of *Salmagundi*, depicting the publisher in the mold of one of Irving's trademark eccentric protagonists, whose foibles, like those of Rip Van Winkle and Ichabod Crane, are worn on his sleeve. Duyckinck printed in full for Paulding's *Cyclopedia* entry the preface's description of "David Longworth, an eccentric bookseller," more in love with literature than with money, whose holdings of literary-related art overflow from his home, one painting from which "had nearly obscured the front of his house with a huge sign—a colossal painting, in *chiaro scuro*, of the crowning of Shakespeare," an Irvingesque caricature of the hero worship of the Bard as a metonym for the crowning glory of English literature.[10] The key to the passage lies in Longworth's Rip-like distaste for finances and in his grandiose embrace of the literary world, which takes on garish and outrageous proportions, like his art collection, of precisely the sort befitting one who would give his blessing to the Lads of Kilkenny and their satirical periodical. For in Longworth, we find "an extraordinary propensity to publish elegant works, to the great gratification of persons of taste, and the no small diminution of his own slender fortune."[11]

"Dusky Dave," however, was actually an opportunistic swindler who beat Irving and Paulding to the copyright and attendant gold mine of *Salmagundi*, teaching Irving a valuable lesson in literary capitalism that he would remember when it came time to publish *The Sketch Book* in England and America simultaneously. Indeed, Irving would take great pains to protect his copyright for *The Sketch Book*, writing letters to British journals that had reprinted his sketches without consent, notice, or remuneration and protecting his work in America through the agency of his brother Ebenezer. If Irving was an exacting capitalist in 1819 London negotiating the placement of the best-selling work of his career, it was only because Longworth had caught him napping, heedless of his own intuition that his profits were vulnerable. "What arrangements have you made with the Dusky for the profits?" he wrote to Paulding, noting "I shall stand much in need of a little sum of money on my return."[12] Before Irving and Paulding were aware of its value, Longworth had taken out the copyright for himself, earning what Ebenezer estimated to be a tidy $10,000–15,000, approximately $250,000 to $300,000 in today's currency. The authors were left with only $100 each, roughly ten times less than Longworth's profit. This would be the last time Knickerbocker authors would fail to recognize their true value in the literary marketplace, for just after the publication of *Salmagundi*'s fourth number, Irving and Paulding made their rounds in the elite circles of Philadelphia, enjoying their newly won prestige in the world of letters. For whatever they lacked in profits on this occasion, it was abundantly clear they made up for in popular and critical acclaim, and thus they threw themselves into maintaining the momentum of their mounting fame, vowing to realize its full financial profits in the future.

The Lads of Kilkenny

"The Lads of Kilkenny," "The Ancient Club of New York," and "The Nine Worthies" were the names whimsically affixed to the literary fraternity that first lodged at Gouverneur Kemble's family mansion. Situated on the banks of the Passaic, "Cockloft Hall" became a kind of bachelor's retreat bankrolled by Kemble's inheritance from his wealthy uncle, who was a British governor in the colonies. The lads "would sally forth from New York and enliven its solitude by their madcap pranks and juvenile orgies," according to Irving's nephew and first biographer, Pierre M. Irving.[13] What began as an elaborate inside joke from the nicknaming of the mansion to themselves—Brevoort as "Nuncle"; Kemble as "The Patroon" or patron; the portly Henry Ogden as "Supercargo"; medical school dropout Peter Irving as "The Doctor"—would rapidly develop into an elaborate satirical mythology of the increasingly eccentric and bizarre Cockloft family that would fill the pages of the first collaborative serial Knickerbocker publication.[14] Irving had just passed the bar exam and joined his brother John in a legal partnership that left him disillusioned with the humdrum routine; Paulding assuaged his boredom at his clerk's job with the United States Loan Office by writing humorous editorials in the newspaper; Irving's older brother William, though not one of the bachelor lads, possessed an inborn talent for writing witty verse.

From such a quintessentially Irvingesque idle aversion to industry arose the collaborative authorship of William Irving, James Kirke Paulding, and Washington Irving of *Salmagundi*. It had sprung from good-natured rebellion against the new republic's increasingly intense work ethic, a sensibility apparent in Irving's letters, in which he would brag about how little he worked at the law, for example, basking in "a sentimental or rather philosophic cigar...over the office fire" and "lolling in cozy armchairs" to the disapproving stare of the books lining the shelves that he imagines as "the ponderous fathers of the law."[15] Much of Irving's charm comes from his persistent refusal to take himself and his pursuits very seriously, especially in these halcyon days of innocence before "Dusky Dave" had made his mark. Indeed, among the most cherished memories of the bachelors at Cockloft Hall is that of cavorting about in the yard much to the neighbors' consternation. Over a decade after their heyday, Kemble would wish "for the time when you, Paulding, Brevoort, the Doctor [Peter Irving] and myself shall assemble there, recount the stories of our lives, and have another game at leap frog."[16] That frolicsome spirit would animate the criticism, sentiment, politics, and satire of *Salmagundi*. The bond of the collaborative group identity was forged in a reformulated conception of the bachelor's life as stimulating and social—however transient and free of fixed habitation—unlike that of Geoffrey Crayon, the isolated and lonely sojourner who came to embody the narrative persona of *The Sketch Book* (1819) over a decade later. Peter Irving's fondest memory centers on such communal harmony, as he recalls "Sundays at the Hall, when we sported on the lawn until fatigued, and sometimes fell sociably into a general nap in the drawing-room in the dusk of the evening."[17]

The Knickerbockers were not only undoing the dominant unsympathetic cultural image of bachelorhood to emphasize a communal, collaborative identity, but were also revising the sense of the bachelor as politically subversive or constantly at war with his vices.[18] When given any notice at all, bachelors have commonly been viewed as social deviants much more threatening than their harmless spinster female counterparts, since unmarried males were often associated with criminal behavior, homelessness, unemployment, and the fathering of children out of wedlock. If not seen as a direct threat to the sanctity of domestic safety, they were seen as an onerous social burden, as in one 1812 *New-England Galaxy* editorial, which called for bachelors to "bear their portion of the burthens of society" instead of selfishly indulging in its "blessings and privileges."[19] Long before Ik Marvel (Donald Grant Mitchell), the author of the wildly popular *Reveries of a Bachelor, A Book of the Heart* (1852), capitalized on the vogue of the bachelor that Irving had previously established with *Salmagundi* and *The Sketch Book*, unmarried men were roundly mocked, as in the 1824 sketch "Character of a Bachelor," which proclaimed them mere "dupes of wretched toad eaters, and slaves to designing housekeepers."[20] Marvel tellingly benefitted handsomely from Irving's "kind note in my behalf to President Pierce" to a "card of presentation to see Dickens" while overseas.[21]

The Knickerbockers seized upon the cultural image of the bachelor as economically vulnerable—easy prey "to designing housekeepers"—and transformed it into an image of enviable and irresistible freedom from market constraints, particularly the responsibility of steady employment in support of a family. Rarely seen as legitimate captains of industry, bachelors were already positioned outside of the market in the popular view, either as derelicts or swindlers. The Knickerbockers turned that economic outsidership into charm, as evidenced by the eccentric quirkiness seen later in Rip Van Winkle's escape from political as well as economic tensions. Irving's famous sketch typifies this iconic antimarket trait of the bachelor aesthetic. Rip's story, in many ways, is a married man's fantasy of escape from the shackles of a confining marriage conjoined with a broader and deeper desire to flee economic responsibility in the market, which had become so essential to the formation of manhood in American culture.[22]

A crucial characteristic of the Knickerbocker identity is a juvenile playfulness, which effectively disarms the sense of the bachelor as a deviant or threat to the social order embodied by marriage. The sociologist Howard P. Chudacoff finds "the link between adulthood and marriage explicit and strong" to the extent that it is nearly universal, appearing "even in so-called primitive societies."[23] Irving's repartee with Kemble in one letter reveals a bachelor banter regarding sexuality they carefully concealed from public view. "You were well received by…many certain young ladies [who] have absolutely declared that you must return here," Irving wrote, insisting that his own stock as a viable beau outshone Kemble's. It may appear that "they longed more to enjoy the light of our countenance though between ourselves, I believe the little scoundrels only said so, to ingratiate themselves in my favour," he declared in a teasing gesture of sexual one-upmanship. Later in the letter, Irving jocosely pleads guilty to two bachelor crimes, expressed as if they were legal violations. "It was plainly proved that I was seen smoking a cigar and…another time when I plead a severe indisposition, I was pronounced guilty of having sat at a young lady's elbow the whole evening and listened to her piano—all which brought me into manifest disgrace."[24] This side of bachelorhood rarely emerged, as the coterie instead took on the appearance of a group of overgrown children in a deft evasion of allegations of homosexuality, deemed a perverse disease at the time. (The circle would eventually have to face the complexities of marriage and homosexuality, which would have a pivotal impact on several careers, as discussed later in this chapter.) Further, their coterie answered to the paradox at the heart of the early republic's national identity, offering an outlet for recalcitrant individualism while also honoring cooperation and unity. While the concept of individualism is so well suited to bachelorhood, a coterie of bachelors reflects the norms of mutuality and conformity increasingly valued during the era of rising capitalism, which emphasized the necessity of cooperation and unity seen in the proliferation of manufactories. Of course, the Lads were not factory workers, nor was their time at all dominated by factory labor. Yet the economy's development in that direction prompted a more humanized, familial alternative version of those capitalist arrangements expressed in the literature and lifestyle of the Knickerbocker bachelors, at once lolling pleasure seekers and a mutually supporting association of professional authors.

In the absence of family support, bachelors increasingly gathered to make their own families. Bachelor clubs formed in response to "economic changes that included the replacement of the pre-capitalist artisanal production system by waged labor and the accompanying uncertainty of employment made it increasingly difficult for young males to accumulate enough resources to marry and start a family." Such clubs could "retain or recreate quasi-family relationships within their urban subculture," as well as forming a method of defraying expenses through cooperative group residences in which members shared costs of housing, food, and cleaning.[25] Kemble was both lad and "Patroon," or chief patron, of Cockloft Hall; his mates, of course, stayed under his roof gratis. Not all of them were as independently wealthy as Kemble, but instead used the retreat as a break from their urban office jobs. Like lodgers at boarding houses, the Knickerbockers shared cultural interests and enjoyed the economic advantages of group affiliation. The lads transformed creative whimsy into the work of writing in a concerted system of mutual professional support. This development of the coterie into a protocorporate enterprise fused the creative fancy, verbal wit, and youthful fun, with a young man's ambition in the market. Indeed, the Knickerbockers would be armed with greater force through their group identity than as separate individuals. They cross-pollinated creative ideas for writing, provided financial support, and made vital connections with publishers. Like genre fiction, the bachelor aesthetic at the core of the Knickerbocker identity gave readers a clear set of expectations for not only the style and subject, but also the ideological leanings of its writers, as reflected in the mores of *Salmagundi*. In this way, ideological reinforcement sustained through the market product arose from an early form of literary collusion for financial stability and political persuasiveness. Specifically, a sense of family and kinship brought distinct social and economic benefits deriving from the original Knickerbocker image without sacrificing an American irreverence and individualism reflected in the juvenile free agency of bachelorhood.

Diedrich Knickerbocker, the fictional narrative persona of *A History of New York* (1812), who is reprised in *The Sketch Book* for the faux sources of "Rip Van Winkle" and "The Legend of Sleepy Hollow," functioned like the fictional bachelors to make unwed men more human, and even lovable in their childish ways. These figures diffused cultural tensions by embracing and domesticating them into the stuff of harmless genial wit. In a discussion on Irving's influence on Melville's early fiction, John Bryant notes that the earlier "*Salmagundi* bachelors place the genial fulfillment of life over social and democratic pretensions [so that] the corrosive effects of faction" are reduced to whim. "The bachelor aesthetic," Bryant explains, "which once connoted misanthropy, implies a comic indifference that is paradoxically communal."[26] This pattern echoes the nation's larger desire to reconcile the demand for freedom and individualism with cultural cohesion.

As the Knickerbocker circle's cultural currency escalated, the group's congenial and communal lifestyle softened the culture's disapproval of single men in society, an attitude visible in bachelor taxes and special laws curtailing their freedom. Irving would always function most effectively as an ambassador of good will, invoking images of domestic bliss, or childlike play—his Rip Van Winkle of *The Sketch Book* passes his days playing with children and dogs miscast in the married life until his fateful trek into the woods would cement his solo status—to diffuse even the most entrenched tensions and biases. Irving's circle made the bachelor appear genial and irresistible, rendering the dangerous cultural figure not only harmless and nonthreatening, but also suffused with amiable charm. They were not without their edge, however, as satire always required a social target. They described their project in the second number of *Salmagundi* as "good-natured raillery," which an error in transcription tellingly transformed into "good-natured villainy."[27] If the bachelor subculture came to represent a threat to family life, the lore of the Lads of Kilkenny, so lovingly retold by Evert Duyckinck in the role of antebellum literature's Plutarch in his *Cyclopaedia* and 1860 preface of *Salmagundi*, urged instead that bachelors could be both close-knit and domestic. Irving's own bachelor life was exemplary of how unmarried free agency could be not only respectable, but highly fashionable as well. Herein lay the key to the distinction of the Knickerbocker name in the literary market.

The bachelor aesthetic was Irving's answer to pressure to produce a unique national literature, at once distancing American letters from that of England, while also reaffirming its kinship as a separate yet sympathetic bond. This was not only a political objective, as Bryce Traister notes, but also an economic one, I would add, since its successful execution meant that Irving would be the first American author to garner immense popularity on both sides of the Atlantic during the period.[28] The bachelor aesthetic was not only a projection of Irving as a single author, but indeed of the collective Knickerbocker coterie.

The bachelor aesthetic employed metaphors of family and kinship as a method of grappling with political and cultural tensions with England through the personification of nations as private individuals engaged in a domestic feud, for example, in Paulding's *The Diverting History of John Bull and Brother Jonathan* (1820) and *A Sketch of Old England by a New England Man* (1822); and Cooper's *Notions of the Americans, By a Traveling Bachelor* (1828). But the bachelor aesthetic would not just be a means of transatlantic ambassadorial dealings. Indeed, it would have a more immediate impact on the local literary and political history in which *Salmagundi* and *A History of New York* are so embedded.

The Knickerbocker mystique arose from a fraternal order that, by its very function, mocked English order with light-hearted humor and without any intended offense. Like a modern-day fraternity, Peter Irving recalls the pseudo knighting ritual of one Knickerbocker. "In the Chinese saloon," pet name for a room at the Kemble mansion, "we made poor Dick McCall a knight, and I, as the senior of our order, dubbed him by some fatality on the seat of honor instead of the shoulder."[29] Such pranks were indicative of the humor of *Salmagundi* that poked fun at tradition in such a way that it diffused tension. The fictional Grandfather Cockloft, for example, continually blows up his grounds to improve the order of the landscape around his fishpond. This portrayal of the oldest member of the Cocklofts in irreverent hues is a comic inversion of the wise and venerable figure of respect embodying tradition. Elsewhere, the congressional military mindset is skewered for glorying in the invention of the torpedo, "by which the stoutest line of battle ship, even a *Santissima Trinitada*, may be caught napping and decomposed in a twinkling."[30] Narrator William Wizard, Esq. goes on to note how this invention "tickled the noses of all our dignitaries wonderfully; for to do our government justice, it has no objection to injuring or exterminating its enemies in any manner—provided the thing can be done economically." The rhetoric of advanced economical and scientific method in the voice of a gentleman narrator comically clashes with the blunt objective of blowing up the British.

Politics, however, was not the objective of *Salmagundi* so much as it was a readily available subject for the trio's fraternal frolic. Irving himself would later look upon *Salmagundi* as a youthful fling, waxing more nostalgic about the bachelor's retreat at Kemble's mansion than the content of their literary production. Irving's lachrymose letter to Kemble lamenting the disunion of the Lads reveals what he really valued: "The lads of Kilkenny are completely scattered; and, to the riotous, roaring, rattle-brained orgies at Dyde's [a luxurious hotel with grand ballroom they frequented for libations], succeeds the placid, picnic, picturesque pleasures of the tea-table." He mourns the passing of "the feverish enjoyments of Madeira and Champagne" and sober return "with faith and loyalty to the standard of beauty quietly set down under the petticoat-government."[31] The nostalgia here is for a past, however, that never died, at least within the pages of the Knickerbockers' writings that continued to ride on the success of *Salmagundi*'s soaring popularity for decades hence.

Homosexuality and Marriage in the Bachelor Coterie

Wit and light hearted satire indeed carried the day for the coterie, but the façade of its carefree bachelor aesthetic cracked under the social pressure of marriage and homosexuality. The fate of many Knickerbocker careers was determined by the ability to mend those fissures and alleviate the pressure. Irving constantly found himself on the inside of bachelor cohorts that gradually dissolved because of the marriage of its members. In 1817 England, for example, he lamented the loss of his dear friend Washington Allston to marriage, noting how he "was the most delightful, the most lovable being I ever knew; a man I would like always by my side—to have gone through life with; his nature was so refined, so intellectual, so genial, so pure."[32] Irving's most recent sympathetic biographer Andrew Burstein explains the effusion thus: "He treated his male friends as wife substitutes. This had to do with intimacy, not sex as we understand it."[33] Ben Harris McClary, writing in the more homophobic 1960s, finds such sentiment in Irving's "overt" conclusive evidence that "an element of homosexuality was one of the cohesive forces which held the individuals together" that formed the latter-day English edition of the Lads of Kilkenny consisting of a mix of five writers and painters.[34] The depth of the bond need not exclude sexuality, as Burstein insists with a dearth of evidence and a royal pronoun in the phrase, "as we understand it." At least one Knickerbocker, Fitz-Greene Halleck, has been identified as a homosexual through convincing recent scholarship by a distant relative, John W.M. Hallock, in *The American Byron: Homosexuality and the Fall of Fitz-Greene Halleck* (2000). There certainly was a homosocial element in the brotherhood of Irving's circles, but the difficulty lies in identifying evidence for a gay culture at a time when a full vocabulary for it did not exist. How seriously should we take Irving's humorous sally—"I hope you and Peter are getting comfortable through the Honey Moon, and find housekeeping pleasant"—in his letter to London artist friend Charles Robert Leslie about Leslie taking up residence with friend Peter Powell?[35] Should it be understood in the spirit of Melville's depiction of the cozy loving pair Queequeg and Ishmael become when they awake in each other's arms during an early scene in *Moby-Dick* (1851)? Yet in Melville's experiences at sea with young unmarried men, there is a strong likelihood that the homosocial bond may have been expressed physically. Further, Halleck was outed in his own time by several literary critics, most notably James Lawson, through highly codified language in reviews that sent him underground after launching a promising career as the most revered American poet next to Longfellow. The evidence suggests that homosexuality was both an in-joke as well as a very real presence in the culture posing unique career challenges for members of literary bachelor cohorts.

Halleck's unmarried status, unlike Irving's, could not be parlayed into a culturally acceptable public persona upon which to build a profitable literary career in antebellum America. He was not a member of the original Lads of Kilkenny, and thus could not legitimate his single status by association with the coterie, and draw on its boyish raillery for materials with which to construct his public profile. Hence the public rapidly became suspicious of his failure to marry. Critical analysis of his poetry turned into an attack on his sexuality led by Lawson, who found his verse irregular, unnatural, and incongruous. Willis Clark was even more open about outing Halleck by calling one poem "a truly amphibious and hermaphrodite composition," as critics increasingly conspired to prove, according to the poet's biographer, that his "form was symptomatic of a personal breach with nature."[36] Halleck's success was considerable—John Quincy Adams praised the power of his "Alnwick Castle" (1823), he was the dinner guest of Andrew Jackson in 1832, and school children recited "Marco Bozzarus" from memory—though only short lived.[37] The most significant poet of any Knickerbocker prior to the Young America circle that began in 1840, Halleck credited Irving for having the greatest influence upon his style. He preferred to associate his works with the Irving of *Salmagundi* and *The History of New York* rather than *The Sketch Book*, mainly because of his affinity for satire. Though capable of writing moving poetry, Halleck never emulated, at least in any sustained way, Geoffrey Crayon's sentiment that peppers sketches like "The Wife." Retrospective romantic reveries inspired by historical monuments and castles, however, did inspire "Alnwick Castle," which was written in the Crayonesque tradition of the wandering

American bachelor, reflecting on the pomp and pageantry of Britain's proud past. Of all the writings of Knickerbockers, Halleck's writing was stylistically the most like Irving's, even more so than Paulding's, which was notorious for first mimicking and then competing with the original Knickerbocker.

Like Irving prior to writing *The Sketch Book*, Halleck thrived on coterie authorship fueled by cohorts consisting of bachelor wits capable of cracking the satirical whip. Just as Irving had collaborated with the (temporarily) unmarried Paulding to create *Salmagundi*, Halleck paired with his close bachelor friend Joseph Rodman Drake during the spring and summer of 1819 to pen a spate of poetic parodies, dubbed the *Croakers*, for the *Evening Post* and the *National Advocate*. Rodman's marriage soon thereafter devastated Halleck much in the way Allston's had crushed Irving. Losing Rodman inspired nothing less than Halleck's best and most popular poetry, first with a parody of Rodman's new bride in the mock epic poem, *Fanny*, and then on the occasion of Rodman's unexpected death, the heartfelt elegy, "On the Death of Joseph Rodman Drake." *Fanny* took the literary market by storm in a tour de force parody of fashionable literary and commercial New York life. Holding up a mirror to the literary culture of the time, *Fanny* exposes pretentions to cultural sophistication amid materialistic business priorities. It even contains a self-promotional (yet disarmingly self-effacing) reference to the *Croakers*, as well as "The new *Salmagundi*," which was Paulding's *Salmagundi, Second Series* (1819–1820), as local productions setting the standard of literary fashion.[38]

Fanny appeared in 1819 at an opportune time to revive interest in the Knickerbocker coterie, since the heyday of *Salmagundi* was over more than a decade ago. The poem targets the erosion of literary standards in the face of the new capitalist ethos epitomized by Fanny's father's ascendance to wealth. Hallock (the poet's biographer) argues that the poem is essentially the frustrated rant of a jilted homosexual lover.[39] The poem indeed works as a sort of psychosexual allegory, and illuminates the dynamics of the New York literary scene beyond Halleck's biography. In addition to venting his frustrations at the loss of Drake to a fashionable, well-connected bride, Halleck's fictional Fanny had a clear public counterpart. Perhaps the most famous actress in the world at the time, Francis Anne Kemble was touted for her leading role in *Romeo and Juliet*, performed on 25 October 1819 at Covent Garden Theatre in London, which was regarded as "the greatest success ever achieved by a *debutante*."[40] Touring America on the wings of her new fame, the English actress became infamous soon for her criticism of American theater and literary culture. This was the Fanny who Halleck had in mind, as he appears to be writing in her voice at times, mocking her rigid disapproval of the elite New York circles, as she was well known for assaulting what she felt were superficial self-stylized fashionables. Halleck would justify "her fears of my reputation as a satirist" upon their introduction by sending up Ms. Kemble's hyperbolic and shrill cry against what she perceived to be a tawdry union of money and literature exhibited by a crass commodity and commercial culture parading its pretentions to literary sophistication.[41] Specifically, there is an explicit exposure of literature's new home with the merchant in the mock epic, which laments in maudlin tones the loss of classical antiquity to technology, commerce (and its attendant materialism), fashion, and the modern languages. The antimaterialist strain is so hyperbolic as to not be taken seriously, but rather, should be understood as a joke on the literary culture's popular sway at the time, which even includes antimaterialistic temperance reform. Indeed, champagne is equated with ambition for its intoxicating effects that bring about delusions of grandeur, illustrated in the image of the crashing chandelier during a party she holds to show off her wealth to interested bachelors. Her status as merchandise is reprised at the conclusion of the poem, as the narrator speculates about the prospect of marrying her and the wealth the marriage would bring.

Fanny reads like the antebellum equivalent of an incisive parody of today's *Cosmo* set, listing the essentials on every antebellum New York lady's resume who lays claim to status as a true cosmopolite. Paulding's *Backwoodsman* is hilariously sent up through its comparison to Homer ("would he ever / Have written, think ye, the Backwoodsman? never"), and Halleck's own fashionability in the literary market also comes on stage as one of the essentials in Fanny's reading including his own *Croakers*.[42] The characteristic Knickerbocker pretentions to naïveté regarding financial matters is even mocked through the narrator's assertion that "Money is power, 'tis said" and confession that "I never tried; / I'm but a poet—and bank notes to me are curiosities."[43] All of this contributes to an assault on the assailant, a dig at Fanny Kemble's condescending dismissal of the American literary scene, and thus a genial and humorous defense of New York's literary coteries. The satire is not finally aimed at disavowing the fashionable elite, for the narrator's idiotic meter comes across as absurd—"And each exerts his intellectual force/ To cheat his neighbor—legally, of course"—but rather, is a playful send up of its foibles betraying a fondness and kinship with it. If anything, the fashionable Knickerbocker circles are paradoxically validated and reclaimed, praised even, for being worthy of notice by Ms. Kemble in all her hyperbolic prudery. This evisceration of Ms. Kemble simultaneously offers a satirical profile of the hip cosmopolite's resume and all its essentials of theater, opera, literature, and foreign languages, all of which are modern, including "Low Dutch and Spanish / And the thought of studying modern Greek and Danish."[44]

Fanny pokes fun at the scramble for literary and intellectual justifications behind a socialite's marriage in a way that echoes the Lads' growing distrust of marriage attendant to their transition from their premarital early twenties into middle age. Irving's fear of losing his associates to marriage was considerable. He confessed that Brevoort's betrothal "had rather the effect of making me feel melancholy than glad," showing his worries openly for the future of their intimacy, since "it seemed in a manner to divorce us forever; for marriage is the grave of Bachelors [*sic*] intimacy and after having lived & grown together for many years, so that our thought & feelings were quite blended & intertwined, a separation of this kind is a serious matter."[45] Marriage, however, did not sever Knickerbocker ties for Paulding and Brevoort; it only changed each author's relation to the coterie and thus the trajectory of his career. Washington and his brother Peter, along with Kemble were the only Lads of Kilkenny to remain bachelors; Irving always had time for social visits with unmarried friend Jack Nicholson, who was close to their circle. Paulding and Brevoort were among the original Lads of Kilkenny who did not vanish from the literary scene, but instead reinvented themselves professionally. The careers of both diverge from the bachelor identity, yet nonetheless reinvest in Knickerbocker stock, spinning new portfolios from their link to *Salmagundi* legend.

Brokering Knickerbocker Stock

James Kirke Paulding knew the commercial value of his Knickerbocker association, as he promptly attempted to reprise *Salmagundi*'s glory with a second series, written entirely by himself in 1819, ironically the year Irving published *The Sketch Book* in England. The volume met with meager returns, but did not stop Paulding from continuing his quest to capitalize upon his Knickerbocker roots. His next offering, *The Diverting History of John Bull and Brother Jonathan* speaks to the influence of Geoffrey Crayon, Irving's pen name and narrative persona of *The Sketch Book*, who expertly diffuses political animosity between England and America, admonishing both nations for transgressions of what he feels should be a filial love and respect between the countries. Paulding's aptly titled *Diverting History* does just that, in an allegory of the United States and England as a father and a son engaged in a private domestic feud, taking Crayon's lead and replacing historical specificity and political agency for a purportedly timeless parable about paternity with universal import. He is not so much showing Irving's influence, as he is producing works fluent with the jargon of the Knickerbocker coterie, the accent of which Duyckinck is sure to capture with observations such as, "In this work the policy and conduct of the United States is keenly but good-humoredly satirized, so much that the whole was republished in numbers in one of the British journals," a fact attributable as much to an adoring public, as to pure larceny in an era of rampant unsolicited reprinting.[46]

In 1822, Paulding went back to the well with *A Sketch of Old England by a New England Man*, purporting, very much in the spirit of Geoffrey Crayon, "to be a narrative tour of the country," with "incidents humorously narrated," prompting "discussion of the social, religious, and political points of difference between the two nations."[47] The building of his career upon his Knickerbocker past ended as he began to speak more openly with his own voice. His 1836 publication, *Slavery in the United States*, all but severed his coterie affiliation in the public eye, as he abandoned the politically assuaging Knickerbocker style for a strident proslavery defense of the peculiar institution that would land him in the company of Carlyle, who had been ousted from another major antebellum American literary coterie, the Transcendentalists, due to Southern sympathies (as discussed in chapter one). In the preface to the 1860 edition of *Salmagundi*, a well meaning Evert Duyckinck attempts to rescue Paulding's waning reputation by excerpting a passage from his prose fiction, only to reveal his wretched and regrettable racial politics. The passage in question was intended to illustrate Paulding's skill at expressing pathos and sentiment, yet the last line of the maudlin scene depicting an old slave's death only reinforces the author's condescending tone toward what he believes is the slave's permanently servile position not only on earth, but in heaven as well: "'What will old negro like me do there [in heaven]?'—Then his eye seemed glad for a moment, and his last words were—'Never mind—I can wait upon the angels.'"[48]

Paulding actively promoted the authorship of the original *Salmagundi* as a joint effort so collaborative in nature as to make the authors' individual contributions indistinguishable. "The thoughts of the authors were so mingled together in these essays, and they were so literally joint productions, that it would be difficult as well as useless to assign to each his share."⁴⁹ Portraying the work as a seamless symbiotic merger of creative minds was not without its commercial appeal for Paulding, who knew that setting himself up as Irving's literary twin of sorts would pay handsome dividends in the literary market. In 1819, Paulding published the second series of *Salmagundi* in this spirit, yet Irving by then had moved on to the most lucrative project of his career in *The Sketch Book*. Irving had felt that their work was too jejune, since he had made significant efforts to sophisticate and evolve the bachelor aesthetic into the persona of Geoffrey Crayon. Rejected, Paulding felt embittered and jealous of Irving throughout his career, remarking that "I never claimed for more than an equal share" of the critical acclaim accrued to Irving.⁵⁰ Paulding's sense of entitlement was not appeased by an adoring public, but instead, was met with an uneven and often indifferent reception by the public. Duyckinck assessed the second series as "a dangerous undertaking, for the very essence of a Salmagundi is the combination of divers ingredients—a product of many minds," a coterie product, rather than an individual one.⁵¹ Salmagundi, which at the time referred to "a mixture of chopped meat and pickled herrings, with oil, vinegar, pepper, and onions," was an apt metaphor for collaborative coterie authorship.⁵² Without the trio working together to diversify the literary ingredients, true salmagundi was not possible. Thus forced into solo authorship, Paulding's writings became derivative, rather than fruitfully linked to the Knickerbocker tradition, as his tepid critical reception led him to write a series of novels over the course of ten years beginning in the mid-1820s. He would finally earn critical respect, if not prodigious monetary rewards, for his later plays, winding up his career on President Van Buren's cabinet as secretary of the Navy, a position, tellingly, Irving himself had previously turned down.

James Fenimore Cooper, also considered a Knickerbocker through his Bread and Cheese Club affiliation, like Paulding, understandably attempted to capitalize on his connection to the coterie.⁵³ With the circulation of so many *Sketch Book*–inspired works in the market, those with real ties to the circle, like Cooper, stood a better chance in the market. Known mainly as the author of once famous Leather Stocking Tales, it is seldom mentioned that Cooper published in 1828 the Geoffrey Crayonesque *Notions of Americans, by a Traveling Bachelor*, yet with a more staunchly aggressive American defense that did not take pains to placate the British. The Crayon formula of Anglo-American cultural criticism disguised as a bachelor's travel memoir in Cooper's hand becomes a more one-sided correction of false British impressions of American culture and society. Unlike Irving, Cooper spins his work without deference to filial piety, donning an attitude of staunch patriotism over ambassadorial reconciliation. Interestingly, Cooper's nationalism committed the coterie sin of disclosing the synthesis of business and literary interests by touting both as American strengths, he predicted, that would prosper. Fitz-Greene Halleck, eagle-eyed satirist, pounced on the faux pas, mocking Cooper's defense of American industry for the absurdity of boasting that "in fifty years, or sooner, / We shall export our poetry and wine; / And our brave fleet, eight frigates and a schooner, / Will sweep the seas from Zembla to the Line," simultaneously triumphing in areas in which Europe dwarfed the United States at the time: poetry, wine, and navies.[54] Something of a lightning rod, Cooper also drew controversy over his barbs at Sir Walter Scott, particularly his attack on Lockhart's *Life of Scott*, which angered prominent New Yorker George Templeton Strong into proclaiming Cooper "meanly malignant enough for anything."[55] Scott's exalted status among New Yorkers was forged primarily by Irving, whose alliance with the author of medieval romantic adventure novels traced back to his orchestration of the American's celebrated reception in Great Britain. Cooper's disdain for Scott's fiction as described by Perry Miller could have also applied to Irving: "Cooper advanced the dangerous thesis that Scott was in fact no romancer at all...that by trying to conceal his one and only gift, he showed himself, as he did in social conduct, a hypocrite, a snob, and a fawner upon dukes and duchesses."[56] Cooper's blasphemy of ridiculing the Knickerbockers' youthful allegiance to Scott voiced a kind of strident nationalism better suited to the coterie's next generation, Young America (1837–1855).

Insider Trading

What began as a series of anecdotes reflective of the Knickerbocker creed's dedication to delight developed into a close and continued relationship with the world of publishing. Frivolous gatherings have led to serious creative ventures before. The Society of Dilettanti, for example, resemble an early English art version of the Lads of Kilkenny. They were a gentleman's club of painters and professionals who gathered in 1734 under the motto *Seria Ludo*, equal parts serious business and ludicrous play. Reminiscence upon their Grand Tours led to sophomoric absurdity, as they dressed up in ridiculous outfits to pepper their outlandish tales. Soon their meetings would inspire and lead to artistic production. One painter, George Knapton, created a coterie-inspired rogue's gallery satirizing many personalities from the Earl of Sandwich in a Turkish turban leering at a glass of wine to Sir Francis Dashwood dressed in a monk's cassock toasting "Matri Sanctorum" while lecherously ogling a disrobed Venus.[57] Like the Lads of Kilkenny, the Society of Dilettanti consisted of a mix of professionals and artists particularly adept in social graces useful for attracting patrons. The Knickerbockers' youthful romp also developed into artistic production and full engagement of the mechanisms of the market to promote their works.

Salmagundi was originally something of a domestic entertainment, a small show to put on without any larger coherence, governed instead by anecdotal amusement. It looks like a family affair, and much of the Knickerbocker aesthetic was faithful to the light narrative characterized by brief and disconnected scenes, interludes, and digressions. This aesthetic is a reflection of the coterie's antimaterialistic strand, its rebellion against occupational specialization reflected in standards of artistic mastery. Irving himself would defend this dilettantish image of authorship later in his career, much in the way he would defend his decision to refuse secure employment throughout his career. His literary style, in this sense, is contiguous with his professional career. Rigorous, all-consuming, narrowly defined positions like the editorial job Sir Walter Scott offered him, or the appointment as the first clerk in the Navy Department Stephen Decatur generously granted him with a handsome salary of $2,400, he argued, would have been anathema to his discursive and divergent imagination. His letter to Brevoort dated 11 December 1824 firmly defends "writing occasionally for my own amusement," asserting his enjoyment of putting "the first conception and first sketchings down of my ideas" compared to "the correcting and preparing them for press" that he finds "irksome," while "publishing is detestable."[58] Late in his career, Irving wrote for Lewis Gaylord Clark from 1839 to 1849, friend and editor of the *Knickerbocker* magazine who suited this sensibility precisely. "I am tired," he confessed, "of writing volumes... there is too much preparation, arrangement, and parade in this set form of coming before the public." Periodical writing, instead, enabled him to "loll at my ease in an elbow chair, and chat sociably with the public, as with an old friend, on any chance subject that might pop into my brain."[59] Novels, furthermore, were out of question, as their specialization into narrowly defined genres, "the manner or school of any other writer," would rob him of the freedom he enjoys writing "sketches and short tales."[60] Vacillating between subjects and relishing the serendipity of creativity were Irving's preferred mode of literary production, an image of authorship consonant with the bachelor aesthetic of untethered rambling for his own amusement. Irving would always defend digression and rationalize his unwillingness to create a symmetrical whole of his works. He tried hard to aestheticize the "miscellany" and sketch as worthy literary genres, but he was not the later genius of Thoreau or Melville in his use of mixed form genre.[61] Instead he was a gossip columnist, a potpourri writer of amiable wit, a master of the quotidian, who believed in the sophistication he could manage in small isolated pieces. This was the opposite aesthetic of Melville, who would shout, "give me a Condor's quill!" and demand "plenty of sea-room to tell the truth in," painting his works, as he liked them best, on an expansive canvas.[62] When it came to promotion, however, there was nothing amateur or small about Irving's support of his Knickerbocker associates and use of them to advance his own career.

The Lads of Kilkenny might appear to be a patrician exclusive group of privileged and idle gentlemen. Yet the history of their business dealings suggests otherwise. The surprising extent of the logrolling, gamesmanship, and use of other people's money to publish and promote their fellow coterie members' works reflected instead a gritty, opportunistic, Yankee business ethic. Their influence was vital in launching and developing innumerable careers, not the least of which was that of Herman Melville. George Palmer Putnam published his first novel, *Typee, or A Peep at Polynesian Life* (1846), for example, only after Washington Irving had read the manuscript as a favor to Melville's brother and sometime agent, Gansevoort. One Southern reviewer, Oaky Hall, lauded Melville as a sturdy Knickerbocker; the author even paid homage to Irving late in life with a prose-poem tribute entitled, "Rip Van Winkle's Lilacs."

As the coterie grew over time, however, the outer limits of its almost tribal loyalty that provided Melville with his first big break were tested on at least one occasion when Knickerbocker money and influence failed to bail out one of its weaker, and more bizarre members, McDonald Clarke, "The Mad Poet." Clarke, an overdressed dandy whose verses were equally ill clad (ending couplets typically reeked with unforgivable similes like "For poets are like stinking fish, / That never shine until they're rotten"), awoke one morning in 1840 to find himself hungry and broke, and immediately sought out Fitz-Greene Halleck for help.[63] After Halleck pressed a two-and-half-dollar gold coin into his palm, Clarke promptly hurried off in search of a meal. On the way, he could not resist handing the money over to a traveling organ grinder playing his favorite song, which Halleck himself had witnessed. Seeing him approach, Clarke ran for cover in a store beneath the Astor House, while the traveling minstrel also fled, thinking he had been handed the gold by mistake.[64] Clarke increasingly found himself in such predicaments, as he continued to lean on the generosity of his Knickerbocker associates, such as Samuel Woodworth, who along with Halleck, was also known to have supplemented the Mad Poet's paltry income earned from writings for newspapers and magazines. Clarke rapidly became infamous for squandering the privilege not only of his coterie ties, but also of his wife's affluent family. His marriage to famous actress Mary Brundage ended in separation, and Clarke's frivolous eccentricity turned to hopeless insanity, landing him in an asylum on Blackwell's Island, where he lived his final years in misery. The moniker by which he signed his publications and upon which he hoped to broker his public profile—posing as nonlinear reckless hedonistic witty "Mad Poet"—could not be converted into a lucrative career without the sort of sane financial management that would come to characterize Irving's illustrious career.

The name "Knickerbocker" itself was a product of the promotional and marketing imagination of Irving. Prior to the publication of *Salmagundi*, he aggressively marketed *A History of New York* with the help of the Lads. His advertising scheme was legendary, as he prepared the book's reception by publishing an editorial describing an odd man, perhaps not in command of all his faculties, who had disappeared from an inn leaving behind an assortment of papers and a book manuscript. Irving's faux author was Diedrich Knickerbocker, the quirky Dutch historian whom Irving later reprised as the quasi source of "The Legend of Sleepy Hollow" and other tales in *The Sketch Book*. Promotion was always a coterie affair for Irving, even before the days of leapfrog on the lawn of Cockloft Hall, as he convinced Lads Paulding and Brevoort to place his tale about the mysterious Mr. Knickerbocker in William Coleman's *Evening Post*, which appeared on 26 October 1809. It describes "a small elderly gentleman, dressed in an old black coat and cocked hat, by the name of KNICKERBOCKER. As there are some reasons for believing he is not entirely in his right mind, and as great anxiety is entertained about him any information concerning him left at the Columbian Hotel, Mulberry street, or at the office of this paper, will be *thankfully*, received."[65]

Brevoort was instrumental in helping Irving realize the full financial potential of his writings later in his career. Brevoort is understood as gradually replacing Ebenezer Irving in the role of his primary literary agent and publicist, which indeed he took over later in his career.

Yet as early as 1812, Brevoort wrote Irving from Paris requesting for him "to find a safe conveyance for a new Knickerbocker & a sett of Salmagundi; I want to present them to Mad. D'Arblay the authoress of Evelena."[66] This was one of the earliest signs of transnational promotional support from within the cohort, in a gesture indicative of his increasingly earnest efforts in advancing the literary fame of his friend that would eventually become his main occupation and life's work. More important than the presentation of complementary copies to D'Arblay was the economy of literary exchange that ensued from his relationship with Sir Walter Scott. Upon meeting Scott and falling into a stimulating discussion in which Brevoort demonstrated his impressive facility with New England Native American Indian history, Scott generously offered Brevoort an ample portion of his well-stocked library of archival gems on the subject he had amassed in preparation for a book, which he had abandoned, on American Indians. Brevoort wisely reciprocated by giving Scott Irving's *A History of New York* at a dinner that included Kemble, a scene he described as another instance of many in which "I dwelt largely upon the intelligence & liberality of our best circles of society" in exchange, of course, for favors he did for them.[67] He also meticulously gauged the circulation of the book in the foreign market for Irving, worrying "that for a beginning the man [i.e., the printer] has been liberal [in his estimate of the size of the first run]," yet "if the work is found to have a wider circulation than the printer contemplated, you have it in your power to increase your subsidy correspondingly."[68]

Brevoort's gift to Scott was an expense gladly incurred by Irving, as he stood to profit handsomely from the exchange, since it so perfectly prepared Scott's reception of Irving's eventual visit to Great Britain with the intent of publishing *The Sketch Book*. Like today's "invisible primary" so influential in determining the actual presidential primary in the United States, Brevoort had ideally prefigured Irving's success in England by winning support for him long before the author's actual arrival there, having done the necessary legwork of intermediary social linking to affirm that "I am now well acquainted with the luminaries of Edinburgh and confess that among them all, Scott is the man of may choice."[69] Irving must have been overjoyed to receive Brevoort's report that he had "presented Walter Scott with a copy of the second edition of Knickerboker [*A History of New York*] in return for some very rare Books," which also included, most importantly, Scott's praise for Irving written in his own hand: "I enclose you a Letter that I received from him since; you must understand his words literally for he is too honest & too sincere a man to compliment any person."[70] The door was open for Irving to become the first American author of an international bestseller. Irving's reception in England, a process in which Scott would prove so pivotal, could not have been better prearranged by Brevoort's decision to compensate his gift with Irving's book.

By 1819, when Irving went to Europe and Brevoort returned to the United States, Brevoort oversaw the full publication process of *The Sketch Book* in New York. He purchased the paper, checked proof sheets, communicated with publishers and booksellers regarding all phases of production and marketing, and even wrote the first positive review of the book in the *Evening Post*, to which Irving himself responded by saying how touched he was by the kind words on his behalf. Brevoort's agency proved more lucrative and reliable than that of even Irving's own brothers, as his friend was essential in escalating his career to world fame after *The Sketch Book*. Irving's *Life of Columbus* received a strong critical reception, for example, due to the intermediary efforts of Brevoort. His letter of 19 December 1827, like almost all his correspondence addressed to his author friend, reads like a statement from a financial institution, as well as shrewd advice from the best connected of stock brokers, his finger on the very pulse of the literary market. In particular, he lauds the virtue of prepublication reviews, of which, Scott not surprisingly had set the precedent. Brevoort mentions that Renwick's "review will appear a short time before the Work itself, but a similar anachronism occurred in two articles on Scott's Napoleon which preceded the publication of the Work nearly six months." The review, Brevoort assured him, would function as the best advertising imaginable, since "Sir Walter's book was greatly aided by the review & many thousand copies have been sold."[71] This particular letter typifies the most effective communication pattern within the Knickerbocker coterie, as it so frequently prioritizes business while also reinforcing the fraternal bond of the cohort. "All our old friends are doing well," Brevoort assures Irving, shifting tone from broker and agent to genial brother reporting on the well-being of the extended family.

Fourteen Wards and Thirty-Seven Bards

Partially a symptom of the small population at the time, there were seemingly far less than six degrees of separation linking any given Knickerbocker to another. The concentration of literary talent in New York City in 1829 led Halleck to quip in the *Recorder* that "our fourteen wards contain some seven-and-thirty bards."[72]

Indeed, it is telling that William Leggett's biographical sketches of prominent American poets that appeared in the New York *Mirror* on 26 January 1828 included Irving—a nonpoet yet very much the hub of literary New York—among the ranks of Brooks, Bryant, Halleck, Percival, Pierpont, Pinckney, Sprague, and Woodworth.[73] Theirs was a small world of interrelated marriages and club affiliations forming a social web of recursive connections. Paulding's introduction to the Calliopean Society in New York, for example, was made possible because his sister had married William Irving, the host who made his home "the general resort of [the] knot of wits and humorists."[74] William not only put Paulding in touch with this literary circle, but also housed him under his own roof and secured reliable employment for him in the form of a clerkship at the United States Loan Office. Shelter, income, and a lively literary circle did not account for all of Paulding's privileges, which also extended into the realm of publication. His first publications landed through the intermediary aid of Peter Irving, editor of the *Morning Chronicle* and later in Washington Irving's *Analectic* magazine. Washington had noticed Paulding's posts in his brother's newspaper and invited him to join the Lads at Kemble's mansion, where they would concoct the first numbers of *Salmagundi*. Paulding married Kemble's sister, and the two purchased their Washington, D.C. home from Commodore Stephen Decatur, who had previously shared a bachelor retreat with Irving in New York. Paulding's first child, Peter Kemble Paulding, was named after Peter Irving and Gouverneur Kemble; his second son, William Irving Paulding, bore the appellation of his most generous patron and provider. Paulding benefitted handsomely from his ties to the Irving family yet failed to capitalize on his high standing in the Knickerbocker coterie as one of its founding fathers. He would become a jealous competitor of Irving's, always an afterthought to his former coauthor's lofty renown.

William Cullen Bryant benefitted from his Knickerbocker ties similar to the way Paulding had in his early career. Fitz-Greene Halleck provided Bryant with his first big break by placing his wildly popular "Marco Bozzaris" in the pages of his *New-York Review and Athenaeum Magazine*. Halleck's star was rising at the time, and Bryant's journal ascended with it. Bryant was a fixture at Cooper's lunches, dubbed "The Bread and Cheese Club," a Knickerbocker congregation that gathered during Irving's travels in Europe. As Bryant gained credibility, he eventually would take over the club when Cooper departed overseas, renaming it "The Sketch Club" in 1826 in honor of Irving, and also as a reflection of the vogue of the literary and visual sketch at the time. Irving himself later placed Bryant's work with a London publisher, effectively introducing him to the English audience.

Fitz-Greene Halleck's entrance upon the literary stage was vintage Knickerbocker. Halleck reprised Irving and Paulding's collaborative effort on *Salmagundi* through his literary partnership with Joseph Rodman Drake on the serially published satirical *Croaker* poems. Paulding and Drake would strategically conceal authorship, until initialing their work to indicate "that we each had a finger in the pie."[75] This was a signal tactic of the coterie, as years later, according to Perry Miller, "one of the games the *Knickerbocker* [journal begun in 1833] played with its subscribers was a mystification as to who wrote what."[76] Halleck himself played that very game with the publication of *Fanny*, about which Brevoort said "he would feel prouder of being the author of *Fanny* than of any other poetical work ever written in America."[77] Halleck's greatest accomplishment, he allowed in one letter, was Brevoort's credibility, the authority of his praise deriving directly from his status as Knickerbocker: "Brevoort," he gushes, "was one of the original 'Salmagundi' concern, and has deservedly the character of a man of extensive literary taste and knowledge. From him"—rather than "a general class of readers [that] does not know good from bad" in his estimation—therefore, "a compliment is worth having," he wrote to his sister Maria.[78]

Yet it was Irving who was the most instrumental figure in launching Halleck's career. The poet confessed to his sister that he had never dreamed of publishing *Fanny* were it not that "the bookseller who brought out Irving's 'Sketch-Book' [Wiley] offered to publish 'Fanny' in a style similar to that work, and I consented to his doing so. The Bookseller stated to me that I was the only writer in America, Irving excepted, whose works he would risk publishing. This opinion was founded, of course, upon the popularity of 'The Croakers,' " and significantly, the good word of Irving, the original Knickerbocker.[79] Tellingly, when Charles Dickens visited New York in 1868, he confessed to wanting to meet Irving, that he "had hoped to see *him*! My dear Irving being dead, there was scarcely any one in American whom I so looked forward to seeing" as Halleck, who functioned for Dickens as the next best author to Irving, a ready substitute for Geoffrey Crayon's creator.[80]

Still more opportunities for Halleck presented themselves through Irving. For example, Wiliam H. Prescott of Boston, publisher of *Club-Room*, solicited poetry from Halleck, pitching a deal for a project "similar to that of *The Sketch-Book*." There is "no writer in America," Prescott assured him, "except the author of 'Fanny,' whose poetry has sufficient merit to entitle it a place in his work." Gleeful, Halleck exclaimed that this is "what one may call the puff direct," a case in which an author finds his own work promoted to himself. Halleck appealed to Prescott because of what his value as a coterie author, whose name would support his subsidiary branch of the Knickerbockers, indicating that the *Club-Room* was initiated by a group of friends, "a knot of gentlemen in this town, most of whom are habitual contributors to the *North American Review*."[81] Prescott praised Halleck's poetry for its "easy conversational wit, and poetry of descriptions, must go alongside of Lord Byron's and Mr. Rose's productions in the same way," very much in keeping with the tenor of the club's formation.[82] The gatherings, like the journal's social and literary purposes, were colored by easy conversational wit, and acquisition of a known Knickerbocker rounded out its profile for a positive gain for both the editor and the poet.

Irving's positive influence over Halleck's career might make it appear that the author of *The Sketch Book* was capable of generating his own fame without relying upon the sort of intermediary aid necessary for the development of so many Knickerbocker careers. But he was no exception. His triumphant return from Europe, for example, was prearranged, just like the English reception of *The Sketch Book*, by his best literary agent, Henry Brevoort. Not a writer, but a friend and liaison to the Knickerbocker circle, Brevoort was the son of a wealthy owner of the valuable New York City real estate. Indeed, his management of the red-carpet welcome, even while in France, is evident in his awareness of how the anticipation of Irving's arrival in America, "the return of Geoffrey Crayon, has made old times and associations of early life the leading topics of conversation among his friends."[83] As the key intermediary in ensuring a Knickerbocker reunion was there to receive him, Brevoort exults not so much in Irving's triumph as his own in thrusting him before the public eye. In absentia from the festivities, Brevoort invokes his coterie membership from overseas, as he "fancied myself seated at the table, mingling with our loyal friends & townsmen in cheering and greeting your long expected return." The occasion would provide nothing less than a ritual celebration reaffirming the life and vitality of the Knickerbocker circle, rather than a cultish hero worship of Irving himself. If anything, expectations for his oratorical address were low, Brevoort noting how "for once in your [Irving's] life I was sorry to find you compelled to perform a part so repugnant to your nature."[84] Indeed, N.P. Willis's coverage in the 9 June 1832 *New York Mirror* of the formal welcoming dinner for Irving held the week prior at the City Hotel in New York describes not a triumphant voice dominating the scene, but one barely audible, "his first few words, which were low, and would have been inaudible but for the perfect silence around, there ran through the whole crowd," whose collective voice significantly takes over with "a murmur of delight."[85] Showcased that evening was not Irving in isolation as much as his authorial identity transformed into a metonymic extension of the coterie of Knickerbockers that had been formed a quarter of a century earlier. Indeed, the evening served notice to "the younger part of our community," the future Knickerbockers, that "have been so long accustomed to hear of him, and to read his thoughts, without the hope of seeing his person, and listening to his voice, that the appearance of the *man* among us is almost like the coming to life of some of those departed poets and authors whose works enrich our libraries, and whose names are cherished as something sacred and apart from those of the living."[86] That night, those new young voices—among them the constituents of Young America—emerged in the crowd as Irving's voice was hushed.

The Astor Factor

Irving's career, like Halleck's, could be effectively traced according to a typology of bachelor's retreats, edifices beginning with Cockloft Hall, coursing their way through the quarters of European royalty (for Irving) and culminating in the sumptuous New York estate of John Jacob Astor. The Donald Trump of his era, Astor had made his fortune in the lucrative fur trade, which grew into an empire in itself. Indeed, the pattern of his patronage was not unlike the one in the U.S. government that readily found employment for New York's men of letters, for example, appointing Paulding chief secretary of the Navy and making Verplank a Senator. Just as Irving functioned as the authorial figurehead from the literary world at the hub of the coterie, Astor was the chief patron from the industrial sector who bankrolled and underwrote much of their work. Halleck eventually retreated from the literary world in 1832 (for reasons discussed earlier) to work as Astor's personal assistant at the age of forty-two, and stayed in that capacity until 1848, when at the age of fifty-eight he moved in with his sister Maria upon Astor's death. Snubbed in Astor's will—the millionaire never forgave the poet for a flip remark by questioning how much money he really needed to live comfortably[87]— Halleck did not die the man of means Irving did. The *National Magazine* dismissed Halleck in 1852 by declaring that "the merchant has swallowed the poet."[88] Alas, Halleck failed at what Irving managed so successfully—lamenting the materialistic ethos of "this banknote world" in his writings while paradoxically pursuing the capital opportunities through the management of his career at the heart of that very world, aptly represented in the Astor position he held for thirteen years.[89]

Irving viewed things differently, as he instead was rather envious of the arrangement, coveting Halleck's "handsome salary" and residence in a "kind of bachelor's hall."[90] Indeed, Irving's nephew, Pierre, later flourished at Astor's mansion while commissioned as essentially a writer in residence to produce a flattering portrait, which Washington stylized in his own hand, of the magnate's fur empire. *Astoria, or Anecdotes of an Enterprise Beyond the Rocky Mountains* (1834) won Pierre a handsome 3,000 dollars, one-third more than he had requested. As one of the first ghostwritten publications in the history of American literature, *Astoria* bore Washington Irving's name, yet was essentially written by Pierre, whose vast majority of the work rules out its classification as a coauthored or collaborative production like that of Irving and Paulding's *Salmagundi*. Irving's career, capitalist and coterie driven to the end, would not suffer the ironic fate of Halleck's.

The connection to Astor, tellingly, came through Henry Brevoort, whose associations with the industrial titan trace back to his travels as a young man with Astor's entourage to the western frontier. "Nuncle," as he was affectionately called at Cockloft Hall, was thus a ready recommender of any fellow Lad of Kilkenny interested in seeking employment within the Astor empire. Without Brevoort's connection to Astor in the economic history of the Knickerbocker coterie, Brevoort would never have been exposed to the Wild West and its rich Native American history. For it was there, on the frontier, that Brevoort's literary interests were sparked, his knowledge and thirst for Indian history swelling to proportions that arrested Sir Walter Scott and led him to hand the young man his rare collection of books on Indian history. Tellingly, Brevoort's aptitude for writing that Indian history was overestimated by Scott, as Brevoort instead devoted himself to the pleasure of being Irving's literary agent, lifelong friend of the Lads, and man of business, a dilettante to the core, with an instinct for gold to match Irving's own.

Chapter 3

Staff Bonds: Bonner's *New York Ledger*

The early Knickerbocker coterie might appear to be a web of literary associates worlds away from the pulp fiction of the commercial writers who staffed Robert Bonner's *New York Ledger*. Fanny Fern, E.D.E.N. Southworth, Sylvanus Cobb, Lydia Sigourney, and the couple Harriet and Leon Lewis indeed appear totally alien to Irving's Lads of Kilkenny and their roving bachelor image of the early Republic. Yet the innovations of the Knickerbockers actually primed the market for the aggressively innovative, even radical, literary capitalism of the mid-nineteenth-century periodical press, epitomized by the *Ledger*. Just as Irving transformed the Lads of Kilkenny into the lucrative literary circle and marketing machine of the New York Knickerbockers, Bonner originally acquired the *Merchant's Ledger* in 1855 and renamed it for the city that was rapidly transforming into the premier commercial hub of the world. The struggling merchantile sheet that cost the twenty-six–year-old upstart immigrant editor only $500 just five years later made him rich and famous, if not a lightning rod for controversy driven mostly by envious competitors mystified by his meteoric rise. The *Ledger* burst onto the scene through what was to be Fern's bestselling novel of her career much in the way the Knickerbockers made their auspicious debut through the runaway popularity of *Salmagundi*. On the cover of the 9 June 1856 issue, Bonner published Fern's first chapter of her novel, *Ruth Hall* (1856), bringing its sales to 50,000.[1] Bonner's long-term circulation goal was 100,000, which he easily exceeded in less than a decade. According to book historian Ralph Admari, the *Ledger*'s value skyrocketed to several million dollars by 1880, the zenith of a reign of commercial dominance over the literary marketplace that extended to the end of the century.[2]

Historically, the Knickerbocker's commercial command of the first half of the century in American literature is well matched by that of the *Ledger*'s for the second half. Yet contemporary critics have not established any continuity in economics or aesthetics between the two camps. The *Ledger* staff has not been discussed as a group recently, except in cursory historical profiles of the magazine.[3] Recent studies instead have focused on Fern, Southworth, and Sigourney in isolation from colleagues like Cobb and the Lewises, who do not appear to immediately support their gender politics. Fern, for example, has been cast as an independent woman and protofeminist rebel in an image, however accurate, that tends to neglect the function of her sentimentality, especially in the context of the *Ledger*'s commercial agenda.[4] Her career indeed shared vital features with those of her colleagues, such as a lucrative advance offer, high salary, short production deadlines, and liberal artistic license. Fern's subversive social commentary could command such a grand, national stage precisely because Bonner aggressively promoted the *Ledger* as a "family paper," emphasizing variety rather than punditry or political polemic, a strategy that effectively packaged her vitriolic column for mass consumption. Fern herself was a commercial author, just as much as Cobb and Southworth were, who wrote with an acute sensitivity to the demands of her readers, furnishing them with sentiment and domesticity on occasion. The *Ledger* offered its writers a condition for literary production that not only revolutionized contributors' salaries, but also empowered them with creative autonomy and freedom to voice their social and political views without censorship or editorial interference.

Examining these authors not in isolation, but within the context of the social matrix of the *Ledger* circle, reveals the surprising extent to which their careers were shaped by their respective positions within a cadre of staff writers acquired under circumstances designed to make them happy, productive, and, above all, profitable. In this sense, I expand Joyce Warren's research on Fern's relationship with Bonner onto the broader terrain of the economic culture of the *Ledger*, a literary circle defined by its status in the marketplace.[5] I explore the shaping of the authorial role through the business practice and attendant commercial ethos of the *Ledger*. The challenge was to manage the tension inherent in the journal's open embrace of literary capitalism as reflected in its proprietor's advertising methods, yet maintain distinction as a family paper, not just in appearance, but through content written by universally respected figures in religion, politics, and literature.

Bonner and his authors emphasized the best characteristics of the business world—its bravery, vigor, shrewdness—and combined it with the code of sympathy and generosity to make appealing a journal that risked alienating readers in what was the most aggressive wedding of literature and commercialism in the entire nineteenth century. Bonner may have used P.T. Barnum's marketing methods, but his stock in trade was literature rather than the bearded lady or Siamese twins, and thus the cultural inclination against openly commercialized and audaciously advertized literature presented him with a greater, and indeed more profound, challenge to reassemble values about literature and capitalism heretofore never explored. Barnum himself offered Bonner season tickets to his "Museum," recognizing Bonner's value as a celebrity who could reach the masses with somewhat wholesome entertainment. Barnum assured the editor that "the improper characters" were excluded "to keep it nice and genteel and patronizing the best class of society" to enjoy this "most gorgeous and interesting spectacular exhibition ever seen in N.Y.," going so far as to suggest that it is "for public *improvement* as well as public amusement."[6] Barnum thus wanted Bonner's presence at the museum not only for celebrity publicity, but to gentrify and sophisticate his product's image through the association with literature. The letter underscores Bonner's higher cultural status than that of Barnum, pointing simultaneously to his colossal commercial power.

Bonner's connection to highbrow culture is visible in the elite literary figures from Irving's genteel circle who had always been affiliated with the *Ledger*. Tellingly, Bonner's first break came from N.P. Willis, the latter-day Knickerbocker who heralded Irving's triumphant return from Europe in 1832. As editor of the *Evening Mirror*, Willis hired the twenty-year-old Bonner to assist in the print shop, read proofs, and set advertisements, for which he showed uncommon speed and creativity,[7] skills he would later use to build the *Ledger* Empire. Knickerbocker poets Fitz-Greene Halleck and William Cullen Bryant graced his pages decades later. Bryant, in fact, was close enough to Bonner to send him a friend's poetry, asking "Can you do me the favor to look over it and say whether you will print it?"[8] Willis also submitted his work for publication, because "the 'Ledger' is a familiar friend in my household I naturally thought of its Enterprising Editor as a professional to handle the case."[9] The *Ledger*'s reach extended to New England and Longfellow, and overseas to Alfred Lord Tennyson, whom Bonner paid an unheard of $5000 for a single poem.[10]

Bonner would battle for literary respect for his *Ledger* by his signing of high profile writers.[11] Dickens, Tennyson, Longfellow, Henry Ward Beecher, and others of world-class renown silenced critics and reflected credit upon his journal. Southworth's *Hidden Hand* brought her popular, if not exactly literary, distinction, as she toured Europe as celebrity author of her international bestseller, which was produced for the stage throughout the States nearly as frequently as the dramatic adaptation of *Uncle Tom's Cabin*. At a time when less than 10 periodicals reached circulations of 100,000, the *Ledger* towered above them at 400,000.[12] Like the Knickerbockers, the *Ledger* staff forged a public profile that appealed to a broad reading public ranging from coach drivers and chambermaids to college presidents and New England poets.

The *Ledger*'s fiction was designed in part to justify its own wealth and offer a moral code of ethics validating the acquisition of riches based on Bonner's example, while warning against the evils of other less noble methods. Indeed, much of the magazine's stories and serial novels, particularly Southworth's Ishmael Worth, the hero of *Self-Made* (1863), feature Bonner figures who nurture and protect the artistic freedom and financial interests of artist/author figures.[13] The narratives tend to encode the prototype of coterie leadership Bonner established—variously figured in the fiction as legal defense attorney, kindly publisher, and fatherly art patron—which can be traced through the social bonding and capital building of the staff's business relations, characterized by generous loans and personal favors that extended into warm life-long friendships. Indeed, the financial fortress the Knickerbockers built around their fraternal love is matched in nineteenth-century New York only by the magnificent marble edifice Bonner erected for the staff whose portraits lined its luminous halls like royal lineage.[14]

"THE GREAT FAMILY PAPER"

Avoiding churlish or lurid associations with pulp fiction, Bonner painted a portrait of his ideal readership in the most wholesome and domestic of terms, insisting that it had been the original principle upon which he built the *Ledger*: "I pictured to myself an old lady in Westchester with three daughters, aged about twenty, sixteen and twelve, respectively." Careful to include piety in the portrait, he imagines them arriving "home from a prayer meeting," as "the mother takes up the *Ledger* and reads aloud to the girls." Allowing that the magazine was not appropriate for small children, Bonner defends its morally upright content in the self-righteous proclamation that "there has never been one line which the old lady in Westchester County would not like to read to her daughters."[15] Readers liked the way Bonner protected their own reputations through such defenses, for everyone knew better, particularly the critics, that the tales of Southworth, for example, frequently included implicitly codified, if not graphically explicit, scenes of rape, abduction, child abuse, murder, insanity, sadomasochism, and a good measure of gleeful blasphemy, including polygamy (made ever popular by Bronte's *Jane Eyre*), and scheming deviants of all sorts, inclusive of vindictive erasable in-laws, and suave swindlers on the make.[16] To be sure, the *Ledger* was no prayer book, and the reading public force fed the code of purity, piety, and submission through temperance tracts from T.S. Arthur, and defenses of domesticity from Catherine Beecher could not more grateful. The sensationalism in the pages of the *Ledger* was hardly an extension of the old lady's Westchester County prayer meeting, as emotional and even physical turmoil, blood and tears ran from Southworth's stories as readily as the adrenaline flowed through the hairbreadth escapes of Cobb's creations.

Yet, Bonner was careful to maintain a basic standard of decency for the paper, in one telling case excising a significant portion of a Cobb serial that left him "angered that Sylvanus Cobb could have written such a chapter concerning the intercourse between the sexes for a family paper." Careful not to admonish his star contributor too sternly, his reprimand came "in the most affectionate way," as he allowed, "you could not have been yourself while writing it." Bonner did indeed have editorial limitations and a principled dedication to the *Ledger*'s image as a family paper, however loosely drawn, he would not trade for profit. "There is not money enough in Wall Street," he proclaimed with escalating hyperbole, "or on the face of the earth, to induce Robert Bonner to publish it," in a stentorian third-person self-reference invoking his public profile, and its near sacrosanct place in the function of his business.[17] Bonner found that leading the life of a puritan (albeit a multimillionaire), much less a purveyor of pulp, was not without its commercial appeal for the benefit of his paper. He was a god-fearing teetotaler and family man who owned multimillion dollar horses—indeed, some of the fastest in the world—and in a show of piety refused to race them for profit, instead entering them in competitions in which the losing owners made charitable donations of $10,000.[18]

Bonner's biggest coup in establishing the piety of the *Ledger* occurred with the signing of his preacher, Henry Ward Beecher, brother of famous bestselling authors Harriet Beecher Stowe and Catherine Beecher. Not one to pass up the profitable opportunity of signing a rising star, even if that celebrity was a clergyman, Bonner, moved by his minister's oratorical charisma, made his best offer to land him for the *Ledger*. The proposal was for Beecher to write an original novel for the *Ledger*, which would appear in installments over the course of the next year. Beecher had never dreamed of publishing fiction—"as a very moderate reader, even, of fictions, I had rarely studied the mystery of their constructions," he confessed—let alone on the most visible national stage in the American periodical press.[19] He thus demurred, referring to the obvious incongruity of his calling with that of professional authorship for the entertainment of the mass market. Bonner, never one to surrender to a refusal, persisted, only to be met with Beecher's prohibitively large price intended to drive the editor away. Bonner characteristically rose to the challenge, his competitive capitalist fire fully stoked, laying out an astonishing $30,000 in advance for the novel under the assumption that the increased circulation would eventually compensate for and surpass the extravagant sum. The flashy advance payment, one of Bonner's favorite tactics in luring big name authors to the *Ledger*, also worked miracles on Horace Greeley, whose *Recollections* looked to be a series obviously destined for Greeley's own *New-York Tribune*. Bonner was up to the challenge of overcoming the conflict of interests, just as he was in the case of Beecher, and after he invited the rival editor to breakfast and left a $10,000 check waiting for him on his plate, the chronically debt ridden Greeley was too financially hungry to refuse.[20] Likewise, after a period of silence, Beecher accepted his advance, crediting God for his decision to enrich his capital gains with the declaration that "miracles will never cease."[21] Beecher then wrote more than expected, for which Bonner happily paid him a bonus. Mission accomplished, Bonner proudly claimed his prize, trumpeting his new alliance with the pious in the last printed words of the bound 1868 copy of Beecher's novel, *Norwood, or Village Life in New England*. "The Great Family Paper" headed an argument for its quality as commensurate with its popularity, since "The moral tone is always pure and elevated," and it features the "leading clergymen of the United States," in addition to its commitment to secure "the BEST WRITERS...cost what it may."[22]

Norwood testifies on behalf of Bonner's character, indeed arguing strenuously against the common view of him as a heartless tyrant of the market. The 1867 Kansas newspaper, *Freedom's Companion*, typifies the attitude of Bonner's skeptics, as it complains of how he "has paid more for advertising than any other publisher in the world, and by thus using the columns of the press as his forces, he has subjugated the reading community and made himself a millionaire."[23] Beecher's last line counters this image with "pleasant associations...fraternal kindness" and most of all "the highest and most enduring charm of a generous friendship."[24] "Generous" here significantly recasts in terms of emotional sympathy and warmth Bonner's reputation that he himself established for paying extraordinarily extravagant sums to his authors. Beecher deftly renders a notorious business practice—about which Bonner bombastically bragged in advertisements, especially of his record-breaking payment of $100 per column to Fanny Fern in 1856—as warm domestic ("fraternal") virtue.[25]

An excerpt from a Beecher letter proves that the clergyman was not merely bought off by the editor. "I have got so used to the *Ledger* that I seem to fit into its columns more naturally than any where else."[26] The line intends to dispel the implication that the preacher had no plans to associate with Bonner beyond this one novel, and instead emphasizes Beecher's comfort with an ongoing affiliation for the *Ledger*. His debut as a popular serial fiction writer only whetted Beecher's appetite for more professional writing for the mass market. "*Norwood* was a practice and preparation which enabled me to write the lives" of notable historical figures, solid training for the sort of popular biography Parton wrote for the *Ledger*.[27] This would be the biggest payday for a pastor in the history of the nineteenth-century literary market, anticipating the alliance of popular mass media entertainment and Christianity that would takeover with megamillionaire televangelists like Jerry Falwell.[28] The authorial role, thanks to Bonner's fearless and undaunting enterprise, began to reach across the professions, wedding what was once a mercantile commercial ledger with Christianity in a singular expression of literary capitalism on the most massive scale ever achieved.

The Bonner-Beecher correspondence reveals the extent to which the minister was financially tied to his editor. "Will you give me a check for $700 (seven hundred) and await the weekly payment thereof until seven weeks have passed?" he wrote, asking Bonner to cover money owed to him from Horace Greeley for contributions in his *New-York Daily Tribune*. The request reveals how Greeley clearly lacked the vast resources that were at Bonner's disposal, which turned the *Ledger* editor into something of a local savings and loan bank for his authors. Financial support paved the way to a genuine friendship and mutual trust between Beecher and Bonner, as evidenced by the sheer bulk of their correspondence, which is ten times larger than any other in the Bonner archive. Their earlier communication frequently found Beecher elated and exultant, as if he had come across a rare treasure. In his verification of the receipt of payment, for example, Beecher positively gushes with joy, noting "I received both checks for 200 and 100," immediately launching into a series of halleluiahs: "What a glorious morning! What a tremendous day!"[29] As their relationship developed, the tones were more muted, the giddy joy at newfound wealth tempered as Beecher discovered authentic friendship with Bonner. "The past year has been one full of trouble," Beecher confessed in one letter, "and of a nature to test true friendship beyond all doubting...and you my dear Sir have stood through 'evil report and good report' as firm as a rock...you have always been kind and generous for which I have been grateful."[30]

The savage inequality of the free market that writers like Orestes Brownson of the Transcendentalists and George Fitzhugh of the slaveholding South would bewail with distinct socialistic leanings was met by the communitarian human sympathy that paradoxically characterizes the *Ledger*'s literary capitalism.[31] Bonner's salaries dwarfed those of his competitors as illustrated by Beecher's $30,000 per novel and Fern's rate of $100 per column, compared to the average of $25. Bonner's piety and family values, his image as god-fearing millionaire, proved a perfect fit for the business of editing a popular literary periodical at a time when literature itself, still a vehicle for moral instruction, was transforming into a commercial enterprise. Morality and money, indeed, never were more compatible than in the *Ledger*, which was broad enough in its offerings to project the image of a family paper, if not exactly an extension of the prayer book or stand-in bedtime fiction. Bonner indeed practiced the domestic principle of caring for his clan, treating them like extended family in innumerable ways. He made loans to all his authors upon request and without question, particularly to the Lewises who squandered their handsome salaries and teetered near financial ruin for decades. He vacationed with E.D.E.N. Southworth, advocated her divorce from her husband who had abandoned her while pregnant, underwrote the exemption of her son Richmond from military service in the Civil War, and even accommodated her in his own home during her last days. Such intimate warmth fostered loyalty among this staff at a time when periodical writers rarely wrote exclusively for one journal, let alone even sign their names to their work. Bonner's system not only humanized authorship in the market, paradoxically it also turned magazine writers into brand names, and in the case of his own journal, created a coterie setting for literary production. Bonner befriended his authors, and even loved them—Cobb's death devastated him so much that it prompted his retirement—within a business setting of eclectic literary creativity and with a liberal editorial policy fostering productivity and satisfaction among its staff like no other journal in America. Cobb was on such intimate terms with Bonner that he asked if he "had any photographs of yourself taken? I want one very much and I should prize one of your wife."[32] For one Christmas Cobb received an expensive set of fur coats and muffs for his wife and daughter. Business relationships, as Emerson pointed out in his essay, "Gifts," too frequently left out the personal touch, omitted the humanity in transactions and exchanges. The only remedy to how "they eat your service like apples, and leave you out," he said, was to "love them," so that "they feel you and delight in you all the time."[33] For Bonner, compensation was an expression of love, in a formulation that appears either impossible or sickeningly obsequious from the ironic distance of a twenty-first–century perspective. But as the letters testify, the personal care of the relationship with Cobb, as with most of his other authors, was heartfelt and totally authentic.

Cobb's relationship with Bonner embodied the ideal partnership in literary capitalism, as it fostered a friendship as warm and loyal as it was mutually profitable. Cobb routinely gave Bonner title options for his pieces, and showed great flexibility in moving between stories and serial novel, regularly soliciting his input as he had for "Forest Adventures" in a December 1862 letter. In this sense Bonner was not only a source of capital, but also a creative consultant, working to make the *Ledger* achieve a unique kind of currency in the culture. A boy working for Cobb, for example, preferred to be paid in copies of the *Ledger*, as Cobb remarked, "he was almost as proud in making the most = most as it is possible for an unprincipled boy to be."[34] The line speaks volumes of Cobb and Bonner's own pride in making "most = most" in their own business. But their professional work was not without tension, as Cobb worried about piracy and writing pace in correspondence from the 1860s, even complaining in one letter that his parents' visit "of course bothered me some" and forced him to take refuge in his study.[35] These were especially prolific years for Cobb and his tone reflects his genuine desire to produce. Cobb's productivity was indeed a mutual business interest, and as such, was deeply connected to his personal life. Bonner was thus acutely aware that Cobb's love of liquor could turn into a professional liability with detrimental effects on his family life. Responding to Bonner's "confidential query concerning my drinking," Cobb assured his friend, "I have in my house some of the best of brandy, whisky, and gin; but I think no more of touching it than I should in going to my kerosene keg for a drink," reflecting that "you are the only human being outside of my own family to whom I would make answer upon the topic."[36] Indeed, Bonner played such an essential role in Cobb's private life that it prompted the author to write a vignette in one letter imagining the domestic effects of leaving his position with the *Ledger*. The sentimental scene details his wife's sorrowful response, as a "tear steals down her cheek," with her exclaiming "there isn't another man in the world like Robert Bonner!"[37]

As merciless with his competitors as he was tender with his staff, Bonner's public persona, as with Irving's for the Knickerbockers, set the tone for the popular appeal of the *New York Ledger* not only as a family magazine. Indeed, like Irving, his own public persona shaped the fictional subjects of his weekly. Southworth's Ishmael Worth, like Bonner, is a rags-to-riches lad; Worth is also an advocate of creative women characters throughout her fiction. Although her writing for the *Ledger* was essentially as an editorial columnist, Fern's own fiction was instrumental in her signing on with the paper. Her first novel, indeed, also tells the tale of a self-made protagonist's rise to the top. *Ruth Hall* (1855) appeared just as Bonner had signed her; his lucrative deal and protection of her from the savagery of stingy rear-guard editors stands as not just a roman à clef against her famous and well-established brother, N.P. Willis, editor of the *Home Journal*. Indeed, it stands as a virtual advertisement for herself and the editorial innovation, imagination, sympathy, and crusading capitalism of Robert Bonner himself. In addition to Southworth and Fern, Cobb crafted tales of ascent from meager origins. His most famous novel, for example, *The Gunmaker of Moscow*, tells the tale of Ruric Nevel, a peasant who rises through his own industry—and crucially, humanity—to become a member of Peter the Great's inner court. These narratives did not pay homage to Bonner just out of gratuity, but tapped into the cultural fascination with self-made men and, crucially, the intersection of morals and money that led to their rise.

The balance of the *Ledger*'s content between Southworth's longer serial fiction and Fern's column had a particularly potent domestic appeal. Readers could enjoy an installment of a Southworth sentimental yarn, while also being treated to Fern's direct intimacy, and even bluntness, that characterizes the colloquial language of her columns. Indeed, the strength of the *Ledger*, like the Knickerbockers' own *Salmagundi* and *Sketchbook*, lay in its variety, its mastery of the miscellany, reflecting diversity and variety in order to create a sense of comfort and communion with a mass readership. Fern approached writing for the *Ledger*, in part, as Terry Novak paints it, like "chatting cozily with the reader in her kitchen with a plate of cookies and a pot of tea."[38] Yet, like Southworth's seemingly harmless domestic narratives,

Fern's newspaper persona may have been intimate, but not in the nonconfrontational, politically evasive way of the Knickerbockers. She instead habitually exposed the flaws of the patriarchal society, from "Tyrants of the Shop" who verbally abuse their female clerks in front of customers, to stingy merchants, and possessive husbands. Fern, after all, made her name, and the *Ledger*'s, through *Ruth Hall*, which earned her the nickname Ruthless Hall for her savage assault of her brother N.P. Willis for failing to aid in her search for employment. Bonner's fictional counterpart, Mr. Walter, replaces the neglectful figure of Hyacinth, Willis's character, revealing by stark contrast the latter's weaknesses. The journey, furthermore, from Willis's rejection to Bonner's acceptance, is mirrored by Fern's own career, which moved through several journals and editors, and their paltry wages, before landing on Bonner. She characterizes that journey in the novel as a search for a literary circle to match her own authorial practice, ethos, and understanding of her social role in such a position. The manner with which work is carried out is pivotal: *The Daily Type* is coarse, ink smudged, and all male, while the *Parental Guide* renders writing as preaching, a sort of Sunday school pulpit funneling its entire purpose into piety. Whereas a daily newspaper bears too much of the grit of immediate events without reflection upon their greater significance, the *Parental Guide* errs in the other direction for Ruth (Fern by extension). These are types of literary coteries for paid authorship in the periodical marketplace flawed precisely by the gender codes they embody. Both are extreme caricatures, not unlike Melville's send up of the rigidity of separate spheres in *Moby-Dick*, as the men collaborate on cleaning decks as if they were preparing for a tea party, and the mincer, in his role of productivity, is adorned by the pelt of the whale's penis, corresponding to the male sphere of market in which spermaceti is processed into material for the production of a commercial commodity.[39]

Margaret Fuller's deconstruction of separate spheres, like Fern's, lauds the special power of the individual capable of acting according to the best traits of both genders.[40] Fuller asserts that gender boundaries break down in the best characters since "male and female" do not "represent the two sides of the great radical dualism" in mutual exclusion. Her notion that "in fact they are perpetually passing into one another" as "two halves of one thought" in which "the development of one cannot be effected without that of the other" since "there is no wholly masculine man, no purely feminine woman," calls to mind how Fern's own stentorian voice of reform and shock can give way to soft nurturance.[41] It raises visions of her fictional counterpart,

Ruth Hall, literally fighting her way out of the office of a tyrannical editor to find better employment, and Mr. Walter, Bonner's character, welling up with tears at the sight of Ruth's impoverished home, his heart overflowing with domestic compassion. But best of all, this gender fluidity is typified by Fern's own writing voice, the revolutionary spirit of which Joyce Warren has compared to gangsta rap, which, significantly, is an image of male artistic production that so aptly describes this feminist author.[42]

Unlike the Knickerbocker circle, gender, if not racial, diversity was well represented among the *Ledger* staff. Southworth and Fern appeared the most consistent of the magazine's women writers, which also included Lydia Sigourney and Harriet Lewis. Bonner made a concerted effort to cater to his female readership, balancing his popular feature, "ADVICE TO YOUNG MEN by Twelve College Presidents," which lent significant credibility to the magazine, with a "series of Twelve Articles, written expressly for Young Ladies, by twelve of the most distinguished Women of the United States, including Mrs. HORACE MANN, Mrs. Lydia Maria Child [formerly of Garrison *Liberator* coterie], Mrs. GENERAL BANKS, Mrs. HORACE GREELEY, and Madame LE VERT."[43] The magazine's content reflected such diversity, as Warren places the *Ledger* somewhere between bland "conventional piety" and "prurient violence and pornography," so that it could be provocative yet suitable for the whole family.[44] Given this broad spectrum, ample evidence of extremely violent material supporting rivals' claims that it pandered to the low brow was offset by plenty of staid moralistic piety Bonner frequently cited to defend against such claims.

"All the Greatest Writers Write for It"

The mix of salacious as well as pious content meant that thrilling fiction always shared space with moral advice columns, given the emphasis on the "corps of popular authors" and the diversity of styles and subjects therein. Bonner regularly trumpeted the diversity of his writers in his advertisements, listing their names and literary distinctions, usually stated in the superlative, to indicate the broad appeal of the journal. In one notice announcing the *Ledger*'s cohort for the coming year of 1869, the contributors of poems ranged from the elite literary William Cullen Bryant, "who is universally ranked as the first of American poets," to John G. Saxe, whose entertaining verses for the masses make no pretention to literary quality (magazine historian Frank Luther Mott calls them a "travesty") yet distinguish him according to Bonner as "the most popular humorous poet in the country."[45] Nonfiction spans the husband-wife duo of popular biographer James Parton, touted as both "entertaining and instructive," and Fanny Fern, whose widely read column needed no introduction other than the assurance that the *Ledger* was indeed her exclusive publisher, as she "has been with us from the start and will continue to write for the Ledger for the coming year."[46] Taking up the most column space and accounting for perhaps the largest portion of the readership besides Fern, Southworth and Cobb were the prose fiction twin-engine of the magazine, driving its success with their sentimental domestic and action-adventure serial novels.

Such diversity lent the *Ledger* an uncanny capacity to escape accurate categorization, enabling Bonner to project it as a family paper given his spread of authors. Mott's groundbreaking history of American magazines thus describes the *Ledger* as tepid on all fronts—"innocuous romance, innocuous adventure, innocuous sentiment."[47] This profile, however, drastically underestimates the often edgy, even racy, nature of its content. Outlaw villain Black Donald of Southworth's *Hidden Hand*, for example, is a charismatic criminal who, even after his attempted abduction of protagonist Capitola, remains so sympathetically drawn that Capitola mitigates his prison sentence and equips him with a horse for his escape. Southworth's *The Lost Heiress* unleashes a torrid stream of child abduction, domestic quarrels, and insanity. Lydia Sigourney's letter to Bonner accompanying her poetry submission to the *Ledger* testifies to this "spirited" side of the periodical, which she worried, might exclude "a more religious character of writing than you might desire." Yet she expresses faith that its readership is broad enough to accommodate her pious verse, "that among your multitude of readers were some of every taste, and that it would harm none" to publish it alongside a searing Southworth saga. The scope of the periodical was so capacious that it could comfortably accommodate Sigourney's poetry.[48]

Like Southworth, Fern was hardly innocuous. She defied the code of domesticity by exhorting women to cease toiling at the "extras"— especially pies and knitting—demanded by Catharine Beecher and other such advocates of the Cult of True Womanhood. In her 1864 column, "Whose Fault is It?" she openly assailed the unequal distribution of wealth in New York City that gave rise to filthy, impoverished living conditions, claiming that funds and sympathy toward the war effort are egregiously misplaced in the presence of such local atrocities. She has stumped for higher wages for women workers in "Women of 1867," and has encouraged unemployed women to seek work; she has inveighed against the merger of materialism and domesticity that left "whole blocks of houses in New York...full of things" that are "too fine for daylight or even for use"; she has exhorted her female readers to seek out vigorous exercise, to stay away from the candy shop, to take responsibility for their health, and to escape financially dependent marriages.[49] Indeed, she is now well known, and even valorized, for fearlessly entering the fray on the woman question, voicing dissent, and courting controversy in her staunch advocacy of women's suffrage. "We are always 'dear, delicate, fragile creatures,' who should be immediately gagged with this sugar plum whenever we talk about that of which it is their interest to keep us ignorant. It won't do gentlemen," she proclaims with dramatic defiance. "The sugar plum game is neigh played out. *Women will vote some day*," she affirms in tones hardly innocuous.[50]

This edgy, confrontational content that attracted readers to the *Ledger* was cloaked in the expansive variety of the paper, which indeed included innocuous advice such as the 1859 piece on the virtue of patience called "Watch and Wait," and Saxe's light poetry that functioned to soften its vitriolic strains. Even more telling of the diverse demographics of the *Ledger*'s target audience was a full-page advertisement that targeted both male and female tastes in fiction as well as the latest in economic and political news as surveyed by the most notable of commentators. Of the fiction, Bonner boasts that "The Ledger is always full to overflowing with literature adapted to every taste," dividing it according to gender with Cobb's "stories of love and adventure which make the pulse of the boys tingle," and Southworth's "romances which the girls read with rapture." For "the grave" of melancholy, gothic tastes there are "the gravities. For the merry, good food for mirth." It then lists an article to appear "which will interest all Wall Street speculators," leading to the more sophisticated fare of politics and literary poetry of "the distinguished authors," who include "Hon. Edward Everett, Hon. George Bancroft, Wm. Cullen Bryant, Rev. Henry Ward Beecher." Such serious "distinguished authors" counterbalance the sensational fiction for "girls" and "boys" in an attempt to straddle not only high and low brow literature, but gender and age categories as well.[51]

The *Ledger* addressed female readership and catered to men in such a way that defied grouping it among the ranks of *Godey's Ladies Book*. Indeed, the first twelve-week series of celebrity authors writing advice pieces was directed toward America's youth. As a conseqence of its success, a new series was implemented to address young women. The magazine also aimed at older established middle-aged men active in business and politics, the clientele associated with the *Atlantic Monthly*. Bonner catered to them by acquiring not only revered literary male authors Tennyson, Dickens, Bryant, and Longfellow, but also statesman and charismatic orator Edward Everett. At the end of his career Bonner considered the acquisition of Everett—former editor of the *North American Review*, Governor of Massachusetts, President of Harvard, United States Senator, Secretary of State, Ambassador to the Court of St. James, and lecturer on behalf of the Mt. Vernon Association—"the greatest card that had ever been played by his or any other paper."[52] For in doing so, the *Ledger* gained affiliations with both politics and New England through Capitol Hill and Harvard it was sorely missing that had made its credibility suffer in the past. Everett, who agreed to write a series of letters to the *Ledger* in exchange for Bonner's $10,000 donation to the Mount Vernon project, whose aim was to purchase the home and tomb of George Washington, was an icon of patriotism. The standard of the paper was indeed raised by Everett's presence, which led historian George Bancroft to contribute to it. Upon Everett's death, Bonner persuaded Bancroft to amend his biographical sketch of the statesman with "reference to his connection with the *Ledger*," a fact conspicuously absent from the other portraits of his life. In his typical display of frank boldness, Bonner assures Bancroft that such a mention is justified by the $24,400 "I paid him for literary labor," along with the many "gratuitous contributions" Everett made to the *Ledger*.[53] He then informs him that he had paid an undisclosed amount to his editor to ensure that a paragraph was included in the sketch making explicit the depth of Everett's connection with the *Ledger*. Bonner could not bear to leave such a ripe fruit un-harvested, and thus swung his promotional repertoire into full motion.

He Had Some Horses

Bonner had reinvented the *Ledger* so that it maintained its loyal following of Fern, Southworth, and Cobb readers, while crusading on a campaign of self-promotion that honored what the culture was ostensibly valuing at the time—politics and piety—by winning over Everett and Beecher, its two most influential orators. These conquests did not replace the commercial thoroughbreds already in Bonner's stable, but complemented them in what eventuated in the most eclectic content in the history of American magazines. This pattern did not escape the notice of inconsolably jealous rivals like *Vanity Fair*, predictably sniffing that, after Everett's engagement with the magazine, the statesman would be known as "Orator, Patriot, Sage, Cicero of America, Laudator of Washington, Apostle of Charity, High Priest of the Union, Friend of Mankind, and Writer for the *Ledger*."[54]

Bonner collected authors like he collected racehorses—his first and best was Fern and his last was Everett. His hobby of buying the fastest horses in the world was contiguous with his love of acquiring prized authors, signified by the naming of one of his most valuable thoroughbreds "Edward Everett." The *Ledger*'s halls testified to his obsession, as they were "adorned with likenesses of his prominent contributors and celebrated horses," tokens of his conquests in both the literary and horse racing markets.[55] The *Ledger*'s auspicious 1856 explosion out of the gate with Fanny Fern leading the pack in the first weekly of its kind, interestingly, was not only carefully charted by flagging opponents like *Vanity Fair*, but also caught the close attention of Fletcher Harper of the famous book publishing Harper Brothers. *Harper's Weekly* flattered Bonner when it debuted 3 January 1857 in direct competition with the *Ledger*, months after his signing of Fanny Fern gained him full control of the market. Harper aped Bonner's format and pitched it toward elite educated readers who, at that early stage prior to the signing of Beecher and Everett, had not been courted by the *Ledger*. The Harper Brothers used their credibility, rather than Bonner's method of massive payments, as publishers of the country's most revered literature to engage the best contributors available. The method won their share of the market, yet it only accounted for a fraction of the popular reading audience, as the *Ledger* more than quadrupled the circulation of *Harper's Weekly*, which started at just under 100,000 in 1857 and peaked at 160,000 in 1872.[56] This indicates that the *Ledger*, mainly through the appeal of its historical and sentimental romances, was the first to capture on a mass scale the proportion of the market currently controlled by the romance book genre. The literary fiction of *Harper's Weekly* could not compete with the romances of the *Ledger*, yet their general format won it a larger share of their market than a conventional format would have. Pictures from woodcuts, fiction, travel, biography, illustrations ranging throughout each issue—precisely the potpourri that distinguished the *Ledger* and set the standard for the general magazine—was the *Harpers' Weekly* formula. Not surprisingly, it also advertised itself as a "family magazine." Little did Fletcher Harper know that he was entering into competition with the century's greatest mind in literary advertising.

Upon hearing that the Harpers had entered the weekly market, Bonner did what he usually did when under pressure: he launched a thousand dollar advertising campaign. At the time, Bonner was notorious for his iterative advertising technique, where he repeated the same phrase, "Buy *The New York Ledger!*" in different patterns, filling entire columns of the paper in as many different venues as possible. Readers could not avoid the incessant repetition of phrases and ponderous patterns in which they appeared. All six columns of page seven of the 6 May 1858 *New York Herald* were cut into symmetrical boxes bearing the same sonnet, "Lo! the poor Indian, whose untutored mind / Sees God in clouds, or hears him in the wind"; and caption, "READ EMERSON BENNETT'S GREAT INDIAN TALE in the NEW YORK LEDGER." At fourteen advertisements per column, the page is covered with a total of eighty-four identical boxes for a striking geometrical grid work effect that would have arrested the casual reader. Another full page advertisement appeared in the 7 April 1863 *Herald*, also employing an iterative style, but only repeating the same brief notice down the length of each column, with captions announcing the contents of the latest issue from "A NEW STORY BY SYLVANIUS COBB, JR." to "SPECULATION IN GOLD—A CURIOUS MATHEMATICAL CALCULATION," to a list of featured authors, rhetorically appealing to the magazine's broad range of interests. The spread renders the impression of overflowing content as echoed in the final salutation, "DON'T GO HOME WITHOUT THE LEDGER to-day. It is full of good things."[57]

It was in this signature style then that Bonner himself placed notices in the major papers announcing the first issue of *Harper's Weekly*. He devised this devious ruse, in part, to call attention to his own marketing method by which readers had come to recognize his product. Now even the staid and proper Harpers, as he made it appear, were shouting out "Buy *Harper's Weekly*!" in repeated phrases running down full columns in serpentine shapes. Astonished at this uncharacteristically commercial display, especially one that employed Bonner's favorite advertising technique, the public praised rather than scorned the high brow Harpers for finally embracing the latest publicity methods. The confounded Harpers quietly accepted their praise and masked their chagrin, as Bonner had successfully brought their paper out on his own terms, signaling to readers before they even opened the first issue of *Harper's Weekly* of its derivative nature.[58] Furthermore, the stunt effectively refuted any accusations that his marketing campaigns were sensational and vulgar by making it appear as though even modest and refined journals were taking the same approach. On a deeper level, Bonner appears to have been using the medium of advertising as an ironic vehicle through which to reverse and thus satirize the conventions of mass-market competition by advertising on their behalf yet in his own characteristic *Ledger* voice. The ventriloquism of mismatching *Harper's* face with Bonner's promotional voice brilliantly displayed how literary merchandise had become inseparable from its channels of publicity, and in a show of dominance over commercial discourse, served as a belittling and intimidating initiation of the Harpers into the competitive periodical market.

Inescapable, yet as diverse as the staff itself, *Ledger* advertising cost Bonner up to $150,000 per year, and ranged as high as $27,000 per week, with his most expensive single notice totaling an astonishing $20,000.[59] Late in his career, Bonner shared a telling exchange about his unorthodox approach to media publicity. "What is the use," a man enquired of the editor, "of your taking a whole side of the *Herald* and repeating that statement a thousand times?" "Would you have asked me that question," replied Mr. Bonner, "if I had inserted it but once? I put it in to attract your attention, and make you ask that question."[60] Endlessly repeating, "Fanny Fern writes only for the *New York Ledger*" and "Read Mrs. Southworth's new story in the *Ledger*" brought advertising to an art form in patterns echoing the mechanics of mass circulation and the endless reproduction of fame as transmitted through the thousands of copies of the *Ledger* cheaply produced and purchased. Indeed, increasingly efficient production meant the prices of ink and paper declined with advances in labor-saving manufacturing machines such as the double cylinder printing press. Bonner was intent on brandishing his seeming extravagance of "wasting" print and paper on repeated statements as a show of excess surplus capital, and thus a clear statement of market dominance. He would spare no expense on ink and paper, especially in advertising, and the payment of his authors, because both were the most visible representations of his money available. Rarely, if ever, did he spend money in any other way. Readers thus could not ignore his signs of wealth, because he so directly correlated them with the caliber of popular authors who wrote for him.

One New York historian and contemporary of Bonner's noted that "His advertisements are so queer and unusual, that when [papers] make a contract with him, they have no idea in what shape the advertisement will come." One exasperated newspaper proprietor even told Bonner he would rather print a picture of one of his horses than drive his readers to distraction with one of his dizzying designs.[61] Bonner's other methods included sample advertising, in which the opening of a story appeared, and a minimalist method in which he left an entire column blank except for several lines. Interspersed with the story excerpt that ran from the first column on page one, to two-and-a-half columns on page four, was an announcement that "the above is all of the story that will be published in our columns," assuring readers that a printing mistake had not occurred. "We give this as a sample. The continuation of it from where it leaves off here can only be found in the *New York Ledger*, the great family paper, for which the most popular writers in the country contribute, and which is on sale at all the stores throughout the city and country where newspapers are sold."[62]

Bonner drew on his special dexterity with typesetting he mastered as a boy to call attention to his own process of production in ironic, nonsensical, and intriguing ways, anticipating Andy Warhol's fascination with mass production and the mechanism of fame captured in his repeated images of Marilyn Monroe and Campbell's Soup cans. Bonner also anticipates Canadian experimental novelist Douglas Coupland's technique of covering full pages of his novels *J-Pod*, and *Microserfs* (among others) with computer code, which draws attention to the technology behind its own process of production, re-arranging it artistically and thus turning it into an art medium. Bonner's modernity can also be witnessed in how he took out half of the 6 May 1858 issue of the *New York Herald*, for example, and interspersed the advertisements every ten pages in the way today's massive marketing campaigns introduce new technological products—Ipod, Ipad, Kindle—piecemeal throughout entire issues. Bonner shares Warhol's Brechtian defamiliarization of advertizing convention to render such an ordinary object as a daily newspaper viewed thousands of times a day, profoundly odd, and even disturbing, yet not without its humor as in his Harpers stunt. He would emphasize blank space, isolating a few tiny ads into one corner of a vast blank column, as if they were trying to hide from the reader. Readers were likely as fascinated as they were revolted by his ludicrous Byzantine patterns dancing down the columns mocking the sober reportorial articles in the adjacent columns. Stacked in an endless variety of patterns like a child's building blocks, his nonlinear ads subverted the serious world of news.

Not Advertising

For as innovative and aggressive as Bonner's marketing methods were in promoting his authors, he employed the equally unorthodox, yet wildly successful, technique of banning all advertisements from the pages of the *Ledger*. The effect was to make the magazine appear non-commercial, to seem as if it were a book with illustrations, an idea not entirely new since the advent of *Godey's Ladies Book*. The exclusion of this dimension of market exchange brought the magazine in diametric opposition to its roots as commercial sheet, literally a *Merchant's Ledger*, which included nothing but lists of items for sale and services of all sorts.

Recreating the commercial space in his competitors' papers by simultaneously raising it to a near art form and a nuisance—one is reminded of David Burns's early performance art days in which he would do nothing but shave on stage, or the late comedian Andy Kaufman's dead pan lost look from which he would break at tediously consistent intervals into 1950s Hollywood musical song, "Here I am to save the day!"—that annoyed as much as it fascinated, meant that he could also re-create the space of his home paper into something more like home and less like the marketplace. The idea was especially appealing to nineteenth-century readers anxious, if not downright fearful, of the market's intrusion into so many walks of life, especially literature and the domestic sphere. The irony was, of course, that Bonner's readers would be led to the space of his anti-commercial "home" of the *Ledger* through his ubiquitous advertisements, which incessantly re-claimed the measured and predictable spaces of the daily newspapers they read.

The advertising-free atmosphere of the *Ledger*'s pages did not "make the price low enough for everyone to afford it," as at least one literary historian has assumed.[63] Instead, the inclusion of advertising would have actually driven the price down, as it does in today's newspapers. The decision not to include them was in fact a costly one for Bonner, yet unmistakably part of his greater campaign to distinguish the magazine from competitors through financial generosity to both readers and contributors. What reader, then and now, would not prefer an advertising-free venue for their entertainment? The gesture was a rhetorical appeal for family reading, which complemented his widely advertised printing of only original contributions for which he offered giant payments dwarfing his competitors. These two facets of the paper signaled that Bonner would attain the best authors, and create the most appealing format for reading them, cost what it may. Indeed, the appearance that money was no object in the production of the *Ledger*, and that Bonner's wealth was seemingly unlimited, and his benevolence equally overflowing, were essential components to the magazine's appeal. Not permitting advertising was akin to his refusal to bet on his horses, reinforcing a popular image that linked him to the fashionable anti-materialistic domestic ethos at the time that shunned the marketplace as filthy and immoral. He thus stood as an example to the culture that leisure should never be confused with financial gain, thus aligning him with the evangelicals he promoted in the *Ledger*. Yet the complex paradox lies in his appearance of perfect ease with capital, which would lead him to write a letter to the *New York Herald* in 1867 correcting their estimate of his income. They claimed that his salary had increased nearly fourfold in a year, from $60,756 in 1866 to $201,736 in 1867. Bonner asserted that the 1866 figure was wrong, and that he had actually earned $155,304.87, almost three times their estimate for the year, "so that I do not return four times as large a sum this year as for last."[64] His point was that he already was extraordinarily wealthy and had earned far more in those two years combined than the *Herald* assumed. Of course, the appearance of established wealth was more fashionable than new money at the time, leading

Bonner to make such a claim. Yet his admirers also celebrated him as a self-made man, as did his staff, especially as reflected in their fictional portraits of him as a daring, bold professional with a heart of gold.

Cobb's blueprint for his stories, particularly *The Gunmaker of Moscow*, reflects the essential components of Bonner's rise. Ruric Nevel, the protagonist, is a "hero of common life...in which the interest depends on the difficulties surrounding the hero and his comrades, who rise from the ranks," according to Cobb's notes headed "Ideas for *Ledger* Stories."[65] Ruric, the gunmaker of Moscow, bears distinct democratic characteristics that transgress the boundaries of hierarchical social rank. An artisan in love with noblewoman Rosalind Valdai since childhood, Ruric seeks the impossible dream of attaining her hand in marriage. Cobb plays on their childhood past to emphasize the couple's natural and innocent mutual attraction free from artificial mechanisms of social class that arranged so many marriages at the time in Russia. Not only Ruric, but also Rosalind, is Americanized in the tale. Hardly the "cold, proud aristocrat" Ruric's mother assumed her to be, Rosalind spent ten years in an orphanage, thus there was "nothing of the aristocrat in her look, nothing proud, nothing haughty."[66] When his rival, Count Damonoff, challenges Ruric to a duel, he appears a democratic action hero out of the mold of Southworth's Capitola, the protagonist of *The Hidden Hand*. Prior to the duel, Ruric receives permission from Officer Alaric to fully engage his considerable skill in swordsmanship, a careful measure added by Cobb to assure that our hero appears law abiding and socially responsible rather than driven recklessly by unrestrained vigilante justice that flouts laws and settles scores through murder.

The mercenary priest, Savotano, is an unmistakable antebellum serial fiction villain, from his shadowy murderous past to his hunchback, "a small deformed man...his features sharp and angular; his eyes dark and sunk into his head; his brow heavy above the eyes," with the "point [on his head] where phrenologists locate Benevolence and Veneration deficient and flat."[67] Savotano plays the groveling minion to the evil mastermind, the Duke of Tula, whose chief sin is economic corruption dramatized by this scheme to establish "himself in high power" by placing "large sums in the hands of the Minister Galitizin for the purpose of carrying out the conspiracy by which the Princess Sophia was to have been placed on the throne." Money in this context is swindled and stolen rather than earned, opposite the wholesome and steady artisanal labor of Ruric.

The Duke of Tula's villainy is etched into both his unprincipled approach toward acquiring capital and his impotent business practice. He invests in a conspiracy that does not transpire. "My property is on the *decrease* fast," he confesses, "I have not enough to live on. Within the past three years I have made some bad ventures," the worst being his loss of vast sums in buying his way to power, the ultimate sin in the American ethos of democratic political economy. Indeed, his economic blasphemy forms the very catalyst of the plot. The Duke stands to win half of the coveted Drotzen fortune mortgaged to Count Damonoff upon the Count's death. He thus sends the Count to Ruric with a forged contract forcing the gunmaker to agree never to marry Rosalind; the Duke's intention is to entice Ruric into murdering the Count for him. The Count appears mortally wounded in the duel, yet he rallies and survives. Faced with this new turn of events, the Duke offers 200 ducats to Savotano to kill Count Damonoff outright, resolving to marry Rosalind himself to acquire her fortune, since "her property is worth the whole of Drotzen twice told—over two million ducats." Such convoluted plots revolving around family fortune were also favorites of Southworth, particularly in works like *The Lost Heiress.*

Ruric reflects the Bonner pillar of virtue of domestic piety when he goes to the dying Count Danomoff and asks his forgiveness. "As God is my Maker and my Judge, I would rather lie down here and die for you," Ruric tells the Count in a Christ-like gesture of self-sacrifice.[68] Ruric then is apprehended and jailed by the Duke, who anticipates cinching Rosalind's fortune. "Ha, ha, ha! The Duke of Tula will have his coffers filled again. Money must come somehow, and how else so easily as this?" he raves, in full violation of the slow and steady accumulation of capital, and the willingness to labor for it embodied by Ruric, and Bonner by extension.[69] At the novel's penultimate scene, Ruric breaks up the forced marriage of Rosalind and the Duke and thus preserves another institution deemed sacred by the majority of *Ledger* readers. Vladimir, the fat monk who had been shadowing the incidents since the beginning, now emerges and tears off his costume, revealing none other than Peter the Great himself beneath the disguise, who restores social, political, and economic order by declaring to the villain, "you are the Duke of Tula no more. A more worthy man wears the ducal coronet from this hour: *Ruric Nevel* shall assume the station you have disgraced, and I know he will ennoble it once more." Peter thus enters as not only a deus ex machina of preposterous and absurd proportions, but also another echo of Bonner as benevolent patriarch, sealing the gunmaker's success in the culmination of his vigilance and investment in him from the beginning. Peter's role is also analogous to Mr. Walter, the Bonner figure of Fern's *Ruth Hall,* who similarly invests personally and professionally in the protagonist and turns over a check for $10,000, the reward she rightly wins at the end of that novel.[70] Her entrance into the ranks of professional authors, a capital circle of established writers, is paralleled by Ruric's entrance into the inner circle of Peter the Great, a political feat he earns himself through the principled pursuit of love and use of professional skill.

Bonner's presence loomed so large at the time that he made cameo appearances in popular fiction well beyond that written by his own staff. As an icon of the self-made man, the mention of his name invoked successful business carried out with moral integrity, embodying the virtues rather than the corruption of the market. In one economic novel, *Kick Him Down Hill; or Ups and Downs of Business*, published in 1875 by Miss M.M. Smith, he exemplifies how solid principles can avert perils of debt. Horace Greeley, written into the novel as a sage voice of reason, discourses on how "Robert Bonner would serve as a valuable text-book to every business man." The portrait he renders reflects precisely the image Bonner had projected of himself in the market since 1855. "He is sober, honest, industrious, of indomitable pluck; the architect of his own fortune; and, to his credit, his fortune was not built up upon the credit system." And although he widely advertised his lavish spending on authors, he was known as one who "never bought a thing he could not pay for when he bought it; never borrowed a dollar in money, and never signed a note in his life."[71]

By the end of the century, his popular memory shifted away from his business acumen, as he began to be regarded as something of a genteel connoisseur, an elite American version of the man of leisure, spending his retirement in his equestrian avocation. An 1897 *New York Times* retrospective of Bonner's career, like most pieces commemorating his life, conformed to the master narrative of his rise from penniless teenage immigrant to genteel equestrian in a parable of American commercial success. The *Times* article went so far as to suggest that he elevated the crafting of horseshoes to an art form.[72] Yet those horses were exceedingly fast before he acquired them, just as his staff had already become certified celebrities—yet had not been overexposed due to their limited venues—by the time he engaged their services for the *Ledger*. Bonner acquired proven successes on the rise who had not yet met their full market potential. He signed Sylvanus Cobb, for example, after the author had made the middling *Flag of Our Union* a smashing success. Since the strength of Fern's columns outshone that of her fiction, she dedicated herself full time to writing sketches of social commentary and criticism. With Cobb and Fern thus engaged, Bonner needed a female fiction writer and took *Peterson's* best serial novelist, E.D.E.N. Southworth, from their ranks. T.B. Peterson's book rights to her serials then became Bonner's prey, which he handily cinched. Soon after Bonner signed Southworth, she wrote her most popular novel, *The Hidden Hand*; Cobb's first contribution to the *Ledger*, chapter one of *The Gunmaker of Moscow*, would become the best-known work of his career, which Bonner announced with a 100 gun salute at City Hall Park in New York that cost him $20,000.[73]

Restricting advertising from the *Ledger* also allowed for a greater emphasis on Bonner's primary commodity for sale: his authors. One of Bonner's more pioneering tactics was to have contributors sign their names to their work, signaling a shift away from the practice of anonymous contributions. Ownership of their writings, in this sense, was directed back to the author and away from the editor, who could alter anonymous articles without the consent of the writer and virtually without limit, so that the results were more coauthored (however hierarchical and undemocratic those power dynamics were) rather than singular productions.[74] The patronizing "blue penciling" that anonymity allowed yielded to a form of literary production more empowering and satisfying for authors. The rearguard found the practice to be an expression of vulgar commercialism, however, and chided how "the names of *all* the contributors are generally paraded conspicuously on the covers" of American periodicals, as Charles Astor Bristed complained in Britain's *Blackwood's Magazine*.[75]

Managing the Ledger Staff

Bonner catered to his staff's needs as they arose, paying for one author's "tuition, books, stationery, drawing and materials" at New York's Mount Washington Collegiate Institute as a Christmas bonus in 1865.[76] The financial history of his relationship with Cobb is striking considering the frequency of requests for funds the author made beginning in the 1860s, "will you send me a draft for $200 paying to Saturday next," and escalating to $300 and $350 by 1864 to $500 in early December of 1867 complete with a hand-drawn finger pointer, a jocular barb at the commercial world they both inhabited. Bonner promptly supplied him with what Cobb described as "the last dollars I owe for the improvements I made on my place and also" funds to "wipe out all I owed to anybody."[77] By 1885, Cobb's requests had risen to $1000 in letters concluding with requisite litanies of physical ailments to solicit Bonner's sympathy. Cohesiveness among the *Ledger* staff was so strong that Fern, in the wake of two miserable marriages and thus perhaps the sharpest critic of the abuses of marriage at the time, would find her third husband in colleague and popular biographer James Parton. Her first husband, Charles Eldredge, died and left her penniless, and her second,

Samuel Farrington, chronically raped her and sent the marriage spiraling into a hostile and malevolent divorce. Conversely, Parton, who married Fern in 1856 shortly after convincing Bonner to sign her onto the *Ledger*, proved nearly perfect, as he would write Fern's biography, and thus bear the honor of the first to commemorate her dazzling and historic career. Parton's initial recognition of Fern's talent that led to her hiring is immortalized in Fern's fictional autobiography, *Ruth Hall*. Fern's current legacy, and that of the *Ledger*'s heyday by extension, owes much to Parton's *Fanny Fern: A Memorial Volume* (1874).

Parton's suitability for Fern stemmed from his admiration of commercial success—as evidenced in his 1871 *Triumphs of Enterprise, Ingenuity, and Public Spirit* and 1891 *Captains of Industry: A Book for Young Americans*—combined with his active support of the professionalization of women's careers that inspired *Eminent Women of the Age* (1869) and *Noted Women of Europe and America* (1883) in which he proclaimed, "The most important result of the better civilization of our time is the increased power of women."[78] Just as Fern achieved historical significance through her protofeminism anticipating later women authors like Kate Chopin and Virginia Woolf, Parton's own popular biographies have not escaped recognition for their contribution to the formation of the genre, and thus have earned him the mantle of "the father of modern biography."[79]

Bonner had a special affinity for popular biography as evidenced by contributions from writers like John Abbott, whose vision of the genre appeared well suited to the *Ledger*'s variety format. His meticulous enumeration of "the reasons I think a spirited sketch of the career of General Bonaparte would now be more popular than that of any other man," however, included emphasis of his "unblemished morals and of exalted principles [to which] the reader can form an attachment." Horace Greeley caught the gaff and upbraided him in his *Tribune*. Abbott thanked Bonner for defending him in a 1 March 1862 letter, but the controversy would not die. Two years later Abbott apologized to Bonner for firing back at Greeley's new assault in the *Independent* and defended his controversial "Napoleon's Napoleon" by urging that he only assumed "men might differ upon historical questions without necessarily being KNAVES."[80] Undeterred, Abbott emerged from the controversy with a proposal for a fresh set of sketches on the Roman Emperors and William the Conqueror. Public discord only fanned the flames of his success, much in the way it had for Fanny Fern's career.

Bonner's support of Fern through controversy extended the life of her career. To celebrate their first fourteen years in business, Bonner sent her a check in 1864, "not exactly as a present, for," as he correctly assumed she "might not like to receive it in that way, but as compensation for some anonymous paragraphs which I want you to write for the *Ledger* whenever you may feel like it."[81] Bonner struck a similar deal with his popular poet, John G. Saxe, offering as much psychological as financial support for his friend and contributor, about whom he had learned "from the Times of this morning that you are unwell and depressed in spirits. Cheer up!—my friend," Bonner sang out, exhorting him to fulfill the social role of the poet by engaging his "faculty of making others cheerful and happy." Then assuming the authoritative voice of his employer, Bonner commands him to "*Turn your attention to that now*," quickly following up with an advance of $500, couched rhetorically as an emotional balm, since "by the time you have sent me poems amounting to that, I have no doubt you will feel better."[82] The corrective measure revitalized the disengaged and unemployed poet.

The *Ledger*'s liberal editorial policy fostering creative freedom along with its flexible, responsive compensation created an environment that encouraged the union of Fern and Parton, and nurtured platonic friendships that patterned themselves after husband-wife roles in such a way that it revolutionized the economics of standard spousal arrangements at the time. Harriet and Leon Lewis, for example, would have been financially ruined had it not been for Bonner's loans. The Lewises personified the *Ledger*'s fictional focus, as together they contributed romance and adventure tales respectively from husband and wife. Yet Leon Lewis was not nearly as prolific as his wife, and was given more to pandering than producing, selling his work—often ghostwritten by his wife—to Bonner in bombastic cover letters, partially poking fun at the editor's Banumesque promotional tactics, with claims that "To this point the interest of the tale has been deepening from the beginning, and it will continue to deepen from this point to the end, making it THE GREATEST STORY OF THE NINETEENTH CENTURY!" to which he allows that "this would be egotistical, of course, if said to anybody but you, but YOU will understand us."[83]

Bonner routinely bailed the Lewises out of debt. At one point, Leon requested that he send $1500 to cover his expenses, which prompted Bonner's query as to what exactly the money was needed for. Leon's litany of losses included his library purchased for five thousand dollars now worth half as much, three houses that declined in value by one-third of their original price (from eight to six thousand dollars) and insurance payments demanding $4,400, and even his furniture, acquired for $1800 now worth only $1200. Bonner rarely asked for such accounting to justify his loans, but the Lewises had far exceeded the normal amount he customarily disbursed. Leon acknowledged this, humbly noting "the above are the principal parts of the information demanded. Personal enough to open my outside debts."[84] Such financial straits were indicative of Leon's reckless pattern of spending and mismanagement of the couple's handsome salary. Breaking a decades-long correspondence exclusively between Bonner and Leon, Harriet boldly revealed this trouble in a haunting letter that would foretell their fates. Like Cobb's sentimental sketch imagining life without Bonner, Harriet also entertains the thought of being cut off from him through her own death, which she anticipated due to a severe illness that required a high-risk surgical procedure. Desiring steady work for Leon, Harriet knew that she was his source of financial stability since she wrote the vast majority of their *Ledger* stories, and that he had squandered much of their income on speculative schemes. "He has wild ideas that seem to him to promise wealth or fame," she wrote, "I have tried to be his balance wheel. What will he do when I am gone?" She ends the missive with a desperate plea to her editor, "to continue your friendship with him, and be patient with him," appealing to the state of her own soul upon her immanent death. "If I could think that you would keep him on with the *Ledger* and see him now and then and keep him busy, I would not dread death for his sake as I do now."[85] The next letter from Leon appears in 1898, a decade after his wife's prophetic letter. In a scrawled arthritic hand, the epistle plays out precisely the future Harriet had foretold as if from the grave, with Leon pathetically begging Bonner for "10 dollars to make my connections," again emphasizing loss, but this time of a sort much dearer than furniture or library values, as "my boy and I are all alone having lost my wife and daughter."[86]

The Lewis's fate was the most heartbreaking of the *Ledger* authors. Bonner faced other equally difficult authors, yet hardly so warm and kindhearted, if not downright pathetic and wounded, in their dealings with him. Mean spirited and unreasonable writers Bonner did not suffer gladly. He dispatched William Henry Peck after granting him what is now considered the mandatory two weeks notice. He rejected Sally Parry's demand for $1000 rather than the $700 he offered her and delayed publication of Eliza Dupuy's manuscript for a full year. Parry complained of paralysis—a veiled threat to not continue—and Dupuy countered with other offers. When she eventually received her contract, Dupuy praised Bonner as "Honorable, true to all duties of life, and as liberal as the day."[87] Parry's sentimental appeal for sympathy was a common ploy among the more desperate of Bonner's authors. Gerald Fallon, for example, bewailed his short finances for returning his "children across the Atlantic," almost begging Bonner, "you would pity me if you knew my exact condition. I have had to work very hard and now I am so unnerved and dejected that I can hardly collect my thoughts and put them to paper," a line that seems less than tenable given his assurance that the malady has not detracted from the quality of his manuscript, which he describes as "well and carefully written, and would not disgrace the columns of the 'Ledger' as a story purely written."[88]

Other writers tried a variety of rhetorical tactics with Bonner, ranging from Parry's form of withholding services and Addey Atwood's threat to "desist from literary labor."[89] Another author, Mary C. Ames, took on a bizarre, almost flirtatious tone in a letter admonishing Bonner for excluding her from his annual list of writers for the new year. Her pitch for the anonymous publication of her manuscript reads as if she were brokering an evening tryst, identities concealed and no questions asked. "Now I think you are amiable enough to see the sight of my initials once a month—(I am not *mistaken*, am I?)"[90] Ames was among the more persistent at haggling with Bonner for higher wages for, of all things, her poetry for soldiers. She assures him that "in visiting the camps I have seen that the 'Ledger' circulates so largely among the troops," testifying that "in one of the hospital tents of a Michigan Cavalry Regiment I found every convalescent with a Ledger copy in his hand" to justify her price of first $10, and then on second thought, $15 for her poem.[91] Ames spent considerable energy trying to insinuate herself into the *Ledger*'s inner circle. Alluding to her work for other journals, she insisted that she had "written for the *people* for too long to believe that I have *nothing* for that dear inner page of yours."[92]

The *Ledger* staff reflected the advertising and management style of its editor; some authors drove hard bargains with him, knowing his salaries were high. Like Irving, Bonner was a source for aesthetic inspiration, as he would frequently make suggestions for stories, for which authors were not only accommodating, but given their rapid rate of production, downright grateful for any creative suggestions that might fuel their productivity. This working relationship, combined with lifelong friendships, and an aggressive, innovative crafting of *Ledger* image for mass consumption. That image reflected both family values and shrewd business rather than cutthroat capitalism and coarse materialism to carry on the very social dynamics that made the Knickerbocker circle a success. Herein lies the key to the most commercially successful New York literary circles of the nineteenth century. Now we turn to its neighbors in the North, the Transcendentalists, with their opposite, yet equally emphatic relationship toward the market.

PART II

NEW ENGLAND CIRCLES

Chapter 4

"The Section to Which We Belong": Emerson's Transcendentalists

Moving from literary New Yorkers to New England's most noteworthy and intricately intertwined literary networks raises important points of contrast, for there was a healthy rivalry between the Knickerbockers and the Transcendentalists. Many from Philadelphia, such as Rebecca Harding Davis, also scorned the Concord clique. Opaque, inconsequential, and most importantly, incomprehensibly abstract were the allegations laid upon Transcendentalists. Davis would even go so far as to write them into her story, "Anne," as self-obsessed narcissists, frauds perpetrating a dangerously egotistical authorial role liable to dupe young talent into relying too much on their "passion" while neglecting the dangers of the market's darkest blind alleys. Melville would similarly send up Emerson as Mark Winsome and Thoreau as his practical disciple, Egbert, in *The Confidence Man* (1857) for their abstruse and vague mysticism much in the way Cornelius Matthews had in *The Career of Puffer Hopkins* (1842). The Transcendentalists surface in Matthews's novel when a hardened book trader bids on "a melodrama, the poem of Bloody Puddle, and the volume of Transcendental lectures" during an auction. The frivolity of his selections, made to appear as inane trash, clashes with the bookseller's serious mercantile demeanor in a parody that mocks commercial literature, especially of the melodramatic sort, as well as dreamy Transcendentalism. The broker trades it as stock "with a fixed and intense look that could not have been readily surpassed by a Spanish inquisitor, or a petty justice reproving a constable," as "the fury of his demeanor was heightened by the close buttoning of his coat." Mr. Fishblatt, a figure of the free market for literature, admires the protagonist's capacity to "tell books by the smell of their leather. And see how daintily he holds an annual up, as a fishmonger does a bass by the tail."[1]

Yet the Transcendentalists flourished, not in spite of, but because of, such venom emanating from New York and Philadelphia. For these increasingly commercial cities—with literary circles arising in direct alliance with market forces (even while espousing non- or anti-commercial conceptions of authorship)—represented precisely the sort of materialism and capitalist corruption against which Transcendental authors famously rebelled. This chapter explores the effects that such an Emersonian conception of authorship rooted in individualism and anticommercialism had on the project of forming the Transcendentalist coterie and promoting its members in the literary market. What was the impact of Emerson's philosophical resistance toward group affiliation, "the section to which we belong," on his function as literary intermediary for the transcendentalist coterie?[2] How might literary collaboration exist in the context of a community founded on the principle "that envy is ignorance; that imitation is suicide"? How could the Concord clique maintain a collegial and collaborative climate given its aversion to the business community's avidity for the "joint-stock company," a method of commercial organization Emerson derided that had come to characterize so much of society's basic functions? How can a coterie function if it is hostile to the concept of collectivism, coloring it as unnecessary compromise and self-sacrifice, a pattern of social interaction "in which members agree, for the better securing of his bread to each shareholder, to surrender the liberty and culture of the eater," a situation in which "the virtue in most request is conformity," while "self-reliance is its aversion"?[3] Fuller's 1843 *Summer on the Lakes* metaphorically reveals Emerson's shortcomings as a leader of a community of artists, particularly his intolerance of diverse artistic subjectivities, and the limitations of his armor-clad self-reliance. These concerns over the viability of a Transcendental coterie encoded in Emerson's and Fuller's writings frame their business practice as literary professionals. Specifically, Emerson responded to the philosophical quandary of leading a group of anticommercial individualists by turning inward and developing the bonds of the inner circle through his editorial innovations of the *Dial* and by drawing in new talent. His blindness to the comparative risks and financial liabilities built into publishers' contracts, however, severely limited his effectiveness as agent and promoter in the broader literary market, as seen in his flawed advice for the placement of Thoreau's *A Week on the Concord and Merrimack Rivers*

(1849) and Fuller's *Summer on the Lakes*. Adding to his difficulties in publicizing Transcendentalists to the broader market was his limited circulation in the social matrices of book publishing compared to his seasoned skills in negotiating the lecture circuit.[4] Fuller's professional career flourished because she acted in contrast to the same advice and opportunities presented to Thoreau, who followed rather than deviated from Emerson's prescribed course.

The Transcendentalists' extreme anticommercial stance was in many ways adaptable to the literary market, as Emerson's international fame as lecturer and Fuller's successful New York journalism career prove. Despite these individual successes, the coterie did not advance as a unit into the New York market from Concord nearly so effectively as it did from Boston, particularly Elizabeth Peabody's 13 West Street bookstore. Conversely, no Knickerbockers would insinuate themselves into the Concord circle, and for good reason. Unlike Concord market, the New York environment lent itself to the mass marketing of literature. New York's coteries thrived on commercial literature such as the serial romance and adventure fiction that made the *New York Ledger* popular and provided canon fodder for the "Reading" chapter of Thoreau's *Walden*. Though not necessarily of the sensationalist breed of fiction the *Ledger* trotted out, the majority of Knickerbockers were nonetheless all popular sentimental magazinists, from Irving and Halleck to Cooper and Willis, whose careers were deeply enmeshed in the mass periodical press. The most noteworthy of their works, Irving's *Sketch Book* (1819) and Cooper's *Last of the Mohicans* (1820), were published in journals before they were published as books. The aloof light charm of Irving's bachelor legacy, further, exuded a studied indifference to social and political tensions that could not have been more at odds with the fully engaged revolutionary writings of Thoreau and Fuller. Knickerbockers, however, could not deny Emerson's almost universally recognized power at the lectern. N.P. Willis's remarks on Emerson typified literary New York's simultaneous respect for the oratorical charisma of his "suggestive, direction-giving, soul-fathoming mind" and sense of him as ultimately insufferable: "We are glad there are not more such. A few Emersons would make the everyday work of one's mind intolerable."[5] Willis's rather generous 1850 review (given his regional bias) of Emerson's lecture on "England" for the Mercantile Library Association reflects how the Concord sage's mounting international fame would increasingly assuage, or at least qualify, Knickerbocker animosity by mid-century.

Evert Duyckinck's *Cyclopaedia of American Authors* (1855), so pivotal in preserving the prestigious memory of Irving, judged the

Transcendentalists as Willis had by undercutting its praise in ultimately less than flattering accounts of Emerson, Thoreau, and Fuller. Duyckinck described the project of "transcendental literature" as having the "obscurity, if not the profundity, of abstract metaphysics," criticizing Emerson's disciples who "wrote hardly less intelligibly," and whose "religious views," furthermore, "had little respect for commonly received creeds."[6] The redeeming value Duyckinck found in Thoreau, as a Knickerbocker predictably would, was in his humor, especially its "English sense," which was the hallmark of Irving's Addisonian wit. Yet no one would mistake Thoreau's caustic social satires with Knickerbocker humor; such disingenuous praise from Duyckinck thus increasingly gave way to frontal assault. "The realities around him," writes Duyckinck as he drops the mask, are "veiled by a hazy atmosphere of transcendental speculation, through which the essayist sometimes stumbles into abysmal depths of the bathetic."[7]

The rivalry inspired and organized Transcendentalist thought, as much of its most salient criticism of commerce addresses the flaws specific to New York market culture.[8] New Yorkers, according to a representative Emersonian retort, measure the individual by their possessions and determine the state of the soul by one's fashion. "These New York people think much of New York; little of Boston. The Bostonians are stiff, dress badly, never can speak French with good accent," he observed, zeroing in on the economic crux of the disparity in which "The New Yorkers have exquisite millinery, *tournure*, great expense, and on being presented, the men look at you, and instantly see whether your dress and style is up to their mark; if not (and expense is part of the thing) they never notice you."[9] Accordingly, Thoreau would devote much of "Economy," the opening chapter of *Walden*, to a diatribe against the New York fashion industry, using New York commerce as the antithesis to his economy of house building and subsistence farming, the controlling images for his experiment in deliberate living. Emerson's disciple found ample material for the philosophical foundation of *Walden* in New York as metonym for the dominant economic culture's conflation of self with dollars and possessions he saw so vividly in the streets of Manhattan while attempting to place his writings there. Thoreau had initially wanted to establish his career in New York because it "was populated by ambitious entrepreneurs and independently minded people who patronized an adventurous culture," as Anne C. Rose describes it.[10] Instead, he emerged from his quest firmer in his belief in the essential incongruity of art and commerce.

Fuller also passed judgment on the Knickerbockers in *Summer on the Lakes*, a prose-poetry pastiche of impressions of her journey to the prairie west of Chicago, a work whose reflections on nature inspired Thoreau's ecological perspective in *Walden*. In particular, Fuller indicts Cooper for soliciting Native Americans as sentimental literary subjects by inscribing in "the Indian a delicacy of sentiment and of fancy... in a white man's view of the savage hero." She similarly assails Irving for viewing them from a "dioramic distance" in a way apparently "wonderful, but inadequate."[11] Elsewhere Fuller laments New York's influence on the prairie as reflected in the tendency of settlers to send their children "to school in some eastern city," suggesting that the investment in "good schools near themselves... instead of copying New York, will correct this mania."[12]

The room to cultivate such economic self-reliance (signified by Fuller's motif of the sprawling Western landscape in *Summer on the Lakes* she links to Washington Allston's visual art) free of external influence was a distinctive core principle in the Transcendentalist ethos. It reflected a disdain for conformist living according to self-abasing imitation of seemingly superior models. Fuller asserts that the prairie settlers should not follow New York's educational institutions much in the way that Emerson insists in "Self-Reliance" and "Divinity School Address" that the American intellect should not replicate European thought. Fuller's claim echoes how the Transcendentalists constructed alternative economic systems of exchange—especially from the materials of nature's example—contrary to the ceaseless striving they saw etched into the anxious brows of urbanites. "To me," Fuller reasoned, "[who is] used to the feelings which haunt a society of struggling men, it was delightful to look upon a scene where nature still wore her motherly smile and seemed to promise room not only for those favored or cursed with the qualities best adapting for the strifes of competition, but for the delicate, the thoughtful, even the indolent or eccentric." Unlike the cramped urban centers, the nature Fuller imagined "seemed to promise room," and did not demand ceaseless struggle in the marketplace for what Irving himself called "the almightly dollar." Instead, this form of nature "did not say, Fight or starve; nor even, Work or cease to exist; but, merely showing that the apple was a finer fruit than the wild crab, gave both room to grow in the garden."[13] To the average antebellum upstart merchant—fictionally typified by Melville's Yankee seed salesman narrator of "The Paradise of Bachelors and The Tartarus of Maids"—raised on the gospel of Benjamin Franklin's economic maxims, such tolerance of indolence, and even sloth, would have appeared downright heretical. The alternative economy of Emerson's knot of dreamers made a strong case against laissez-faire capitalism, yet material necessity demanded they make concessions to, if not fully embrace certain aspects of, the free market.

The Genesis of Emerson's Knot of Dreamers

What complicates the appearance of this seemingly neat dichotomy of intense battle between the Knickerbocker and Transcendental literary circles polarized primarily over their understandings of market conditions and the authorial role was that Emerson—in addition to his role as founding father and philosophical inspiration behind the Concord circle—paid for everything.[14] It is well known that he bankrolled Thoreau's trip to New York City to launch his professional career, supplied the land upon which he built his cabin at Walden Pond, lent the Hawthornes liberal sums, only to be exceeded by the financial support he paid Bronson Alcott for his experimental commune, Fruitlands, which abruptly aborted. The source of Emerson's money was the estate of his first wife, Ellen Tucker, who left a fortune upon her death at the age of twenty. After winning it from his sister-in-law's husband in a legal battle, Emerson bought the homestead in Concord that soon became known by all in the transcendental coterie as "Bush," wielding his financial power in the early years much in the way Irving deployed his unmatched celebrity status to support his Lads of Kilkenny who had communed together at Cockloft Hall. Emerson's money supported all five of the authors—Louisa May Alcott, Margaret Fuller, Henry David Thoreau, Nathaniel Hawthorne, and Emerson himself—who made their homes where Lexington Road meets the Cambridge Turnpike. Without Emerson's 1836 legal settlement that granted him possession of his late wife's fortune,[15] it is unlikely that the Transcendentalists would have formed into a cohesive coterie, if at all. Like the New York circles of Part I that coalesced around serials and journals from *Salmagundi* and the *Knickerbocker* in Irving's clan to the *New York Ledger* of Bonner's unit, the Transcendentalists' primary print medium was the *Dial*.

As the print embodiment of the Transcendentalist coterie, the *Dial*'s existence derived as much from Ellen Tucker's estate (not to mention Lydia Jackson's magnanimous hospitality at Bush) as it did the earliest meetings of the Hedge Club. For herein lay the financial and social foundations of the coterie, enabling an antimaterialistic ethos precisely because it was so well funded, attracting followers who in essence became Emerson's alternative congregation, a surrogate for the Unitarian Church he had abandoned. Emerson's acquisition of newfound wealth coincided perfectly with his desire to build a coterie around the radical ideas that led him to resign his post as a Unitarian minister. Emerson scholar Mary Kupiec Cayton convincingly argues that Emerson's hunger for new associates originally grew from the early deaths of his two close brothers, Charles and Edward, and later, his departure from his own congregation. "Among the first of Emerson's attempts to replace the associations he had lost through his forfeiture of the settled ministry," Cayton observes, "was his membership in the Hedge Club, or the Transcendental Club, as it later came to be known."[16]

So with deep pockets and a small group of like-minded radical Unitarian ministers, Emerson was in an ideal position to form the nucleus of the Transcendentalist coterie. The Hedge Club first met on 20 September 1836 to receive Emerson's former Harvard Divinity School classmate, Frederic Henry Hedge, from Maine to discuss his growing disaffection with the Unitarian Church, particularly its restrictive atmosphere that thwarted the free exchange of ideas in his Bangor congregation. Hedge had obtained his position the year prior partially through Emerson's intervention. Dubbed "Germanicus" by Margaret Fuller, Hedge was the only member of Emerson's circle who had studied Goethe and the German romantics in Germany and thus was indispensible for the foundation of Transcendental thought. Hedge also shared Emerson's rebellion, at least initially, against conservative Unitarianism, as the two struggled with their respective congregations similarly, both complaining that their parishes discouraged the free exchange of social and economic criticism and the construction of alternative progressive principles of living, particularly with respect to the free market. The Hedge Club, in this way, was not harmless, but rather consisted of a corps of radical thinkers subverting the core of conventional American culture, from its materialism and relentless capitalism to its routine, mechanical, and stultifying Christianity. Joining Emerson and Hedge at their first gathering of this soon-to-be-public secret society were other unconventional thinkers who would later become radical reformers in their own right, including labor advocate, Orestes Brownson, and educational innovator, Bronson Alcott. The founder of Brook Farm, George Ripley, also attended along with Convers Francis and James Freeman Clarke. Francis and Hedge would eventually split from the group because they stopped short of Emerson's intellectual extremism and Alcott and Ripley's social radicalism. Much in the way economic and professional circumstance conspired to remove James Kirke Paulding from his place among the founding members of the *Salmagundi* circle, Hedge did not sustain his seminal influence over the Transcendental

Club. Opting to compromise with his flock, he did not abandon his calling and reinvent himself professionally as Emerson had. Hedge, unlike Emerson, made concessions to his congregation and found a middle ground that enabled him to remain pastor until 1850, where his lived a quieter and more stable life outside the coterie than his more famous Concord friend who now faced the challenge of forming it into a cohesive unit with a recognizable market presence.

Philosophical Friction with the Market

Transcendentalists, and Emerson in particular, were not naturally inclined toward coterie authorship. In some ways, they could be best understood as an accidental coterie, a group of individualists conjoined as much by their aversion to pretentious conventional social interaction as by their thirst for the divine within themselves and nature. Emerson and Fuller both struggled with interpersonal communication and the cultivation of intimate relationships.[17] They were repulsed by the conventions that constituted the social graces, readily admitting, if not proudly displaying, their weaknesses in this area. A superlative lecturer, Emerson was diffident in the company of others in informal situations, a condition he described in his journal in "some public persons born not for privacy but for publicity who are dull and even silly in tete-a-tete."[18] Fuller's loosely autobiographical story of Mariana in *Summer on the Lakes* renders "a strange bird," whose "schoolmates were captivated with her ways; her love of wild dances and sudden song, her freaks of passion and of wit." Yet her public performances for them could not sustain their friendship: "they tired of her. She could never be depended on to join in their plans" given her "love of solitude" that eventually "displeased her companions."[19] Emerson's self-diagnosis similarly describes dull intimate relations despite brilliant public performances in which "the teeth appear, the eye brightens, a certain majesty sits on the shoulders, and they should have a wit and happy delivery you should never have found in them in the closet."[20]

Unlike the garrulous and ever amiable Knickerbockers, whose identity hinged on the wandering bachelors' oral storytelling capacity, the Transcendentalists' social disposition—which emerged directly out of their individualistic ethos—did not incline them toward coterie formation. Indeed, Thoreau's own famous intolerance for social intercourse has been well documented; at one point he confessed he was born to stay at home. Hawthorne's shyness was so pervasive that it provided the controlling metaphor for an entire biography on the author.[21] The ongoing purpose of the early Hedge Club meeting even gave Emerson pause, who admitted in a letter to Hedge that "I have never found that uplifting and enlargement from the conversation of many which I find in the society of one faithful person,"[22] a sentiment he developed and expounded upon in "The American Scholar." Not only did Emerson privilege the intimacy of one-on-one conversation, preferably during walks in the woods like the many he took with Fuller before drawing her into the circle, he also loathed the thought of having his own identity attached to that of a larger association. He asked rhetorically, "Is it not the chief disgrace in the world, not to be a unit—not to be reckoned one character—not to yield that peculiar fruit which each man was created to bear, but to be reckoned in the gross, in the hundred, or the thousand, of the party, of the section, to which we belong; and our opinion predicted geographically, as the north, or the south?"[23]

This philosophical and personal mismatch with coterie formation raises some vexing issues: How did Emerson and the Concord writers reconcile their individualism to their literary allegiance recognized in the aggregate? To what extent did they make concerted efforts to commune and cohere as a recognizable "unit," as the literary "section to which we belong"? How could the project of forming a coterie be reconciled with the debilitating effect of group identity Emerson described in the "American Scholar"? Emerson produced a coherent statement (or antistatement) defining the circle's belief in "The Transcendentalist" in response to pressure to issue a clear definition of the Transcendentalist creed. George Templeton Strong is representative of the view of Transcendentalism from outside of Concord in this respect, remarking in his journal that a joint lecture by Bronson Alcott, "the father, I suppose, of Yankee-Platonism and hyperflutination," and Reverend Brother Bellows "on the subject of tonight's discourse being announced in a sphinx of a printed card as 'Descent,' which left it uncertain whether we were to be enlightened about family history and pedigree from an aesthetic standpoint, the canons of art applicable to bathos, or the formulas expressing the law of gravitation." The prominent statesman and president of Columbia University could not puzzle out the subject, which discoursed upon "'whole men' (analogous, I suppose, to 'entire horses')," as he facetiously echoed the New York view of the coterie's ponderous principles. Emerson's "Transcendentalist" apparently answers to Templeton's desire, shared by the broader literate public, to make its "signs of genius, power of illustration, and the expression of kindly and hopeful temper" at the heart of Transcendentalism more "intelligible to plain people" so that "it would be a useful discipline to them."[24] Yet "The Transcendentalist" likely raised more questions than it answered as a coterie self-portrait and mission statement defining core principles to foster wider appreciation of the products of Transcendentalist authors in the literary market.

The capitalist condition was inescapable to all coteries in the literary market, yet Emerson appeared to be doing precisely that by deconstructing the positivist pretentions of "the sturdy capitalist [who] no matter how deep and square on blocks of Quincy granite he lays the foundations of his banking-house or Exchange must set it...on the edge of an unimaginable pit of emptiness." Many, including Strong, scratched their heads at the position Emerson defined as one that "does not respect labor, or the products of labor, namely property, otherwise than a manifold symbol, illustrating the wonderful fidelity of details the laws of being."[25] Crucially, the coterie definition he renders not only refuses an orientation toward the market that implies some sort of participation in the commercial world beyond reading it as an elaborate system of symbols, but also negates even the possibility of considering Transcendentalists as a collective coterie. "You will see by this sketch," he writes, "that there is no such thing as a Transcendental *party*," a point he means in more than just a political sense. Transcendentalists have a natural aversion to forming groups and are "unsocial worshippers" who "shun general society," yet only because it is "a choice of the less of two evils."[26]

The break, it would seem, from market conditions was clean and absolute in Emerson's writings. But at a closer look, his misgivings of the market are less consistent and more accommodating than his distaste for "general society," which takes on a looming, almost evil presence in his work, representing a deep threat to individuality and self-culture through its unremitting demands for conformity. The market, on the other hand, he can make concessions for, allowing that the divine spiritual life and the working economic life can mutually enhance one another. He urges that the "worst feature of this double consciousness is, that these two lives...really show very little relation to each other; never meet and measure each other; one prevails now, all buzz and din; and the other prevails then, all infinitude and paradise; and, with the progress of life, the two discover no greater disposition to reconcile themselves." The potential here of enabling the two worlds of spirit and market "to meet and measure each other" is considerable, yet Emerson never wedded it to a business practice that might have advanced the Transcendentalist coterie (rather than his own lecturing career, which was quite successful) more effectively. Instead, his final plea was for "thoughts and principles not marketable or perishable" in an age of economic expansion, of hunger for another "subscription of stock...a new house, or a larger business."[27]

Unlike Walt Whitman, for example, who effectively merged exultant and expansive spirituality with audacious self-promotion through commercial discourse,[28] Emerson only recognized the potential in such a wedding. He stopped short of realizing it in managing the commercial life of the Concord coterie because he sensed that such an enterprise would produce a collective literary commodity too closely aligned with the acquisitive materialism of the larger culture.

Capitalism and the formation of social groups are major concerns, if not obsessions, throughout Emerson's writing, mainly because he was so sensitive to the real financial costs of his views toward both. Forming a coterie was fraught with the struggle to develop the self in relation to others, and intrinsic to that problem was the notion of hierarchy. He muses that friendship is a vertically oriented system of hero worship, an odd process of self-abasement and idolization. Were a companion "high enough to slight me, then could I love him, and rise by my affection to new heights. A man's growth is seen in the successive choirs of his friends...why should I play [with my friends] this game of idolatry?"[29] Further, he admits that when "much intercourse with a friend has supplied us with a standard of excellence, and has increased our respect for the resources of God" so that we might convert it into "solid and sweet wisdom" it is a "sign to us that his office is closing, and he is commonly withdrawn from our sight in a short time." Emerson finds this pattern of interpersonal relations utterly organic, and without shame. Its truth is brutally honest and its implications for the development of a literary coterie are grave indeed. Were this hierarchical and self-interested pattern somehow adaptable to a more horizontal and democratic model, the rhetoric would be more hopeful in its application to the construction of a functional literary coterie.

Such understandings of friendship and their problematic implications for the formation of a literary coterie are complicated by the economic dimensions of Emerson's "Man Thinking" in "The American Scholar." Insofar as he "plies the slow, unhonored, and unpaid task of observation...and relinquishes display and immediate fame," he is the polar opposite of Robert Bonner's *New York Ledger* authors, who thrived on recognition, money, and speedy literary output.[30] Significantly, Emerson does not take this sacrifice as a badge of honor, but with a sharp pang of regret that syntactically registers through his only break in the passage describing the life of "Man Thinking." "Worse yet, he must accept—how often!—poverty and solitude" in a life that refuses to conform to "the ease and pleasure of treading the old road, accepting the fashions, the education, the religion of society." He takes consolation in "exercising the highest functions of human nature" knowing that he has triumphed over "the vulgar prosperity that retrogrades to barbarism."[31] According to this formulation, money is mutually exclusive to the true literary life, and must be sacrificed for this ideal of authorship.

Emerson's fractured syntax and exclamatory "how often!" is the most emphatic of this long paragraph in "The American Scholar." It is significant, further, that such an emotional outburst should come as a *lament* for the inadequate financial compensation of Man Thinking. Emerson's hope, it would thus appear, is that the scholar might be better provided for materially, if not lavished with a Bonneresque salary or obsequious Irvingesque celebrity associated with "bank-stock and doubloons, venison and champagne." Compensation should be material as well as spiritual, according to the logic of his wincing "how often!" regret, yet in no way conflated with worldly excesses and "the base estimate of the market of what constitutes a manly success" as opposed to "the presence of the soul."[32] The scholar needs enough income to continue comfortably, if not extravagantly, in his pursuits so that he might enjoy "the privilege of going on," as nineteenth-century popular author Lucy Larcom describes it.[33] Emerson is objecting to the "display and immediate fame" embodied not only by the *Ledger* staff, but also by the commercially dominant Knickerbockers of the prior era as well. It is not that Emerson was blind to their financial successes. More to the point, he instead refused to count their products as literature. For within the commercial context, "Genius leaves the temple to haunt the senate or the market," a condition in which "literature becomes frivolous," driven by sensation, spectacle, and sentiment alone.[34] Fiction writing, indeed, seems anathema to the Transcendentalist project altogether, especially in Thoreau's regret that the mechanization of literary production—its unprecedented rise in efficiency through labor-saving inventions such as the double-cylinder steam press—raced ahead of the creative capacity to fill those new pages with ink worthy of reading. "If others are the machines to provide this provender, they are the machines to read it," he reasoned.[35] Can genius haunt the market and still be sacred, or at least not profane the temple? Only if it is offered up in the spirit of loving "God without mediator or veil," a situation virtually impossible given the rise of the literary intermediaries that began to drive the publishing world like never before.[36]

Fuller's Coterie Quandary

Margaret Fuller shared Emerson's apprehensions about coteries, calling into question the project of forming associations, which had always been suspect to Emerson. Fuller's misgivings about artistically inclined individuals within close social environments sheds light on the problems inherent in the formation of the Transcendentalist coterie and its function in the commercial free market. Forming a coherent group of radical individualists she knew was fraught with the sort of obstacles visible in her own difficulty establishing herself in her peer group as a girl, alluded to above in her story of Mariana in *Summer on the Lakes*. Indeed, the worry of Fuller, as with Emerson, is that the individual will chafe against the rigid conformity of the larger group, as embodied by Mariana's environment's effect on her "ardent and too early stimulated nature" within the context of "the restraints and narrow routine of the boarding school."[37] Mariana's school environment is diametrically opposed to that which she observes in the inclusive and tolerant "natural community" consisting of "several happy families, who had removed together...ready to help and enliven one another." These denizens of the farmhouse where Fuller's entourage took shelter on her tour of the prairies speak volumes of this sort of potential in human communities. The tableau fits the ideal Transcendentalist coterie as an agrarian socialist utopia, a cooperative labor program based upon the principle of equality. Yet like so many signs of hegemony that creep into the Blithedale farm life in Hawthorne's thinly veiled fictional assault on Brook farm, Fuller spots hierarchical domination in the way "the women did no like the change, but they were willing," grudgingly submitting to their arduous roles for the sake of the children, a self-sacrifice made "'as it might be best for the young folks.'"[38] The Seeress of Prevorst's story that follows is a small, seemingly digressive vignette that tells a similar tale of the nightmare of misunderstood subjectivity, though in vastly understated and muted tones by comparison.

It is not by accident that Fuller's succession of images in *Summer on the Lakes* of dysfunctional social arrangements detailing the squashed inner lives of isolated and rejected individualists prefaces her famous parody of Emerson as *Self-Poise* to her *Free Hope*. The dialogue between the two characters speaks to her supple romantic pragmatism in contrast with Emerson's inflexible armor-clad individualism. His principle that one should "Sit at home and the spirit-world will look in at your window with moonlit eyes" admonishes the adventure of running "out to find it," because "the spirit world, rainbow, and golden cup will have vanished and left you the beggarly child you were." One can "do no better service than to hold himself upright, avoid nonsense, and do what chores lie in his way," according to *Self-Poise*. That, in Fuller's view, does not leave "room enough for the lyric inspirations, or the mysterious whispers of life." Specifically, she pinpoints the obsessive sense of self-control in his vision that leaves him hardened to such mysteries. Crucially, the missing piece of Emerson's vision is his incapacity for self-surrender, an emotional state that is at once social and aesthetic, like falling in love. "To me it seems that it is madder never to abandon oneself, than often to be infatuated; better to be wounded, a captive, and a slave, than always walk in armor," she writes.[39] Though her hyperbole can be misleading here, Fuller's rhetoric should not be mistaken for seeking the command of a male, or grudgingly deferring to patriarchal authority as the farmer's wives do in the earlier vignette. Instead, she refuses to be cast in the role of Emerson's cold and hardened isolated patriarch. Her point also bears on the importance of community as a condition that flourishes in proportion to its members' capacity to give themselves to one another, to fall in love, as it were, with all the faith and risk that entails. Too much self-possession, in her view, denies the healthy social function of communities.

Indeed, Fuller not only extols the pleasures of losing oneself in a kind of surrender to infatuation as an aesthetic principle, but also highlights its importance as the bonding principle of well-run communities that are at once tolerant and nurturing. In fairness to Emerson, Fuller's expectations for the new social network of authors may have been too high when she first assumed a place in the Transcendentalist inner circle. "Since I have been an exile so long from the social world and a social world is now suddenly thrust upon me, I am determined by the help of heaven to suck this orange dry...I abandon myself to what is best in you all," she gushed with wild idealism, building up the Concord coterie into a kind of social utopia.[40] Such surrender and compassion were the qualities she had wanted, but seldom received, from the men of Concord, with whom she had significant individual interactions, but never on a group level to match her lively role in Elizabeth Palmer Peabody's conversations. Indeed, she observed in *Woman in the Nineteenth Century* (1845) that "the triumphs of female authorship" have been "great and constantly increasing" despite the persistence of male gatekeepers who have "pronounced them unfit" for their entry into the public sphere.[41] Her characterization of Emerson as *Self-Poise* stuck in his home and on himself contrasts with her own opposite professional trajectory away from Concord. She would venture into the New York literary market and find work and a new home there, soon traveling thereafter to Europe where she would fall in love and marry amid political turmoil and revolution all at a time when alternative forms of community were being widely discussed, especially according to the theories of Charles Fourier and Karl Marx.

Whereas Emerson proved the wrong man to head a functional and inclusive coterie as portrayed in *Self-Poise*, the figure of Morris Birkbeck in *Summer on the Lakes*, a "truly valuable settler" from England, possessed all the qualities necessary to lead a community that honored, rather than misunderstood, the wild variations of artistic subjectivity. In these two figures Fuller's concept of the ideal literary coterie becomes apparent. Emerson shared Birkbeck's qualities as "An enlightened philanthropist, the rather that he did not wish to sacrifice himself to his fellow men, but to benefit them with all he had, and was, and wished," and even his "visionary" belief that the divine resided in "all the creatures...who ought to be happy and ought to be good, and that his own soul and his own life were not less precious than those of others." Birckbeck's credo, "Every man his own priest, and the heart the only church" is strikingly Emersonian in its emphasis on deinstitutionalized individual spirituality and self-culture. Yet Birkbeck's portrait deviates from Emerson's, according to Fuller, precisely because the immigrant's aims, unlike Emerson's, "were altogether generous," reflective of a community-loving ideal patriarch. Rather than lock himself in the armor of his own self-reliance, Birkbeck is forever vigilant of the health and happiness of his people, a quality poignantly expressed through the circumstances of his own death. Having fallen into a river he and his son were attempting to cross, Birkbeck began to drown in the rushing current. His son alertly plunged in after him, "exerted all his strength to stem the current and reach the shore at a point where they could land; but, encumbered by his own clothing and his father's weight, he made no progress." When the futility of his son's efforts became apparent to Birkbeck, "he, with his characteristic calmness and resolution, gave up his hold of his son, and, motioning to him to save himself, resigned himself to his fate." The body was found, and "on the countenance was the sweetest smile," an image that became an iconic emblem for Fuller of "ready and serene" resolve "to lay aside even life, when it is right and best." This was the patriarch that Emerson—for all his armor and dissent—never was to Fuller. Birkbeck loved unconditionally, happily dying to preserve his son's life in this instance, a metonym for the larger community he served. The smiling face of Birkbeck "touched my imagination," Fuller confessed, "and has often come up, in lonely vision" to restore her in ways Emerson was incapable of, highlighting for her the value of human compassion, sympathy, and even surrender.[42]

Fuller's admiration for Birkbeck bears special significance for her perception of the flaws of the Transcendentalist coterie. She readily acknowledges the need for "tranquil enjoyment of intellectual blessings, and the pure happiness of mutual love," knowing that individualism's heroic qualities also have a dark underside. "Solitude," she admits, can become "lonely and deserted" without a willingness to engage the social, political, and economic exigencies of the outer world. Such engagement in her view demands "patience to learn the new spells which the new dragons require," a formula for the growth of a thriving immigrant community with profound implications for that of the Transcendentalist literary coterie, which hardly lived up to the "natural community" she witnessed in *Summer on the Lakes.* The key to growing that sense of community is in the tenderness, sympathetic love, and knowledge of that larger world, evocative of the literary market Emerson was unable to fully exploit for the benefit of his cohort. "American men and women are inexcusable if they do not bring up children so as to be fit for vicissitudes," Fuller proclaimed, describing a resourcefulness and pragmatic savvy she found wanting in the imagination and priorities of Emerson. Indeed, the incapacity for expansion outward into the commercial world of resources appears in the very language of Fuller's most direct assault on Emerson: "You, Self-Poise, fill a priestly office. Could but a larger intelligence of the *vocations* of others, and a tender sympathy with their individual natures be added, had you more love, or more of apprehensive genius, for either would give you the needed *expansion*" both as outward sympathy and professional growth, "and delicacy [to] command my entire reverence." Like others in the circle, she resolves to "deny and oppose you... for you tend, by your influence, to exclude us from our full, free life." She speaks for Thoreau, the Alcotts, Channing, and the Peabodies when she says, "we must be content when you censure, and rejoiced when you approve." Fuller declares her independence by "passing on to interest myself and others in the memoir of the Seherin von Prevorst," a tale of a bed-ridden woman suffering deeply from her peculiar spiritual condition at the very edge of the physical world, with one foot in the afterlife, a bold sign of the artistic sensibility denied, censured, and isolated into a torturous medical condition.[43] She puns on the word "pass" here to imply her self-liberation from his habitual passing of judgment upon her and others in the Concord clique. Fuller rhetorically wields Frederica Hauffe as a figure of rebellion, and even retaliation, against Emerson, as suggested by her own prefatory remarks. I would argue that this figure of misunderstood subjectivity is not only an extension of Fuller's own psychological past of her blocked or frozen mourning of her father's death in 1835, as Jeffrey Steele has argued.[44] The Seeress, a clairvoyant haunted by spirits, who "was at all times more awake than others are" can also aptly describe the creative condition shared by most of the acutely impassioned Transcendentalist authors, who seem in their best works occupying both a meditative abstract world apart, and a pragmatic earthy presence. Thoreau's morning work and the cry of Chanticleer in *Walden* speaks to his acutely tuned senses and heightened awareness, while his famous reveries that conflate terra firma with the sky above evoke a clear entrance into a dream world, however mediated by nature. "For it is strange to term sleep this state which is just that of the clearest wakefulness. Better to say [Frederica] was immersed in the inward state" of the sort Thoreau and Fuller engaged while wakefully dreaming at the height of their creative powers.[45]

If anything sustains the suffering Seeress, it is Dr. Kerner, another figure of paternal sympathy, drawn in direct contrast to the Emersonian *Self-Poise*. In response to a sad verse she writes of the mean spirited rumors abounding, Kerner answers Frederica with his own: "To us thou seemest true and pure, / Let others view it as they will; / We have our assurance still / If our own sight can make us sure."[46] Further, Kerner understands her affliction as a poetic process involving "the projections of herself into objective reality" in a view that presents a figurative understanding of authorship—even under such bizarre circumstances of animal magnetism and clairvoyance—that is pragmatic and profoundly respectful of the woman's powerful intellect. Indeed, her uncanny facility to see the spiritual world and to use language in such an unusual way he attributes to "no gift from without," not bestowed by a mystical source, "but a growth from her own mind." For her curse, he discovered, was indeed a gift of creative vision, the rare capacity to "attend to what is simple and invariable in the motions of their own minds," and still more unusual ability to "seek out means clearly to express them to others."[47] This is the writer's gift and its tragic results given the lack of a sympathetic social context.

Spinning the *Dial*

The social context of Fuller's professional situation within the Concord Transcendental circle revolved around the *Dial*. When she first began her editorial duties for the *Dial*, Fuller received a spate of encouraging letters from Emerson, many of which reflected the tone of his meditation on "Heroism." Fuller's desire to identify with other past women writers surfaces in his sense of "the fair girl who repels interference by a decided and proud choice of influences, so careless of pleasing, so willful and lofty, inspires every beholder with some what of her own nobleness." After being so encouraged to "come into port greatly," Fuller moved into a more influential role within the coterie as editor and cowriter with Emerson.[48] At this time, however, their conversations increasingly turned into debates, and the *Dial* became the site of Emerson and Fuller's famous clash over Thoreau's "Persius." Fuller found her editorial authority overruled by Emerson, who opposed her persistent refusals of young Thoreau's submissions and eventually forced them into the pages of the journal.[49]

Fuller's professional relationship with Emerson was strained by the unusual circumstance of an antebellum man and woman maintaining a close collegial relationship, which for Transcendentalists consisted largely of sharing isolated walks in the woods. Lydian's emotional outburst at one awkward and telling dinner highlighted her accumulated stress from playing hostess to legions of transcendental guests, including Fuller, who made her more acutely feel the pangs of outsidership. Asking Fuller to join her for a walk in the woods, Lydian abruptly cut off Fuller's reply. "'I am engaged to walk with Mr. E. but'—(I was going to say, I will walk with you first), when L. burst into tears. The family were all present and looked at their plates. Waldo looked on the ground," Fuller recalled in her journal. Fuller's insistence that she join her only made her angrier. "I do not want you to make any sacrifice, but I do feel perfectly desolate, and forlorn, and I thought if I once got out, the fresh air would do me good, and that with you, I should have courage, but go with Mr. E.," Lydian retorted, her anguish and frustration now on full display. "I will not go."[50]

Emerson's relationship with Fuller flourished from their first meeting in 1836 for four years, until October of 1840. The crisis mounted out of Fuller's decision not to move to Concord despite Emerson's efforts to locate living arrangements for her near his home. "Fuller's decision in part was based on the need to limit his influence on her which she sometimes found overwhelming," according to Judith Mattson Bean.[51] A source of that pressure came from Emerson's original conception of the *Dial* as a journal that would be responsive to the suggestions and demands of its immediate community. While such a democratic spirit had its strengths, it also had the unintended consequence of opening channels for sexist criticism of the journal's supposed feminine quality. Under the duress of such claims, Emerson pressed Fuller to alter the journal's format to appease its male readers.[52] Fuller knew these objections were baseless and that the philosophically dense and earnest journal bore nothing of the entertainment style and format of ladies magazines—flush with fashion plates and advice columns on etiquette—dominating the periodical presses. If anything, the journal reflected her dedication to the transcendence of the limitations of gender that she praised in authors like "Shelley, who, like all men of genius, shared the feminine development, and, unlike many, knew it."[53] This approach, anticipating Virginia Woolf's claim of the next century that all great writing transcends the limitations of gender, was beyond the grasp of many of her male contemporaries. Theodore Parker, for example, saw the *Dial* as "a band of men and maidens daintily arrayed in finery [compared to] a body of stout men in blue frocks, with great arms and hard hands and legs." When he launched his own *Massachusetts Quarterly Review*, he described it as a "*Dial* with a beard."[54] Fuller's growing discomfort with her editorship, which otherwise benefitted from Emerson's loyal support, thus set the stage for her refusal to move to Concord that initiated their rift. Emerson's "Friendship," which advocated distance from companions, would directly emerge out of this crisis.

From when she began editing the *Dial* in late 1839, among the happiest days of Fuller's career in the periodical press was her departure from that post in 1842. She had learned that her best efforts to balance the journal's budget, along with its policy of not paying contributors—one strikingly opposite of the *New York Ledger*'s policy of liberally exceeding common authorial wages—did not garner enough profits to justify her own $200 salary she had been promised. Many of Emerson's failed protégés who found their way onto the *Dial*'s pages made the journal's content even less marketable, as witnessed by the dubious fates of their professional careers.[55] Further, the *Dial* seems to have been in an ideal position to market its anticommercial leanings as other coteries like the Knickerbockers had. The paradox of taking advantage of the increasingly commercial periodical market through non- or anticommercial conceptions of authorship—as seen in the popularity of the Knickerbockers' carefree and very much unemployed sauntering bachelor image—might under better circumstances have aided the *Dial*'s plight. Yet the pastiche method, the level of abstraction, and the emphasis on in-progress portfolio fragments, all conspired to ruin any possibility for the Concord clique to find a broader audience through the *Dial*.

Before taking over editorial duties of the *Dial* from Fuller, Emerson made his boldest innovation for the journal in an article entitled, "New Poetry," which appeared in the October 1840 issue. In an attempt to boost circulation, Emerson called for more literary and intellectual news, inviting the submission of works in progress that might otherwise have been hidden within private journals. As such, his aim was "to make it less a showcase for finished work and more a clearing house for like-minded souls," as Robert D. Richardson has aptly described it.[56] Emerson's larger purpose in establishing that clearinghouse, I would add, was to unite the fragmenting Concord cohort. Another effect, perhaps unintentional, was to make the *Dial* more provincial and idiosyncratic. Instead of expanding the circle, he sought outside writers whom he might integrate and acculturate into the coterie to strengthen its inner bonds. Emerson was specifically steering the *Dial*'s toward an amateur's open forum, utilizing the periodical as a means by which to foster local literary conversation. Emerson was responding to a perceived lack of collegiality and an unwillingness to collaborate within the circle with this measure designed to realize the untapped creative potential of the coterie.[57] He posted the intriguing solicitation "for a new department in poetry, namely *Verses in the Portfolio*" since the democratic "revolution in literature is giving importance to the portfolio over the book."[58]

Emerson's call for the "unpremeditated translation of...thoughts and feelings into rhyme" worked directly against an elitist exclusive coterie concept that many have mistakenly applied to the Transcendentalists. Emerson's solicitation was emphatically inclusive and democratic, openly rebelling against "the straitest restrictions on the admission of candidates to the Parnassian fraternity."[59] Changes in the book market prompted his appeal, essentially a corrective measure against the publishing industry's narrow range of celebrity authors who were effectively silencing "the one in five who may inscribe his thoughts...in a private journal" versus "the one man in the thousand who may print a book."[60] He thus called for verse not written for publication, but first impressions or even false starts and fragments. The advantage of such contributions, he argued, was "that they testified that the writer was more than artist, more earnest than vain; that the thought was too sweet and sacred to him, than that he should suffer...to see a superficial defect in the expression." Packaging, image, name recognition, and a long list of published books in this sense are "the prescriptions that demand a rhythmical polish [that] may be set aside."[61] Such anticommercial poetics, almost Whitmanian in their desire for intimacy outside of the codified intermediary networks of literary production that bring a work its "finish" and its author fame—"the cold types and wet cylinder between us," as the voice of "Song of Myself" envisions it, lamenting how "I pass so poorly with types...I must pass with the contact of bodies and souls"—react against surges in expansion and protocorporatization of the antebellum literary market.[62]

However anticommercial the solicitation was, Emerson still paradoxically called for literary production and publication, yet in a journal that was in the business of escaping the trappings of conventional literary business. "We have fancied that we drew greater pleasure from some manuscript verses than from printed ones of equal talent," he wrote, ironically urging poets to transform their manuscript verses into printed ones. This new department of the *Dial* was thus intended to make the mechanism of literary production a transparent medium for the "unpublished" amateur, all the while doing exactly the opposite by publishing works to advance professional careers within the coterie. This instance exemplified how Emerson did attempt to wed spiritual truths and social forces otherwise apparently at odds in the Transcendental coterie.

Though their dance between airy idealism and self-interested practicality was not always smooth, Emerson believed that great dividends could be attained when the ideal and the material divide of the "double consciousness" breaks down so that the two "meet and measure each other" from otherwise separate worlds in which "one prevails now, all buzz and din; and the other prevails then, all infinitude and paradise."[63] Indeed, Emerson actually admired the independence and freedom of action if not the material possessions of the wealthy, as he urged that "power is what they want, not candy—power to execute their design, power to give legs and feet, form and actuality to their thought; which, to a clear-sighted man, appears the end for which the universe exists, and all its resources might be well applied... Is not then the demand to be rich legitimate?"[64] John Patrick Diggins has provocatively explored parallels between the ambition of the Transcendentalists and America's early Protestants whose antimaterialism inadvertently turned out a spirit of capitalism because "the Calvinist came to feel he could work his way out of the very situation of predestination into which God had willed him," as portrayed in Max Weber in *The Protestant Ethic and the Spirit of Capitalism* (published as a two-part essay in 1904–1905). But the Transcendentalists themselves did not "make the same mistake as the early Puritans in assuming that they could follow their calling, uphold the work ethic, strive to prove themselves, and somehow avoid the unintended consequences of their striving."[65] The richness of the Transcendentalist dialectic indeed accommodated select methods of the business world that resonated with their energy, vigor, and spirit of adventure without giving way to acquisitiveness for its own sake. Despite its inward focus, the poetry portfolio department of the *Dial* embodies precisely how the mechanism of the literary market—particularly the function of the coterie to spread notoriety and attendant professional success—could "meet and measure" the aims of the idealist by socializing otherwise private, and thus sacred, poetic utterance. The purpose of drawing in new talent thus counters the common tag of insularity affixed to the Transcendentalists, as Emerson's aim was clearly to enrich and diversify his ranks, if not to propel his authors into the wider publishing world. Thought leads to thing, private verse to publication and coterie presence, even in the protective enclave of Concord deliberately carved out as a refuge from the biting wind of capitalism. This context conditioned Transcendentalism, no matter how averse the coterie's credo to acquisitive trade.

It is important to emphasize that Emerson rarely thought of the management of his own career or the status of the coterie as concessions to commercial culture, let alone market transactions. Nonetheless he consistently poured over his financial ledger, tracking every transaction with meticulous care, a habit that directly served his own success on the lecture circuit and in print. Emerson invited contributions "written on important and agreeable topics" that would make "fine texts for conversation"[66] since, as Judith Mattson Bean notes, "He considered the *Dial* to be a vehicle for continuing conversation."[67] Ellery Channing (the younger) made his poetic debut in the Concord coterie within Emerson's new portfolio verses department of the *Dial*. As he had done with Carlyle and Fuller, Emerson successfully drew Channing into the enclave of Transcendentalist thinkers. Emerson would promote Carlyle's career on the national stage through book publishers with greater success than he had for any of his disciples.[68] Emerson's editorial framing of figures like Channing expressed his philosophical principle that "the failures of genius are better than the victories of talent," and that glimpses of an author at work are indeed the most authentic portraits we have of the human being behind the writing, since "Art is the path of the creator to his work."[69]

This emphasis on sharing writing in progress espoused a conception of authorship that was indeed social and even collaborative despite the centrality of individualism in the Transcendentalist credo. Interestingly, Emerson reconceived of the *Dial* as an extension of the private journals the coterie commonly kept. Like Thoreau's journals, Emerson's "were, in part, collaboratively conceived in that he interwove, in the manner of a conversation, quotations with his own ideas, extracted correspondents' letters and other people's journals into his own, and allowed some intimates within his circles to peruse them, hear them read, and comment upon them," as Ronald J. and Mary Saracino Zboray point out.[70] Yet these journals, like the Romantic aesthetic of portfolio writing to which Emerson had adapted the *Dial* upon taking over editorial duties from Fuller, were written for the inner circle, not the wider public, their social trajectory aimed inward rather than outward toward expansion into a cosmopolitan market. Indeed, Fuller herself acknowledged that the coterie never followed Emerson's success in the market. In a review of *Essays: Second Series* (1844), she asserts that Emerson's star outshone that of the collective Concord coterie. Writing in New York City years after her departure from Concord gained her the clarity of vision to perceive that "a similar circle of like-minded books" to Emerson's "must and do form for themselves, though with a movement less directly powerful, as more distant from its source."[71]

Material necessity, in part, expanded Fuller's sense of audience for the *Dial* that initially shared Emerson's inner focus on developing an exclusive coterie of like-minded thinkers without reaching the masses. Larry J. Reynolds has argued that she perceived the journal's audience as "a large circle of ideal friends. For her, the American public was hopelessly vulgar and ignorant, and she was reluctant to address it at this time."[72] The final qualifying phrase here is crucial, because she indeed embraced the notion of reaching a broader audience *at a later time*, namely as an author for Greeley's *Tribune*, famously lauding the periodical press as "the most important part of our literature [and] the only efficient instrument for the general education of the people."[73] Thus she was not nearly so priggish and insular as Reynolds paints her, but instead genuinely interested in finding a wide circulation for the *Dial*, at the very least, to make it a financially viable venture. Indeed, upon the realization that she fell short of this goal, she left her position. According to Fuller's morally upright and responsible business ethic, the $3 per year quarterly publication had not sold enough under her care to justify the already meager $200 she had been promised. Despite her Romantic aesthetic of portfolio writing, she nonetheless was not content catering local potpourri to the insular Concord coterie. Yearning for a broader regional focus, Fuller solicited Hedge for a contribution to the *Dial*, urging that "it is for dear New England that I wanted this review," according to the assumption that she could, as editor, have easily supplied the piece, admitting "for myself, if I had wanted to write a few pages now and then, I had ways and means of disposing of them."[74] Beyond New England, the New York market to which she was eventually drawn was indeed validating to her professionally, since it proved to her that her ideas and work could find both a wide and appreciating audience. Her best and most productive years as a writer immediately followed her liberation from the *Dial*, as *Summer on the Lakes* and *Woman in the Nineteenth Century* blossomed after she ceased editing the *Dial*, and her position with Horace Greeley's *New-York Daily Tribune* began in 1848. Her career continued its outward expansion toward the eye of the revolutionary storms in Europe. At the *Tribune*, and as correspondent reporting on the revolutions that began in 1848, she would write some of the best social, political, and literary criticism of the entire century prior to the shipwreck that took her life in 1850.

Yet Fuller's departure from the *Dial* did not mean that she braved the waters of the literary market relying solely on her own powers. Indeed, her continued use of her Concord connections embodies how "the bounds of intellectual life remained permeable in Antebellum America" since "communities of thinkers encouraged experimentation and supported individualism" like her own, as Anne C. Rose explains.[75] Fuller's publications after her departure from the *Dial* directly involved Emerson in the role of literary agent. Her professional success provides a fascinating study in contrast to that of her coterie colleague, Henry David Thoreau, for they responded oppositely to strikingly similar generous offers from Horace Greeley and identical shortsighted book publishing advice from Emerson.

Unlike Fuller who embraced Greeley's offer to become a steady contributor to the *Tribune*, Thoreau would not accept a similar deal, and instead pressed ahead for the publication of *A Week on the Concord and Merrimack Rivers*, fatally, even desperately, turning to Emerson for help in securing a contract with one of his former publishers, James Munroe. Instead of half profits, Munroe had offered in 1849 to publish *A Week* at the author's own expense, payable through the initial profits earned from the book. Such an arrangement was dangerous for an author like Thoreau whose circulation in the market at the time was limited to the *Dial* and a few other magazines, and nonexistent in the book market. He had just rejected an offer to publish with Ticknor and Fields under the condition that he pay $450 to cover production expenses; now the lure to sign with Munroe for advance payment for costs was too tempting. Emerson dispensed with reckless advice: "I am not of opinion that your book should be delayed a month. I should print it at once, nor do I think that you would incur any risk in doing so that you cannot well afford. It is very certain to have readers and debtors here as well as there."

Fuller wisely sidestepped an almost identical incident with Emerson while trying to place *Summer on the Lakes* with a publisher. Faced with two offers, one from Emerson's James Munroe, and one from Little, Brown, Fuller was faced with a profound dilemma. Little, Brown not only had the advantage of a wider distribution range in the South as well as New York, but their contract was not as financially risky as Munroe's deceptive deal. Little, Brown offered 10 percent royalties on retail sales after recouping expenses, demanding her to bear no additional financial responsibility for unsold books. Munroe's half-profits deal, however, seemed to promise a greater return, yet was nearly identical to the 10 percent royalty Little, Brown offered. Most importantly, Munroe also committed Fuller to repay the publisher for half the losses in the case that sales failed to cover expenses and break into the profit margin. Emerson trivialized the financial risk and provincial distribution network of Munroe as he had with Thoreau, and pushed strenuously for Fuller to sign with his own publisher. Fuller rejected his advice, and signed with Little, Brown, a decision that saved her from paying for half of the poorly selling book's losses, which Munroe would have demanded of her.

Munroe, as it turned out, served Emerson well only because he had established himself through the periodical press as America's "most steadily attractive lecturer" according to the *Atlantic* monthly.[76] Emerson's crusade to counter the sensationalism of popular newspapers through his lectures paradoxically had the effect of vigorously circulating his name and spreading his fame because the events were so widely reported in the press. He expressed concern in his journal that "cheap literature makes new markets" and expands the audience into an anonymous mass beyond the "box office" so that "now it appears there is also slip audience, & galleries one, two, three; & backstairs, & street listeners, besides." Writing for such a mass audience, he mused, would be like delivering "a lecture, if I will, to 70,000 readers."[77] His fame spread almost despite himself; his loyalty to Munroe and sense of him as the preferred book publisher of the Transcendentalists likely sprang from Munroe's peripheral place in the commercial market, as seen in the company's reluctance to fully engage the available mechanisms of commerce to promote its authors.

Thoreau somehow made humorous light of the humiliating consequence with Munroe that Fuller narrowly escaped when he self-effacingly proclaimed to be the proud owner of "a library of over nine-hundred volumes, over seven-hundred of which I wrote myself."[78] Also, unlike Thoreau, she would eventually take up a generous offer to write for Horace Greeley and turn it into one of the most satisfying ventures of her career. In fairness to Emerson, it must be emphasized that however suspect his talents as literary agent were for Thoreau and Fuller, he did in fact successfully help Thomas Carlyle place his work with influential publishers that were instrumental in the spread of his renown in America.[79] Further, Emerson displayed remarkable skill in bringing together some of the most radical individualists in America for fruitful and provocative exchanges that would lead to greater successes elsewhere. The successful integration of outsiders like Channing and Carlyle, one could argue, is not even as impressive as his triumph of bringing Fuller and Peabody into the all-male coterie of recalcitrant Unitarian ministers in a culture averse to women joining gentlemen's clubs.[80]

The *Dial*, like Munroe, was not a potent promoter of talent, but instead built internal bonds, and engaged a wider audience almost accidentally. The key distinction, therefore, in the Transcendental coterie was its all-consuming anticommercialism, a willingness to live as "man thinking" as much as material necessity would allow. As the two most notable forays into the book market by Thoreau and Fuller indicate, and as the fate of the *Dial* shows, seeking payment could be accommodated for in the fiercely antimarket ethos of the Transcendentalists, not just as a necessary evil, but as the key to perpetuating the writing life and surviving in a culture not yet ready accommodate the concept of writing as the primary vocation and means of living. "The man who would be literary must earn his living first—pursue an honest occupation... His necessities thus provided for, literature may be to him the most delightful and ennobling amusement" was the dominant formulation, to which the Knickerbocker coterie's image, if not reality, naturally conformed through their collective identity of the financially secure bachelor dilettante.[81]

Coterie writing in Concord promised an immediate and intimate audience, as represented in the *Dial*, and not an anonymous mass public. Especially relevant in this regard is the Zborays' claim that "it is a mistake to take the anonymous market as the primary audience for such work [as Emerson's and Thoreau's]; it was, rather, face to face relations of the literary circle," or at least the replication thereof in the *Dial*, "with the market playing—if anything at all—a mere supporting role after, perhaps, other different coteries." One of those different coteries was the Knickerbockers, whose discord with the Transcendentalists is discussed at the beginning of this chapter. The literary New Yorkers, further, *were* the market to the Transcendentalists, offering a template against which to work out their anticommercial ethos in the context of "the small variants within the local intellectual climate of Concord, Massachusetts." That ethos took its keynote from the commercialization of literature well under way in New York City, which not only functioned as the antithesis of the Transcendental coterie identity, but also constituted a social matrix of the publishing world that would, ironically, supply the setting, audience, and inspiration for Fuller's later success and innumerable Emersonian oratorical performances. "If the role of coteries is kept front and center... it promises much insight into common amateur and social authorship practices," bringing new meaning to the study of "canonical authors' works as sources for the study of social history."[82] It is to 13 West Street, the Boston bookstore of Elizabeth Palmer Peabody, locus of conversation, collaboration, book acquisition, lending, and publishing—a coterie world at the edge of amateur and professional, canonical and common categories of authorship—that we now turn.

Chapter 5

Boston and Beyond: Elizabeth Peabody's Promotional Practice

Far more successful than Emerson at nurturing and promoting careers in the marketplace was Elizabeth Palmer Peabody, whose "conversations" held at her Transcendentalist bookstore were instrumental in publicizing New England intellectuals. Beyond the fact that she did not pay for everything, what differentiated Peabody from Emerson as a literary intermediary was that she elevated conversation to an art, both as an intellectual subject and as a means to create social change and influence public values. For as famous as Emerson was, he certainly did not circulate as much among the literati and intellectuals of New England, nor did he share her dedication to the art of conversation on such a consistent level. As such, Peabody was ideally equipped to bring New England's writers in contact with the publishing industry in Boston and beyond. Specifically, Nathaniel Hawthorne's career owed much to her promotional tactics and influential market connections that also linked her to Horace Greeley. Perhaps the best connected of all the Transcendentalists, Peabody landed Hawthorne a position at the Custom House through correspondence with George and Elizabeth Bancroft, whom she had engaged to participate in one of her literary conversation clubs. From 1825 to 1850, Peabody was one of the most enthusiastic literary clubwomen in America, with affiliations in the Transcendental Club, and the Salem and Boston Lyceums. She organized the Saturday Club at the home of Susan Burley, into which she drew the reclusive Hawthorne, exposing him to the social matrix of the publishing industry that would launch his literary career. Gatherings at Peabody's West Street bookshop cultivated Fuller's early feminist thought that would lead to *Woman in the Nineteenth Century*. It was during such discussions that the idea of the experimental commune, Brook Farm, was conceived. Harvard Rhetoric Professor Edward Tyrell Channing befriended her and she advised him on his best orations, interestingly, on the subject of the virtues of unrestrained mixed-sex conversation free from the excessive formality and attendant condescension of performative and pedantic lecturing. Inspired by one of the readings of his wife of a George Ticknor lecture to a mixed audience, she was taken by the ensuing discussion in which women felt "no restraint about talking and improving by their conversation." With "no pedantry in their conversation," she wrote to her friend Maria Chase, "you will not find any ladies there whose business is dress and visiting—all have some serious pursuit or other which is engrossing."[1]

This chapter engages new research by Charlene Avallone revealing the surprising extent to which Peabody's obsession with the art of conversation structured her religious, social, and pedagogical thought to suggest that such expertise also vitally served her intermediary roles as editor, publisher, promoter, and marketer.[2] Specifically, the socially progressive dynamics of "conversation" she espoused put her on equal footing with influential literary men who would otherwise not be so disarmed in her presence, thus providing a more liberal context for dialogue than the broader culture typically allowed. Avallone has established that Peabody's "extensive conversational culture engaged her in both masculine scholarly traditions and feminine discoursive traditions and shaped her contributions in print as well as talk."[3] The considerable range and depth of the conversational culture Peabody inhabited has profound implications for her promotional practice and powerful influence in the literary market through her print publications and club contacts.

Reconeptualizing conversation as a forum for free mutual exchange displaced the common antebellum oratorical convention of the (usually patriarchal) pedantic speech in interpersonal communication between the sexes. Peabody adapted to her own business practice Fuller's sense of conversation as dialectical and mutually responsive, cultivating for her promotional method Fuller's own healthy aversion to passive subordination demanded of "mere sounding boards" and satellites to "ruling orbs." Fuller's distaste for such monologues surfaces in her criticism of Goethe's biographer, Johann Peter Eckermann. Though Fuller allows that he was an effective secretary, she criticized Eckermann for merely recording rather than responding to and challenging his subject's "light of genius."[4] Bruce Ronda has identified a similar strain in Peabody's "aversion to persuasive rhetoric" that, I argue, avers docile listening for the sort of active interlocution she inspired later at the Temple School. Peabody reinvented the discourse dominating antebellum culture from evangelical preaching to commercial advertising into a more inclusive democratic form ideally suited to the promotion of Transcendentalism in the literary market, which would become the main focus of her career.[5] In the process, she became the most prominent female literary agent, before that occupation was formally open to women and when male editor-publishers primarily assumed that role, in antebellum New England.

Peabody's favoring of the intimacy of conversation over the subordination of rhetorical soliloquy and monologue marks a unique romantic reaction to market forces that shaped so many of the conceptions of authorship coteries espoused at the time. Similar to Irving's use of anticommercial rhetoric for the purpose of coterie promotion, Peabody's leveling of discourse from a hierarchical standard thwarted persuasive rhetoric in such a way that enabled her to win over the hearts of her interlocutors, usually to benefit someone other than herself. Conversation was not only an effective method by which to promote the thinkers who frequented her Boston bookstore on 13 West Street. It was also essential to the social formation and function of a literary circle solidly achieving its aesthetic, reform, and financial goals.

THE BUSINESS OF 13 WEST STREET

Despite her near hero-worship of the charismatic Unitarian preacher Reverend Dr. William Ellery Channing—"slander and envy and jealousy and hatred cannot *imagine* a spot upon his character" she gushed in one letter—Peabody likely savored the poetic justice of publishing decades later Channing's warning against the pitfalls of the book trade.[6] The warning appeared in a letter in which he flatly tells her not to open the store, since "I have a distrust of your business talent; and this I say not to discourage, but that you may seek counsel from those who know your worldly gifts and the demands of this business."[7] What eventually became the most successful venture of her career, in both financial and literary senses, was initially fraught with hazards, not the least of which was the culture's unpreparedness for a female bookseller. Channing warned that "in this age of proprieties difficulties should be started which I cannot anticipate." Her triumph was not over Channing so much as that more formidable gender barrier of which he spoke. Channing actually shared Peabody's belief in the principle that "a variety of employments [should be] thrown open to women, and if they may sell anything, why not books? The business," he continued, "seems to partake of the dignity of literature," and thus transgresses more acceptably into the public sphere than if she were proposing to open her own church, or practice law or medicine.[8]

Also at the heart of Channing's warning was his acute awareness of "the misunderstandings and ugly things said of" what were known as "Margaret's Conversations" held at West Street prior to Peabody's decision to sell books from that location. Fuller's "object of making women set themselves seriously to cultivate their minds by literature, the fine arts, and an independent view of their duties in life, was very dear to him."[9] Channing indeed provided a key source of advocacy for what has been habitually presented as Peabody's entirely self-reliant enterprise. He was particularly effective in encouraging her to adapt Transcendentalist ideals for more functional operation in the publishing world. Indeed, Channing called into question the overly idealistic rejection of the market by Bronson Alcott and George Ripley in such a way that provided an outlet for Peabody's "worldly gifts" in the professions of literary agent and retailer. "Wisdom is nothing if it is not practical" was a maxim of his Peabody found especially motivating.[10]

The notion of beginning the free market enterprise of 13 West Street ironically sprang from discussions of the evils of capitalism. These thoughts led to Ripley's proposal for Brook Farm based "on the principle of *co-operation* instead of *competition* of interests; making agriculture the foundation, but paying all labor the same wages by the hour—the more intellectual and artistic work involving so much reward in itself." Channing's suggestion that Ripley not abandon his position in the Purchase-street Society, but "employ his great conversational powers in changing his pulpit exercises for such a conference meeting" encouraged Peabody's own adaptability and pragmatism, her uncanny capacity to adapt Transcendentalism to the increasingly capitalistic literary market. This was the "pragmatic and synthetic thinker [who] combined ideas, tried things out and sought to build intellectual alliances" that her most recent biographer has described.[11] Working more aggressively within the system to advance Transcendentalist ideas now presented itself as a viable option to Peabody. The paradox did not escape her notice, as she commented that "when commerce seemed about to be *reformed out*, I had come to Boston on my first commercial enterprise, to which some collateral circumstances conspired to open a prospect of success in obtaining the means of subsistence."[12] Peabody appears to appreciate the irony of fighting against the tide of the market at the very moment of her entry into it. Yet the explanation for how this tension resolved itself so fruitfully in her career lies in the method by which she engaged the market. Viewing the process of "obtaining the means of substance" through "commercial enterprise" as something of a necessary evil, Peabody sought to make a virtue of necessity, and humanize the inescapable market that defined so much of her existence. Instead of passively allowing the exigencies of conventional publishing's codes of conduct to dictate her fate, she ventured forth on her own terms to reconstruct those codes precisely to carve out space for a female literary intermediary like herself. This was not a hypocrite concealing her own crass self-interest under the veil of then fashionable antimaterialism, but rather a pioneer creating a woman's professional occupation where none had previously existed. Hers was the spirit of nonconformity and commitment to equality that distinguished Fanny Fern's justification of female authorship in *Ruth Hall* (1855).

Such a commitment to equality was visible in Peabody's frank and open conversation that included Ripley and Channing and inspired her to reach across the gender divide of separate spheres ideology segregating intellectual and commercial culture. Her concept of conversation as fostered by the Fuller-led discussions, significantly, preceded the conception of opening the salon as a store. Most coteries worked in the reverse, as in John Murray's 50 Albemarle Street in London in the 1820s, which functioned first as a publisher and bookseller's shop, which grew into a hub of informal gatherings that included Washington Irving, Sir Walter Scott, and Lord Byron. West Street was a curious hybrid between Transcendentalist cooperation and free market competition; the principles of Peabody's business practice offer a fascinating study in the mix of these seemingly averse and mutually exclusive paradigms. The Transcendentalist emphasis on intuition, for example, finds its way into Channing's business advice to avoid proceeding only as if "rules and machinery are worth little; that the principle within us will meet intuitively the wants of the moment." He highlights the importance of punctuality and precision, especially the entrepreneurial principle that "engagements must be met at the very moment...people must know where to find you, and what to expect," an apt description of the duties of business administration and management. Evoking the Transcendentalist principle of antimaterialism, he warns Peabody of the implications of moving from the more socialistically oriented literary intermediary to merchant and proprietor. Her connection to the community and role as patron and promoter, he trusts, will rescue her from rampant greed and individualism that is anathema to Transcendentalism. "Were your business to be more independent," he speculated, "I should also fear for the ascendancy of your imagination" toward avarice and egotism. "Our country is a land of 'golden' dreams, and you might give in to these, were you to set up for yourself; but in your character of agent, you would not be much tempted."[13]

The West Street bookstore was not just a bookstore, but also a general store reflective of the diverse group that gravitated there for conversations. Since "the Transcendentalist movement generally favored freer relations between the sexes, the store attracted a mixed group," as Anne C. Rose describes it, as colorful as the literary marketplace in which it was situated.[14] The shop was ideally situated in the market to spread Transcendental thought. By 1840, the area between Washington and Tremont Streets in Boston was showing early signs of the glittery marketplace it would become in the next decade, resembling Nathaniel Hawthorne's *The House of the Seven Gables* (1852) portrait of "a kind of panorama, representing the great thoroughfare of a city, all astir with customers. So many and so magnificent shops as there were!" Peabody found herself amid the onset of consumer culture's "groceries, toy-shops, dry-goods stores, with their immense panes of plate-glass, their gorgeous fixtures, their vast and complete assortments of merchandise, in which fortunes had been invested; and those noble mirrors at the further end of each establishment, doubling all this wealth by a brightly-burnished vista of unreality!"[15] Her shop was located on "publisher's row" where Ticknor and Fields would eventually lodge their business along with dozens of other dealers including Gould and Lincoln, Crocker and Brewster, Crosby and Nichols, and James Munroe. All these publishers sold books out of their parlors and hosted impromptu meetings on topics ranging from Unitarianism to social reform to children's literature. Peabody's bookshop may have appeared to be an afterthought and a means of making modest profits on the considerable trafficking of intellectual culture through her family's parlor. But she invested her fortune in making a retail business out of coterie culture, a decision of great significance particularly for moving Peabody's career as Transcendentalist patron and promoter squarely into the commercial realm. She never conceived of herself as a professional author. Instead, her work as a literary intermediary necessarily conjoined with the forces of the free market, and found one of its purest and most profitable expressions in her role as a retailer.

When Peabody entered the book retail trade, she faced the bookseller's challenge of representing Transcendentalism through the selection and display of her inventory. Making that inventory attractive became a priority since the antebellum "bookstore played on people's penchant for...the Barnumesque enjoyment of watching sleights of hand," as Ronald J. Zboray explains. Like Hawthorne's mirrors that double the wealth of stocks into "brightly-burnished vistas of unreality," Zboray notes that "Here the magic was applied to a shop's representation of the fragmented state of knowledge. But the theater of the bookstore—the realization that, after all, the retailer earnestly desired to *sell* books—and the sense that all players understood it as such made book buying something of a ritual of epistemological unification, one effected and mediated by the commodification of knowledge within a marketplace."[16] As its proprietor, she arranged her store to reflect the Transcendentalist reach across the Atlantic to a broader print culture than the relatively narrow one accessed by Concord's *Dial*. That epistemological unification was global, as witnessed by the foreign language inventory Peabody stocked; it was also local, as seen in the store's function as a hub for the denizens of Boston and Concord to engage in intellectual exchange.

Though not exactly the print cultural equivalent of P.T. Barnum's museum (as Bonner's *New York Ledger* had become for periodicals), Peabody's bookshop still occupied similar territory at the crossroads between local and more systematic forms of business attuned to a wider market. Like her later promotional campaign for the kindergarten movement, Peabody packaged Transcendentalist thought for the middle classes in her movement toward a more sophisticated and systematic form of literary agency and marketing than New England had seen in the past. Indeed, as Bruce Ronda notes, "West Street was undoubtedly Peabody's most successful business venture and brought her into contact with even more of the literary and political lights of the Boston area."[17] Those connections the store fostered best served the careers of Fuller, Channing, and the underwriters of Brook Farm, most notably George Ripley. The stock Peabody carried reflected the coterie members themselves. The painter Washington Allston was behind the art supplies for sale, for example, since he had insisted that she cater to his colleagues. Among the books she sold were those bearing her own publisher's imprint with the store's name and address. Coterie culture and family life were contiguous as reflected in the merchandise; Channing suggested items for sale that appeared on her shelves, which shared space with her father Nathaniel's homeopathic medicines. The large parlor off the entry that held the famous Fuller-led conversations was a few steps from the back rooms where the Peabody family lived beginning in July 1840. A distinct fictional echo of this arrangement is in Hepzibah's transformation of part of the Pynchon house into a general store. Striking in this confluence of family, retail business, and literary coterie is not so much its amateurish character, but rather its capacity to cater to so many interests without losing sight of economic necessity.

Hepzibah Pynchon's general store in Hawthorne's *The House of the Seven Gables* reflects Peabody's diversity of stock drawn directly from the suggestions of her patrons. For Hepzibah, the wise old Mr. Venner (Channing?) dispenses with advice on the best business practice. Hawthorne could very well have had Peabody's store in mind, as her successful management skill resonates with Venner's seemingly homespun wisdom that is surprisingly innovative and responsive to current market developments. Hawthorne was well aware of Peabody's professional enterprises from which he directly benefited. (The two were so emotionally intimate that they would have likely married had she not introduced him to her younger sister, Sophia, who eventually became his bride.)[18] Further, Hawthorne had worked in weights and measurements quite successfully himself and thus could appreciate such nuances of a well-run store, as intoned by the venerable old man. "'Give no credit!'—these were some of his golden maxims,—'Never take paper-money! Look well to your change! Ring the silver on the four-pound weight! Shove back all English half-pence and base copper tokens," Venner directs Hepzibah, admonishing her to be wise to the confusion of diverse currencies intersecting through the new Republic. Time is the most precious commodity that can be transformed into profit, he reasons, so "at your leisure hours, knit children's woolen socks and mittens! Brew your own yeast, and make your own ginger-beer!" He tells the perpetually scowling Hepzibah, "Put on a bright face for your customers, and smile pleasantly as you hand them what they ask for! A stale article, if you dip it in a good, warm, sunny smile, will go off better than a fresh on that you've scowled upon."[19] Peabody's manner in minding the store similarly grew increasingly enthusiastic and would echo her garrulous and effusive style of patronage in club circles and gatherings.

Peabody's management style seemed the epitome of Venner's sage business advice. For example, she was careful to supply the demand for foreign books where few existed at the time, and was savvy enough to buy advance sheets and stereotype plates from across the Atlantic, have them printed, and sell them from her own shop. "I came to Boston and opened the business of importing and publishing foreign books," she recalled, "a thing not then attempted by any one. I had also a foreign library of new French and German books."[20] The ample population of literate Bostonians fluent in modern continental languages, then a staple to all undergraduate curricula, along with the dearth of foreign language bookshops in the area, more than sustained her enterprise. Transcendentalists were turning out an increasing amount of publications inspired by European Romanticism; Emerson had subscriptions to all British quarterlies and regularly received shipments of books from Europe (quite interesting in light of his strident eschewal of foreign models in the "American Scholar"). Sensing the need of a clearinghouse for these materials to serve the Transcendental coterie, Peabody was also alert to the expanding market of readers fluent in their native continental languages. The relative weakness of the book market that drove Emerson away from book publishing and into lecturing also encouraged Peabody to sell periodicals in addition to books. The relatively high prices of books—typically running from one to two dollars each, approximately $25–$30 in today's currency—meant low volume sales, which prompted her to stock cheaper foreign and domestic journals. She deducted that the voracious intellects of her clientele meant their finances would struggle to keep pace with their reading, and thus offered both periodical and bound volumes for either loan or purchase. Too frequently 13 West Street has been described as a "library," but it was certainly not in the sense of a public library associated with free lending. Channing had misgivings not about charging patrons for loans, for he supported such an opportunity for profit. Instead he worried that "a circulating library" would be vulnerable to the "corrupt taste of readers, who often want books which one would not like to circulate," a fear that stems from his distrust of the masses whom Peabody's business would inevitably engage.[21] Peabody was instead careful to charge patrons for loans of all printed materials at a significantly lower rate, of course, than purchase price.

Likewise, attendance at the "conversations" indeed required a fee for admission. West Street was not, despite its central humanitarian purpose and thrust toward broader social reform, a philanthropic enterprise. Caroline Healey Dall recalled the admission fee was anything but nominal. After gaining popularity from three years of conversations, Peabody immediately saw their greater market potential in widening the coterie's scope "to be composed of both ladies and gentlemen." Thus she changed the all-lady daytime meetings into evening affairs to include men unencumbered from work hours with the women. So by 1841, Peabody and several others launched the plan for ten conversations at George Ripley's home to capitalize on how "the affection and loyalty" of the young women had grown into "a most gifted and extraordinary circle." Since Fuller "had great need of money," Dall recalled, "tickets of admission cost twenty dollars each, a very high price for that time. It was in the bookroom of Elizabeth Peabody that I first heard the discussions." At only eighteen years old, "I was very young to join such a circle," Dall noted, suspecting that she was valued more for her monetary than her intellectual contributions. "Elizabeth had more regard, I think, to Margaret's purse, than to my fitness for the company," Dall wrote in a show of modesty nonetheless revealing of Peabody's promotional pluck.[22]

Although Fuller regarded those meetings at Ripley's home as failures, they represent Peabody's vigorous effort to expand the scope of the coterie by crossing gender lines. The March 1841 series of conversations was the culmination of a prior set of what can best be described as essentially informal adult education classes led by Fuller that began in November of 1839. Peabody would open her bookstore one year later and record with such precision and engagement the content of those conversations that critic Charles Capper has called her "Fuller's Boswell." Transcription was a vital part of her role as "every aspiring Transcendentalist's patron," a function as important as setting and collecting admission fees for the events and managing the finances.[23] She understood these notes would not suffice without a backup scribe, and thus recruited the young Dall to the task. The pressure and importance of transcription was never more apparent when Fuller had captured during a conversation a formulation of nothing less than the meaning of life. Yet when called upon to restate it the next day, Fuller "said she had forgotten every word she said," but would try to replicate it nonetheless. "She then went into the matter, and, true enough, she did not use a single word she used before," as Emerson retells Peabody's anecdote. Even with her considerable efforts to record this definition of life, Peabody could only admit to having captured "fragments" of the "full, clear, and concise" utterance itself.[24]

The Intermediary's Art

Peabody did not have a uniformly favorable reputation; she was considered eccentric "flighty and overenthusiastic" according to her latest biographer, and a "character" whom Emerson found exasperating.[25] "You would think that she dwelt in a museum where all things were extremes & extraordinary," he complained of her prose style.[26] Extraverted and fully engaged with the market, she defied Victorian standards for the ideal withdrawn and commercially disengaged lady of letters described by Sarah J. Hale in the *Ladies' Magazine* according to separate spheres ideology: "Our men are sufficiently money-making. Let us keep our women and children from the contagion as long as possible."[27] Peabody's manner, though not exactly Bonneresque in its audacity, was for an antebellum woman literary publicist persistent and often brazen, flouting "the masquerade of separate spheres that required that *business* be left out of their public conversation," as Steven Fink explains.[28] At one point she virtually held vigil over Emerson after foisting a copy of Hawthorne's rather tepid "Footprints on the Seashore" on him. Emerson acknowledged that thanks in part to her promotional efforts, he had heard praise for his fiction, but held firm in his belief that "there is no inside to it" and that its dialogue was lacking. "It's no easy matter to write dialogue; Cooper, Sterling, Dickens" struggle at it, but certainly "Hawthorne cannot," he said. He nonetheless links Hawthorne to quite elite company in butchering the art of fictional conversation, which ironically Peabody and Fuller had mastered it in its real form.[29]

Peabody's persistence with Emerson was indicative of her "ability to appreciate original thinking in others, draw it forth, publicize it, and transmit it."[30] She capitalized on the opportunities such conversation invited to promote what she believed were the most socially efficacious of causes, from Thoreau's civil disobedience to Fuller's feminism to Washington Allston's art to William Ellery Channing's gospel of Christian socialism. Through her aid, Thoreau's "Resistance to Civil Government" was published; her prolific transcription of conversations, as noted, established Fuller's reputation as a conversationalist. Alcott's Temple School, named for its location in Boston's Masonic Temple on Tremont Street, furthermore, enjoyed its best publicity in Peabody's *Record of a School* (1835–1836). Fuller's entrance into the Transcendental inner circle was made possible by Peabody's insistence that she join her on a three-week stay in Concord. Emerson acknowledged Peabody's instrumental role as Fuller's informal agent and publicist by certifying that she had successfully convinced the clique to "share your respect for Miss Fuller's gifts & character."[31] Peabody also ushered Fuller into the professional world of letters by urging *New England Magazine* editor Park Benjamin to publish her works. Peabody's intermediary work on behalf of her brother's employment landed her in the home of Henry Hedge, whose visits to Boston with Emerson's circle would become the first Transcendentalist Club. Arguably, it was through this connection that the entire Transcendental circle originally formed. As the unofficial gatekeeper of the coterie, Peabody cross-examined Lydia Jackson on her fitness for the circle and asked her for a statement of her religious beliefs.

As Anne C. Rose aptly observes, the gesture represented the wider significance of entrance into the coterie, since her request of such a statement from Jackson was "like a test of admission to a church" designed to impress upon her "that she was marrying into a movement where convictions mattered."[32] This test aptly illustrates the power and centrality of Peabody's intermediary roles ranging from agent and promoter of Transcendentalist talent to informal admissions officer and registrar.

Peabody launched not only Fuller's but also Hawthorne's professional career, peddling *Twice Told Tales* in a tireless promotional campaign that accessed the most powerful publishing figures and outlets available, including Horace Mann and the *New Yorker*. Her efforts are well known, yet her method has not been emphasized, particularly her use of the romantic image of authorship to fight against the flow of commerce even as she entered into it. She was not simply operating within the exigencies of the emerging literary market, but drove its leading edge as a woman promoting a male author in a masculinized publishing industry. Peabody's March 1838 letter soliciting Mann's inclusion of Hawthorne's fiction in his book series for school libraries wields the rhetoric of a modern literary publicist managing the image of her author for mass consumption. Her pitch casts the "young man in this town" whose work "surpasses *Irving* even" as a diamond in the rough, a part-time author rather than a full-time professional since the trade "does not seem to offer a means of living—he has not thriven with bestsellers." This was a special talent, she assured Mann, whose exposure may be limited, but it is because he only "occasionally has dropped a gem into the passing periodicals." She presents his literary talents as "involuntary," entirely natural and in no way bent toward commercial self-promotion associated with pseudo-geniuses. His work is immune to market corruption, she argued, given his natural aversion to the business of letters. Hawthorne's new enterprise takes on a hue of moral wholesomeness in its "attempt at creating a new literature for the young—as he has a deep dislike to the character of the shoals of books poured out from the press." This rhetorical distance from the market receives even greater emphasis later in the letter when she suggests that Mann should approach "Capen [who] is a bookseller of *principle*—the only man I know in that line capable of being liberal...I think a suggestion from you to *Capen*—who thinks every thing of you—to endeavor to enlist Hawthorne by good offers to write for the young—would perhaps secure him to his work." The "only man in that line" who operates on "*principle*" indeed becomes elevated above the rest of the underhanded booksellers according to her logic. By raising Capen above the illiberal unprincipled trade, she flatters Mann by suggesting he too is so prudent, since this exceptional merchant "thinks every thing of you."

Although Hawthorne "has no genius for negotiation with booksellers," Peabody can hardly contain her enthusiasm for the profit potential of his "genius for such an enterprise that could not fail to make a *fortune*." He would be pleased by modest compensation, "at least that would satisfy so very moderate desires as his," she assured Mann.[33] Although Mann would eventually demure on the deal, Peabody pressed her suit elsewhere by forwarding a similar conception of Hawthorne as the isolated romantic author in a *New Yorker* review. In it, she plays on the mystery of his biography, making it rife with intrigue innuendo and rumor: "we have heard that the author of these tales has lived the life of a recluse" very much in the British romantic tradition of "Wordsworthian philosophy... one of Nature's ordained priests, who is consecrated to her higher biddings."[34] She similarly portrayed him to Mann as possessing "a passionate love of nature [that] together with some peculiar circumstances have made him live a life of extraordinary seclusion," an ideal portrait of the artist as a young romantic storyteller.[35]

Peabody's promotion of Hawthorne illustrates how she "served as mediator between the radical and original thinkers of the New England Renaissance and a middle-class, educated public committed to certain reforms." The "key word for a deeper understanding of Peabody is *mediation*," especially in light of the wide range of figures she backed, including Channing and others in the abolitionist movement, well beyond the woman's network she orchestrated.[36] Peabody's promotion of Native American Sarah Winnemucca's autobiographical *Life Among the Piutes* (1883) has been examined as an example of Peabody's ability to work within and against the vestiges of the "Cult of True Womanhood" as established by Catharine Beecher's *Treatise on Domestic Economy* (1841). Katharine Rodier has convincingly argued that Peabody and her sister Mary Peabody Mann "validate anew their own efforts by fostering a dynamic of patronage more readily available to women in the United States only after the Civil War."[37] Peabody thus brought otherwise obscure radicals, romantics, and reformers to the American public.

The American public's obsession with religion, which captured Alexis De Tocqueville's attention as he toured the young Republic, factored into Peabody's concept of advocacy. Behind her professional agency was her belief in social harmony that grew from her Christian socialism, which was so pronounced that Ronda has identified it as a forerunner to the utopian novels of Christian socialists such as Edward Bellamy. Whereas Peabody's sense of community was originally inspired by Channing's Christianized socialism, she would transform it into her own unique ethos that validated her promotional practice. In her view, Jesus was an ideally socialized individualist, perfectly orchestrating his own relations with his disciples to encourage their formation into a close-knit mutually inspiring circle. She saw in his ministry a model for the type of loving leadership anchored in the substantial trusting relationships, support, and inspiration that might form the guiding principles for the ideal literary coterie.[38] Transcendentalism, once established with commercial authority in the market, she believed, could humanize trade, whose condition reflects the state of the nation's soul since "the coin is a delicate meter of civil, social, and moral changes," as Emerson had noted.[39]

Was Christ the ideal coterie leader, as in Emerson's role, or perhaps the perfect intermediary, as in Peabody's? Perhaps both, but more importantly, she knew from her relationship with Jones Very of the dangers of acquiring a messianic self-concept, and respected the limitations of emulating Christ's model. Peabody's capacity to see the depth of significance attached to a fully socialized existence as embodied by Christ brought her in contact with a variety of figures who shared similar views. The most bizarre of these was Very, the diminutive and spiritually possessed poet who became known as the man who thought he was the second coming of Jesus Christ. On 27 December 1837 he delivered a lecture for the Salem Lyceum entitled, "Epic Poetry." "Being on the front seat with my father," Peabody recalled, "I said 'Let us go ask him to go home with us'" at the conclusion of his talk, drawing herself into contact with him as she had countless other intriguing literary figures not so much like an agent discovering talent for her own profit as an enthusiast eager to hear more. She "stepped up to him" and "He grasped my outstretched hand like a drowning man" in a tableau of Peabody typically engaged in her intermediary art of building social capital. He "accepted the invitation" and that evening pleased her with his enthusiasm for Emerson and subtle "interpretation of Shakespeare."[40] She had judged him on such strengths that bore little evidence of the insane mysticism that would overtake him and send him into an asylum within the next year. Very's frightening distortion of Emerson's ideals into runaway egotism in many ways represented the religious equivalent of the Weimar Republic's twentieth-century bastardization of Emerson's concept of the "oversoul" to fuel their nationalistic bravado. Fully convinced that he had emptied out his former self to become a vessel for God, he approached the woman who had extended her hand to him as if she were saving a drowning man less than a year prior. This time, he was doing the saving. On 16 September 1838, Very proclaimed, "I come to baptize you with the Holy Ghost and with fire." Peabody was terrified. "I trembled to the center—But it was my instinct—not to antagonize but to be perfectly quiet—I felt he was beside himself and I was alone in the lower story of my house." After a pause, he suggested that she should feel a change in her spirit. "I replied gently, 'I feel no change'—'But you will'—said he hurriedly—'I am the Second Coming—Give me a Bible'—There was one in the room to which I pointed. He went to the table where it was and turned to Christ's prophecy of the Second Coming—and read it ending with the words, 'This day is this fulfilled in your hearing'—I was silent but respectful even tenderly so."[41]

The liberal Christian ideal that brought Very into the Transcendentalist fold went awry with his insane egotism that took on the most bizarre conception of Transcendental authorship, far stranger indeed than the Knickerbockers' own "Mad Poet." For after proclaiming his status as the anointed one, Very "unfolded a monstrous folio sheet of paper, on which were four double columns of sonnets—which he said 'the Spirit had enabled' him to write," and ironically had impressed Emerson enough to have had them published. Very composed the verses at the height of a phase that had "nothing of self-exaggeration—He seemed only rather to have obtained self-annihilation & become an oracle of God."[42] Regardless of who precisely was occupying the body of Jones Very at the time he composed those verses, he nonetheless found himself worthy enough to become a vessel of a higher voice. In the wake of the crisis, Channing intervened and Emerson made every effort to nurture Very back to sanity, hosting him at his Concord residence for protracted stays, but to no avail as the young poet was not fit for public society and thus retreated to living with family after his stay in an asylum. The coterie culture had in many ways created this monster, with Emerson and Peabody its Dr. Frankensteins, as the illness took over and he eventually disappeared from the Transcendentalist circle. Hauntingly, when Very unfolded the monstrous folio sheet, he was enacting Peabody's idealized conception of writers "directly confronting God, the universal Author" as vehicles for the divine "expressed everywhere," who work "in the presence of divine thoughts and meanings [making] even the words he utters luminous of Divinity," which she forwarded in her article, "Language," in the *Aesthetic Papers*.[43]

Forced to leave Very behind, Peabody forged ahead undaunted, still active in attracting inspiring Transcendentalist talent steeped in the infinitude of the Holy Spirit. Ellery Channing, perhaps the male literary figure she supported most, was gaunt and spiritually effusive like Very, yet had never convinced himself that he possessed messianic powers. Whereas Very never realized his professional potential, Channing was on the forefront of reform, fully engaged with the mechanism of the literary market thanks to Peabody's publishing efforts on his behalf. Peabody published his 1836 book, *Slavery*, in which he applied his characteristic Transcendental liberal Christianity to the abolitionist cause. Channing advanced the social benefits of embracing African Americans through the communitarian premise that "Christianity is the manifestation and inculcation of universal Love" and thus "the spiritual principle in man is what entitles him to our brotherly regard."[44] Channing's argument was fueled by the elements of the Social Gospel forwarded by such figures as Baptist minister Walter Rauschenbusch, whose work questioned laissez-faire competition by interweaving social theory, American history, and culture with biblical interpretation. Such Peabodian Transcendentalism, as Bruce Ronda calls it, was a forerunner to Christian Socialism, or the "Social Gospel," which shaped the communal principles of Brook Farm in opposition to "the gospel of wealth" that cast the poor as sinners causing their own demise rather than ascribing causality to the unequal distribution of wealth attendant to the larger capitalist system.[45] These self-less communal leanings propelled Peabody's enthusiasm for Channing's book and mobilized her full arsenal of forces on the literary market.

Peabody's work on behalf of Channing to publish *Slavery* speaks to the difficulties that lay in her way as a female operating as an intermediary in the antebellum book trade. After publishing the first run of a thousand copies of this work that resonated so deeply with her own belief in reform and socialized sense of Transcendentalism, Peabody was immediately under pressure to sell them as quickly as possible. Channing had received queries from antislavery societies in New York and Philadelphia "for leave to print editions, each of twenty thousand copies," presenting a golden opportunity to reach a massive scale of national distribution, but "said it must not be done until my edition of a thousand copes had been sold," as Peabody recalled. Her trouble moving the stock amounted to gender discrimination against a woman in the book trade, since "booksellers would only take copies of me on sale to be accounted for in six months; for the publishers seemed to conspire," as Fanny Fern's *Ruth Hall* (1855) also attests, "to discourage a woman from attempts to publish." Remarkable in this episode is Peabody's acute awareness of the tide of public interest and her sense of urgency in meeting the surge in demand for abolitionist cheap editions on a mass-market scale. "I feared that if the popular tide was not taken at once," sales and thus the "dearest end—to serve the Antislavery cause—would be frustrated." Her willingness to absorb the loss herself speaks to her faith in the force of that new mass audience to eclipse her own small business. Indeed, a short run of 1,000 expensive copies, she knew, could never compete with 40,000 produced in a cheap format with wider distribution and more powerful advertising outlets. Her allowance for "the Societies to go on with the cheap editions and risk the loss of mine," which "was never entirely sold" not only served the purpose of abolition by utilizing the full potential of the market forces, but also bowed to stronger competitors in the interest of her author, a self-sacrifice that speaks volumes of the generosity and loyalty that distinguished her style of literary agency.[46] Channing's *Slavery* eventually went to the societies, and James Munroe and Company in Boston also published a run of the book.

Peabody emerged from this transaction with the satisfaction of knowing that she had removed herself as an intermediary occlusion slowing the marriage of supply and demand between Channing and the society's readers that seemed so immanent. In this case, defying Channing's insistence that she sell out her copies before releasing the work to the wider market showed a shrewd business sense for tapping the right resource in the most timely manner. For not only did this move serve his interests, but also corrected his underestimation of the sales potential in the surging "popular tide" of mass demand she perceived in the culture for abolitionist works. She would not miss the opportunity to meet this demand at its peak rather than waiting out the unfair delay ("to be accounted for in six months") the gender biased booksellers imposed. The statistics reporting the exploding circulation of abolitionist journals in the periodical press at the time indicates the accuracy of Peabody's estimation. The "popular tide" was indeed rising, as indicated by Anti-Slavery Society's 1839 report that "there now exists not less than 9 weekly, one semi-monthly, and 4 monthly papers, mainly, if not exclusively, devoted to abolition. With the exception of the monthlies, which are chiefly for gratuitous distribution, these papers have a circulation of not less than 25,000 copies, and are supported by subscriptions to the amount of more than $40,000 per annum."[47] Peabody's realistic sense of the broader market helped her rebound from this transaction, as it alerted her not only to the considerable competition in bestselling genres by mass producers, but also to the routinely sexist treatment she would continue to receive from booksellers who felt entitled to demand discounts or refusing her offers outright because she was a woman. Undaunted, she reasoned that "if I could not publish" under fair circumstances, "I could import; and that Mr. Allston had offered to give me help by his letters to secure reliable artists' materials" from London to diversify her inventory. This was a case of "the brave, industrious and persevering" qualities Emerson identified in commerce, a "game of skill" in which "probity and closeness to facts are the basis, but the masters of the art add," as Peabody continued to do, "a certain long arithmetic."[48] Her adjustment to the obstacles before her embodies the spirit of professional self-reinvention of Emerson's "sturdy lad from New Hampshire or Vermont, who in turn tries all the professions...in successive years and always like a cat falls on his feet, [and] is worth a hundred of these city dolls."[49]

Peabody's energy adaptability and imagination in publishing prompted Emerson himself to call on her to rescue the financially beleaguered Transcendentalist journal, the *Dial*. Much has been made of Emerson and Fuller's distaste for Peabody's writing—only three of her innumerable submissions were accepted for publication in the *Dial*—but less has been made of their praise for her publishing. The demand for her business skill arose when it became apparent that the *Dial* was a sinking ship that nobody could save. Weeks, Jordan, and Company, the *Dial*'s first publisher went bankrupt in October of 1841 and Margaret Fuller, the editor at the time, promptly suggested that Peabody take over as publisher. As she had done for Channing, Peabody divulged the true market condition of the literary product, accurately assessing as she had for Channing the immediate financial status of the journal and prescribing the best course for potential for growth. Before she came on board as publisher, the flagging Weeks, Jordan, and Company had cooked their accounting books and deliberately masked the tailspin the *Dial* was actually in. Along with James Freeman Clarke, Peabody examined the records to reveal that the the original publishers' estimate of subscribers was double the actual amount. The return of $750 on these subscriptions barely covered the $700 for paper and printing costs and Fuller's salary, let alone Peabody's own. By October 1842, Peabody revealed that the journal was unable to cover costs and in fact was operating at a deficit. Her suggestion to shift temporarily away from subscriptions, which had fallen sharply to 220, to single copy sales signaled the need for broader distribution in the retail market. Writing to Thoreau who had taken over editorial duties temporarily while Emerson away on a lecture tour, Peabody persuaded him to impress upon Emerson the urgency of the *Dial*'s finances, whose "regular income does not pay the cost of its printing & paper." In the letter, she suggests that single sales will rejuvenate subscriptions, since "there are readers enough of it to support it if they would only subscribe." Enhancing the quality of those single issues sold might convince readers to subscribe, since "only by doing so can they secure its continuance."[50] Although Emerson blamed Peabody for the *Dial*'s failure to sell single copies because she had neglected to secure the arrival of the April 1843 issue with retailers by the first of the month, the journal in fact was beyond rescue by that point and thus her mistake could hardly be construed as fatal. Emerson had Munroe, his own publisher, take over the publication of the *Dial* in the wake of this debacle. Here is yet another instance in which Emerson had resorted Munroe during a publishing crisis, which once again was a death knell. His suggestion that Thoreau publish *A Week on the Concord and Merrimack Rivers* with Munroe would also prove fatal for the life of that book in the market, as it also would have for Fuller's *Summer on the Lakes*, had the author not wisely refused his urging.

The last issue of the *Dial* appeared a year later in April of 1844, at which point hindsight made it clear that Peabody had inherited a sinking ship that nobody could save. She was instrumental in divulging the truth of its circumstances and imaginative about regenerating subscriptions. What is important is not the failure of the *Dial* under her watch—for she inherited an irreversible situation made so by the fraudulent sales figures of its original publishers—but that she had performed so impressively as a publisher and agent through West Street that she would be called forth to rescue the journal, and in the process of saving it, be the first to assemble an accurate diagnosis of its fiscal condition.

New Conversations, New Ventures

Quick on the heels of the *Dial*'s demise, Peabody moved directly into plans for a journal of her own, which she would call *The Aesthetic Papers*. This involved gathering the greatest minds to bring greater meaning, especially broader social and political import, to the philosophical understanding of aesthetics. As such, the quality and range of authors she engaged for the first, and what would become the last, issue of the journal that appeared in May of 1849 was ambitious indeed. Her contributors, including Emerson, Hawthorne, and

Thoreau, reflected the considerable power she wielded in the male-dominated scholarly discursive tradition. Her model for size and type was *The British and Foreign Review*, which fit the flexibility and organic literary production that issued forth from the conversational culture of her West Street bookshop. Unlike a weekly journal struggling to fill a set number of pages at a clip frequently more rapid than the production of significant news reports, opinion, and valuable fiction could support, the *Foreign Review* stood as an ideal model for the *Aesthetic Papers* to emulate because it only went to press with a number "whenever a sufficient quantity of valuable matter shall have accumulated to fill" the desired size.[51] Thoreau's criticism of the periodical press in *Walden* resonates with this concept of publishing not at arbitrarily spaced regular intervals but only when enough valuable submissions have accrued. He sarcastically apes the language of a *New York Ledger* serial tale to mock its emphasis on quantity over quality in "Reading." "'The Skip of the Tip-Toe-Hop, a Romance of the Middle Ages, by the celebrated author of "Tittle-Tol-Tan," to appear in monthly parts; a great rush; don't all come together.'"[52] *Aesthetic Papers*, Peabody's policy affirmed, would make no such mistake.

Aesthetic Papers represents Peabody's executive powers of management and development of social capital in a professional expression of an early tendency she herself identified years prior in her diary in which she noted, "I am a very orderly person."[53] This early diary from 1836 contains important clues reflecting not only the origin of Peabody's philosophical construction of conversation as a leveling, inclusive, and democratic discourse. It also reveals the extent to which she refused to be silenced by men. Her views would find their ultimate expression in scholarly discourse in *Aesthetic Papers* for which she served as editor and contributor in an otherwise all male line-up of authors. Her method of dealing with dissent in such a position of authority was accordingly open, since she designed the journal to be a forum for discussion and meaningful exchange, rather than a propagandistic outlet for like-minded thinkers. As such, her inclusion of what would be Thoreau's most politically potent and controversial work appeared as "Ch. X, Resistance to Civil Government; a Lecture delivered in 1847. By H.D. Thoreau, Esq." That oppositional and defiant spirit was also captured by Sampson Reed's "Genius," which argued against the great man theory, suggesting that it was blasphemous. Reed's position was consonant with the journal's opposite trajectory away from silence in the presence of a demigod of the sort Fuller had identified in Goethe's biographer, or the type that Garrison's hegemonic editorial practice for the *Liberator* demanded.

In her "Prospectus," Peabody goes so far as to invite dissenting contributions, registering her distaste for the tyranny of editors who never allow for opposing views to enter their pages, in which "judgments should be reconsidered or overruled, where articles, written in bad spirit, should meet with just reprobation."[54] Here she redefines periodical authorship as dialogic, bringing the editorial role out of its bully pulpit and into the democratic conversation. "As it is," she explained, "reviewers, and editors of journals, are a class of men who are never called into account."[55] *Aesthetic Papers* would deliberately work against that trend, while employing other conventions in the commercial period market, like the inclusion of her own advertisement for *First Nursery Reading Book*, on a back page of the number, "Just Published at No. 13, West-street."[56]

Peabody's distaste for "classes of men never called into account" can be traced to an incident she recorded that represents the origins of her commitment to open discourse between the sexes. An otherwise lovely mid-April day in 1836 darkened dramatically when a quarrel erupted with Bronson Alcott over the professional ethics of the medical community. The conversation turned toward the subject of the relative desirability of extending the human life span through medical technology. The timing of the altercation was telling, for it occurred the day she recorded her resolve to move professionally away from pedagogy and toward a scholarly and intellectual life. "Having recently given up my long followed plan for keeping school," she had pursued instead "the plan of devoting my own time to a more regular prosecution of study than I have had an opportunity for, since."[57] Yet entering the male tradition of scholarly discourse meant contending with the contentious, the prohibitive, and the censorious. The ensuing altercation with Alcott thus served as both an initiation into, and a case study of, the sort of unfair tactics that she would likely face within this world. From it emerged not only her theory of democratic conversation, but significantly, the key tenets of her broader understanding of "Language" forwarded in her article in *Aesthetic Papers* and their far-reaching implications for her approach to her work as literary agent.

"Mr. A" had engaged Peabody in the moral implications of the expansion of human life to "two centuries." She "deemed it not a desirable thing to live so long, but rather a misfortune," to which Alcott retorted that "the reluctance to live another century would be a *suicidal sentiment*." By living fewer years, she returned, one is more "grateful ... of the years Providence seems to have allotted." In an odd and even funny turn, Alcott then lauded the profession of doctors to extend the life span. "I objected to it," she said, and "replied that I had heard him say they fed like Vampires on the community for the sake of money—and I had also read in his articles expressions of a like kind." Alcott replied that she "entirely misunderstood him" and that "every profession was a greater evil than good—only that the individual here or there did any good—but that most persons in the professions did harm."[58]

This part of the exchange spoke volumes of Peabody's sense of hypocrisy and double-speak of the Transcendentalist perspective on professionalism. On the one hand, Alcott supported a kind of fantastical vision of immortality through the endless expansion of human life. His vilification of the professions ironically registers his fear of the authority they increasingly possessed in the culture. Yet her exposure of his support of the medical profession as disingenuous by quoting his own prior venom toward quack doctors back to him—a tactic, if accurate, unfailingly rankles the opposition—prompted his frenzied recanting on the meager grounds intoned through the arrogant paternalistic insult that she "entirely misunderstood him." Alcott's diatribe against the professions as "a greater evil than good" appears to have had a moving effect on Peabody's dedication to professionalizing the Transcendentalist coterie and mediating its entrance into the commercial world. Interestingly, Alcott distinguishes between two kinds of doctors: the avaricious who will falsely promise an extended lifespan only to enrich themselves, and the "individual here or there" within the profession who might promise the beginnings of immortality through medical science.[59]

The man who would mastermind Fruitlands, the short-lived Brook Farm–like experiment in agrarian communal living, comes off here with a stock defense of the exceptional individual, the nonconformist who will do good despite his profession. This deeply problematizes the notion of a group identity, and indeed has profound implications for the paradox at the heart of the Transcendental coterie's self-concept. If every profession were a greater evil than good, then what did he make of the professionalization of authorship, and more particularly the increasingly commercial careers of the members of his own Transcendentalist literary circle? What did he make of the stark realization that sooner or later Emerson would not be able to pay for everything, and that they would have to face the market as professionals without the direct aid of his capital? What did he make of facing the market with Emerson's endorsement rather than his capital and the prospect of relying on intermediary intervention for optimal positioning in the publishing matrix by figures like Peabody herself?

Peabody's exchange with Alcott ended with her ardent defense of professionalization, strenuously objecting to his assertion that "the bulk of every profession felt not responsibility and did harm for money's sake." Peabody, by extension, was also defending the formation of professional associations against allegedly narrow financial self-interest at the expense of humanitarian service. She claimed that "such reckless persons" as Alcott had referenced "were the exceptions of the professions" opposite what would become her own role as promoter of authorial talent. Their conversation highlighted for her the uneven playing ground in conversation between men and women, and also galvanized her belief in the potential good that might come of the developing professions. She resolved to operate according to a different set of principles, by refusing to enter into conversation armor clad like the persona of "Self Poise" in Fuller's *Summer on the Lakes*, an iconoclastic self-reliant Emersonian voice incapable of the sort of self-surrender and generous aid that Fuller found in the magnanimous immigrant communitarian spirit she sees in Morris Birkbeck. The resolution of their discussion sent Peabody fleeing to her room (she was lodging with the Alcotts at the time) and scratching out the entire exchange in her diary. "I found I felt very uncomfortably; as if I had been treated very uncivilly," she wrote. The effect was totally averse to the spirit of the original meetings of the Hedge Club's dedication to uncensored expression because she "resolved that in the future I would take more pains to be silent on a subject on which it is possible for Mr. Alcott to differ from me, or I from him."[60] Meaningful conversation thus ceased to exist between the two, as Peabody's self-silencing embodied precisely Fuller's assertion that, at their worst, men's effect on women "has a tendency to repress their impulses and make them doubt their instincts, thus, often, paralyzing their action during the best years."[61] Thankfully, Peabody's silence was only temporary on this occasion, as she had the self-possession to record the injury and increasingly engage men in scholarly intellectual discussions leading directly to literary production.

This early journal entry was the seedling of what would become a fully developed theory and practice of interpersonal communication expressed in Chapter 11, "Language" of *Aesthetic Papers*. "Language helps us think, by its generalizations, which condense knowledge of particulars into general propositions," she writes, reflecting her belief in conversation grounded in a material objective. "The *artifice* of the poet is to make the *subjects* of his poem command undeserved attention," a notion that aptly describes the art of advertising, the core of the language of commerce so critical to introducing, recommending, and circulating literary talent, at which she showed more than a knack, but a particular genius, connected as it was with her appreciation for the artistry of conversation. That artistry specifically was rooted in the pragmatic, in the meeting and measuring of word and thing of thought and action. It would make sense, therefore, that the woman who believed that "the human mind is in relation to nature as the stone-cutter or the artist to the quarry; and language is at once the representation and vehicle of all that has been quarried" and thus is significant only in its capacity to "come into relation with *things*" would also be the one to usher Transcendental language from its quarry of thought into the retail and commercial publishing industry via her unique promotional practice.[62] In this way, Peabody shared Fuller's hope that "when the same community of life and consciousness of mind begins among men" as it has with women, "arbitrary limits and ignorant censure [will] be impossible; all will have entered upon the liberty of the law, and the harmony of common growth."[63] Such arbitrary limits and censure prevailed not only in Peabody's quarrel with Alcott, but also in Fuller's conversation series for both sexes hosted by George Ripley that the men wound up dominating "both because of their own proclivities and because they often did not feel that women were worth listening to," as Joel Myerson has succinctly explained it.[64]

In addition to promoting Transcendentalism by inspiring Peabody's dedication to literary agency, Peabody's rift with Alcott also bore the tragic import of the demise of the Temple School. The conflict resulted in the tangible loss of momentum they had gained two years prior in their work together at Temple School. Ironically the capacity to draw out children and establish liberal discourse with them in a school setting was Alcott's forte and source of Peabody's original admiration of him, much in the way she had originally admired Channing's capacity to speak to her Sunday School pupils. In the classroom, she and Alcott formed a democratic pedagogy fully invested in what students had to say on their own, a pattern to which Martin Bickman pays homage in his superlative *Minding American Education: Reclaiming the Tradition of Active Learning* (2003). In 1834, Alcott and Peabody's classroom was animated by what pedagogical theorists now recognize as an early form of constructivism. On a typical day, Alcott asked students to write in their journals about "the effect of the external world—upon the internal life—is made more obvious to their own perceptions—by putting down in permanent form the pictures which form in their minds, and the thought and feelings they excite. (They all stopped and looked with much interest as he spoke and said they *understood* the advantage)." Peabody's parenthetical afterthought stands as nothing less than miraculous here, as she notes how his questions focus on "the mental processes of the individuals described [in the stories they read] or the mental process of the author of the story."[65] Our current educational system, Bickman would concur, might find this a model worth emulating in teaching critical thinking and writing.

This auspicious beginning ended soon after, however, when a controversy erupted regarding the publication of discussions on birth. Peabody knew that her own engagement in such a discussion would have been perceived as scandalous, and thus resigned from the Temple School before the discussions were printed. Four months prior to the altercation discussed earlier, Peabody wrote a letter in August 1836 requesting Alcott refrain from publishing the physiological details of the lesson in *Conversations with Children on the Gospel*. As her private journal shows, by this time she had fully severed her capacity to speak with him as an equal intellectual again. Literary historians have understood the August letter variously as a token of Peabody's conservatism, claiming she wished to suppress such details about the formation of the body "on simple grounds of propriety."[66] Upon closer examination, however, the letter reveals her business guile and acute respect once again for the power of the mass readership in a letter bent on professional self-preservation. Propriety indeed is at stake for Peabody, but less as a principle to be backed for its own sake. She, therefore, wished not so much to censor discussion of genitalia with children as a general principle as much as she wanted to preserve her own reputation from potential scandal that it may have aroused. Her language in the letter is tellingly self-interested in this regard, and justifiably so, as she recognized that Alcott's career might suffer perhaps a fatal blow given the already considerable attacks he had endured. Objectionable contents, she urged, should be excised; "at least...they must be entirely disconnected with *me*," and "in all these conversations where I have spoken, I should like to have that part of the conversation omitted."[67] Knowing she would provide easy prey for critics, she defended her name as a commodity in the marketplace to assure "that on you rests all the responsibility of introducing the subjects" that could threaten the livelihood of her reputation as an educator and thus her future endeavors.[68] Though dedicated to the democratic progressive potential of conversation across the ages and sexes, both in and out of the classroom, Peabody was also alert to the professional consequences of an inadvertent spark catching fire by the mass reading public, whose forceful gusts she would never underestimate during her entire career, unlike Alcott and so many other Transcendentalists.

Marshalling Peabody's Legacy

Peabody's radical revision of power dynamics of intellectual conversation between the sexes goes far to rescue her image from that handed down from Megan Marshall's master narrative of the Peabody sisters. Emphasizing her role as thwarted lover of Hawthorne positions her within the patriarchal parameters of silence typified by the men's behavior at the Fuller conversations hosted by Ripley. In other words, we should not miss that Hawthorne was not just an object of romantic desire for Peabody, but also a business associate and friend, whom she trusted and respected. In many ways, she treated him the same way she did the women in her New England network. Hawthorne admired her business skill; she was not the perennial frustrated bridesmaid and eventual spinster Marshall makes her out to be. Measuring a woman, and this one in particular, according to her capacity to attract a man is an unfortunate misapplication of the marriage ending of so many antebellum romances to very real human biography. In Peabody, we have an antimarriage ending that is nonetheless more full of warmth and companionship than any conventional marriage might have brought her. Indeed, her biography embodies the truism that "a woman needs a man like a fish needs a bicycle."[69] She was the greatest literary agent in antebellum New England, more successful in this regard than Emerson. To let her portrait be taken over by her personal failures does her a disservice.

The marriage ending even governs the denouement of Marshall's biography itself. "What was Elizabeth *really* thinking?" Marshall asks after citing overwhelming evidence that Elizabeth's private thoughts about Mary's wedding to Horace Man were totally supportive.[70] Typical of responses to marriage at the time, Elizabeth's sentiments were tinged with regret at the loss of her sister's role as direct confidant and companion. Such a reaction was so conventional, in fact, that Washington Irving even registered precisely this note upon the loss of one of his Lads of Kilkenny to marriage. Was the ambivalence in granting her blessings to the newlywed Mary Peabody Mann saturated with repressed jealousy and unrequited desire? Only if we forcibly superimpose that narrative onto her and refuse to take her unremitting joy in their wedding at its word. The sisters toasted to their marriages and gloated in their new privileged status over Elizabeth. But did Elizabeth herself consent to such a characterization as leading an inferior life, one intrinsically *not* happy? No evidence suggests she did.

But in 2006, one year after her stunning biography, Marshall admitted that the "love triangles" have attracted "much attention over the years" since they "have a distinctly Jane Austen-ish cast to them." Finally setting the score right with regard to Elizabeth's true priorities, she allows that "whether she inwardly wished to be married is a matter of speculation," and that "romantic connection was not primarily what she sought" in Horace Mann, but instead reached out to him since he had shown so much "praise of her writing and endorsement of her ambitions...in a sisterly way," which I would argue, needs also to be construed in a professional and collegial way. Further, Marshall even recants her portrait of Hawthorne leaving her at the altar for her younger sister, an image she herself had reinforced in her biography, allowing that though his increasing interest in Sophia pained her, "the greatest pain of all was losing Hawthorne's friendship, not his love." Marshall's repositioning, however, still intimates that Elizabeth inwardly wished to marry, especially in the assertion that she refused "to admit feelings of loss or rejection," protesting "*perhaps too much*" that Mann's "gray hair and sorrow" were unappealing to her.[71]

The unrequited lover, Elizabeth, played that role so well in Marshall's biography and elsewhere in so many retellings of the Peabody sisters' love triangles precisely because she was the most professionally ambitious, the oldest, and even the strongest physically and longest living. As such, she was a woman before her time, a literary professional before such existed, and an Evert Duyckinck of New England, doing for Transcendentalism what Lydia Child did for Abolitionism. Marshall's tableau of Elizabeth at her happiest depicts her at work in a room of her own at the Alcott's plying "the pen for bread and butter" unencumbered.[72] To Marshall's credit, she finally granted Elizabeth the coda she deserved, one ironically more consonant with earlier and significantly older scholarship by feminist critics like Helen R. Deese, who looked at her love interests as trivialities, so many "persistent rumors" linking her romantically to Hawthorne and Mann "largely discounted by scholars" who honor the fact that "Peabody vigorously denied" them.[73] This was indeed a woman for whom literary business was all consuming, and thus she needed not just "friendships" in the "scholarly life" she wished to lead. More precisely, Hawthorne and Mann, like Channing, Emerson, and Alcott, were associates essential to the execution of her extensive literary business enterprises. Indeed, the master narrative of the Peabody sisters obscures this titan of the

New England literary marketplace by setting up her professional accomplishments, particularly those as literary agent and promoter that profoundly shaped careers around her, as the backdrop for her failed love interests, a kind of bizarre punishment for her aggressive encroachment into the forbidden public sphere. The assumption that she always already wanted marriage is tantamount to saying that she was incomplete without a husband. I would argue, instead, that most of Peabody's feelings of being incomplete issued from the transformation of her role as literary partner to that of sister-in-law, which she knew, would inevitably subsume the former given the overwhelming influence of cultural convention.

Peabody's role as editor and publisher in her own right were consonant with her connection to literary clubs and societies, through which she performed remarkable results as a protoliterary agent. Her own work as literary agent naturally led to her work as literary biographer, and thus fueled her preservation of the memory of Ellery Channing in a memoir that not only celebrated his life, but also her own fond memories of her work on his behalf in the publishing world. Nowhere is Peabody more efflorescent in *Reminiscences* as when she recounts the market's readiness for his abolitionist work, *Slavery*. For herein she knew with her heart and mind the rising tide of popularity now more than ever could be met through the mechanisms of the literary market to fuel the abolitionist cause, which was the greatest reform movement in American history. It is to that battle waged through the exigencies of the literary market that we now turn, beginning with William Lloyd Garrison's print warriors, Channing and Peabody's allies against the peculiar institution.

Part III

Political Economy: North and South

CHAPTER 6

PRINT WARRIORS: GARRISON'S ABOLITIONISTS

Elizabeth Peabody was slow to embrace the abolitionist movement, and preferred to allocate her talent and energy as a literary intermediary toward other social reform movements as the Civil War approached. There was no shortage of pens at the ready in the war of words, however, as William Lloyd Garrison famously rallied his troops through the *Liberator*, the most efficient mass media instrument for abolitionism. The market conditions mediating the magazine's circulation were analogous to that of the *New York Ledger*, which it echoed with much of its sensationalistic content and strident tenor. In his seminal study of the mass literary market's impact on the antebellum canon, *Beneath the American Renaissance*, David S. Reynolds characterizes this style as "dark moral reform," in which many writers including Thoreau and Whitman employed images from popular fiction of the sort commonly appearing in *Ledger* stories by Sylvanus Cobb and E.D.E.N. Southworth.[1] Garrison openly acknowledged that many found the *Liberator* to be "conducted in bad taste, almost in bad spirit" due to the sensationalism of such headlines as "Blood! Blood! Blood!," "Burning Alive," "Horrible Butchery," and the darkly gothic "A Ghoul in Real Life."[2] He even defended the "severity of my language" that intoned the hyperbolic stentorian voice of a born agitator.[3] Garrison lamented that the language itself could not scream louder, which he found "lamentably weak and deficient in regard to this matter. I wish its epithets were heavier—I wish it would not break so easily."[4] He minced no words about his unyielding belief "That the compact which exists between the North and the South is a 'covenant with DEATH and an agreement with HELL'—involving both parties in atrocious criminality—and should be immediately annulled."[5] Bent on rallying the masses to his cause with almost Whitmanian self-promotion and crowing in a voice as loud as Bonner's, Garrison predicted with characteristic bravado "my name shall one day be known so extensively as to render private inquiry unnecessary; and known, too, in a praiseworthy manner. I speak in the spirit of prophecy, not of vainglory—with a strong pulse, a flashing eye, and a glow of the heart."[6] There was no shortage of swashbuckling individualistic charisma in Garrison, who was as defiant and audacious as Ahab howling on the quarterdeck of the *Pequod* in Melville's *Moby-Dick* (1851). Yet how compatible would this larger-than-life messianic persona prove to be in constructing a collective haven for a community of writers—often in sharp conflict with each other—backing the common cause of ending slavery?

This chapter casts Garrison's struggle to manage his literary circle within the context of heated sectional abolitionist strife. The *Liberator*'s controversial reputation stemmed from Garrison's own contentious vision of professional authorship. His defiant, messianic approach to literary production informed the manner with which he managed his staff, a method that effectively alienated the powerful Lydia Maria Child and Frederick Douglass while encouraging lesser figures like Henry Wright and Nathaniel Rogers to exaggerate the circle's defining characteristics of sectarian hostility and radical individualism. Garrison's management style conditioned his circle's relations and bore his unmistakable extremist stamp. Wright, for example, overstepped the group's already loose sense of propriety in his slanderous attacks on the clergy in the 1840s and 1850s, yet the group kept him in the fold because he was nonetheless operating within their established social norm that condoned frequent personal attacks on rival abolitionists. Rogers, on the other hand, found himself summarily expelled for attempting to implement an extreme "no organization" policy, while Child was driven out for refusing to abet the circle's culture of antagonizing fellow abolitionists. Despite his extremism, the reckless Wright could be accommodated only because his tactical breach had not violated the group's derision of the Massachusetts clergy, who were among the most formidable foes of the *Liberator*. Child and Rogers, on the other hand, deviated from the circle's norm in ways it could not tolerate. Child, to whom the majority of this chapter is dedicated, had challenged the very foundation of its ethos by refusing to direct her energy and imagination against fellow abolitionists, while Rogers committed the unpardonable sin of applying

Garrisonian individualism to the circle's method of administration, which threatened to obliterate the group identity altogether. However awkward and unwieldy the *Liberator* circle was due to its commitment to the individualism of its constituents, Garrison knew that its members would be powerless without their group identity. While coddling the inconsequential and inconsolable Wright, Garrison drove away loyalists like Douglass and Rogers and drastically underestimated Child's capacity to form her own circle through a magazine that would surpass, if but momentarily, the *Liberator's* subscriptions and thus his own considerable power to reach the masses.

Garrison's "Little Shop" in the Reform Market

Like his Southern counterpart, George Fitzhugh, Garrison was part self-aggrandizing showman and part zealous crusader. Fitzhugh and Garrison's flamboyance in the literary marketplace, however, was rooted in sharply contrasting business practices that distinguished their leadership from each other. Those methods of doing business in their respective circles reflected the ethos of the larger social and economic culture of their respective regions. In a situation that typified the chaotic cacophony of reform interests in the broader Northern culture, Garrison's circle would be plagued by internal hostilities that led to a fractured, unwieldy set of interests resulting in the loss of several key figures who struggled to find suitable niches from which to back the cause.[7] Whereas Garrison's print warriors fought among themselves and rival abolitionist circles, Fitzhugh's apologists maintained cohesion reflective of the South's collectivist consolidation of resources for socialized cooperative capitalism. The South was by no means ideologically homogenous, yet it was characterized by a broader unity that sharply differed from the North's commitment to social and economic laissez-faire liberalism that gave rise to countless, and often conflicting, reform interests.

Also like his Southern counterparts, Garrison engaged every available mechanism of mass production and commercial advertising to make the printed word scream as loud as possible. After Garrison expanded the *Liberator* to the outer limits of size and typeset, he mobilized the full extent of accessible labor and technology resources to maximize production and distribution rates.[8] During the debut year of the *Liberator*, Garrison thus called for more presses to enter the market, especially ones run by free blacks. He exhorted African Americans to "multiply periodicals among yourselves, to be conducted by men of your own color. The cause of emancipation demands at least 100 presses." The time was ripe, he urged, to "put your children to the trades; no master mechanic will [lack] colored with education."[9] Signs of Garrison's soaring ambition in 1832 after this first year of production were thus visible not only in the twofold expansion of the *Liberator* to a massive 20-by-25-inch "Royal" sheet, but also in his repeated claim that "the cause demands a hundred daily presses" to produce more copies of the new giant paper faster than ever.[10] Typesetting the paper himself meant he could indulge his penchant for stentorian all-caps proclamations. The latest paper cutting machines, stereotyped plates, Hoe and double-cylinder steam presses propelled the *Liberator*'s rate of production to 1,000 papers per hour, five times the old hand press's yield of 200 per hour. By 1835, the market was flush with abolitionist pamphlets produced by the American Anti-Slavery Society, which was freshly infused with a $30,000 donation from philanthropist Arthur Tappan, who would bankroll the cause with vast sums from his own fortune for decades to come. The mass mailings of the evangelical societies, and eventually Tappan's own religious periodical of the American Tract Society, provided the antislavery movement with the model for their distribution method.[11]

With presses engaged at full speed, and generous donors behind him, it would seem that only the South would be the biggest threat at this point. Northern literary culture, however, was transforming into an increasingly diverse commercialized competitive network. Other literary circles in the North, such as the the Knickerbockers and the Transcendentalists, were factionalizing and subdividing toward mid-century just as political and moral reform groups had. Melville and Duyckinck's radical Young Americans broke from the Whiggish soft-focus sentimentalist Knickerbockers and hurled some of their mightiest barbs at them, most notably in Melville's "Hawthorne and His Mosses" and the belligerent fictional satires of Cornelius Mathews. Concord Transcendentalists now had the Bostonians of the Peabody-Channing circle to contend with. The rising ethos of individualism met with a surge in the proliferation of reform groups whose number reached unprecedented heights in the decades before the Civil War. This meant capitalist culture pitted special interests in competition with each other like never before.[12]

This shift drew the ire of Emerson and Thoreau, who scoffed at the marriages of reform to commerce and morality to marketing. Thoreau famously said that if he knew a reformer were visiting him with the intention of doing him some good, he should run for his life. In that spirit, Emerson complained that "each 'cause' as it is called—say

Abolition, Temperance, say Calvinism, or Unitarianism—becomes speedily a little shop, where the article, let it have been at first never so subtle and ethereal, is now made up into portable and convenient cakes, and retailed in small quantities to suit purchasers."[13] Notably, "Abolition" heads his list of reform groups; the "cakes" packaged and sold for consumption took the form of abolitionist magazines at the time, which multiplied exponentially throughout the 1820s. Local antislavery societies shot from 100 in 1826 to 2,000 in 1840, a year before Emerson delivered the lines above in a lecture intended to distinguish Transcendentalism from the myriad of reforms flooding the market like so many "little shops."[14] Emerson responded to the feeding frenzy of reform with typical Transcendental aversion and skepticism of the movement's propensity to harness the power of the market to advance its aims. Those aims, he claimed, often appeared more interested in self-styled distinction and public prominence (based on principles "at first never so subtle and ethereal" before becoming bewitching commodities) than in real social consequences. Further, the producers of those "cakes" competed savagely with each other for patronage, as various brands of reform in similar categories also vied for distinction in the increasingly commercial periodical market.

The market competition inherent in the commercialization of the reform movement meant that contention, not consensus, typified the North during the era. Abolitionists did not work toward compromise as much as they dug deeper trenches to defend their camps against each other even as the South's plans to fight for an independent Confederate nation loomed on the horizon. Indeed, Garrison himself even initially resisted Lincoln's unionist declaration of war because it compromised his own ardent advocacy of peaceful disunion that formed the basis of his rally cry, "NO UNION WITH SLAVERY."[15] It is telling of the factionalized sectarian nature of Northern antislavery reform that its foremost leader and spokesman would be disgruntled with the president's course of action that ultimately led to the passage of the Thirteenth Amendment to the Constitution to forever abolish all slavery in the United States. Perhaps most striking is that at various points throughout his career, Garrison detested Lincoln, Douglass, and Child, arguably the three greatest antislavery forces of the period, while even turning on his own mentor, Benjamin Lundy.

If Garrison felt entitled to defy so many prominent abolitionist figures, it was only because so much of his original principles were rooted in the defense of libel as a subcategory of free speech, which he cast as a metonym for the broader concept of liberty. Tappan's financial support of the *Liberator* interestingly traces back to the first time

Garrison was jailed as an enemy of the state for maliciously slandering the "good name" of Francis Todd, the owner of a well-known slave ship. As Emerson had done for Thoreau, Tappan bailed out Garrison from the Baltimore jail where Garrison wrote, "whatever relates to the freedom of the press is intimately connected with the rights of the people."[16] Literary historian Robert Fanuzzi has identified Garrison's ruminations in captivity as the origin of his persecution complex, which led him to devote the vast majority of his editorials during the *Liberator*'s first year to the defense of libel. The crime of libel was consonant with his antislavery agenda, as Fanuzzi explains, since it "established the libertarian credentials of his editorial mission and, by extension, the cause of the New England abolition movement, which he straightaway committed to the defense of free speech."[17] His jail cell writings object to "the growing tendency in many courts, to stifle free inquiry, to dishearten every effort of reform, and to intimidate conductors of newspapers." This defiance of civil institutions that constrict individual freedoms echoes the libertarian spirit of Thoreau's "Resistance to Civil Government."[18] Tappan eventually bailed Garrison out of his forty-nine day incarceration. Garrison could reconcile Tappan's patronage with his radical individualism by understanding it as payment for his public good, the benefaction of his crusade against slavery and the defense of liberty against an unjust government. Garrison's obsession with defending libel, I would add, established the keynote for the belligerent style of authorship and hostile culture of the *Liberator* circle.

Though his enemies were many, Garrison garnered supporters with deep pockets, as he relied on patrons like Tappan his entire career. Even after the Civil War, his own farewell editorial in the *Liberator* on 29 December 1865 was a veiled solicitation of financial support, as it sentimentalized the penniless origins of the paper that had ended profitless. Readers responded by initiating the collection of a "National Testimonial" for Garrison in 1865, amassing $31,000 over the course of two years. Garrison's career was thus bookended by patronage from Tappan's initial bail out to the public's "Testimonial" after the war. Garrison paradoxically was dedicated to self-promotion and theatrical public displays of extremism, yet did not have the financial management skill to realize the kind of profit or circulation that Child's *National Standard* was rapidly amassing in her short tenure there. In essence, Garrison was more adept at constructing and empowering his own presence in the market as an embattled lightning rod of controversy for the cause than he was in autonomously acquiring capital. If Garrison had chosen the antislavery movement as a method of becoming a famous author, then he did so without realizing financial wealth from the enterprise. Although he never succeeded in turning the *Liberator* into a profitable enterprise, Garrison had intended from the start to engage commercial mechanisms to their fullest extent to reach the broadest audience possible. His aggressive advertising in the *Liberator* and self-promotional stunts, however, earned him more notoriety than cash.

Garrison promoted the *Liberator* to transform it into the main commercial vehicle for slave narratives in the broader antebellum print culture. The slave narrative was not automatically well received, nor even well understood by the reading public. In fact reports of life in bondage by former slaves inspired a great outcry of skepticism about potential frauds or ghostwritten accounts. Harriet Wilson's fictional autobiography, *Our Nig, or Sketches in the Life of a Free Black* (1859), is candid about the prevalence of profiteering free blacks in New England posing as ex-slaves, including her own husband, Samuel, who delivered illiterate harangues against the evils of the peculiar institution despite never having set foot in the South. Skepticism of such imposters along with the mounting distrust of charlatans in the broader market society posed a considerable challenge to Garrison's objective of winning over his audience through slave narratives. Thus, he harnessed commercial rhetoric, a force that had become increasingly central to the culture, and saddled it with antislavery morality to promote these books in the pages of the *Liberator*. Garrison scholar Augusta Rohrbach astutely notes that "Garrison gave advertisers leeway to draw moral or ideological connections to the antislavery cause as their means of persuasion," because he knew reactions to slavery could effectively join forces with the increasingly powerful rhetoric of advertising to stimulate market demand.[19] The reading public's lust for sensationalistic thrillers could now be redirected toward moral reform and even piety, which promised to transcend the idle decadent self-indulgence groups like the American Tract Society associated with fiction reading.[20] The results were astonishing. From 1850 to 1860 the publication of slave narratives doubled, thanks in large part to the *Liberator*'s promotional campaign. The *Liberator*'s advertising of these narratives exploded from less than a column, to over four columns, spilling over onto another page as well. Although the magazine listed miscellaneous goods and services from hair tonics to cough remedies typical of antebellum monthlies, the majority of the items for sale consisted of print merchandise with sophisticated advertising. A preponderance of books appeared not because of their connection to Garrison or the *Liberator*, but because they were ideologically suited to the mission of antislavery.[21]

Despite commercializing the slave narrative genre and bringing a radical self-promotional charisma to the abolitionist periodical press, Garrison was happy to appear more interested in winning moral high ground than financial profit. As Charles Sellers points out, "abolitionism burgeoned especially among people trying, like Garrison, to reconcile self-making egotism with ancestral altruism through the intense Christian piety of Fenneyite benevolence." In this way, Garrison helped spearhead the movement to "ascribe success or failure wholly to character," rendering himself something of a messianic martyr for the cause—willfully throwing himself into harm's way by courting angry mobs and imprisonment—and thus focusing "altruistic indignation on chattel slavery."[22] His individualism was not projected as a defense of capitalism, per se. He only favored capitalism for its liberality, for its *free* market. The sufferings of free blacks in the North, or of the legions of white wage laborers who captured Orestes Brownson's sympathy and compassion, he only ascribed to flaws of individual character, with no mention of the inherent inequalities in the distribution of wealth laissez-faire capitalism brought. Garrisonian Wendell Phillips represented his position on the issue in his claim that only individual "economy, self-denial, temperance, education, and moral and religious character" and not socialistic government intervention could save the beaten down worker in the North. "Does capital wrong them?" he asked. Then Franklinesque "economy will make them capitalists," he concluded.[23] Fitzhugh and company would find this an inadequate argument indeed, as they attacked its failure to address the systemic causes of brutal working conditions in the North. The Garrisonian apology for market corruption based on the morality of individual character played perfectly into Garrison's two-pronged literary business practice. Moralism provided the key to his solicitation of patronage, while individualism drove his striking public persona and defense of libel as a means of both perpetuating his controversial career and symbolically supporting free speech as the root of liberal society. This business practice formed Garrison's editorial vision that would shape the belligerent culture of the *Liberator*'s circle of writers.

The more Garrison could sell the *Liberator* by agitating Northern sensibilities, the nearer he moved toward attaining his goal of disunion with the South. One of his favorite publicity stunts was to burn the Constitution in public, raving to astonished onlookers about the evils of this "covenant with death."[24] Calling for the cessation of all free states, Garrison argued that it was immoral of Northerners to pretend to be dissociated from slavery, whose participation in the government implied their active economic support of it. Northern tax dollars, he testified, were used to fund the suppression of slave insurrections and the enforcement of the Fugitive Slave Law. "People of the North!" he shouted, "if the South be wholly dependent upon you for protection in prosecuting her bloody enormities, who are the real slaveholders, the real slave-traders, the real slave-drivers, the real slave-plunderers, but YOURSELVES? You cannot extricate yourselves from the position with a repeal of the Union," he insisted.[25]

Whereas Garrison's sensationalism and capacity to attract attention could match that of story papers like the *New-York Ledger*, his management of his writers fell short of the companionable and generous editorial styles of Child or even the openly commercial Bonner. Garrison, as historians such as R.J. Wilson have noted, often prioritized the promotion of his own public reputation and celebrity status over that of the larger abolitionist objective.[26] The ideological war to end slavery directly depended on Garrison's relationship with the staff of *The Liberator*, which thrived when contributors felt his sympathy, and suffered when they perceived his disapproval. Disputes with his writers were symptoms of his intermittent rhetorical narcissism, which bore a direct impact on the ideological diffusion of Northern antislavery forces. Garrison would become world famous for his intransigence toward the South, but was unable to mollify that rigid and disapproving demeanor in dealing with the philosophical diversity of his own contributors such as Child and Douglass, whom I discuss in greater detail later in this chapter.[27]

Garrison attempted to purify and homogenize abolitionist thought at the *Liberator* against the tide of rhetorical sources available at the time that were intermingling and transforming at alarming rates. His desire to homogenize the slave narrative was especially visible in his censorship of Douglass's speeches. Elsewhere telling signs emerged suggesting that rhetoric was not crisply dualistic, but surprisingly tangled even between North and South. William Ellery Channing, Elizabeth Peabody's transcendentalist colleague and abolitionist author of *Slavery* (1836), was the first American to embrace the work of French sociologist August Comte, who would later inspire proslavery's "sociology." The confluence of thinking was uncanny and telling of the diversity of intellectual sources fueling the war of words leading up to the Civil War. This overlap placed North and South in the odd predicament of differentiating otherwise similar strands of their arguments for the nation's ideal social structure.

Within the North especially, there was also pressure to establish distinction among the various approaches to the abolitionist cause, which triangulated the movement into three major circles. Significantly, a movement that began with the seemingly unstoppable trio of Garrison, Child, and Douglass would end with their separation. The causes of that separation were not only ideological, but also hinged on Garrison's autocratic managerial method and business practice. From the American Anti-Slavery Society, three circles emerged.[28] The most prominent was Garrison's New England moral perfectionists, who increasingly defined themselves against Child and Douglass after their departures in the 1840s. Child, who never formally joined a larger antislavery society than the Boston Female Anti-Slavery Society she entered in January 1844, would become the target of Garrison's orthodoxy for her views toward the union and political party organization. Douglass defected from Garrison to Gerrit Smith's more political upstate New York circle. A third circle, which presented itself as less controversial and problematic for Garrison, consisted of evangelicals in New York City and Ohio led by the Tappan brothers and Theodore Weld. But even they would draw fire from Garrison's crew.

Garrison knew that a culture of contention and agitation prevailed over these sects; he was born for the fight and was aware that his vitriol might very well kill him, as he predicted his own fame only "if my life shall be spared." Garrison extremism played well against the South, but also set the tone of no compromise for dealing with fellow abolitionists. Garrison's ego loomed large in the formula. Garrison's famous voice of power thus also functioned in the capacity of an editor as crushingly unilateral. One wonders how writers could feel any sense of creative or philosophical liberty under the editorial fist of a man who vowed to be "harsh as truth, and as uncompromising as justice. On this subject, I do not wish to think or speak, or write, with moderation...I will not equivocate—I will not excuse—I will not retreat a single inch—AND I WILL BE HEARD."[29]

Garrison knew such extremism made him vulnerable to physical assault, and even murder. His intuition proved correct on 21 October 1855. At a meeting of the Boston Female Anti-Slavery Society, some 5,000 "gentlemen of property and standing" stormed in on the affair and converged on Garrison.[30] He escaped lynching but could not evade the torture and humiliation of being tied to a rope and dragged through the city streets of Boston. Less than two weeks after the event, he ensured to report the wrongdoing in the *Liberator* as evidence of the noble aims of his New England cause in contrast to the brutal and guileless mob mentality of the South. Garrison's tactical journalism impelled the South to no longer resort to such physical violence against him. From this victory, Garrison assumed a new piety and self-righteousness in print, as a sense of fearlessness and invulnerability began to pervade his writing. Knowing the mob would not stalk him, Garrison's "own intransigence had increased correspondingly," as George Fitzhugh's biographer has noted.[31]

But the lynch mob still hounded Garrison, only in other forms. Rumors that abolitionist literature had arrived at the U.S. Post Office of Charleston, South Carolina, sparked a riot involving the burning of heaps of mail in the street. Garrison and Tappan were hung in effigy not only as an intimidation tactic, but also as a signal to Garrison that copies of the *Liberator* arriving through the mail would be intercepted and destroyed. Indeed, the next month, a meeting of Charleston officials legislated that the general public sentiment of "abhorrence and detestation" toward the North's efforts "to deluge our State with Incendiary publications" warranted the appointment of a twenty-one–person committee designated to search, seize, and burn all objectionable materials arriving in the mail. The *Liberator* was contraband in Charleston, as a $1000 reward was offered for the identification or capture of any individual in possession of abolitionist literature, especially with the intent to distribute such materials.[32] Unlike Child, Garrison thrived on such notoriety and loved being hated. Henry Mayer, his most recent biographer, has emphasized that he deliberately made himself an issue in the debate over slavery. "There shall be no neutrals," he proclaimed in a moment of supreme self-definition echoing Emily Dickinson's most powerful poetic odes to her "imperial self." "Men shall either like or dislike me," he declared, joyfully affirming his notorious status, and reveling in the fearsome and intimidating public persona he had forged through the press. He took special pleasure in the shock of visitors realizing they were speaking to the maligned editor of the *Liberator*. "They had almost imagined me to be in figurine a monster of huge and horrid proportions," he registered with satisfaction. "But now finding me decently made, *without a single horn*, they take me cordially by the hand, and acknowledge me a 'marvelous proper man.'"[33] A savage in the public eye feared and loathed by his enemies, he enjoyed disarming people with a genteel domestic side. Weaned on Benjamin Franklin's myth of the self-made man, Garrison revolutionized the commercialization of abolitionism by being the first to generate revenue from aggressive and broad advertising of print goods in his journal, and mastering techniques of courting controversy through the sort of self-promotional stunts that had made P.T. Barnum infamous.[34]

George Fitzhugh, author of *Cannibals All!, or, Slaves Without Masters* and Garrison's Southern arch-nemesis, could perceive precisely the fault of extremism Child found in Garrison, in this case his rejection of the New England clergy, whom she had tried to placate rather than irritate as he had. "The extreme wing of the...Abolitionist party," Fitzhugh explained, "are called Garrisonians." Their leader, he continued, "edits the *Liberator*, which is conducted with an ability worthy of a better cause. He and his followers seem to admit that the Bible and the Constitution recognize and guarantee Slavery, and therefore denounce both, and propose disunion and no priests or churches as measures to attain abolition."[35] The blow was aimed particularly at Garrison's conflict with the local clergy, who objected to the strenuous participation in the cause by women. Fitzhugh's straw man attack seized on this animosity to "prove" that Garrison willfully opposed the Bible's supposed recognition and guarantee of slavery. Garrison was hardly rejecting religion because it somehow unproblematically supported slavery, as Fitzhugh alleged. Far from rejecting the Bible because it supported slavery, Garrison was embroiled in a controversy with local clergy that nonetheless gave Fitzhugh an opportunity for the accusation of sacrilege. The dispute involved several conservative preachers sensing Garrison's usurpation of their moral power and concomitant seizure of the woman question. Their aim was to loosen his grip on the American public, but the conflict that ensued only tightened it.

Early Strife

In the summer of 1837, Angelina and Sarah Grimke stormed the nation with a whirlwind antislavery speaking tour that attracted massive crowds. The tour in no time became notorious for its outspoken female participants, who sparked the furor of conservative clergymen. Claiming the sisters spoke with passion unbecoming of their sex, the General Association of Massachusetts Congregational Clergy protested that they were attracting a "promiscuous" audience and driving away conservative abolitionists. The clergy drafted a letter indicting the Grimke sisters of usurping their own roles as spiritual and moral guides, and also alleging that the women at these events did not conduct themselves in a lady-like manner. The language of the letter, both a retrograde invocation of separate spheres of gender ideology and a veiled advocacy of proslavery, is defensive and antifree speech. Professional paranoia saturated their demand for "deference and subordination...in the relation of the people to their pastor." An acute distrust of women in powerful public speaking roles drove their disapproval of ladies "assum[ing] the place and tone of man as a public reformer [in which] she yields the power which God has given her for protection, and her character becomes unnatural."[36] Patricia Okker has observed that "in contrast to the social acceptance...women editors experienced, those women who spoke to (or were perceived to speak to) audiences other than women and children at times elicited harsh rebukes." This was mainly because "women editors often established their editorial authority by relying on Victorian constructions of woman as inherently moral and domestic."[37] Indeed, the position of editor, as Child learned, did not violate gender codes, whereas the role of travelling speaker, as the Grimke sisters soon learned, encroached into the territory of male discourse with its embodied and impassioned expression. The rhetorical conventions of public speaking on behalf of an urgent reform measure such as abolitionism indeed called for the passion Charles Grandison Finney envisioned when he said that the best preachers often appear to be fighting bees in the pulpit.[38]

The image of women engaging in impassioned public speech as a form of fighting prompted the male antebellum clergy to object to the Grimke sisters' speaking tour. As a female editor, Child did not face such gender discrimination, however, as women editors including Sarah Hale, Anne Stephens, Elizabeth Peabody, and Margaret Fuller had become much more common in the market due to the culture's acceptance of women as moral instructors, albeit domestic ones. The public accepted performances by women in theater and opera, but the lyceum circuit and live orations were forbidden. Child was thus well received as the editor of the *Standard* both because it was a disembodied public role, and because women had already established themselves so closely with the cause, as evidenced by the Boston Female Anti-Slavery Association. Okker explains that "given both nineteenth-century ideologies of gender and the history of American women, periodicals focusing on family and domestic issues, religion, social reform (including suffrage), and literature were the most popular kinds of periodicals for nineteenth-century American women to edit."[39] It follows, therefore, that Child would draw the *Standard* away from the controversy and struggle for dominance associated with the *Liberator* and toward the type of periodical that women tended to edit at the time. The assumption may be that men dominated the periodical industry, when in fact there were more than 600 women editors of American journals during this period.[40]

Child inherited the *National Anti-Slavery Standard* as an embattled and fatigued instrument whose very origin arose from an unresolved schism. The orthodox Christians who withdrew from the American Anti-Slavery Society to form the Foreign Anti-Slavery Society took the *Emancipator*, the former journal of the AASS, with them leaving the AASS without a periodical. Thus Nathaniel P. Rogers opted to head up its replacement, the *National Anti-Slavery Standard* that debuted in 1840. The journal had been in existence for one year before Child took over on 20 May 1841. Rogers's disposition was not fitted for the crossfire of debate that raged between, and even within, the camps over union, nonresistance, politics, and exclusive black or female organization. Describing Rogers's personal sensitivity to criticism in a letter, Garrisonian insider Edmund Quincy admitted, "We have always handled him like a cracked tea cup."[41] Rogers was averse to controversy, but unlike Child, his response to the climate was defensive and hypersensitive.

The original *Standard* prospectus, written in 1840 by managing editor James C. Jackson during Rogers's overseas journey, distinguished the journal as tolerant and accepting of a broad range of antislavery views based on "universal fraternity of the human race, irrespective of sect, party, sex, color or country." Such peaceful and inclusive aims, however, were undercut by his second commitment to the defeat of the "spirit of the new organization as inimical to the broad and noble platform from which the Anti-Slavery enterprise first started."[42] His target was the orthodox American church that denounced the public lectures of females, and condemned Garrison for his violent "abuse of gospel ministers and excellent Christians not ready to unite with anti-slavery societies."[43] Much of the blame for the unsavory treatment of the clergy was leveled at Garrison only because he was the figurehead of the Boston clique. The most acerbic venom actually issued from the pen of Henry Wright, who nearly was eliminated from the circle for attacking not only the clergy, but also "the religion of the Bible!"[44] Wright had also weakened his standing in the circle by backing Rogers, who had previously been ousted from his editorial position at the *Herald of Freedom* for espousing a "no organization" policy, positing that organized antislavery activities thwarted free speech and wasted valuable resources of time and energy through the making of agendas, reports, minutes, and elections. Unwilling to bring their dedication to free speech to this level, the Garrisonians disclaimed Rogers's position because they feared it would weaken their collective political voice. The limitations of individualism and free speech had thus been drawn through the expulsion of Rogers, confirming that Garrisonians, despite their individualistic rhetoric, believed that real political power was achieved in groups and that solitary activism was impotent in the face of collective force.

Wright backed Rogers initially, especially because his own openly heretical anticlergy stance was well suited to Rogers's antinomianism.

But Wright remained in the clique because he was better connected to its inner circle, as he frequently lodged with Garrison. Aside from Phillips, Wright was Garrison's closest antislavery confidante, and by 1847, he reestablished himself with the group and accordingly conformed to its distaste for Rogers. Indeed, Wright would contribute to rumors that Rogers had been hiding an estate of $20,000 to appear needy so he could more effectively solicit patronage. Most of all, Wright could be pardoned for his sins—including a scandalous spate of extramarital affairs that temporarily wreaked havoc on the *Liberator*'s reputation— whereas Rogers deviated unpardonably from the Boston clique's ideology by backing an alliance of white laborers and black slaves for the overthrow of the ruling classes. This revolutionary plan was anathema to Garrisonians, who instead backed "internal rather than outward reorganization [because it] is needed to put away the evil that is in the world."[45] Individual spirituality, the Garrisonians believed, needed to be morally reformed and purified before any such institutional change should be implemented. Indeed, the Garrisonians' rally cry to expel the South from the Union sought no major changes in the current Northern market condition, and indeed scorned any attempts at altering, either through government intervention or political activism, the market's institutional structure that left the poorest 81 percent of Boston's population with less than 5 percent of its total wealth.[46] Thus Rogers's call for a joint white worker and black slave rebellion flew in the face of the consistently sacrosanct Garrisonian vision that reform should take place within the individual soul and not in the form of tax payer boycott, labor union strikes, and socialist utopia communities. For as organized as the *Liberator* staff was around "Father Garrison," they certainly had little faith in the sort of organization that might empower the masses for broader Northern economic change.

The larger vision of Rogers that accommodated both aggressive individualism (through "no organization") and worker revolution (through unified black and white labor rebellion) might have eclipsed Garrison's circle had he not fallen prey to petty sectarian squabbling. The *Standard* appeared an oasis from the storm of debate brought by the "new organization," yet fell on hard times precisely because it refused to disengage from ongoing controversy. Thus the journal's avowal of the original principles of the "old organization" and movement toward pristine abolitionism failed to be accomplished without open assaults against the "new organization." Rogers, who hated disputes with fellow abolitionists, nonetheless courted them with his excessive defensiveness that grew into a highly offensive and belligerent posture. Indeed, his position toward the "new organization" reads like a vendetta. He proclaimed this sect to be a more dangerous "*enemy* of the antislavery cause" than "slave-driving" itself, vowing to "unmask new organization. That is the business of antislavery." Engrossed in this battle, the journal's effectiveness would soon wane, especially when managing editor Jackson antagonized black groups for organizing without admitting whites into their ranks. The right to exclusive organization, he argued, violated the principle of universal inclusion and open acceptance, which only fostered more sectarian exclusion and divisiveness. Rogers's sensitivity to criticism transformed the *Standard* into precisely the combative defensive venue he had not wanted it to become. Garrison's example had so profoundly set the tone for the management of antislavery periodicals and their attendant authorial circles that sectarian strife thus became something of an unthinking habit to most abolitionist editors like Rogers. Handing over the reigns to Child, Rogers assumed she would take up the battles he had waged and strive to subdue the rivals who bested him. He thus advised her to eschew her "womanhood" in the "warfare before her" like "the maid of Orleans...when she led France to the rout and expulsion of England from her shores."[47] Child, however, would manage the paper in order to invite and inspire, much less to rout and expel her own Northern neighbors in place of the real enemy to the South.

Abolition's Child

Child's 1833 publication, *An Appeal in Favor of That Class of Americans Called Africans,* sprang from the most fruitful period of her relationship with Garrison. Their mutual admiration reached its height in 1829 when Garrison was taken by her essay "Comparative Strength of Male and Female Intellect," a work he found so moving that he reprinted it in the *Genius of Universal Emancipation,* the journal he edited prior to founding the *Liberator.* Hailing her as "The first woman of the republic," Garrison was sure to conscript Child's services when he launched the *Liberator* two years later.[48] Child's *Appeal*, which many regard as her magnum opus, particularly the chapter, "Prejudices against People of Color, and Our Duties in Relation to This Subject," was an expose of racism fueled by her place on the inner circle of the fiery *Liberator.* The piece bore the influence of Garrison through its technique of moral alarm that rang out the bitter truth that no "other people on earth indulge so strong a prejudice with regard to color as we do."[49] The chapter placed Child directly in the fray, as her argument to end all racial discrimination not only demanded the elimination of professional restrictions for blacks, but also the repeal of antimiscegenation laws. The latter proposal placed

Child at the epicenter of controversy, which intensified upon her support in 1838–1839 of women's active roles in abolition, especially as officers and committee members. In 1840, the American Anti-Slavery Society's division over the issue deeply disillusioned Child, who began to search for another venue outside of such incessant controversy.

Unlike Garrison, Child did not commit her career to the defense of libel as a principle upon which to build a dedication to liberty and thus abolitionism. Indeed, she roundly disapproved of Garrison's habit of showcasing sectarian quarrels in the *Liberator*, a practice she felt was a terrible waste of the talent and energies of the cause. "Oh! How my heart is grieved by these dissentions! I wish our dear Garrison would record them more sparingly in his paper," she lamented in an 1839 letter to her friend Lucretia Mott regarding a clash over whether the circle should try to regain the conservative clergy and enhance its public image by reversing its positions on nonresistance and women's participation in the movement.[50] Amos Phelps and Henry B. Stanton led the movement to reconcile with the disgruntled clergy by appeasing the demands of the collective 1837 letter. But the movement not only alienated many in Garrison's circle, it gave rise to a melee that absurdly led to Garrisonians and preachers accusing each other of undermining the larger antislavery mission by overemphasizing their narrow sectarian interests. The situation left Child "sick at heart, discouraged, and ashamed," she confessed to Ellis Loring the same year. Although Child initially reviled the movement to placate a sexist hidebound clergy, she increasingly felt the dispute itself reflected the virulent social culture of the Garrison clique. While chiding the shameful "sectarian zeal, and cunning, and obstinate perseverance, with which Calvinism seeks to build itself up and shut others out," it became obvious to her that "the spirit is manifestly wrong on both sides."[51] Noting "that every move Garrison can make against" the rival party "re-acts against the Liberator," Child would learn from this quagmire in her own editorial work. She would limit such disputes to the margins of the *Standard* rather than showcasing them with reprints of rival dissent followed by savage rejoinders. Garrison's zeal for the defense of libel that began his career, indeed, would become the very motivation for Child's departure to the *Standard*.

Before Child took over the *Standard* from Rogers, she wisely settled differences with Garrison, paving the way for his approval of her wildly successful journal. In a letter read at the January 1839 Massachusetts Anti-Slavery Society that Garrison later published in the *Liberator*, Child requested that Garrison's enemies tolerate how his "religious views differ from most of us" to enlist their support in the man who originally spurred them on, the one whom "every true-hearted abolitionist" must laud for his "clear strong voice of warning and rebuke...woke us from our slumbers."[52] This defense was not consciously calculated to win his support for the *Standard* as much as it was a genuine plea for peace among the ranks of antislavery. Ellis Loring, Child's close confidante, shared this sentiment and disapproved of the belligerence of Rogers and others like him. Loring thus "longed for a dignified and temperate discipline of principles," especially in "dispassionate statements of facts" in order to civilize the discourse culture. "If the Anti Slavery organizations cannot find better business in the future than they have been engrossed by, for a year or two back, they will assuredly die," he warned. This stern admonition aptly described the spirit with which Child began her work on the *Standard*.[53]

One of the first principles Child instilled in the *Standard* in her "Prospectus" was to relegate "very small space" to discussion of "divisions in the anti-slavery ranks" since, she argued, they were already so well covered by abolitionist journals at the time. Indeed, the finer points of colonization, disunion, women's and blacks' exclusive groups, voting, nonresistance, and church issues had all been rehashed in the abolitionist press, with many articles finding their way into multiple journals due to rampant reprinting for the purpose of directly addressing opposing views. Child knew well that the market was saturated with such fare and that readers did not need another outlet engaged in more of the same. As such, she promised to lay out facts "disentangled from personal controversy, as much as possible."[54] Thus Child's vision for the *Standard* was not only averse to the hairsplitting tedium of narrow sectional disputes based on principle, but it was also a savvy business decision aimed at differentiating the *Standard* from other similar products in the literary market.

Her diplomacy in the "Prospectus" of the *Standard* was not without its market appeal, as it effectively defused controversy by explaining that, according to the history of major ideas, camps typically cluster into progressive and conservative movements. According to Child, it was perfectly natural, and indeed expected, for one movement's exploration of contemporary applications and "all the collateral bearings" of any new revolutionary concept to be checked by another's harkening back to original principles for more cautious forward progress. Child suggested that the Grimke sisters, whose public speaking sparked the great schism in antislavery, represented a progressive "go ahead" spirit of innovation, while the reluctant clergy "looked back to St. Paul to arrest the progress of this innovation." Her bias for the Grimke sisters, though well concealed, was visible in her description of their pioneering spirit that "boldly asked, 'What if I do differ from St. Paul? So he differed from Peter on some points.'" But she was quick to play the middle ground and put the primary objective of antislavery in the spotlight. Two years prior, Jackson's prospectus had failed to do precisely this, when he vowed to defend against the malignant new organization. Child masterfully disarmed readers by declaring that "all conservative minds are not necessarily narrow and base, nor are reforming minds honest and true," while heralding in no uncertain terms an assault on the common enemy that had left "the slave still in chains, counting the time of his redemption by minutes, while we count it by years."[55]

Child courted a readership through the *Standard* that was relatively unfamiliar with antislavery not only to recruit the undecided to join the abolitionist cause. She also relished the opportunity to be the first to educate noncommittal readers from a nonsectarian point of view, inculcating them with the principles of her *Anti-Slavery Catechism*, which she reprinted, and glossing the basics of the cause in her column, "A, B, C, of Abolition."[56] She also worked in a fictional mode with editorials like "The Deserted Church" in which she imagined slavery's future through the controlling image of a decaying and isolated Southern church, left for dead and overgrown with weeds and haunted by bats and ravens. The import of the piece conveyed the inevitable decline of religion in a culture that had profaned Christianity as a tool for its own self-perpetuation. In such instances, Child aimed to prevent noncommittal readers from "ignorance and indifference," among the worst sins of antislavery. Her chief motive was to defend against misrepresentations of the cause to the uninitiated that might fill "honest minds with prejudices, by presenting false statements, and making up false issues" so that "a large proportion of intelligent citizens honestly believe that our principles and measures are totally opposite to what they really are."[57]

Child's early success garnered praise from Unitarian minister and Transcendental associate Ellery Channing, new organization leader Lewis Tappan, and Garrisonian Wendell Phillips. Though she won much support from such key figures across the warring camps through her literary distinction, impartiality, and broad readership, she also raised the ire of some of its more radical loyalists. Oliver Johnson complained that the *Standard* was "often complimented at the Liberator's expense" and was too "*agreeable*...under Mrs. Child's administration" because it lacked the *Liberator's* moral commitment and oratorical "fire," catering instead to the complacent "half-and-half-, milk-and-water sort of abolitionists." Among Johnson's chief worries was that the marketing of the journal would take over its moral crusade. "I don't want our papers to become too popular," he groused, "lest it should require too much time and sacrifice hereafter to take care of their reputation."[58] But tending to the magazine's reputation meant focusing literary pieces, and explications of the movement's foundational universal tenets demanded far less "time and sacrifice" than airing the latest controversy with the new organization and managing its fallout.

Child's competitors showed bitterness over being surpassed for the lead in the abolitionist periodicals market that soon transformed into ideological warfare, which eventually forced her to step down from her editorship. As quickly as Child was welcomed by the new organization as a third party to defuse tension with Garrison's circle, the proinsurrectionists from the *Liberator* began an assault that would turn into a pivotal stand on the issue of disunion. The Liberty Party's Gerrit Smith particularly challenged Child's editorial scruples of playing the middle ground through his "Address to the Slaves of the United States" delivered at the 1842 Peterboro AASS convention. Child found Smith's speech so offensive that she deviated from her noncontroversial format by reprinting it in the *Standard* with her rejoinder. In his "Address," Smith exhorts slaves to steal from their masters any necessities to aid their escape to the North, constituting theft as justifiable retribution for their sufferings in captivity. What made his appeal morally problematic to Child was that it went further by encouraging theft from random individuals while in transit toward liberty in the North. Smith encouraged stealing "the horse, the boat, the food, the clothing" to aid their journey, which to Child were not worth the cost of the stigma attached to such criminal behavior.[59] Child also objected to the impracticality of such a letter that invited interception by vigilant masters who would likely respond by tightening their grip on their slaves. Further, Child was concerned that Smith's "Appeal" would "diminish what little confidence" the Northern readers had in "the discretion and practical wisdom of abolitionists."[60] Most appalling to her was the thought of already criminalized African Americans in a culture already rife with racial discrimination, the scope of which she accurately measured in *An Appeal in Favor of That Class of Americans Called Africans*. Dedicated to nonviolence, Child's concerns that blacks abide by the law proved prophetic, as Kentucky slave Nelson Hackett successfully escaped to Canada by riding his master's racehorse. Upon arrival, he was promptly arrested for the theft of the horse and his master's gold watch that he had intended to exchange for cash along the way. Even the typically tolerant Canadians could not overlook the escaped slave's possession of stolen property (though his own body constituted precisely that). Embodying the failure of Smith's Douglass-esque advice, Hackett, although no longer a slave as he stood on Canadian soil, effectively had transformed himself into a fugitive in the process of attaining liberty.[61]

With little real momentum to be gained from Smith's reckless proposal, Garrisonians returned to their founding principle of repudiating the Union. Child had caught wind of this movement, and was careful to assuage any potential friction with them by advocating disunion in an unsigned editorial she ran in the *Standard* entitled, "The Union." In it, Child supported a break from the South, a position she had advocated years earlier when she was on the inner circle of the *Liberator* during its earliest days. Now, however, she would align herself with Garrison's circle to mollify its radical edges with the insistence on a peaceful separation with the South to end the Constitution's legal, economic, and thus moral, complicity with slavery. To illustrate such complicity, Child cited Garrison's favorite examples in support of disunion: the use of Northern tax dollars to suppress slave insurrections and the nationwide enforcement of the Fugitive Slave Law. Both of these required the cooperation of the North, they claimed, and actively perpetuated the existence of the peculiar institution.

Much to Child's chagrin, Garrison threw himself into the movement to repeal the union. She did not differ so much with the proposal for disunion as she did in his presumptuous attempt to make it every abolitionist's first priority. Child's protection of the plurality and diversity of individualistic abolitionist views was now under direct threat, as Garrison threw caution to the wind with his undemocratic and unilateral proclamation that all abolition would now make "the REPEAL OF THE UNION between the North and the South, the grand rallying point until it be accomplished." His intention to funnel all abolitionists' efforts into disunion was now explicit. "We are for throwing all the means, energies, actions, purposes, and appliances of the genuine friends of liberty and republicanism into this one channel, and for measuring the humanity, patriotism and piety of every man by this one standard."[62] In charging that it was "imprudent" of him to proclaim disunion "the chief business" of abolition "*before* the Society had at all deliberated what was best on a subject so very important," Child had defied the essence of his authority as the de facto leader of abolition and its most charismatic ruler. She did not disguise her disgust with his method, calling it "rash to throw out such an enunciation, without any explanation of the *means to be used*," strongly implying that Garrison's urgency suggested the use of violent force. Child had boldly accused Garrison of violating the principle of democracy by imposing his agenda on the majority without having first obtained their consent by observing that a tyrannical "set in Massachusetts were going to measure every man's 'humanity patriotism and piety,' by their willingness to dissolve the union."[63]

Garrison's insistence that his proposal for disunion represented the collective interest of antislavery, despite overwhelming evidence to the contrary, gave the antiabolitionists of the *New-York Courier and Enquirer* fresh and apparently conclusive evidence that their opponent's "avowed object" was "treason to the Union of the States."[64] The inflammatory nature of the *Courier*'s retort alarmed Child into believing that this new controversy could erupt into another riot like the one that tore through New York City in 1834 after a mob stormed an abolitionist meeting. In an effort to ease tensions and avert such violent upheaval, Child collared James S. Gibbons, chair of the American Anti-Slavery Society executive committee, for aid in writing up a circular making clear that Garrison's position on disunion was in fact not reflective of all abolitionists. Specifically, they insisted that the repeal of the Union was not the main objective of the next society meeting, since it was "an object... entirely foreign to the purpose for which [the AASS] was organized." Gibbons and Child boldly warned that the agenda for the annual meeting would not pursue this issue and instead would engage more pertinent matters, regardless of coercive measures to implement Garrison's plan. Their expectation of a fierce response was clear in their vow not to be "deterred from the fearless discharge of duty by threats of violence."[65]

Responding much as they expected, Garrison laid out an enraged ultimatum restating how the North's complicity with a Union that supports slavery necessitated a split with the South. His vitriolic method of forcing disunion as the White Whale of abolition was Child's main objection.[66] She was not opposed to Garrison personally, since "I have no *disposition* to 'wash my hands of Garrison' for the simple reason that I have the highest respect for his ability, the most perfect confidence in his integrity of purpose, and a general unity with his principles." Instead she only desired that the issue of disunion be dealt with in a tolerant manner in which it could be "fully and freely discussed." Garrison made explicit that there was little room for the "calm, rational appeal" of "intelligent and judicious" voices, and that a collaborative approach was anathema to what Child described as his "cat-hauling" style.[67]

In light of this controversy, Child's departure from her post seemed inevitable. Although Garrison had made amends with her by suggesting that the market was big enough to accommodate both the *Liberator* and the *Standard*, reality suggested that his all-caps shrieks, frequently in bad taste, and at the highest volumes possible, would likely drown out her more sophisticated, reflective literary image. Ideally, if there were other papers like Child's in the market, she might have enjoyed a longer tenure at her position. As it was, intense divisiveness set the standard in the market. The last two controversies that ensnared Child spoke to that culture of disrespectful infighting, and finally broke her tolerance. The first involved a proposal of "come-outism" forwarded by Garrisonian Maria Weston Chapman, which pressured all abolitionist organizations and periodicals to cut ties with religious sects and political parties that did not condemn slavery. Much like her reaction to Garrison's blunt promotion of his pet issue of disunion in the name of AASS, Child found "come-outism" to be "narrow and coercive."[68] Rogers was particularly supportive of Chapman's proposal, as it reinforced his antiassociation radical spirit of institutional disaffiliation, which became so extreme that it prompted his dismissal from Garrison's ranks. Rogers had always been miffed at Child's treatment of the *Standard*, which she resolutely refused to turn into a belligerent weapon aimed at the "new organization." He had pressured her with "come-outism" in a manner she found particularly corrosive, since it was clear that Rogers was driven in part by personal spite toward her.

Personal vendettas were a bugbear to Child from the beginning of her work for the abolitionist movement and would finally encourage her departure from it. Specifically, Edmund Quincy's attack on Arthur Tappan that gloried in the financial demise of abolitionism's original benefactor struck Child as a malicious swipe reeking of Schadenfreude. Quincy failed to see Tappan's financial decline as a somber occasion marking an ironic and sobering reversal of antislavery's philanthropic origins. Instead, Quincy sniped at Tappan, relishing his demise since Tappan had transformed the *Emancipator* into a "new organization" venue, an unpardonable sin in Quincy's view. Although Child had developed by now serious ideological differences with the Garrisonians, she was not so myopic as to miss how Tappan had generously lent Garrison the funds to launch the *Liberator*. Totally demoralized by Quincy's disrespect for the integrity of the movement's history, Child admitted this was but one of innumerable personal attacks that "took the last scales from my eyes" to see abolitionists "fighting in the spirit of a *sect*, a spirit which I abhor in all its manifestations."[69] Interestingly, her last editorial, "SECTS AND SECTARIANISM," swore off all organizations just as Rogers had. Her purpose, however, was to exit the periodical market for the literary book market and seek a publisher of her collected "Letters from New York" column that had appeared in the *Standard*. Rogers, on the other hand, had advocated "no organization" as a method of more efficiently assaulting the "new organization," a way of turning the

Garrisonians into a sect of guerilla warriors who were not burdened by bureaucratic procedure and thus free to barrage the likes of Tappan from a scattered front consisting of lean individualists.

It is important to note that Child did not step down only for ideological reasons. Her method of doing literary business not only was too progressive for antislavery's politics, her financial approach also proved to be effective in ways that others around her could not fathom. Indeed, when she took over the *Standard*, she inherited an $800 debt from Rogers's mismanagement of the paper. She quickly turned that into a profit, which just as rapidly diminished once John Collins, who had helped manage the paper from its onset, intervened and pressed her to abandon cautious management for his "scheme of large adventure."[70] The paper thus overreached its capacity and left Child $2000 in debt. In many ways, her departure was similar to that of Elizabeth Peabody's resignation from her position as publisher of the *Dial*. Like Child, Peabody realistically acknowledged the journal had fallen into worse financial condition than she could manage. Margaret Fuller had also left her editorship of the *Dial* when the journal's narrow circulation and emphasis on the inner circle of Concord appeared to her to come at the expense of winning a wider market leaving the paper, in her view, in an irretrievable deficit. In all three cases, these women proved astute fanciers of these periodicals, and had it not been for the interference of Collins and Emerson in their management of them, they might have flourished. Child's winning formula of careful financial management and innovative content, particularly her popular column, "Letters from New York," would never be approached or replicated in another abolitionist magazine.

Garrison to Douglass: "Tell Your Story, Frederick"

Like Child, Frederick Douglass began his career in antislavery with Garrison and would finish it without him. Also like Child, Douglass harbored serious misgivings about Garrison's tactics. Douglass began work for the abolitionist movement selling *Liberator* subscriptions while writing his *Narrative of the Life of Frederick Douglass*. He admitted in the later edition of his autobiography, *My Bondage and My Freedom*, that he had been swept away by Garrison's charismatic power and even fell to "hero worship" of the abolitionist leader like so many free blacks had at the time. This was because Garrison came to represent to blacks an embodiment of the *Liberator*, the most powerful abolitionist periodical in the world, "a voice, a movement, a community, and indeed a person [promising to] render them as a free people," as Fanuzzi explains.[71] "His paper took its place with me next to the Bible," Douglass recalled of the prominent place of the *Liberator* in his life, extolling "the mind of William Lloyd Garrison." "Learning to love him through his paper," Douglass wrote, "I was prepared to be pleased with his presence." Ironically, the more intimate Douglass became with the real man behind the idealized *Liberator* persona, the more it confirmed for him the need to break from his attachment and hero worship.[72] Seventeen years after being ignited by Garrison's oratorical fire, Douglass could see that Garrison's power lie in his capacity to captivate the crowd and win with his flamboyant style wide-eyed admirers like himself when he was living in New Bedford at the time. Douglass recalled that most in attendance at a Garrison oration were astonished. It was an effort of unequaled power, sweeping down, like a

> tornado, every opposing barrier, whether of sentiment or opinion. For a moment he possessed almost that fabulous inspiration, often referred to but seldom attained, into which a public meeting is transformed into a single individuality—the orator wielding a thousand heads and hearts at once, and by the simple majesty of his all controlling thought, converting his hearers into the express image of his soul.[73]

The seventeen-year historical perspective on this tornado that was Garrison exudes a repressed sense of skepticism in the overdetermined description, a sense that all of this spellbinding "majesty" and "fabulous inspiration" dangerously hammered out the diversity of the audience through the delusion of omnipotence over "every opposing barrier." Indeed, Douglass, of course, initially relished the honor of sharing the stage with Garrison, yet his misgivings show through in precisely his desire to deviate from the Garrisonian agenda. With admiring crowds and *Liberator* staff writers forming a "single individuality" expressing the editor's will, Douglass soon found that his desire to speak on his own was effectively censored by the internally combative culture of abolitionist discourse. Indeed, Northern skeptics of Douglass's credibility posed a threat to Garrison's authority and thus it was agreed that the former slave would remain factual in his accounts despite the urge to "denounce slavery." When Garrison would whisper in his ear, "Tell your story, Frederick," he meant for the ex-slave to refrain from unleashing rhetorical fireworks of the sort reserved for Garrison's performance. "Give us the facts," his handlers told him, "and we will take care of the philosophy." He admitted that "I could not always obey, for I was now always reading and thinking. New views of the subject," not always replicating those of the Garrisonian circle, "were presented to my mind."[74]

Douglass wrote *My Bondage, My Freedom* from the vantage point of moving from a pawn of Garrison's, a P.T. Barnum curiosity and evidentiary exhibit valuable only for the raw facts of his enslaved past, to a fully autonomous abolitionist philosopher, agent, and activist. As such, he was acutely aware of the schisms that daunted Child. Douglass eventually found his ideological match in Gerrit Smith, whose support of the Constitution, union, the use of violent means to end slavery, and political party organization were diametrically opposed to the *Liberator*'s position on those issues. Douglass would dedicate *My Bondage, My Freedom* to Smith in gushing terms, expressing gratitude for a patron who treated him not so much as embodied evidence useful only for his eyewitness testimony, but as a force unto himself demonstrable through the skill with which he edited his own periodical, the *North Star.* "To honorable Gerrit Smith," he effused, "as a slight token of esteem for his character, admiration for his genius and benevolence, affection for his person and gratitude for his friendship...this volume is respectfully dedicated by his faithful and firmly attached friend, Frederick Douglass."[75] By 1857, Douglass could see, just as Child had, that "present organizations may perish, but the cause will go on. That cause has a life, distinct and independent of organizations patched up from time to time to carry it forward," which, apart from its ephemeral and often profane sectarian political manifestations both agreed was immortal and sacred.[76]

Whereas Child's reinvention of the abolitionist press met with discord that sent her into a book writing career as her primary vocation, Douglass would find a fruitful niche in Smith's New York circle. Such maneuvering between sects and attempts to discredit one and other in intense competition, however, was not the environment that characterized the Southern literary marketplace in which George Fitzhugh and James DeBow operated. Debow would find a generous donor to launch his journal just as Garrison had, yet the management of their careers was cooperative and conciliatory compared to their Northern counterparts. They promoted rather than persecuted each other more in the spirit of Tappan and Garrison's original collaboration and Child's later editorship of the *Standard.* Literary business was not, surprisingly, ruled with an iron fist, nor was it hegemonic in South. But it was indeed every bit as self-promotional and tapped into the media networks of print culture that would spread its proslavery ideology and forge the very culture and creed with which the South identified itself. It is to that proslavery print culture, and its own stentorian audacious ringleader, George Fitzhugh, that we now turn.

Chapter 7

Proslavery and the Pen: Fitzhugh's Apologists

When literary entrepreneur James D.B. DeBow originally conceived of starting a practical commercial periodical as an alternative to the *Southern Literary Messenger*, he never dreamed that it would transform into proslavery's most powerful weapon against the North and the instrument by which Southern culture came to define itself in the years leading up to the Civil War. Politics were the last thing on his mind in the early going. Instead, he was mainly concerned with maintaining a solvent and financially sound enterprise to avoid suffering the economic troubles that plagued the *Messenger*, the prestigious rival magazine associated with Edgar Allan Poe. DeBow was acutely aware of the anemic finances behind the *Messenger*'s literary prestige and never became enamored with the renown of contributors like Poe, whose personal finances dissolved while his star rose. DeBow thus pragmatically dedicated himself to prudent fiscal principles to weather the stormy Southern literary market in the first number of *DeBow's Commercial Review of the South and West*, which resembled a glorified commercial and agricultural almanac. He would accordingly fill the modestly printed ninety-six octavo pages of the January 1846 debut issue with useful information about commercial and agricultural resources for Southern and Western entrepreneurs. What began as a lean version of *Hunt's Merchant's Magazine*, however, would soon transform into the South's most potent weapon in print culture by the dawn of the Civil War. But before achieving such a status, it would have to avoid an early grave by appealing to the practical business needs of a wide untapped market of readers in the

South and the West. Distinguishing his journal from "Able monthlies and quarterlies, devoted *exclusively* to literature, in its higher walks of fancy, or its statelier tread of philosophy, [which] have run their brief career and have almost expired in the very throes that gave them birth," DeBow vowed that his enterprise would endure. This magazine, he promised, would not sacrifice profitability, as *Messenger* did, for impractical aesthetics. Above all, he would not exclusively regard "remuneration, if it comes at all, as the starved devotee to literature and science too frequently greets it [in] the simple consciousness of extending the influence and the empire of letters."[1] *DeBow's* would instead devote itself to the use of businessmen and agrarians first, and address literature second. Like the fate of the *American Anti-Slavery Almanac*, however, this early devotion to facts and statistics, commercial method and practice, gradually yielded to the increasingly impassioned rhetoric that would come to characterize the vitriolic debate over slavery.[2]

This chapter argues that the movement toward narrative contributions on the moral value of slave labor in *DeBow's* sprang from the economic perspective inherent in its original commercial agenda. That perspective reflected a distinctly collective, even collusive, market orientation instrumental in shaping the South's associationism that fueled its propaganda in the years leading up to the Civil War. The economic ethos was marked by a distinct inclination toward socialism that united the South,[3] propelled *DeBow's* and its primary contributors to success, and thus posed an ideological threat to Garrison's circle and the North at large. The South attacked the Northern market's avarice, narrow individualism, and rampant abuse of its working class in favor of a domestic benevolent paternalism that extended into an argument for a larger more protective government. The method by which Fitzhugh's apologists conducted their literary business also bore the stamp of collectivism. The region's book trade was sorely lacking in resources, since paper mills for production and railway and roads for distribution were scarce, and populace, as the North was more than double its size as John C. Calhoun frequently noted in support of his minority region's right to hold slaves. Economic survival in the literary market, therefore, depended on the consolidation of capital, sharing of resources, and sympathetic collaboration. Unhampered by the individualism that splintered and fractured Garrison's staff and other New England circles like the Transcendentalists—especially evident in ideologically homeless figures like Orestes Brownson caught between advocating wage or slave labor—the close-knit Fitzhugh clan's collectivist economic vision supplied the South not only with the lexicon for its defense of slavery, but also with a deeper and more urgent embrace of kinship and extended family as the very foundation of its regional identity.

The Collective Construction of DeBow's Review

For all the fiscal prudence espoused by DeBow in the first number, his journal immediately fell on hard times. *DeBow's* and its circle of contributors owed their existence in part to an eleventh hour financial rescue from certain dissolution by a wealthy businessman and statesman named Maunsel White. DeBow did not actively court White's patronage, but instead began in earnest to bring his entrepreneurial dreams to fruition on credit alone. Fresh from his attendance at the Commercial Convention of the Southern and Western States in Memphis in 1845, DeBow carried the meeting's optimism and energy directly into his new enterprise. DeBow had played an integral role in the convention, which was attended by John C. Calhoun, whose objective was to establish methods and identify resources for keeping pace with Northern industry, especially in transportation, manufacturing, and agriculture. The pooling of information at the event struck a cord with DeBow; he, too, could continue the conversation in the print media, thus enriching the prospects for the region's economy, while venturing forth bravely onto the free market himself. The seeds of *DeBow's* were planted, and capital would continue to prove essential to their cultivation.[4]

During this early phase of *DeBow's*, editorial policy distanced the paper from "party movements and maneuvering and party tactics," calling for "an active neutrality."[5] The goal was to strengthen the Southern economy without taking sides in party politics. DeBow's belief that his magazine could develop the Southern economy through the collectivization of resources and the latest commercial knowledge nonetheless had profound political implications at both the national and local levels. Nationally, his agenda economically set the stage for war, and regionally, it advanced the literary careers of the magazine's inner circle of writers, who were to become the foremost war propagandists. Thus Maunsel White's financial intervention to save *DeBow's* from ruin did not have immediate militant designs, or even conscious conspiratorial motives, but was totally consonant with this larger economic objective.

White's aid was a business transaction that epitomized the Southern collectivist vision of capitalism. White had made his fortune through his sugar cane plantation, but well understood the rigors of free market enterprise, as he had arrived as a thirteen-year-old penniless Irish immigrant and immersed himself in the full spectrum of Southern commerce first in Kentucky as an accounting clerk and later in New Orleans, where he did business in molasses, pork, corn, cotton, and rice. White typically conceived of commerce in the aggregate, always advocating the consolidation of resources for the good of the larger whole, no Yankee individualism tarnished his honor in fostering Southern kinship. *DeBow's* published White's biographical profile in 1858, citing a letter in which the former veteran of the War of 1812 and confidante of Andrew Jackson extolled the virtue of capital. He saw "commerce [as] the all and all of prosperity," and the larger collective denizens of the South, like those of New Orleans, "the spontaneous, yet youthful, vigorous offspring."[6] Indeed, White had played the role of benefactor to many struggling merchants and farmers in the Old South ("his purse has often been at their service") generously spreading his wealth "of nearly two million dollars" and establishing a reputation among "the most respectable merchants of New Orleans for a half century." What was not so clear was his political position on slave trafficking. By the time White's biographical sketch was published in 1858, *DeBow's* had eagerly sought out prominent figures to advance the proslavey argument. Accordingly, the sketch cast White's support of commerce as advocating the "opening of the new sources of the supply of labor and thus...the slave trade."[7] White indeed owned 200 slaves at his Deer Range plantation, yet was in fact clearly against regarding them as his property, a position echoing Fitzhugh's benevolent paternalism. "I have made myself a solemn promise never to sell a Negro," White testified, nonetheless carefully separating the slave trade from his own (and the South's by extension) dependence on it for its livelihood: "it is a traffic I have never done. I would rather give them their liberty than sell them."[8]

White considered his patronage of *DeBow's*—which rescued the journal from a six-month dormancy that had tested the limits of its creditors and left the editor literally on the brink of starvation—to be an investment in the commercial growth of the region dissociated from the moral depravity of selling human beings. White had become something of an iconic Southern philanthropist in the mid-1840s, having recently retired from his role as active partner in Maunsel White and Company to focus on his own sugar cane crop at Deer Range Plantation. DeBow's anemic budget and noble commercial aims made him a perfect project for White, who responded in November 1848 to the urgency of his financial situation.

Fortified with White's investment, DeBow was determined not to disappoint his patron. The period that followed was lean; he and associate R.G. Barnwell lived in a desolate chamber above J.C. Morgan's bookstore in Charleston, Louisiana, "looking on no other furniture than a modest mattress on the floor, on which the two companions rested at night. They literally lived on bread alone, with a little butter, however, to soften the dryness. Never did two persons exist on so small an expenditure, their daily outlays rarely exceeding twenty cents—that is, ten cents each," Judge Charles Gayarre recalled.[9] Morgan, White, and Barnwell were thus immediately vital to the survival of *DeBow's*, since they respectively provided the office, funds, and assistance necessary for the establishment of a war room from above Morgan's shop for their assault on the literary market. From that dank setting, DeBow took pains to garner as many subscriptions as possible covering as much of the region as travel permitted by his tireless agents, Price and Foster. The publishing firm of Weld and Company noticed the gathering momentum and pitched in their support with money and machinery. DeBow's brother would also enter the picture and the enterprise began to take flight by the early 1850s. The ambition of reaching 5,000 subscribers was now well within reach and fueled by the momentum of this growing matrix of distinctly Southern antebellum cooperative capitalism.

By the 1860s, *DeBow's* had established the largest circulation of any journal in the South based on steady subscriptions that sold for five dollars per year. Its sparse advertising during the 1850s developed into an ample bounty by the end of the decade. With the most valuable advertising space available in the South, DeBow was now able to charge twenty dollars per page, offering substantial discounts for long-term contracts. Goods and services for sale reflected the South's surging economy. By 1860, the magazine devoted at least twelve pages to advertising, which were flush with notices for "sewing machines, pianos, machinery, liquors, patent medicines, insurance, and books to the extent of a dozen pages." In 1853, "West" was dropped from its title, as DeBow resolved to focus on not only his own Southern readership. He also paradoxically expanded his already brisk clientele by winning a substantial Northern audience consisting mainly of New York businessmen, the antebellum forerunners of the Gilded Age Yankee entrepreneurs who would flood the South during reconstruction.[10] If the constituency of Northern subscribers were the invisible patrons of *DeBow's*, then certainly the magnanimous

Maunsel White, a Southern celebrity in his own right, was among its most visible financial supporters. While White had provided the initial capital and star power to launch the magazine, Fitzhugh and George Frederick Holmes rhetorically propelled it to new heights.

Fitzhugh's own reputation owed a great deal to Holmes's tireless promotion of the former's first book, *Sociology for the South* (1854), which he reviewed glowingly no less than five times at strategic intervals, each highlighting a different strength through the media to win over the mass audience. Holmes's masterful barrage of the literary market publicized Fitzhugh without saturating or trying the patience of the mass readership. As assistant editor of the *Southern Quarterly Review*, Holmes used his credibility in the periodical press to place his first glowing review in the Richmond *Examiner*. In three and a half columns, he praised Fitzhugh's illustration of the demise of the industrial working classes in Britain and Europe while vindicating "a larger, a healthier, and a more profound philosophy than that which has affected to past sentence of condemnation upon them."[11] This review speaks volumes to the mutual promotion of the *DeBow's* circle that moved beyond the early cash investment, legwork, and office space necessary for launching the journal. Southern cooperative capitalism[12] now moved into the realm of collective literary production and shared intellectual property. According to this business practice, Holmes had no misgivings about lavishing praise upon *Sociology for the South*, even though it bastardized ideas he himself had published in 1850 under the title of "Observations on a Passage in the Politics of Aristotle Relative to Slavery," whose argument proceeded from Aristotle's contention that "Nature has clearly designed some men for freedom and others for slavery:—and with respect to the latter, slavery is both just and beneficial."[13] Holmes showed no resistance toward Fitzhugh's liberal borrowings and potential misreadings of his original work, but he instead recognized the polemical potency in the Virginian's rhetoric.

Holmes then reached the more sophisticated literati of the *Southern Literary Messenger* in his next review, which was a more densely woven tribute to the book suited to the higher literary standards of their readership compared to that of the *Examiner*. Fitzhugh could not contain his joy upon seeing this review in such a prestigious magazine that all but cemented his credibility and fame. "My Dear Holmes!!" he sang out, "First, let me thank you for your kind and able Review in the Messenger. I subscribe to every word of it. You have greatly strengthened my main position—the Failure of Free Society." Fitzhugh quickly alluded to the coterie ties of their ascendant circle of writers. "You and Hughes, and I in the last year, it seems to me, have revolutionized public opinion at the South on the subject of Slavery." He then went on to marvel at his spreading influence, mainly as a function of the periodical press in which "not one paper vindicated Slavery in the abstract,—now all endorse my book, and thereby endorse slavery in the abstract." Acknowledging the essential role of Holmes's promotion in the process of spreading his fame, Fitzhugh was well aware that without this systematic marketing campaign he would have remained obscure. Fitzhugh thus observed his own success "is all owing to the powerful and hortatory review with which you backed it at once in the Examiner." He casts the reviews as nothing less than masterpieces of publicity, declaring that in the case of Holmes's latest work, "the review far surpassed the work reviewed."[14] Holmes then went directly from the mass generalist *Examiner* and exotic literary *Messenger* onto the *Quarterly Review of the Methodist Episcopal Church South*, whose editor John McClintock regarded Holmes as one of his best contributors. Holmes had similarly used his sway with John Thompson, editor of the *Messenger*, to publish his review. He finished this tour de force campaign with a notice in his own *Southern Quarterly Review*, which was edited by William Gilmore Simms, former Knickerbocker and Lad of Kilkenny who had drifted South to become an ardent loyalist of the region and one of proslavery's fiercest advocates.

As illustrated by Fitzhugh's borrowings from Holmes, the *DeBow's* circle openly shared intellectual property unlike their Northern counterparts, who savagely defended their individual perspectives from rival abolitionists. Proslavery writers understood intellectual property to be a common good open to mutual exchange. Thus their correspondence does not detail borrowings and the specifics of authorial influence. Though not widely catalogued outside of the writing itself, the evidence of the claims so many of the proslavery writers—Bledsoe, Grayson, DeBow, Armstrong, Stringfellow, Cartwright, and Elliott—were making in their work indicate not only Fitzhugh's profound influence over the South at this time, but also the culture of collectivizing intellectual property as shared rather than individually wielded in the market to establish product differentiation. The coterie nonetheless worked to produce writing that would have a singular effect, especially on the book market. *Sociology for the South* was wildly popular in Richmond, Fredericksburg, and Washington, selling out its first edition in a few months. Fitzhugh kept close watch over sales, speculating that "it sells better because it is odd, eccentric, extravagant, and disorderly. Its hop, skip, and jump manner is exactly like Aristotle's Politics and Economics," the very work that Homes himself had used in 1850 for "Observations on a Passage in the Politics of Aristotle Relative to Slavery." Holmes could see that Fitzhugh had captured more than his own ideas by tapping into the rhythms and cadences of Aristotle's discourse with a panache his own essay lacked. Thus Holmes was content to promote Fitzhugh not out of self-sacrifice but to see his Aristotelian defense of slavery win the masses cloaked in his friend's vibrant, extravagant rhetoric.

Historians of the Old South have tried to isolate Fitzhugh from the *DeBow's* circle of contributors, claiming that his socialistic utopia of slaveholding society, along with his flamboyance and often-reckless rhetoric, alienated him from his more staid, eloquent, genteel colleagues. His brassy showmanship, self-promotion, and theoretical impracticality, an older generation of scholars have argued, put off Holmes and Hughes, the more quintessential Southern gentlemen.[15] Missing in this formulation is the fact that Holmes had been the circle's most aggressive marketer of Fitzhugh through his reviews. Further, Fitzhugh's visionary writings influenced the entire circle of writers, even DeBow, the least literary of them all and the most skeptical of socialism. This knot of writers thus openly pooled intellectual resources for production into high and low cultural markets from university textbooks to philosophical treatises to mass periodicals like *DeBow's*.

Fitzhugh's sense of indebtedness to Holmes prompted his endorsement of his friend's candidacy for a reputable position of chair in history and literature at the University of Virginia. His exuberant and superlative praise for Holmes appeared in a prominently placed *Examiner* editorial. "Could we secure such men as Geo. F. Holmes at the University," he gushed, "we might expect to send out champions of the South, [because] Holmes combines as much of great learning, power of reasoning and originality of thought as any man in America."[16] Here was an early expression of Southern kinship concomitant to the cooperative capitalism that gave rise to *DeBow's* circle as the shaping force behind Southern print culture essential to the Confederate ethos. How could this culture of kinship that governed literary business transform into a larger socialistic ethos? How did *DeBow's*, "the South's most vigorous journalistic economic promoter advocating expansion of southern manufacturing in the 1850s," as the Genoveses have recently described it, thus become the vehicle for criticism of individualism and laissez-faire capitalism?[17]

Planting Southern Capitalism with Socialist Seeds

The principle of benevolent paternalism was not limited to defenses of plantation slavery. For what were White and Holmes respectively to DeBow and Fitzhugh but protective father figures providing shelter from the free market? This drive for mutual aid found more formal political expression during the height of the Civil War in Fitzhugh's 1862 proposal for "the organization and consolidation of capital" toward the construction of an economy tailored to the imagined Confederate Nation. Since the American political economy favored Northern business' "merchants and manufacturers, whose daily receipts enable them to make frequent payments...but not the business of planters," he proposed to make an alternative "financial system suited to the industry and wants of the South" by creating "an agency to consist of an encorporated [sic] company with sufficient capital, to be invested in good public and private securities with braches in the several Confederate States and Europe."[18] His formulation here matches the business practice behind the construction of *DeBow's* circle characterized by collaboration and resource consolidation. From its inception, cooperative capitalism set the keynote for the cohort's business practice, from White's gallant eleventh hour rescue to Holmes's barrage of promotional reviews to Foster and Price's zealous solicitation of subscriptions to Wells and Company's generous contribution of printing equipment. Such business practice reflected Fitzhugh's support of larger government as an extension of his socialistic vision of the ideal plantation family.

The socialistic leanings of *DeBow's* circle were so dedicated to big government that the majority of its constituents remained unionist until the late 1850s. Fitzhugh made the choices clear. On the one hand, "Let Alone [that] is made to usher in No-Government" and essentially the anarchy and mob rule associated with the "Wild West's Vigilance Committee of California" and such abominations attendant on liberal society as "Free Love." On the other hand was "more of government," which finds its expression in slavery in the South and increased legislation in the North because the "masses require more of protection, and the masses and philosophers equally require more of control." The North is "too little governed" desperately forming "mobs and vigilance committees to protect rights which government should."[19] Proslavery followed Fitzhugh's lead in sounding the socialistic keynote of Thomas Carlyle's assault on the free market and urging that "more of government is needed," for "we, too, are a Socialist (for free society), but we would screw up the strings of society, not further relax them, much less cut them 'sheer asunder.'"[20] Fitzhugh was careful not to be misunderstood as advocating the socialism of Northerners like the Brook Farm Fourierists, whose associationist solutions he disavowed as anarchic.

Such proslavery socialism advocating paternalistic interventionist government fueled support for the union that lasted up until the final years before the Civil War. The focus of Southern thought in the 1840s and early 1850s was not devoted to plotting a Confederate conspiracy for secession, so much as it was focused on arguing for the union to support the legality of slavery. John C. Calhoun had tied slaveholders' interests to those of the greater United States; James Chestnut, Sr. admitted after the war that he "wanted all the power the United States would give me—to hold my own."[21] The unionist position was especially consonant with the "vigorous government participation in economic development" Fitzhugh wanted, which echoed Henry C. Carey's belief that the government should plan and promote internal improvements, develop financial marketing facilities, and foster transportation, particularly the building of the railroad.[22] The opposing contention "that government is best which governs least" became something of a Northern rally cry from the *United States Magazine and Democratic Review* of 1837–1859 to Emerson's 1844 "Politics" to Henry David Thoreau's famous opening line of "Resistance to Civil Government," originally published in Elizabeth Peabody's 1849 journal, *Aesthetic Papers*. Thoreau's essay led to his searing abolitionist defenses of the North's most visible militant revolutionary in "A Plea for Capt. John Brown," and "The Last Days of John Brown." New England Transcendentalists and proslavery advocates shared a hatred of industrial capitalism's crushing competition and grossly unequal distribution of wealth. Fitzhugh's assertion that "the frequent accumulation of large fortunes, and consequent pauperism of the masses, is the greatest evil of modern society" could have plausibly been penned by any of the Transcendentalists. This overlap did not escape Fitzhugh's attention, and he made a concerted effort to differentiate proslavery from what he called the many narrowly subdivided and frivolous reform agendas in the North, symptoms of free society's chaotic and bizarre masquerade of self-interest run amok in thousands of wayward and ill-conceived clusters.

Fitzhugh highlighted such reform movements in the North as evidence of the rampant social disease caused by industrial capitalism that would inspire such corrective measures. Since "the old crazy edifice of society, in which they live, is not longer fit for human dwelling, and is imminently dangerous," its denizens are rushing headlong like rats "with haste and panic into every hole that promises shelter," finding refuge in mesmerism, harmonialism, and the Spiritual Telegraph.[23] In the context of a society governed by narrow self-interest, he argued, the reform impulse ran amok among the chaos of innumerable –isms, so rampant and conspicuous that Fitzhugh called them "our trump card."[24] He derided Shakers, free love, women's rights "and all of the other Isms which propose to overthrow and rebuild society and government, or to dispense them altogether." He targeted Horace Greeley's *New-York Tribune* as "the great Organ of Socialism" as an anarchic distortion of his own socialism whose radicalism threatened to cut the strings of society "sheer asunder."[25] Like Fitzhugh, Holmes also underlined the limitations of the North's view of socialism, rejecting their solution as absurd "unmitigated Pandemonium."[26] Holmes even showed concern that Fitzhugh's aggressive alignment of slavery with socialism could be misread as a destructive and radical revision of society rather than the picture of quiet control and harmony they intended. Further, Holmes worried that the identification of socialism with slavery might provide inadvertent support for destructive visionaries.

Fitzhugh's adaptation of socialism surfaces in *Slavery Justified* in which he portrays the plantation as a "beau ideal of Communism; it is a joint concern, in which the slave consumes more than the master" and is thus always content in a protective society characterized by "peace, quiet, [and] plenty. We have no mobs, no trades unions, no strikes for higher wages, no armed resistance to the law, but little jealousy of the rich by the poor. We have but few in our jails, and fewer in our poor houses...Slaves never die of hunger, scarcely ever feel want" in contrast to "FREE COMPETITION," a masquerade of equality that is "but giving license to the strong to oppress the weak."[27] This "beau ideal" hijacks Communism's principles of shared resources, community, and love, to appear superior to free society's wage labor system. Fitzhugh took the claim that free labor was less costly than slave labor not as a liability to the system, but as a token of its commitment to a more equal distribution of wealth. To this end, "he concluded—as did Karl Marx—that, therefore, free workers suffered greater exploitation than slave," as the Genoveses explain. It stood to reason, therefore, that "Slave labor was more expensive than free because masters treated laborers more humanely."[28] The portrait of Southern society here shares much in common with Bostonian Edward Bellamy's socialist utopia in *Looking Backward* (1867) that lashed out against competition, urban squalor, and economic friction caused by the widening disparity of the social classes and uneven distribution of wealth. Indeed, Fitzhugh's consonance with New England's leading socialist thinker is manifestly evident in the abolitionist press's refusal to publish indentured servant Harriet Wilson's *Our Nig* (1859) because it assaulted the Northern capitalist condition for free blacks so convincingly.

Fitzhugh's overlap with thinkers like activist Orestes Brownson, who would doggedly defend the rights of Northern wage laborers, is telling in this case. The innumerable arguments like those of Brownson and the free black author, Wilson, combined to form something of a trump card for Fitzhugh, as they voiced precisely his anticapitalist contentions from a Northern point of view. (Although Fitzhugh was unlikely to have read *Our Nig* due to its tiny circulation, he nonetheless was well aware of similar testimonials to the atrocities of Northern labor conditions). The closer one examines Wilson's market critique in light of Fitzhugh, the more it looks like a proslavery document.[29] Brownson's own dedication to the rights of Northern laborers in light of the brutal capitalist condition in fact brought him to the brink of embracing slavery. If Northern wage labor were not easier to escape than chattel slavery, and if there were no alternative but the two systems, Brownson would have dedicated his "preference to the slave system over that of labor at wages."[30] His ardent commitment to the plight of industrial workers came from his deep compassion for their crushing circumstances, which left him, and them, little reason to support abolition given the urgent need to cure the more immediate social ills of poverty and squalor. "Why is it," he asked rhetorically, "that so few of the real workingmen here are abolitionists?"[31] he asked, highlighting the elite class bias represented by the abolitionist movement, which Fitzhugh dubbed "Oi Polloi rats."[32]

DeBow's became Fitzhugh's medium for voicing his compassion for the laboring slave, and his assault of the elite North that turned a blind eye toward the sufferings of wage laborers. His attack on Northern industry reached its fullest expression when the editor granted him carte blanche access to the journal for the publication of his writings. "What the author of 'Cannibals All' writes and sends us," DeBow informed his readers in 1859, "we publish without hesitation, knowing him to be a bold, fearless, ingenuous [*sic*], learned, though somewhat eccentric writer."[33] No other noneditor authors enjoyed such privilege with any journal at the time; even the close-knit Transcendentalists were subject to rigorous screening by *Dial* editors, as Thoreau's difficulty placing his work there attests.

Of the hundreds of articles he published in *DeBow's* during the next three years—which by today's standards reads almost like a blog—Fitzhugh typically advanced arguments driven by a vision of cooperative capitalism with distinctly socialistic strains. If he was not railing against Northern industry, he was singing the praises of the domestic tranquility of plantation slavery, or proposing new government institutions to intervene into the commercial management of Southern business. The latter contributions led the charge for advancing the cotton industry through coordinated selling and investment patterns to build agriculture into manufacturing, particularly paper mills.

The "Florida Scheme," a particularly socialistic expression of this movement, proposed that one company should control the entire Southern crop through state charters. One contributor to *DeBow's* worried that Northern legislation might impede the plan, given "the present state of public feeling" of mounting resistance to slavery and socialized economic institutions. They aimed to establish "a charter to a great trading company, which proposes to monopolize all the cotton trade of the United States, and which, according to the showing of its friends, is to divide enormous profits."[34] Reinventing the concept of monopoly, Southerners colluded to abolish excessive oligopolistic competition that might weaken and divide them. From a united front they could increase cotton prices through the collectivist tactic of reducing planting and thus surplus supplies generated by large crop yields and European imports that drove prices down. The solution of "planters withholding a portion of their crops from market," as described in the *DeBow's* article, was universally recognized as impossible without concerted organization. The Florida Scheme *"cannot be carried into effect by individual action."* Therefore, "procuring the necessary concert" for planters to act in unison and synchronizing their withholding for the largest benefit of the whole to avoid individual losses was deemed essential.[35]

This collusive practice was initially born out of economic survival rather than dreams of destroying the North. These concerted socialized economic plans were originally methods of recovering from the storm of British occupation that wreaked havoc on their plantations so that they might keep pace with Northern industry. The South's deficiencies ranged from severely limited transportation networks to low literacy rates and a populace two and a half times lesser than the North's. John C. Calhoun would expound on this fact in defense of the South's minority status, playing victim to the tyranny of the North's disproportionately large population.[36] Whatever the South lacked in these areas, it compensated for, or at least attempted to, in coordinating the cotton trade in such a way that was contiguous with Fitzhugh's ideal domestic economy of steadfast support and providence. The South refused to stand by idly and watch its brethren smolder in an ash heap of economic ruin. Fitzhugh made clear in *Sociology for the South* that "Our system of improvements, manufactures, and mechanic arts, the building up of our cities, commerce, and education should go hand in hand."[37]

The building of *DeBow's* into a literary alliance for the defense of the Confederate States would take on precisely this cooperative complexion, spanning all phases of literary production, from paper production and printing to promotion and advertising. The six glowing reviews of Fitzhugh's works penned by Holmes in all the influential journals, along with DeBow's open invitation for Fitzhugh to publish his writings in his magazine at will (making him something of an informal coeditor, as he would contribute over a hundred articles from 1855 to 1867), gave Fitzhugh unprecedented publicity in precisely the venues that would most effectively promote his career. Since *DeBow's* boasted the widest circulation in the South, his capacity to publish virtually everything he wrote from 1859 on invested him with the mantle of the voice of the South. The three men worked together to make Fitzhugh's influence as powerful and broad as possible, not only to galvanize support for the South, but also to antagonize the North, and even win over converts. His impact on the North was profound. *Sociology of the South* raised Abraham Lincoln's ire more than any other proslavery book according to the president's law partner, and *Cannibals All!* incited William Lloyd Garrison's rage to the extent that the book received "considerably more attention than any other book in the history of the *Liberator*," according to C. Vann Woodward.[38]

OF PAPER MILLS AND SOUTHERN COMTEANS

The consolidation of resources and cooperative capitalism that helped construct the infrastructure of a sustainable literary marketplace tailored to the South's readership is not only visible in the early business of *DeBow's*. It is also apparent in an ongoing interest in big government, like the federal agency Fitzhugh proposed to support Southern commerce, and a myriad of other cooperative economic proposals with distinct socialistic leanings. One of the more explicit proposals toward this end appeared in an unsigned contribution to the January 1857 *DeBow's* issue entitled, "Mobile and Dog River Factory." In it, the author solicits investments in the Mobile Paper Mill in a kind of commercial declaration of independence from the Northern market. "The facilities presented for the manufacture of paper in the vicinity of Mobile are superior to those of any other part of the Union," the author proudly announced, highlighting its ideal situation near several streams that "provide an abundance of pure water" and access to "the material or stock necessary to make paper from 50 to 100 percent lower [in price] than at the north." The materials for the project would come from "an area of 300 miles of surrounding country, in which the worn out negro cotton clothing, and all other used up cotton garments," along with "the waste of cotton factories...could feed several ordinary paper mills." He notes that cotton production at Dog River Factory alone accounted for 43,000 pounds of such materials in 1856, which together with other sources "could be purchased at very low rates." Further, investment in Southern paper production promised to reverse the overreliance on paper coming primarily from the North, which gouged buyers forced to pay exorbitant prices for its extensive distribution covering up to 1,000 miles. Discarded "negro cotton clothing" and waste from the ubiquitous Southern cotton mills alone ironically offered the stuff of economic liberation from Northern tyranny over paper production, and by extension, the publishing industry. The Southern literary market might win independence from the North literally from the backs of slave laborers to remedy a condition in which "our printers and publishers are now entirely dependent on paper makers of other States, who often take advantage of the dependence, and foist upon them a worthless article." The true value in such an enterprise, he urged, lies in the power that accrues to the entire process of Southern literary production, in which "publishers [can order and obtain] such qualities and descriptions of paper as they might require" for a mutually profitable and economically efficient cooperative arrangement.[39]

The movement to diversify the cotton-based agricultural economy with manufacturing was widespread at the time in the South. Historian William Freehling has called it "The Great Reaction," which, as Tom Downey describes it, was "the need for...a domestic industrial sector, to wean the state from cotton monoculture and diminish its embarrassing reliance on the North for its manufactured necessities."[40] But the South was less interested in weaning itself from cotton than it was in expanding and diversifying its economy into the manufacturing sector. The great problem of the South was indeed how to raise the price of cotton, but investments in enterprises like the Mobile Paper Mill exemplify this sometimes reluctant embrace of manufacturing, which was considered by many a lamentable replication of evil Northern industrialism. South Carolinian James Henry Hammond typifies the calls for support of manufacturing in the South. "It makes an immense difference in the prosperity of any people, and especially an agricultural people," he remarked, "whether their workshops are at home or in other countries." The industrial manufacturing of the South, it became clear, would distinguish itself from the individualistic Northern laissez-faire scramble through a sense of collective mission, a cooperative capitalism woven from the fabric of cohesion, a brotherhood of factory owners "united in the same community with a class of industrious and enlightened agriculturalists." As in the Mobile Paper Mill proposal, industrialists and agrarians would work together and "mutually enrich and strengthen one and other" so that "citizens and our investors [would] encourage such investments" in cotton factories, which, by 1850, had proliferated significantly. The economy thus advanced from cotton plantations to cotton factories and—especially for the development of the literary marketplace to better serve the mass production needs of a periodical titan like *DeBow's*—paper mills. It is not by coincidence that the solicitation for investors in the Mobile Paper Mill would immediately precede "Book Notices." All ten volumes listed bore a New York publisher's imprint. By the 1850s, the South would collaborate to construct a literary market as the clearinghouse and core of their domestic industrial sector. That literary market's bestselling product would become *DeBow's*.

Like the general design for economic growth in the South, Fitzhugh's apologists were bent on mutually enriching and strengthening one another. Their views, however, were by no means uniform, and indeed would strain under the pressure to synthesize as cessation and war approached. The circle of *DeBow's* contributors, including Edmund Ruffin, Albert Taylor Bledsoe, William J. Grayson, George D. Armstrong, and Thornton Stringfellow, all acknowledged the influence of Fitzhugh's first book, *Sociology for the South, or the Failure of Free Society* (1854), but did not universally praise it. DeBow himself groused that the author was "a little fond of paradoxes, a little inclined to run a theory into extremes, and a little impractical."[41] Others complained of its inaccuracies, inconsistency, and overexuberant support of socialism. Yet Fitzhugh was making more explicit only the collectivist inclinations inherent in the commercial agenda that united them in the first place. Laissez-faire capitalism in the tradition of Adam Smith did not suit the needs of proslavery nearly as well as socialism, which, of course, resonates well with an institution that would systematically strip the autonomous rights of a large portion of its population. The free market, Fitzhugh argued in his magnum opus, *Cannibals All!, or Slaves Without Masters* (1857), was out of control and unnatural, while "slavery is the natural and normal condition of society. The situation of the North is abnormal and anomalous."[42] The appeal was magnetic, and galvanized the circle according to a paradigm of cooperative capitalism that ironically sought to humanize an otherwise barbaric capitalist condition with the kind nurturance and protective domestic tranquility of the benevolent paternalism that would come to characterize the main defense of slavery.

Any misgivings toward Fitzhugh's socialism were voiced mainly by DeBow, Jacob Cardozo, and Nathan Ware, who tried conversely to support slavery through Smithian economics. As the Genoveses note, "DeBow, almost alone, argued that industrialization would strengthen slavery; the others explicitly or implicitly believed that it would eventually render slave labor unprofitable."[43] They were less successful, however, than Fitzhugh since laissez-faire capitalism so commonly allied itself with the social contract theory of John Locke, which stipulated that citizens were entitled to private property and the autonomous pursuit of wealth and prosperity. Espousing Smith generally meant espousing Locke as well, and thus threw into question the viability of the slave system that places blacks outside of the system of social contract. Thus Cardozo and DeBow "strained to find support for unfree labor within the Smithian science of wealth," as Jeffrey Sklansky notes, while Fitzhugh's socialism painted a pleasing, gentle contrast to the harsh and barbaric world of the Northern market.[44]

The social theory of Auguste Comte, which sought to counter vestiges of the corruption that led to the French Revolution, provided the basis for Fitzhugh's defense of big government and cooperation between owners and laborers. Comte prescribed remedies for social ills he diagnosed in the economic and psychological dimensions of what he believed were repeated patterns in history. Indeed, Fitzhugh's portrait of the antebellum North appeared much like that of prerevolutionary France with its lawless and vicious treatment of the laboring masses and shameless tolerance of aristocratic decadence and self-indulgence. The "southern Comteans," as they called themselves, were all frequent contributors to *DeBow's*, despite the editor's initial skepticism toward their economics. DeBow nonetheless was well aware of the groundswell of support for the Comteans, the foremost of whom were Fitzhugh, Holmes, and Henry Hughes, and thus spread the influence of his journal through their names. Further,

DeBow's commercial interests, though not as effective in advocating slavery, complemented and completed their economic views. DeBow's practicality tempered Fitzhugh's idealism and affinity for Carlyle, whom most Comteans admired. The title for Fitzhugh's *Cannibals All!* came from Carlyle, whose dialectic was rich enough to accommodate both men, since DeBow had also chosen a quote from the Scottish philosopher for the early cover of his magazine proclaiming, "Commerce is King."[45]

The cohesion of the Comteans fueled their success. DeBow, for example, adjusted his laissez-faire leanings—seen in his opposition to trade unions and government intervention—to accommodate Fitzhugh's compassion for the laboring classes. DeBow admired both Holmes and Fitzhugh, for despite the editor's support of the market and limited government, he shared the common ground with them of compassion for the poor. This sympathy for laborers, of course, was vital to the defense of slavery. Even the rather digital economically driven DeBow found occasion for humanistic sentiment. "The poor must be fed," he conceded, "the miserable must be relieved or humanity ceases to perform her noble mission" in order to fulfill "an obligation to provide for the labouring classes."[46] Through such support of aid to the needy, DeBow effectively reconciled his Smithian economics with the Marxist social perspective of Fitzhugh and Holmes. Difference should not be overemphasized here, as the ostensible evidence reveals that DeBow championed both men by publishing them liberally, indeed the most sincere sign of support an editor has within his disposal. Unlike commercial icon Maunsel White who balked at slave trafficking, DeBow believed that merchants, the most ardent supporters of proprietary rights, were natural allies of slaveholders. But he was also careful to adopt Fitzhugh's belief in transforming slaves into the extended kin of the proverbial plantation family.

Holmes was a frequent correspondent of Fitzhugh's and one of his closest confidantes; the two shared trade secrets on rhetorical weapons and tactics, and even confessed the depravity of their own cause. In an 1855 letter to Holmes, Fitzhugh wrote, "I assure you, Sir, I see great evils in slavery, but in a controversial work I ought not to admit them."[47] The North's division into "hundreds of little guerrilla bands of Isms, each having its peculiar partisan tactics" justified such guile, Fitzhugh reasoned, and compelled them to "vary our mode of attack from regular cannonade to bushfighting, to suit the occasion." He compared proslavery's persuasive tactics to a series of rapid assaults—"in which facts, and argument, and rhetoric, and wit, and sarcasm, succeed each other in rapid iteration"—from a variety of stations, a metaphor aptly describing *DeBow's* diverse, yet cohesive circle of authors that formed a multilateral and diversified front in battle for the common goal of protecting the South's interests.[48]

These field generals of print held prominent status in the region, as their successes indicate. Henry Hughes's seminal *Treatise on Sociology, Theoretical and Practical*, published in 1854 when he was a twenty-five-year-old lawyer, was the standard social science textbook in the higher educational curriculum of the South until the end of the nineteenth century. Its own attempt to naturalize economic and racial domination took on the tone of hard-edged academic theory compared to Fitzhugh's rhetoric of love and affection. "Order is the essence of organization," Hughes pontificated in a typical staccato declaration of social law that characterizes the volume. His inflexible language had a huge following in Southern universities eager for a "science" of their social system. (DeBow himself would even occupy the chair's position at the University of Louisiana, now Tulane University, an honor that contradicts his twentieth-century reputation for lacking "the gifts of oratory and of politics, the twin keys of greatness in the South of that day."[49]) "In every society there must therefore be orderers and orderees," Hughes proclaimed in words measured to assuage any sense of guilt for the peculiar institution's oppressive power dynamic. "Some must order, some be ordered. These are subordinates, those superordinates. The supreme orderer of society is the sovereign power. This power associates, adapts, and regulates."[50] In this vein, Hughes believed slaves and the laboring classes should be insured or "warranted" to make a living, since economic development relied heavily upon their productivity. The government, he asserted as Fitzhugh had, must be interventionist to orchestrate a collectivist society and "labor obligations [by] establishing hours of work and rest, setting wages, and regulating and supervising the whole of economic life."[51] Competition and collectivism became staples of the Southern college curriculum that "taught free-market economics but rejected free-market social theory," the Genoveses explain. "Southern professors—unlike their...northern colleagues—made a case for having one without the other since they took slavery for granted as a superior social system."[52]

Unlike Fitzhugh, Hughes justified power through his dogged, sanctimonious prose that criminalized laissez-faire capitalism because it endorsed business transactions between blacks and whites—"economic amalgamation is sexual amalgamation" was his flat equation. Fitzhugh conversely wielded the language of protection and benevolence, exuding warmth that invoked filial love for slaves.[53] "Love," he purred, "and veneration for the family is with us not only a principle, but probably a prejudice and a weakness."[54] Fitzhugh attacked liberty in the North for unleashing a more lurid brand of love as seen in the rise of the "New York free love saloon."[55] His condemnation of the sociological effects of this sort of affection, like Hughes's objection to doing business with blacks, established a framework of academic social science theory (that, along with Comte, was some of the first of that species ever penned). Fitzhugh frequently identified Northern Christian socialism's liberalism with excessive tolerance for the sexual perversity of "love saloons," sounding the note repeatedly in variations of "Free Love Villages...patronized and approved by the 'Higher Classes'" in a portrait of free society engaged in the "total overthrow of the Family and all other existing social, moral, religious and governmental institutions."[56] Yet female slaves like Hester in Frederick Douglass's *Narrative* were routinely exploited for their masters' erotic gratification and for breeding. These charges were perhaps the most hurtful to the South; Mary Chestnut, famous antebellum plantation diarist, would lament the moral corruption of Southern men who engaged in miscegenation.[57] Masters, in the Genoveses' words, "deeply resented the charge of deliberate slave-breeding by other than generally respectable methods designed to encourage a stable family life."[58]

Few defenses of such specific "breeding" practices arose from proslavery, which instead emphasized the South as home to the true domestic institution in comparison to the immoral condition brought about by the Northern free market. The domestic trope and appeals for larger government shared the common ground of associationism. As war neared, these appeals mollified an otherwise increasingly imperialistic visions, especially the grandiose political prophecy of a Southern empire extending from Central America to California and other bizarre plans for the annexation of Cuba and the importation of Chinese coolies. These theories crowded the pages of the 1849–1851 issues of *DeBow's*, a phase notable for the magazine's decided shift away from agricultural and commercial fare toward proslavery arguments. DeBow capitulated to this increasingly political intellectual climate in the years leading up to Fitzhugh's 1853 *Sociology of the South*, the first of his two major books. Fitzhugh's insistence upon benevolent patriarchal relations with slaves as family members rather than as property captured the popular imagination in 1850 and 1851 when his first independent publications appeared. Both were pamphlets issued out of Richmond later placed in the appendix of *Sociology for the South*. These works likely prompted DeBow to recant his hard-line commercial stance for the more (quasi)humanistic emphasis on slavery as a domestic institution.

Fitzhugh's influence on DeBow is evident in the editor's July 1850 article, "The Origins, Progress, and Prospects of Slavery," which was Part II of his four-part series on "Slavery in the United States." The series established the template for proslavery thought that his journal would encourage for the next decade. It set out to achieve a balance between common requisite defenses that had become clichés of the coterie and the fresher insights advanced by Fitzhugh that sought to distance itself from allegations of force, cruelty, and dominance. DeBow makes what were then conventional defenses rooted in religion (God's curse of the black servant Ham to a life of slavery and the Isrealite's slave trafficking foremost among them), classical antiquity, and colonial American history. But he is clear to note, however, just two months after his article appeared that the religious argument had grown stale. He rather reluctantly accepted an unsigned piece for the September 1850 issue entitled "Slavery and the Bible," noting, "This paper has been handed us for publication, and, as it contains a summary of the Bible argument for slavery, we give it place, though the subject is growing hacknied."[59] If biblical defenses were becoming retrograde and inconsequential—a stand-off between Northern and Southern theologians had been devolving into teleology—then the cutting edge lie in works like Fitzhugh's 1849 pamphlet, *Slavery Justified*, a dynamic assault on the free market aimed toward humanizing slavery's coarse barbaric image. Free society, he argued, had failed given the examples of the French Revolution and the corruption of the Northern states. He located the failure in the economic friction and political strife that eventuated in a ragged social condition in which "all society is combined to oppress the poor and weak minded." The North's individualism of "'Every man for himself, and devil take the hindmost' [that] is the moral which liberty and free competition inculcate," he roundly rejected. Benevolent paternalism of Southern slavery thus becomes a beacon of hope in all of this chaos, a safe haven for blacks who would otherwise be mauled by the free market as autonomous citizens because "half of mankind are but grown-up children [and thus] liberty is as fatal to the Negro as it would be to children."[60] Both whites and blacks equally suffer under the condition of Northern free market capitalism according to Fitzhugh, whose argument implies that poor whites should also be enslaved for their own protection from economic exploitation. Fitzhugh, however, stops short of drawing that conclusion in the chapter, "Negro Slavery" in *Cannibals All!*, in which he makes a case for the "peculiar" predicament of the black race that necessitates their institutionalization under masters and overseers for life.[61]

Although DeBow's article never flirts with the possibility of enslaving poor whites as Fitzhugh does, DeBow nonetheless combines his colleague's signature rhetorical tactics with his own unmistakable love of the ledger and quantitative statistics. Less concerned with commercial competition with the North, Debow's statistics illustrate slave versus free black populations to demonstrate that slavery was already present in the North and all but forced upon the South from the nation's colonial era forward. His goal was not to show how slavery could be a means toward greater profits to defeat the mighty Northern industry. Northern slave trading from the prior era emerges as much worse than the current Southern one. "Rhode Island, the greatest of all slave traders," he wrote, "'doubted if slaves should be baptized, as then they might become free,'" in a heinous deprivation of God's grace for the sake of their captivity.[62] Southern slaves, DeBow asserts, are always deemed worthy of Christ.

DeBow is careful to dissociate proslavery from belligerence at this stage in the early 1850s, though when war approached, he was perhaps the most bloodthirsty of Southerners, sounding his battle cry with fury by establishing the "Southern Confederacy" department of his journal. Although his venomous support of secession preceded that of Fitzhugh, who was the longest unionist holdout among both the Comteans and *DeBow's* circle, DeBow never attached slavery to Southern economic competition against the North after his 1850 article. This new allegiance to Fitzhugh's paternalist argument prompted DeBow to separate his familiar advocacy of cotton's commercial importance from the issue of slavery. This was tactical, of course, and DeBow recognized its rhetorical power by leading off his 1850 article with the claim that slaves were more than property to be worked into the ground and dominated into submission. In a direct echo of Fitzhugh, DeBow urges that the notion of slaves as soulless property is abhorrent "because it gives the absolute power and control, not only *over*, but *in*, the subject without any limitation or restraint...it exists by my will, and I may change, alter and *destroy* it. No such power is, or perhaps ever has been, claimed or exercised over the slave since the Christian world first abandoned the barbarous doctrine that an infidel was not entitled to the rights of a human being."[63]

The shift here is remarkable, for it signals that slaves are human beings with rights to be respected, individuals not to be tyrannized, spirits not to be commoditized. For the apologists' propaganda mill, this meant slaves would be discussed not as a valuable labor resource to be capitalized upon for the production of cotton to defeat Northern industry, but as members of the human community within the protective enclave of the Southern plantation family. DeBow's affinity for commercial metaphors surfaces in his image of the slave as apprentice, a collaborative colleague in trade. Of course, the image is utterly bankrupt given the aims of authentic apprenticeship toward mastery of the trade and autonomy to sell one's skill in the free market, much in the way Frederick Douglass struggled to do in the caulking trade (that initially robs him of the fruits of his labor) in his *Narrative*. DeBow's apprentice slave is thus much like Fitzhugh's slave in that he is a perpetual child caught in a state of stunted growth. The contours are strikingly similar, the justification equally galling. He reasons that "the power exercised over a slave is far more analogous to that exercised upon an indentured apprentice than to any power claimed over a mere chattel. The apprenticeship may be as *involuntary* as the slavery in its incipiency and its continuance, and very often is. The apprentice and the slave are both for a term of years, the one being for a life term," he affirms. In true Fitzhugh fashion, we find even this commercially savvy, hard-bitten self-made editor rail against the despotic rule of "the capitalists, all the world over, and especially in England, over his operatives."[64] DeBow was no factory owner, but his advocacy of both slavery and cotton metaphorically made him such despite his refusal to present them as mutually dependent economic entities.

Peculiar Innovations

DeBow's rhetoric of the permanent apprentice to describe slavery was crucial to spreading a more dignified image of black identity in the South. Blacks were worthy of learning trades, if not fully mastering them, and thus were capable of education in DeBow's view. Although DeBow and Fitzhugh's circle did not advocate such permanent apprenticeships in medicine, law, or the ministry, a more radical faction of proslavery did. Their most potent voice was Harrison Berry, whose antiabolitionist slave narrative, *Slavery and Abolitionism, as Viewed by a Georgia Slave* (1861), is the only one of its type extant and has remained virtually invisible to scholars. An African American born into slavery on David Berry's Georgia plantation, Harrison was ten years old when he "was placed in the law office of John V. Berry, son of the former."[65] As an office assistant, he had been exposed to legal rhetoric as well as proslavery argumentation throughout his life.

His enthusiasm for the Bible eventually led him into a career in the Protestant ministry after the Civil War. His slave narrative thus provided crucial testimony positioning him as something of an expert witness on behalf of proslavery with the oratory of a preacher and the precision of an attorney. Berry defends slavery based on Divine Law, citing religious principles of fellowship and brotherly love to frame his unionist antiagitation argument. "It is well known that the New Testament teaches peace—peace—peace, prosperity and happiness," he pontificates. "To preserve peace in a country," he insists, "even at a sacrifice, is the best mode of sustaining the country."[66] This peaceful pose, however, is undercut by his vicious attacks on the most visible abolitionist figureheads, including his Northern counterpart, Frederick Douglass as well as Abraham Lincoln. One letter of authenticity in the volume's front matter proudly relates that Berry "would let Fred Douglass and other Abolitionists know, that the slaves of the South were not fools enough to believe that they were benefitting them, or even intended to try to benefit them."[67] He lights into Lincoln's Inaugural for its crude anarchy of mob rule, "a mixed up affair of colored and white" that he deplores with a class bias cultivated from his apprenticeship in his master's law office. In addition to Douglass, he takes on another free black Northerner, Charles L. Redmond, for his comment during a Boston antislavery convention. The erudite Berry deplores the "blasphemous language" and coarse crudity of Redmond's barb, "'remembering Washington as a Slaveholder, I could spit on him.'" The slight was met with the mirth and glee of all but the well to do and "conservative men who groaned" with disapproval.[68]

Berry functioned as living evidence of black refinement in the context of slavery, just as Douglass did in the free North with his eloquent speaking and writing. "In the native wilds [of Africa] he is a savage," one endorsement for Berry asserted, "with no hope for improvement. A free man among white people, he is inferior, and cannot rise to a level with his neighbors" due to inherent disadvantages built into an unfair and racist market for employment that Douglass himself railed against. The uneven playing field meant the black man worked "when in health under disadvantages that few can overcome, and when sick, he has no one to care for him." All the abolitionist efforts serve to "only draw the cords of servitude more tightly around him."[69] Berry indeed provided through lofty rhetoric and impassioned Christian appeals to peace backed with an impressive theological frame of reference precisely the evidence the South desired to back one of proslavery's more innovative pretentions to liberalism and the uplifting of the black. Berry assures us that slavery has made him better and provided him with a life superior to those free ones of Africa and the North.

Berry supplied pundits like E.N. Elliott of Mississippi, editor of *Cotton Is King*, an 1860 collection of proslavery arguments, with ready evidence of the "results [that] have already been achieved by American slavery, in the elevation of the negro race in our midst; as they are now as far superior to the natives of Africa, as the whites are to them."[70] Dr. S.A. Cartwright of Louisiana, a contributor to *Cotton Is King*, favored the education of blacks (if not their emancipation) because of the benefits that purportedly accrued to an individual like Berry. Cartwright accounted the value of the "educated negro, one whose intellect and morals have been cultivated, [to be] worth double the price of the wild, uncultivated, black barbarian of Cuba and will do twice as much work, do it better and with less trouble."[71] Further, "it is not the ignorant semi-barbarian that the master or overseer intrusts [sic] with his keys, his money, his horse or his gun, but the most intelligent of the plantation—one whose intellect and morals have undergone the best training," he reasons.[72] This measure was designed to conscript the slave into the plantation's process of managerial capitalism. Education not only inculcates trusted managers of the valued estate, but also produces speakers on behalf of the peculiar institution at large in its more eloquent exemplars like Berry. Berry argues for peace, and promotes slavery as a condition conducive to the education and civilization of blacks. The teleology and self-serving logic of all of these arguments for training of slaves into skilled or managerial labor, of course, makes a charade of advancement.[73] Well-developed individuals may advance, but have no means of transcending the system of servitude. Individuals may succeed, if only to see the fruits of their labor and their power systematically feed back into the perpetuation of slavery's existence. Indeed, advancement is limited to positions as aggrandized security guards of the plantation and protocorporate middle managers to galvanize the institution with bureaucratic support for its own self-preservation. Such education stops short of granting blacks any autonomy or real power in both cases, but instead exploits them to perpetuate and enhance the power of the peculiar institution. Proslavery was ingenious at hi-jacking black uplift for labor beyond manual fieldwork in order to attach a managerial position to some slave work to better serve the plantation's financial interests while also providing a fresh moral defense through the appearance of professionally developing slaves. (Tellingly, much of corporate America would apply the same plantation mentality to the treatment of their employees in the next century, as dramatized in David Mamet's acerbic Reagan era play, *Glengarry Glen Ross*.) Proslavery, in essence, had thus invented a "professionalized" vision of the slave's role, as embodied by Berry's position as fixture and permanent apprentice of the legal offices of his owner. After all, no convincing black proslavery narrative would have come from the pen of an African condemned to pick cotton his entire life. Berry readily acknowledges his privileged position and, since he writes from within the hegemonic confines of slavery, he can do no more than advocate for peace. Indeed, the range of his argumentation is shackled by proslavery's rhetorical parameters, and thus he winds up supporting the existing power structure much in the way Catharine Beecher supports patriarchal dominance and the lack of female voting rights in her antebellum *Treatise of Domestic Economy*. Just as Berry would adopt a regressive hegemonic conservatism with the rhetoric of peace, Beecher would similarly instruct women to "assume the office of a mediator and an advocate of peace" and avoid agitation at all costs. She takes her authority from the gender code of behavior that would suggest that vehement opposition to anything, let alone slavery, was not lady like. She sharply rebuked Angelina Grimke in 1837, for example, for "exciting and regulating public sentiment," which she believed was a gross impropriety that overlooked the importance of "promoting a spirit of candour, forbearance, charity and peace" in tune with the cult of true womanhood.[74]

Berry's argument conformed to Fitzhugh's widely popular claim that servitude was universal and thus inevitable,[75] which led authors like Chancellor Harper of South Carolina to characterize the South as anticapitalist. Compulsory labor, according to Harper, and *"servitude* is the condition of civilization," but the social structure built around it need not be antagonistic and competitive.[76] Fitzhugh believed that human nature was not indeed vicious, but only that the Northern capitalist climate warped and perverted it into being thus whereas the South brought out humanity's natural inclinations toward sympathy and love.[77] Harper's argument is typical of the South's—and its most visible literary coteries'—self-definition in opposition to "the intense competition of civilized life, and the excessive cheapness of labor" in the North, where "men will labor for a bare subsistence, and less than a competent subsistence." The "domestic institution" of slavery bore the costs of providing material comforts throughout the full life span of its laborers, "rearing them in infancy and supporting them in sickness or old age," as Harper writes in a nearly identical claim to Berry's. Conversely, "the employer of free laborers obtains their services during the time of their health and vigor" only, leaving them in the cold during their most vulnerable times. Further, Harper argues that slaves are insulated from the fluctuations of the market unlike Northern laborers, whose earnings and jobs vanish when the economy slows. "If the income of every planter of the Southern States were permanently reduced one-half, or even much more than that, it would not take one jot from the support of comforts of the slaves," Harper brags with characteristic hyperbole. Labor's higher value in the South, according to such arguments, is consonant with the image of agrarian peace and tranquility, an idyllic pastoral portrait at odds with industry. The agricultural superiority of the South, primarily dictated by the favorable growing climate was often cited as proof of how "nature herself indicates that agriculture should be the predominating employment in Southern countries, and manufactures in Northern." Whereas "commerce is necessary to both," the manufacturing industry "of articles of luxury, elegance, convenience, or necessity" of the North sharply contrasts with Southern agriculture that "has less of the commercial spirit" in Harper's view.[78] The South thus becomes associated with a distinctly socialized economy averse to exploiting cheap labor and peddling its manufactured goods to an increasingly materialistic mass of consumers. Yet Harper's allowance that "commerce is necessary to both" resonates with DeBow's aggressive promotion of paper mills and other manufacturing plants in the South, such as the Dogwood Mill discussed earlier. Chancellor Harper's portrait of the South driven by less of "the commercial spirit" was thus not entirely accurate in a larger sense, as competition and commercial interests comprised the chief subject of *DeBow's*, which was the most widely read journal in the antebellum South. The South did not have *less* of a commercial spirit, but more precisely, a commercial spirit of a decidedly *different* kind that was more socialized and cooperative. Indeed, commercial production was a focus. But did this mean slaveholders were more laissez-faire than they were letting on, more like the Northern industrialists they assailed? Production method may have indeed matched that of the North, but cooperative capitalistic practice was wider reaching and more collaborative than in the North, especially in its drive for more coordinated big government. Indeed, thinkers in the North may have promoted socialistic answers to the free market's woes, but the South's business practice accorded more closely with socialistic principle, ironically enough, in their unique manner with which they socialized the formation of mill and manufactory production, two mainstays of industrial capitalism.

Given the pervasive influence of the *DeBow's* circle on a diverse range of authors like Berry, Elliot, Cartwright, and Harper, the notion of a literary circle should be reconsidered in the case of the antebellum South. The diversity of thought that issued forth from *DeBow's* served the purposes of the wider literary market, and became fodder for an expansive network of literary producers in and beyond the periodical press. By giving Fitzhugh the privilege to publish anything he wrote, DeBow turned his journal into a veritable propaganda factory, producing the ideas that the region would then reproduce and disseminate even in more literary venues like the *Southern Literary Messenger*. At least one contributor to the *Messenger* grew weary of the repetitive and circular nature of the proslavery arguments that saturated their pages, testifying to the *Messenger*'s distaste for bowing to this and other popular trends they lagged behind in the periodical press. DeBow's commercial emphasis was now wedded to the mission of educating the entire region on "all the standard treatises" in defense of slavery so that the South might better "know the 'reason' of her 'faith.'"[79] The *Messenger* never took on the proslavery mission with quite this zeal, as its editor, John R. Thompson, typified how its contributors felt their literary interests had been subsumed by proslavery propaganda. Thompson weighs in on how such arguments have "been stated over and over again...viewed from all possible lights, turned this way and that, considered from beginning to conclusion and from conclusion the beginning." He complained that the *Messenger* had been saturated with what *DeBow's* had enthusiastically embraced due to its consonance with their commercial interests. "Upon the abstract proposition of slavery, its justice, its humanity, its happy social consequences," he complained, there was "nothing to be said that cannot be found in the volumes of the *Messenger*."[80] The *Messenger*'s financial woes that DeBow was so openly committed to avoiding brought it to the brink of collapse in September 1861. Thompson's anxiety was desperate and his hostility toward rivals vehement in detailing what the journal needed to do to recover. He sarcastically assured readers that recovery would come in adopting "all of the most trashy, contemptible and popular features of *Harper, Godey, Frank Leslie,* the *Herald, Home Journal, Ledger*," and others, promising to "have nothing but pictures the latest news and fashions" along with "little dabs of light literature *a la* Fanny Fern."[81] He takes on a mock Bonneresque tone in proclaiming that "no expense...be spared" in offering "any sum for Mrs. Emma E.D.N.O.P.Q.R.S.T.U.V.W.X.Y.Z. Southworth." Thompson is all too aware of his thriving Southern rival *DeBow's*, observing that during the onset of war "even the staunchest journals have been compelled to retrench and economise"; even the mighty "DeBow's *Review* is published but once in two months" in order to survive compromised economic conditions of the trade that left editors with "bad ink, a scarcity of paper and of printers, a great falling off in contributions, and almost a suspension in payments."[82]

So where Fitzhugh set the standard for the propaganda mill, Southern literary markets were challenged to diversify literary productivity, from the construction of their own paper mills to the expansion of the book trade into proslavery novels. J.W. Randolph was one of the largest and most successful publisher-booksellers of the South during the antebellum period. Randolph's success came in large part from his legal line of books that changed from a Virginian to a Confederate focus, but he also sold regional and political histories in great quantities. Although novels refuting *Uncle Tom's Cabin* appeared on his stock lists, only three out of fifty-eight titles about slavery were issued by Randolph's company, which suggests Southern readers were not singularly obsessed with the issue of slavery in the book market, while virtually insatiable for the topic in their periodicals.[83] Southerners, like their Northern counterparts, looked to journals for coverage and commentary on timely issues and controversies like slavery, and purchased books mainly for what they hoped would be their timeless value. This was in part due to the fact that the average book cost over ten times the price of a single issue of a magazine like DeBow's, and that magazines and newspapers were ephemeral reading, which readers discarded and did not store and admire like books. It is telling that the bestselling novelist of the South, Augusta Jane Evans, rose to fame through the popularity of *Beulah* (1859) and *Macaria; or, Altars of Sacrifice* (1864), which were not polemical proslavery works like Catherine E. Rush's *North and South* (1859), or J.W. Page's *Uncle Robin in His Cabin in Virginia and Uncle Tom without One in Boston* (1858). Evans's corporatist collectivist plots and themes advocated big government and backed Comte's theory of "carefully guided social change to overcome social antagonism," as Genovese describes it.[84] If Evans bore the impression of Holmes and Fitzhugh, her novels also resonated with the entrepreneurial spirit of DeBow, as they equally recognized the power of commerce in the development of the South's collective soul, as witnessed in one character's off-hand observation that "commerce and agriculture" were the staples of Southern autonomy.[85]

The novels countering Stowe only amounted to a small wave in the sea of the Southern literary market. For the most part, the readers of the region were thus clearly taking their information about proslavery and war developments, and indeed the very credo of Confederacy, from *DeBow's*. Significantly, Stowe would inspire Southern women writers to enter the fray not only in fiction, but also in the far more widely consumed periodical press. Just one month after Stowe's novel appeared in serialized form, Louisa McCord became the first female contributor to *DeBow's*, issuing an assault not so much toward Northern women as toward Britain's position in the matter. By the mid-1850s, however, such arguments, along with McCord's status, gave way to the insurgency of Fitzhugh, Holmes, and Hughes, which eventually took over when the Kansas controversy mounted and became increasingly focused on slavery.

Randolph's success did not issue forth from fiction or proslavery propaganda, but instead, his stock in trade that sold best was almanacs, agriculture, and business related titles, precisely the area in which DeBow had originally invested. The book trade did overlap with the periodical press in the form of Thornton Stringfellow's *Scriptural and Statistical Views in Favor of Slavery* (1856). Stringfellow was a statistic citing preacher and regular contributor to *DeBow's*, bearing a curious combination of evangelical fervor and quantitative rigor that DeBow especially appreciated since he had grown weary of conventional biblical apologists. That curious combination of economics and spirituality, of ethics and politics is precisely what guided the rise of Southern ideology before the Civil War. Were it not for the cooperative capitalism with its socialistic business practice and systematic standard of mutual support and promotion, the vehicle of *DeBow's*, and the career of Fitzhugh would not have flourished to the extent that it did. The unique approach to the literary market and coterie culture, the management and editorial practice of the journal itself, all speak to the larger shifting attitudes toward the market prevalent in the South at the time. Their reinvention of commercial culture toward a more socialized model than that of the North was thus essential to the formation of Southern ideology prior to the Civil War. The Gilded Age, as we will see, brought even more pronounced manifestos of socialism in literary coteries like Bellamy's Boston Club. It is to such literary institutions and their promotional practice on behalf of creative writing careers that we now turn.

Conclusion: The Boston Bellamy Club, Rand's Objectivists, and Iowa Writers' Workshop

The unifying principle behind Garrison and Fitzhugh's circles, in part, was competitive spite, a pattern confirming Eric Hoffer's dark observation that "Hatred is the most accessible and comprehensive of all unifying agents."[1] The prospect of a common enemy did indeed galvanize some writers behind a single cause, as in the case of Fitzhugh's apologists, but it also splintered and factionalized others like Garrison's abolitionists, who quarreled over how, precisely, they should combat slavery. The Transcendentalists, despite their reputation for preposterous optimism that Melville satirized in his novel *The Confidence Man*, shared an aversion to the commercialization of culture, literary and otherwise, as they encouraged each other on to greater and more daring assaults on the market. Emerson had particularly harsh words for abolitionists peddling their cause through commercial channels. In "Self-Reliance," he denounced the "angry bigot who assumes this bountiful cause of Abolition" for slaves in Barbados with "a tenderness for black folk a thousand miles off" when America's own cried for their attention. "Varnishing their hard, uncharitable ambition" for the benefit of distant slaves, these abolitionists traded genuine sympathy for the lacquered veneer of transnational commercial enterprise, Emerson argued.[2] That "angry bigot," as Martha Schoolman recently observed, may not "refer to any particularly offensive abolitionist, but rather to any Garrisonian activist true to his or her leader's methods."[3] In refusing to allow a "sect" or "community of opinion" to eclipse his own individual voice, Emerson chided writers who hid behind their larger affiliations and thus diminished authorship into little more than a group stamp. "The section to which we belong" becomes the brand name of authorial identity by which the consumer can anticipate the rhetorical position of the writing itself, all too often with deadening regularity according to Emerson, so that "If I know your sect, I anticipate your argument."[4] Beyond simply advocating for individualism, Emerson employs the language of coterie competition much in the way Garrison had by denouncing the moral position of a rival circle to promote not only his own ethical superiority, but by extension, that of his Transcendentalists.

More than a series of ongoing verbal jousts of hostile attacks and defensive retreats, competition between antebellum literary circles manifested itself through the hotly contested and precarious concept of sympathy, which had become something of a cultural fetish at the time. Far from a social matrix of competing doctrines of hate, the major American literary circles of the nineteenth century allocated much of their resources toward establishing the prevailing and definitive approach to human sympathy.[5] If I know your sect, Emerson might have said, I anticipate your argument *about sympathy*. The question of true compassion—authentic bonhomie rather than narrowly self-interested "hard uncharitable ambition"—was ironically the source of the most heated competition in the literary market because each coterie's ethical status was at stake in its definition. Such ethical status was intimately linked to winning the moralistically inclined American mass readership. Much of antebellum literary competition centered on which circle could package and promote sympathy the most effectively.[6] Indeed, Emerson's own acerbic upbraiding of a particular sect of trendy and increasingly professional abolitionists in "Self-Reliance" (in perhaps his most notorious growl) promoted his own alternative form of brutally honest compassion in which "Your goodness must have some edge to it, else it is none."[7] Refusing to permit the Garrisonians to speak for his own Transcendentalists, Emerson denounces their claims to moral high ground and thus the nation's hearts and minds. Although Emerson's distanced skepticism toward abolitionism in general softened into something of a reluctant acceptance by the late 1840s, he would nonetheless never want to be mistaken for a Garrisonian, a loyalist to Tappan's "new organization," or one of Gerrit Smith's up-state New York militants. When viewed in light of coterie competition, such signal moments of romantic disaffiliation in canonical writings like Emerson's appear contiguous with the periodical press's culture of contention that figures like Garrison fostered, and others, like Child, fled. Authors like Child were inclined to return to the original principle of sympathy—toward slaves and fellow abolitionists—because the hostile sectarian competition that came to characterize the literary market threatened to eclipse it altogether. True sympathy was worth rescuing not because it offered an escape from the market, but because it promised a civilized and humane method of coming to terms with it.

Antebellum authors frequently referenced competing circles in their writings, conscripting them as allies and marking them as rivals, building bridges for social capital and, in some cases, tearing them down. Such gestures were so pervasive that they became embedded in the literature itself as emblems of coterie allegiance, each distinguished by a unique approach toward the management of exigencies of emergent industrial capitalism for a sympathetic American culture and society. Coteries transacted literary business both by competing with rival circles and by promoting their own talent in ways that indicated their full engagement in the culture's larger preoccupation with economic survival during this key phase in the development of capitalism. Quarrels took place everywhere from Emerson's essays to the polemics of Garrison's *Liberator*. Knickerbockers found themselves scrambling to maintain the aura and mystique of their early golden era, with writers brokering and bartering to draw on Irving's magic for their own careers. The *New York Ledger* would become a titan of the periodical market in part because its editor, Robert Bonner, could acquire the most popular writers from competing magazines, making his a veritable New York Yankees of antebellum journals. This era witnessed not only Bonner's pioneering editorial capitalism, but also Elizabeth Peabody's pioneering work to bring women a greater voice in her own Transcendentalist circle at her Boston bookstore. Indeed, laissez-faire opened the market to women like Fuller and Peabody who not only entered the editorial ranks, but also revolutionized methods of literary agency, proving that savvy business could put men and women intellectuals on equal conversational footing. Frontal assaults on rival coteries were carefully appended with alternative moral systems of belief inevitably bearing on alternative economies. The South was the most dexterous in this regard, as *DeBow's* filled its pages with Fitzhugh's benevolent paternalism of warm plantation domesticity with the Southern land of plenty drawn in sharp contrast to the cold, needy industrial North.

If the antebellum South, along with factions of the Transcendentalists led by labor advocates like Orestes Brownson, had planted the seeds of socialist thought by exposing the limitations of individualism and free market capitalism in antebellum America, the stunning emergence of Edward Bellamy in the Gilded Age would cultivate it to near fruition. Bellamy emerged in the context of rampant industrialization that led to the 1886 labor strikes associated with the Haymarket Affair in Chicago in which dozens were killed. The riot "became the focus for all the raging passions of the day, including radicalism, mass immigration, and labor activism."[8] The outbreak of violence captured

Bellamy's imagination and inspired him to publish *Looking Backward* shortly thereafter in 1888. Readers of his socialist utopian novel then formed the Boston Bellamy Club, which led to the first concerted socialist literary movement. The movement would make its most significant impact not in literature, however, but in the realm of politics, by creating a party that would back a potential candidate for the president of the United States. Not only proslavery writers but also most literary circles in this book anticipate the Bellamy Club's Gilded Age antimaterialism that eventually took on potent political dimensions leading to the formation of the socialist party in 1901 under Eugene V. Debs. The anticommercial Transcendentalist writers, for example, share misgivings about the market—its excessive materialism, endless division of labor, dehumanizing mechanization of production, debt, unequal distribution of capital, spiritual impoverishment—voiced in *Looking Backward*. At the ideological opposite end of the spectrum, Bonner's literary capitalists of the *New York Ledger* celebrated the free market in ways that anticipated Ayn Rand's Objectivists of the next century. Literary circles now are highly controlled, credentialed, and institutionalized in higher education creative writing programs. The Iowa Writers' Workshop continues to produce the most successful careers in the literary market by subjecting students to a harsh critical climate designed to disabuse them of romantic ideals of authorship and thus prepare them for the competitive rigors of today's publishing industry. This brief history to the present of American literary circles, of course, is not intended to be comprehensive, but rather seeks to highlight the most influential and diverse literary movements that emerged from their nineteenth-century forerunners who had also first forged their identities in response to key shifts in the development of capitalism.

Bellamy's *Looking Backward: 2000–1887* has been called "one of the most important literary events of the century," especially in terms of its "direct intellectual influence on numbers."[9] Bellamy scholar Sylvia E. Bowman has positioned it as the most influential single work on the political formation of the American left, noting that Bellamy held much greater sway over the United States than even Karl Marx. Bellamy's appeal had much to do with the distinctly nationalistic brand of collectivism he promoted in the pages of his tremendously popular bestselling novel. Enthusiasm for the novel developed into clubs, which initially aimed to educate its members in the principles of an economy run entirely by the federal government and the advantages that accrue to a mutually supportive, noncompetitive social environment like the one detailed in Boston of the year 2000 in *Looking Backward*. Club members rallied around the charismatic Bellamy just as the *Liberator* and *Ledger* staffs modeled both their politics and their approach toward authorship after their respective editors. Likewise, Rand would transform an informal New York reading group into the most radical capitalist cult of twentieth-century America. Social activism and zeal were the mainstays of both circles. By the time the Iowa Writers' Workshop formed in the middle of the next century, the urgency and the intensity seem to have been drained out of the American literary circle along with such star power, with the notable exceptions of Ginsberg's Beats and Frank O'Hara's Greenwich Village bohemians. It would seem that once institutionalized and couched in the gauzy inconsequential pedagogy of humanities higher education, authorship becomes soft, domesticated, and thus as harmless and vacant as the stares on the faces of the husband and wife agrarians of the Midwest prairie in Grant Wood's iconic painting, *American Gothic*. The Iowa Writers' Workshop, however, circulated a different story, granting degrees for creative writing, which had been done for years for the fine arts, but never for imaginative prose and poetry. The Workshop would rapidly transform itself into a Julliard for authors. Rather than isolating writers from the market, the Workshop became the market, as savage competition ensued between students in the race for this gold-plated degree that all but guarantees success in the publishing industry. The cliché advice to budding professional writers continues to emphasize the importance of a powerful agent; better advice would be to obtain an MFA from the Workshop, perhaps the most powerful agency in the history of American literature from 1941 to the present, marking higher education's appropriation of the role of professional publicist.[10]

Bellamy's Socialists

The Boston Bellamy Club may have begun as a fan club of *Looking Backward* enthusiasts, but it rapidly turned into a niche of producers in its own right. The Club's passion for the novel was not a consumer's fanaticism that characterizes today's J.K. Rowling followers, for example. Instead, the Bellamy cohort took its cue from the "industrial army" of the novel's socialist utopia, and thus gathered with an uncommon zeal for collaborative production. In its developmental phase from 1888 to 1891, The Bellamy Club consisted of intellectuals already deeply invested in the author's collectivist vision and who, therefore, naturally shared resources and labor in accomplishing their agenda of spreading the morality of socialism, educating new members, and producing and disseminating publications. The founders consisted of fifty members led by Cyrus Willard, journalist for the *Boston Globe*, and Sylvester Baxter, a reputed editorialist for the *Boston Herald*, who just one month after their first meeting formed the Nationalist Education Association. This more politically earnest moniker reflected the group's support for Bellamy's goal of socializing American democracy, while also recommending the author's strident nationalism. The NEA elected Bellamy as president and immediately began the publication of the *Nationalist* under the seasoned and expert guiding hands of Willard and Baxter. The inner circle was careful to screen out dilettantes and fans from its ranks, only allowing members into the NEA who had ample time and willingness to work for them, and especially welcoming those with finances to bankroll their enterprise. The plan worked. Word spread quickly and support was evident in the rise in attendance from the inaugural meeting of 50 loyalists to the 2,000 who attended the second annual gathering at Boston's Tremont Temple in December of 1889.

Initial interest in the Boston Bellamy Club sprang from a group called the Theosophists, who advocated the peaceful overthrow of the capitalist system Bellamy's novel had suggested would naturally occur by the year 2000 once citizens realized the damaging results of the free market—labor strikes, urban blight, poverty caused by the grossly unequal distribution of wealth—were intolerable. Thomas Wentworth Higginson described this group as "a band of young proselytes who, instead of believing that what [Bellamy] says is too good to be true, believe that it is too good not to be true; and are ready to proclaim its teachings as at least a temporary gospel of good news."[11] Led by Willard, the Theosophists were particularly attracted to Bellamy's aggressive eradication of class-consciousness, tension, conflict, hate, and injustice. A strong Bellamy following grew in California when the concept of industrial cooperation captured the imagination of Theosophists there, who had been encouraged to join the Nationalists by H.P. Blavatsky, author of *The Key to Theosophy* (1889). Blavatsky's treatise, which sparked a string of Theosophist society branches throughout California, eventually organized themselves into Nationalist Clubs directly backing Bellamy. The movement took on real political dimensions by 1892, as the Nationalists assembled a platform of 1,654 delegates consisting of radical leftists from all walks of life ("white and black, native and naturalized, lettered and unlettered, professors, farmers, artisans, doctors, newspaper men, women, and a millionaire") who nominated General James P. Weaver of Iowa for president.[12] Weaver would become the first third party candidate to win twenty-two votes in the electoral college since the Civil War. With the votes of this new Populist Party peaking, Bellamy was stunned when he discovered its numbers had been suppressed from the general public. A bureaucratic convention that had become fixed in material print culture, in this case the Western Union Company's ledgers prepared under the auspices of the federal government, suppressed these gaudy numbers from the media because they had lacked a column for a third party. Hence, the media heralded the decline of the party, and the false rumors dramatically curtailed the Populists' momentum. The media in conjunction with the government would thus conspire to undercut the greatest opportunity for a competitive third party the United States has ever seen. Since then, the Socialist Party has splintered and divided, and has never had such a powerful backing by a single mass of voters as that of Bellamy's 1890s heyday.

Just as the forces of print media gave birth to the socialist movement in America through Bellamy's bestseller, *Looking Backward*, print media would also kill the socialists' greatest opportunity to seize power when the missing third column of Western Unions poll dispatches undercut the Populists' building momentum. Print media's commercial realm, acerbically vilified in *Looking Backward*, ironically proved kinder to the socialist cause than government bureaucracy, in which Bellamy backers had placed so much faith. Indeed, laissez-faire capitalism fanned the flames of the socialist movement through the sale of Bellamy's novel, while a superannuated government document spelled its doom. Interestingly, the formation of the Populists into a third party arose directly from the periodical press, as Bellamy had taken over the publication of Willard's *Nationalist* by 1891 under the new name of *The New Nation* with a more political bent and a practical application of the philosophy. The journal inspired others to create their own local Nationalist organs, totaling over fifty from coast to coast. All major New York and Boston newspapers had at least one Nationalist on its staff. The culture of collaboration and industry fueled this movement toward the realization of its founding principle that "competition is simply the application of the brutal law of the survival of the strongest and the most cunning," preventing "the loftiest aims of humanity [to] be realized." The movement that started as a literary club of enthusiasts for a winsome utopian novel had come dramatically close to establishing a permanent third party presence in American politics, and indeed had inspired many of the New Deal social programs legislated after the Great Depression precisely because it carried out so boldly the forth pillar of its credo. "No truth can avail unless practically applied," therefore, became more than a slogan as socialists set about to replace "the system founded on the brute principle of competition" with "another based on the nobler principle of association."[13]

The Bellamy following openly espoused this "nobler principle of association," because, according to William Morris's *Manifesto of the Socialist League* (1885), "if we wish to avoid speedy failure, [then] frankness and fraternal trust in each other, and single hearted devotion to the religion of Socialism" along with "industry in teaching its principles" would be "most necessary to our progress."[14] Education and zeal were also prominent features of Ayn Rand's Objectivist movement, but her following dropped off in its inability to reconcile the organization of its own ranks with its founding principles of radical individualism, competition, and free market capitalism, principles diametrically opposed to the associationist movement of Bellamy. Rand's radical capitalists, all believers in the moral sanctity of selfishness, ironically surrendered to hero worship of this goddess of the market, behaving in strict accordance to her Objectivist philosophy in ways that inadvertently took on socialist dimensions. At its worst, Rand's cultish circle operated almost like a Communist cell with more rigid and hegemonic dimensions than Bellamy's socialism, which conversely was rooted in Christian fellowship and love. Whereas Bellamy's socialists were still competing for the hotly contested definitive ethic of sympathy, by the postwar twentieth century, Rand's capitalists chided the overemphasis on compassion and self-sacrifice that they believed had deleterious effects on individual genius. The project of inspiring the individualists of the world to unite posed a profound paradox that threatened to cripple the very function of the group's social dynamic as it had for the Transcendentalists.

Rand's Radical Capitalists

If the Bellamy Club was characterized by a culture of collaboration, Rand's Objectivists were distinguished by a culture of contention that was paradoxically at its most harmonious when the disciples first gathered to hear Rand read from her manuscript in progress for what would later become *Atlas Shrugged*. Nathan Blumenthal and Barbara Weidman were at the forefront of the fawning acolytes, who led a cadre of UCLA undergraduate students inspired by *The Fountainhead*. Her novel had been steadily climbing to the top of the bestseller list, and was purchased by Warner Brothers for $50,000, a tremendous sum at that time. Blumenthal and Weidman moved to New York City to continue their studies, and Rand, along with her husband, followed them. It was a bizarre decision indeed for a rich and famous bestselling novelist, and now screenwriter, to follow a pair of college student fans across the country. Further, the impulse to follow was anathema to the core principles of Objectivism rooted in the defense of egoism and selfishness. It was especially ironic that the circle—which included future White House economist Alan Greenspan and gathered weekly at Rand's smoke-filled Manhattan apartment in a salon setting—would call themselves with less irony than they intended "The Collective" the year after the *Fountainhead*'s publication in 1943. Her followers lost themselves in Rand, and even began to merge identities with each other. Blumenthal and Weidman, for example, would marry in 1953 and adopt the surname of Branden, a three-way blend of their own last names with Rand's. "The Collective" began to develop a hegemonic code and took on an increasingly institutionalized profile through the formation of the Nathaniel Branden Institute, or NBI (he had changed his name from Nathan upon his marriage). He would play an instrumental role in enforcing the credo of egoism by "treating" members of the circle who were suffering from low self-esteem, a measure and practice both corrective and psychological in the application of Objectivist philosophy to "therapy." Playing the role of Rand's henchman and disciplinarian, Nathaniel administered "loyalty tests," which in effect put members on trail in Rand's living room. Bonner would also make efforts to boost his writers' self-esteem, often with lavish bonuses, or new assignments that challenged or expanded their work for his *New York Ledger*. But Bonner's gestures were made informally and almost always with good will. Rand's circle, on the other hand, were given to pouring over their guru's novels to assess which of their members required reeducation, vindictively forwarding their names to NBI for correction.[15]

While Bonner's *Ledger* was not given to such scapegoating, Southworth, Cobb, and Fern idolized their editor and heaped praise upon him in various forms within their writing. Southworth loved Bonner like a brother in the manner of Fern's affection for Mr. Walter in *Ruth Hall*. Likewise, Nathaniel initially admired Rand in this way. But in an odd twist, Rand fell for Nathaniel, a married man twenty-five years her junior. True to the principle of following individual whim and subjective desire, Rand openly pursued him, flouting social conventions of monogamy and marriage on the Objectivist grounds that they were needlessly self-sacrificial. She would regularly meet with Nathaniel while her husband, fully cognizant of the affair that was taking place, fled to a local bar. She had no qualms about justifying her behavior to her husband as a form of self-reward she had been denying herself for too long. He turned to alcohol, while Barbara began to suffer from panic attacks. When Nathaniel later pulled back from Rand, she threatened to dismantle NBI. He exposed her, and soon her credibility in the circle declined as she savagely excommunicated anyone who supported Nathaniel, instigating a bloodletting that signaled the end of the Objectivists. He then wrote an expose biography of her to recant *Who Is Ayn Rand?* (1962), an earlier promotion of Rand he coauthored with Barbara sanctifying her as a goddess of the market.[16] In their heyday prior to this dissolution, there had been Objectivist sports teams, movie nights, dinners, and dances; the individualists, amazingly, did unite under the dollar sign Rand wore in a diamond encrusted broach on her lapel, a garish icon of wealth anticipating such audacious jewelry preferred by the more successful rappers of today's hip-hop set. At her funeral stood a six-foot flower arrangement in the shape of a dollar sign. On Thoreau's tombstone reads the single word, "Henry," an equally telling representation of his position toward the market, materialism, self, and coterie, also an iconic product of American literary culture at the opposite pole from Rand.

Shattering any cohesiveness achieved by Rand's circle was the conflation of the Objectivist principle of possessiveness with the control and near ownership of members as if they themselves were acquired capital. This, along with the tendency toward regimentation, tangled into a contradictory mess of theory and practice corroding the coterie's culture and social dynamic. Rand's name nonetheless was instrumental in producing prominent careers for the Brandens and Alan Greenspan. The Brandens' *Who Is Ayn Rand?* had helped explain and promote Rand to the general public. After the break, Barbara's 1986 *The Passion of Ayn Rand* and Nathaniel's 1989 *Judgment Day: My Years With Ayn Rand* advanced their careers at Rand's expense. More recent works, both published in 2009, by Anne C. Heller, *Ayn Rand and the World She Made*, and Jennifer Burns, *Goddess of the Market*, position Rand more accurately in the history of radical capitalist thought. The history of Rand's biographies speaks to the extremely polarized attitudes toward the author, who has provoked responses ranging from zealous evangelizing hero worship to exploitative desecration.

For all her encouragement of the young admirers who formed the "Collective," she discouraged several young writers of note. In the early days of the "Collective," for example, Rand had actively promoted Kay Nolte Smith, an original contributor to *The Objectivist* journal, but by the late seventies had withdrawn her patronage.[17] Rand's encouragement of the members of her circle continually stopped short of the active promotion of their careers. Instead she built them up as extensions of herself. She recalled that for "Barbara, career-wise, the turning point was when I saw the first few pages of that short story which you started and didn't finish. It was those pages that convinced me that you're going to be a great writer, and you've been developing, since then, everything I saw in those pages." But such a mystical vision of professional authorship, Barbara knew with the clarity of several decades of historical perspective, was not the equivalent of ardent, pragmatic support, or even aesthetic nurturance. "Not even Ayn, with her perceptiveness and impressive powers of prediction, could see a 'great writer' in the few pages of a short story I wrote," Barbara confessed. She could also see that Rand had built up Nathan into a larger than life figure not unlike Howard Roark. Rand indeed had described Nathan in heroic tones: "I thought he was a genius from the first evening." In him she saw a "creative, initiating intelligence, total independence, the firsthand look of a creative mind, a mind constantly active on it own power. Nathan is the man to whom I want to leave my intellectual inheritance, whom I want to be my intellectual heir," she said, simultaneously identifying him as the father of her intellectual children (she originally called the Collective the "children of *Fountainhead*") and her intellectual child. Gushing with oedipal recklessness, Rand envisioned Nathaniel as both progenitor and progeny by conflating self and other, literary and sexual power, for a volatile cocktail of seduction and patronage that would devastate the Objectivist circle.[18]

Self-interest, both sexual and economic, was at the heart of Objectivist life. Like all of the coteries discussed in this book, Rand and her circle defined themselves according to their orientation to the market, which in this case was the full embrace of the creative and artistic application of unfettered self-interest at the core of laissez-faire capitalism. Objectivists rarely supported each other professionally, unlike many of the literary circles of this book; Rand's followers received little of the professional and economic support that Bonner and Fitzhugh's associates enjoyed. This is mainly because Rand herself saw her disciples not so much as talent to develop, or careers to commercially promote in the literary market, but as reflections of herself and her own fiction. She turned her disciples into "fantasy figures in her mind to whom she gave reality by means of fiction—just as she formed a fantasy replacement of her real self and demanded to be seen as the archetype of virtue and rationality—just as she formed a replacement of Frank [and Nathaniel] in the image of her novelistic heroes," Barbara recalled, "so she seemed to be forming fantasy figures of Nathaniel and of me and attempting to live within that artistic conversion." Ironically, this capacity to blend fiction with nonfiction that crippled the social relations of the inner circle was initially also her greatest professional asset that launched her fame. Not since Bellamy had any author in America so effectively packaged economic philosophy into bestselling fiction, as she sold over 20 million copies of her books by 1986. Her capacity to blend genres in this way to seduce the masses echoes her amalgamation of the imaginative world of her novels with her own personal relationships that led to the luring of Nathaniel into an affair he would forever regret. It was clear, however, that she only loved him and Barbara insofar as they functioned as creative fodder. They were muses, indeed, but ones she brazenly abused and disrespected. Tellingly, Rand signed a picture of herself to Barbara revealing precisely this tendency. "To Barbara— You remind me of myself and I wish [for] us both that you remain that way. With love—Ayn. June 21, 1951."[19] One Rand loyalist noted that she "could be immensely empathetic if she saw things in you that were like her. But if she didn't see herself in some aspect of you, she didn't empathize at all. You weren't real to her," or more paradoxically, at least not real enough to be one of her fictional characters.[20]

Rand's fondness for Nathaniel not only sprang from his seeming embodiment of her novel's heroes, but also from his critical role in promoting her works in the literary market. By the middle of the 1960s, Rand had grown weary of writing books from scratch, yet continued producing essays that Nathaniel published in the circle's periodical, the *Objectivist*, which proved critical to her success in the book market. After bringing out her essays in the *Objectivist* as they were completed, he then gathered them into collections to be published as books every two or three years. It then dawned on Rand after several editions appeared that Nathaniel was aggressively profiting from her fame. "You're an intellectual entrepreneur, and I'm one of the factors of production you're organizing." She knew better than to object, however. "That's all right," she allowed, "go ahead—I don't mind," quite content with her steady salary she earned from the *Objectivist*. "I always wanted a source of income separate from my books. Without the newsletter, I wouldn't have that, and without you, I wouldn't have the newsletter. I would never have started it on my own."[21] Nathaniel worked with such zeal on publishing the journal and collected essay volumes not only for his own profit, but also because he felt compelled to atone for his sin of failing to live up to the literary promise Rand had originally expected of him. Again, an odd reversal emerges here, as the protégé becomes the patron's publicist, a twist even stranger when one tries to imagine Thoreau promoting Emerson's career, an option he emphatically rejected when Horace Greeley suggested he write a biographical profile of Emerson for a series on influential contemporary figures in his *New-York Tribune*. Yet the pattern is consonant with Bonner's staff and their volumes of stories and columns that more than reflected credit upon his public persona.

By working to keep the *Objectivist* alive, Nathaniel provided Rand with an outlet for her preferred literary mode, and thus extended her career considerably, while also forwarding his own NBI. At the time, business was booming for NBI as well, as his courses were now offered in fifty-four cities and expanding onto the international market. NBI functioned as the institutional arm for the Objectivists, much in the way the Naropa Institute (originally the Jack Kerouac School of Disembodied Poetics) of Boulder, Colorado, had for Allen Ginsberg and the Beat Generation writers. The revealing tales of "The Collective" told by Nathaniel and Barbara find their Beat counterpart in *When I Was Cool* (2005), the memoir of Sam Kashner, one of Naropa's first students. In it, the chagrined alumnus recounts grisly tales of his abuse at the hands of Herbert Hunke and Jack Kerouac. One such tale is of a hallucinogenic ritual designed to train the neophyte in self-reliance that involved leaving Kashner stranded by the side of an isolated road in the mountains high above Boulder. The ritual vision quest proved more reckless than epiphanic, however, since his mentors refused to even leave him with a map and instead told him to rely on his spirit to find his way back. Such initiation rituals are no longer part of the Naropa curriculum, as the institute is now fully accredited and does healthy competition with creative writing programs like Sarah Lawrence College and the Iowa Writers' Workshop for today's best budding poets and fiction writers. Interestingly, as NBI was becoming an international force, Paul Engle—a literary outlaw and entrepreneur with Gatsby-esque ambition whose library contains a well-thumbed copy of *Hopalong Cassidy*—had just transformed the Iowa Writers' Workshop into the most potent producer of literary talent in the world.

NBI, it should be noted, was never established to nurture literary talent, so much as it was a mechanism for spreading the philosophy of Objectivism. Although Naropa essentially started as an outlet for Beatnik thinkers and writers in the mountains, its pedagogical mission gradually developed as outsiders, usually young romantic visionaries like the Brandens, increasingly flocked into the fold. The Iowa Writers' Workshop, on the other hand, did not necessarily develop out of a literary coterie, but instead sprang from the isolated agricultural confines of the University of Iowa. An unlikely location to become such a powerhouse of literary talent, the University of Iowa's low profile belies a tradition steeped in progressive, even radical, social innovation. Few are aware, for example, that Iowa was the first major university to award a doctoral degree to an African American in the United States (Ph.D. in Political Science), and boasted the highest enrollment of women in graduate programs during the first decades of the Gilded Age.[22] Progressive university administration, however, is no substitute for a viable living coterie. As the Workshop's prestige rose after World War II, the famous writers gathered. The results are indisputable: in the last quarter century, 5,000 books were published by Iowa MFAs compared to 200 by Emerson College creative writing graduates.[23] Iowa has produced two Pulitzer Prize winners Marilynne Robinson in 2005, and Paul Harding in 2010. How did the Workshop produce such successful authors? Or were these authors already destined for success upon entrance into the program? By what method did the Workshop promote its graduates' careers, if at all?

INSTITUTIONALIZING THE LITERARY CIRCLE IN IOWA

The University of Iowa's Program in Creative Writing, informally known as the Iowa Writers' Workshop, set the standard for similar programs nationwide and in the process transformed the history of the literary circle in America. Informal organic cliques like the Lads of Kilkenny are no longer as visible in today's literary culture precisely because such elite creative writing programs in higher education have drawn the majority of young talent into their ranks. Authors have increasingly rejected the starving artists' life in Greenwich Village for what appears the safer alternative of pursuing prestigious MFA degrees for admission into the elite inner circle of the publishing industry. Whereas administrators of more powerful programs like Iowa's candidly admit that they do not produce talent by "teaching" writers because their students already are highly accomplished upon admission, these program officials actively tout the prestige of the Workshop's credential through its association with famous authors, suggesting its worth as currency in the literary marketplace. Much of the Workshop's power lies in the affiliation it provides with a social network of established influential and well-connected faculty *and* students.

Many have commented on the dubious pedagogy of creative writing in higher education. Critic David Haven Blake, for example, balks at the thought of a present-day Walt Whitman attending seminars in which his classmates would "workshop" his free verse.[24] The tyranny of ill-defined mantras like "show don't tell," and the use of metaphors to teach the craft have been ridiculed not so much for their usage, but for the seemingly undeserving institutional authority they bear in a university setting. The soft, highly subjective "write what you know" side of creative writing programs that has become their liability today did not originate in Iowa, but instead is a later development that occurred in the last few decades. The Workshop's roots trace back to 1861 when the first literary clubs consisted mainly of students engaging in debates and public speaking to sharpen their skills. The Zetagathian Society and the Polygon "writers' club" gathered for amusement and recreation rather than as a training ground for professional authorship. Despite their leisurely bent, these groups, particularly Polygon, formalized the process of reading aloud and fielding suggestions for improvement. The workshop method that grew from this became an engine for publication in the next century when the Program in Creative Writing commenced. Hardly the esoteric therapy sessions so many of these have become today, the Workshop of director Paul Engle's era (1941–1965) that advanced the program onto the national and global stage was characterized by challenging, rigorous faculty and peer criticism. Surviving the program increasingly brought stardom as its reward. If any fault lay in the Workshop, it was that its pressure-filled competitive environment became too abrasive in its desire to avoid becoming a "place overrun with aesthetes come not to work but to dabble their delicate fingers in the Iowa River, which flows through the campus."[25]

When Thoreau read his manuscript for *A Week on the Concord and Merrimack Rivers* to Emerson in his hut at Walden Pond, for example, he did not expect his mentor to advise him to show and not tell, nor to find his voice. Indeed, Emerson did neither, but instead made general comments, not necessarily to be implemented as revisions, and thereafter exclusively addressed the project in terms of its placement with potential publishers.[26] Charlotte Bronte read her manuscript in progress for *Jane Eyre* (1847) during this time to a close group of family and friends. Notably, her refusal to follow their suggestions, particularly the dubious advice to make Jane less ambitious, paradoxically fueled her creation of one of the century's greatest and most subversive heroines. Rand's readings of her *Atlas Shrugged* drafts were conversely without much tension at all since her audience responded with unmitigated adulation like the fawning and docile "children of *Fountainhead*" she affectionately regarded them to be. Rather than challenging her or suggesting she change course, her acolytes benignly cheered her every move. Outside of the academy, peer criticism was unlikely to have much of an impact on the completed literary product, despite such notable exceptions as Ezra Pound's vast excisions of T.S. Eliot's first draft of *The Waste Land*, which made the work more collaborative than most might have assumed.

Unlike the feedback from Bronte's listeners, the Iowa Writers' Workshop's systematic and voluminous criticism had a moderating influence on its writers, especially during the postwar decades. The growing national influence of the Workshop meant that such moderation and centrism effectively neutralized the radical paradigm that had been established in American literature during the prior era. Radical mid-century circles like Rand's Objectivists, for example, can be traced back to notions of creative writing fostered in the 1920s and 1930s that were deliberately oppositional and even countercultural, heroically defying the "mob mind that does not wish us to devote ourselves to great achievements," as *Ledger* author Sylvanus Cobb's grandson, Stanwood, wrote in *Discovering the Genius Within You* (1932).[27] The Workshop discouraged the charisma of authorial voice, especially the use of first person, through a regimented program that tamed deviance, actively moderated excesses, and discouraged extremism, both aesthetic and political. Mark McGurl has recently called this the "Iowa Style," a reaction to the radical approach toward authorship Cobb described and Rand embodied, and thus "a correction of those pages in American literary history with red pen."[28] One course at Iowa was recently advertised as writing "boot camp." McGurl aptly describes the early days of Workshop culture as designed to systematically hammer out irregularities and reinforce "modulation by way of negative feedback in which the output of a system is to some degree reversed before entering it as input."[29] An author like Hemingway, who developed his craft not in the academy but in Gertrude Stein's 1920s Paris literary salons, employed a diverse range of styles and voices, from a detached third person limited to an intimate first person narrative persona. By contrast, the strikingly homogenous literary corpus of Flannery O'Connor bears the stamp of her Iowa training during the postwar era. Never deviating from the third person limited form of the Workshop inculcated in her, she would produce even measured prose, ironic distance from first person narration, and the segmentation of her stories into discrete, coherent units, reflecting the Workshop's culture of constraint. McGurl goes so far as to compare her sentences, measured staccato statements, to so many spankings, noting that her stories divide themselves into aesthetic "unities" prepackaged and galvanized for the critical siege of her seminar peers.[30]

Regardless of this somewhat reckless assessment of O'Conner's craft, McGrurl is right to say that the institution indeed shaped the literature itself. I would add that these tight and tidy products of the Workshop were invariably salable; editors of the mid-twentieth-century were attracted to works that were not extreme, showed depth, yet were highly disciplined. The disciplinary aesthetic regime was not as cruel, nor as sadomasochistic as McGurl paints it, however. He extracts far too much innuendo, for example, from a photograph of a young tweed jacketed pipe smoking Engle stationed at his steel typewriter with a bullwhip coiled beside it. Much of the program's rigor, I would argue, had to do with the needy financial situation the program itself faced as a fledgling establishment within a university unable to house it in any better confines than a mobile army barracks unit left over from the war. A telling tableau of the University's perennial failure to match fiscally the rising status of the program occurred when Robert Frost was forced to address the University on a makeshift lectern in the mobile barracks unit the Workshop called home. Engle tirelessly lobbied administration for funding, carrying with him into the offices of the deans and president briefcases full of publications by his pupils and dumping their contents on their desks to solicit their support.[31] From his first day as director during the war, Engle was always in desperate financial straits, and thus became acculturated to constantly selling the program not only to administration, but also to students, parents, corporate sponsors, and, crucially, famous authors.

Far from a perverse fascination with punishing his students for pleasure, or exacting control over the program for its own sake, Engle was a visionary with a pragmatic economic side. He would nightly retreat to the converted shed behind his home that he referred to as the "hog house" to transact the business of promoting the Workshop, exploiting all leads and ties, soliciting corporate America's titans with grant proposals, and even pitching greeting card jingles to Hallmark to open up opportunities.[32] In his ongoing quest to make the program solvent, Engle bartered and brokered his students' writings for publication; he wrote to one mother pleading for tuition dollars to readmit one dropout.[33] The Workshop offered a remedy for authors facing a literary market coldly indifferent, if not utterly blind, to brilliant young talent without connections and endorsements. Yet Engle had a shortage of staff and meager resources with which to fulfill his mission, making for methods that were often blunt. He had no colleagues to coordinate with for a more democratic process to allocate student funding, for example, than to line them up outside of the barracks and hear their pleas one by one, making unilateral and highly subjective decisions on their fate. This process, like the ones that would come to characterize the administration of the program itself, was far from a perverse pleasure, and certainly not a preference but an economic necessity.

So was Engle operating a dictatorship diametrically opposed to the nurturing community that Bonner, Irving, and Peabody had fostered and that Fuller had hoped for in Concord? Is it fair to classify Engle's administration of the Workshop as a cultish autocracy routinely abusing its members and demanding rigid uniformity like that of Rand's Objectivists? Nothing in the archive of Engle's papers in Special Collections at the University of Iowa would suggest that he was a Cold War ideologue. (McGurl, who lays claim to the most recent history of the Workshop, did not bother to consult these documents prior to eviscerating Engle for running a virtual Cold War concentration camp). Engle in fact was under investigation by Senator Joe McCarthy's House Un-American Activities Committee and was forced to defend the Workshop's right to use taxpayer money to fund speaking engagements for Communist party affiliates.[34] Engel's alignment with business sponsorship harnessed national recognition for the Workshop Partnerships with business at the time, especially to support creative writers, represented his radical and innovative use of corporate capitalism and not a humiliating concession to hegemonic forces of evil profaning an otherwise pure vocational pursuit of letters. Engle's statement that "in an open society such as ours, writer, businessman, and university can join to make an environment which is useful to the writer, friendly for the businessman and, and healthy for the university" need not reflexively and unimaginatively be dismissed as so much pandering.[35] Indeed, Engle was innovating the business of letters by reimagining the social function of the creative writing circle in light of new developments in capitalism as most successful coteries had in the prior century.

Aside from being a tireless professional advocate of Workshop writers, Engle was a personal companion to them. Kiyohiro Miura's experience in the program confirms the warm side of Engle who "'looks after his student, even their pots and pans.'" Once Engle secured scholarship money for him, Miura, fearing he was losing his native tongue, refused it since he had determined to return to Japan.

"I'll make your career," Engle said in a desperate attempt to keep his protégé, promising far more than the scholarship. Miura eventually returned to Japan and successfully landed an academic position despite not having earned even a master's degree. Engle made good on his promise, however, as his letter of recommendation was instrumental in Miura's hiring. In it, his former mentor certified that he had completed the Japanese equivalent of the requirements for an advanced degree under his tutelage. But the dark side of Miura's testimony corroborates that of Hampl and others discontent with the Workshop. Jealousy and squabbling for Engle's affection mixed with hostility toward his methods. His criticism of one student was so harsh that it was understood as an ultimatum by all present. Engle's greatest asset, his capacity to wed business with letters, was regarded by many as his worst liability. There were allegations of "Paul's making use of his students, taking them with him to the firms he targeted and having them recite their poems in front of the company executives. 'We aren't in show business,' a girl in the group said." One particular student had "refused to play the role of the bard" but nonetheless became the eventual beneficiary of Engle's recommendation of her work to a prestigious literary journal.[36]

Engle continued to promote his students in the market in this aggressive, and ultimately successful way. His negotiations with Columbia Pictures on behalf of his students, for example, enabled students to submit work for payment without question; no manuscripts were refused, nor were revisions demanded. Columbia paid students $500 per manuscript for adaptation into screenplays in addition to $250 to be "deposited in the University Treasury as a fund to help young writers now here." "Television can use all kinds of stories," Engle assured them, urging that such a concession to the mass market bore no shame, since "Faulkner and Hemingway stories have been utilized" similarly. (Elsewhere in his correspondence, he glories in this coup of securing such a substantial guaranteed payment for unedited manuscript submissions.[37]) Such a lucrative arrangement was possible only because Engle's own writing had become a major source of revenue for Hallmark's Hall of Fame television series.[38] Engle generated professional success for his students despite their resistance in some cases. Quarreling over a student's manuscript in which he saw great potential, Engle proudly flourished a letter of acceptance from *Esquire* of that very story by the end of the semester, having submitted it without the student's knowledge.[39] The revision and workshopping was not only academic, but wedded the seminar classroom directly to the publishing industry in innumerable cases. "We aren't in show business" may have been the refrain shared by particularly self-important students harboring romanticized notions of authorship above and beyond the market and mass media. But as Engle's own sense of the market proved, and according to Ralph Ellison and Norman Mailer's conclusion reached in Iowa City in 1959, writing had already irreversibly become show business.

The key promotional breakthroughs by Engle affirm that writing was indeed show business, and his self-described "delicate and imaginative aggression" was ideally suited to it.[40] In February 1952, *Poetry* devoted half of a special issue to the verse written by Iowa Workshop writers. A 17 July 1955 *New York Times Book Review* article written by Engle touted the productivity of Workshop students for publishing seven novels, numerous poems, and short stories in respected magazines.[41] And perhaps his biggest coup for national publicity came on the 4 December 1959 Conference covered by *Esquire*, *Newsweek*, *Writer's Digest*, and major Chicago and Des Moines newspapers. It is thanks due in large part to the global renown Engle built that the United Nations Educational, Scientific, and Cultural Organization (UNESCO) named Iowa City one of three of the world's Cities of Literature in 2007 along with Edinburgh, Scotland and Melbourne, Australia. Engle himself would be nominated for the Nobel Peace Prize in 1976 for the transnational reach of the Iowa International Writing Program, cofounded with his second wife, Hualing Engle.

One of the ironies of the Workshop is that its current administration is reluctant to acknowledge that its success was built upon Engle's literary capitalism. Rather than masking it, Engle himself foregrounded the very question of literature's association with the mass media in the 1959 *Esquire* conference. Though he never openly espoused a Bonneresque commercialization of literature, he nonetheless was fully engaged in it, as a series of notes among his papers indicate his firm grasp of the paradoxes of high culture literature's transformation into a mass phenomenon. In them, Engle summed up the economic condition of authorship in 1954: "the economic facts of *periodical* publication were strongly against the new writer; and among the 'professionals' editorial lines, at least in the big circulation fields, seemed drawn definitely in favor not of the serious professional writer, but the professional hack...For the first time in Am. Publishing history, writer has chance to make a living—minimal one, but nevertheless-without resort to magazine conformity." Abating his worry that popular writers would crowd out new literary authors like his own pupils, however, was the realization that the standards for fiction were on the rise. "Mags can reduce themselves to conventional hacks formula, and nothing more (and be outdone in this field by cheaper paperbacks); or, since the pb is predominantly novelistic rather than shortstory, periodical can elevate its fiction to the intellectual level of its non-fiction, assuming the unified intelligence of the reader. 'Professionalism' has its admirable aspect" in both worlds of "Hemingway Faulkner, et al, or professional writers, as much as Faith Baldwin, Buddington Kelland."[42] His optimism in the mass market's promise for serious authors is reflected in his own lecture tours, intellectual affairs that were also wildly popular, a formula reminiscent of the one Emerson had perfected a century before. Engle was particularly adept at "combining fairly complex academic ideas with a mode of popular presentation," as John P. Barden, Dean of Cleveland's Western Reserve University noted of his lecture style.[43]

At the *Esquire* conference, "The Writer in a Mass Culture," Ralph Ellison and Norman Mailer drew similar conclusions, despite serious misgivings about literature joining forces with the mass media. Dwight MacDonald was perhaps the most fearful and elitist of all, asserting that "We now are threatened with something even more insidious, and that is what I call mid-cult, or middle brow culture [that] combines the worst features of high culture and mass culture. It combines the pretentiousness of high culture and the vulgarity of mass culture." Mailer responded by arguing, "we all agree the mass media is a dreadful thing...but to say the only answer is to have an elite is nonsense." He emphasized that the "elite that grew in privacy," the sheltered coterie totally detached from the market "is a thing of the past" since today's talent is instantly "swept up into the mass media." Such "elite that grew in privacy" inhabited seventeenth- and eighteenth-century England and France, but by the nineteenth century in America, most literary circles oriented themselves toward the market. Mailer called Kerouac and Ginsberg elite because they developed "private and separate from the main body of American life" in total opposition to the mass media "that do not allow you in any way to be extreme."[44] Mailer does not advocate a middlebrow solution, but suggests that a new "high culture" exists that has defined itself in opposition to market mechanisms, exactly according to the sort of elite rebellion against commercial forces I have traced from the Knickerbockers on. This rebellious stance was not without its commercial appeal, and through such poses coteries carefully managed themselves into the market, wary of each other's positions and maneuvers.

Particularly resonant with essential findings of this book was Ellison's view that "we can't really separate the two" categories of high art from low art, a position that calls into question the political intensions behind the vilification of mass media. "It's not quite as dismal as it seems," he said, since the mass dissemination of literature may have a democratizing effect. "I don't believe that you can really in this country separate the political from the artistic," he added.[45] Ellison cited Whitman as poet of the masses, who nonetheless could not reach them very successfully, and Melville, who defied the market with *Moby-Dick*, but "really suffered for his position." Nineteenth-century literary circles all reached for the masses with varying success through their politically inflected preoccupations of bachelorhood, patronage, sympathy, conversation, and race. Mailer confessed, "I'd like *everybody* to read my books," as did Ellison, who added an important caveat: "I personally would like to be read by as many people as possible but on my own terms."[46] That common object, inevitably, required a full engagement with the mechanisms of promotion and publicity in the literary marketplace.

To that end, the Workshop offered a "manner of publication without losing too much blood," fostering, in Engle's words, "useful competition that at the same time freed [writers] from the imperatives of the marketplace."[47] Engle would make precisely this same rhetorical appeal in a letter courting no less than Sinclair Lewis to join the Iowa faculty.[48] This shelter and security from the market was subtler than it may have appeared, for the seminar classroom was so engrossed in simulating the rigors and criticisms of the real market that it became directly linked to publication. Insulation from the market was not an end in itself; production into the market and the acquisition of prestige associated with publication in serious journals and presses was instead the priority. Indeed, status within these classes led directly to publication. "Pets" emerged from the Workshop who acted and dressed the part of young prodigy, calculating their ascendance by immersing themselves in faculty writings and by addressing their mentors "not dutifully, but forthrightly and even speculatively."[49] The economy of exchange of criticism in the seminar classroom was thus conditioned by extracurricular maneuvering for social status. Engle's own promotion of the Workshop relied precisely on such a nonmonetary gift economy among students, administrators, and publishers. Engle's contemporary, William Charvat of Ohio State University, conducted business in a manner Leon Jackson suggested also hinged upon an elaborate array of gifts and favors. He demonstrates convincingly that Charvat's own theoretical "flattened and desocialized model of authorship" nonetheless was generated by a man who ironically "understood the social dimensions and the multiple economies of authorial practice intimately."[50] In contrast, Engle's theory matched his practice, as he promoted Iowa for its uniquely socialized vision of authorship, which was well suited to the world of commerce. The program's check on favoritism of "pets" was its rigorous peer criticism, a brutal, yet leveling and democratic rite. John Leggett, for example, emphasizes that the result is an army of authors market ready, toughened to the rigors of adverse feedback that may either inspire or demoralize in the authentic professional context of the free market. The end justifies the barbaric means, in this sense, because the Workshop "is very much akin to publication, to the sense of immediacy about publication," instilling a desire to find a cluster of respected minds and write to them, envision them as the audience, and thus motivate one "to the top of your form."[51]

Life in the program was not just a matter of surviving direct and often harsh criticism; it was a matter of establishing oneself in the peer pecking order through publication. The Workshop was, according to graduate Joe Bellamy's recollection, "a rigid status system that depended on publication, a world where if you publish, you have status. If you do not publish, you have no status. So in a kind of Pavlovian way, it sets up an intense desire to publish, a hunger for it." Jack Myers captured exactly the potential for controversy intrinsic to such a system in which many "felt that competition had no place in the life of an artist and their work and egos suffered under the severe pressure of trying to survive in this atmosphere." Iowa City became the drinking town that it is thanks not so much to Big Ten college football as to postwar Engle comrades learning to "drink just as deeply to failure as to success, because I think we all felt that we were really only pitting ourselves against our last best effort."[52] Glasses were raised to victory and defeat in the publication wars more than to the petty scrapes of workshop skirmishes. Herein lies a critical point distinguishing the Workshop's orientation toward the market: the very nature of its shelter from the free market predisposed its members to perceive the rigors of the real publishing industry more acutely and thus train more specifically for survival in it.[53] Although the prevailing character of the Workshop was competitive, the nature of that competition nonetheless drew the cohort toward the common goal of publication. Sympathy, the ideological lynchpin of existence for most nineteenth-century coteries, had thus found its way into literary production once again in the twentieth century.

As Engle's example and the case studies of this book have shown, the creation of prestige was paramount to the success of literary coteries. Pierre Bourdieu's formulation of the literary field aptly illuminates the patronage and promotion driving the production of prestige. Herein are the "struggles which aim at transforming or maintaining the established relation of forces: each of the agents commits the force (the capital) that he [or she] has acquired through previous struggles to strategies that depend for their general direction on the position in the power struggle, that is, on his [or her] specific capital."[54] So when Iowa Writers' Workshop students lined up outside Engle's temporary army barracks, which functioned as the program's headquarters, to make their best appeal to him for funding, they were enacting the same ritual that had begun when the Knickerbockers drew upon Irving's capital, both social and monetary, to gain prestige for their own careers. Both were committing capital acquired through previous struggles to strategies whose trajectory or "general direction" depends directly on the nature and form of that capital. The prestige all writers of this study sought was intrinsically linked to competition first for symbolic status in the subfield of restricted production, located at the inner workings of the coterie level in my study, as in Bourdieu's schema. At this level "authority based on consecration or prestige is purely symbolic and may or may not imply possession of increased economic capital."[55] Not until a place in the coterie's hierarchy had been established and the author's relation to the leading agent had been confirmed could the writer effectively produce into and for the mass market. There is a distinct difference, for example, between Irving's original cohort who assembled for their own amusement and those who later assaulted the mass market with their individual productions. Similarly, Thoreau's earliest poetry was designed to please his patron, Ralph Waldo Emerson, compared to his later essays that he furiously peddled in the publishing industry of New York City. My argument has been that the prestige, celebrity, and consecration of honor in the broader literary market is carefully developed first at the coterie level, at which knowledge, competency, and disposition—Bourdieu's "cultural capital"—is acquired and learned. Status and prestige, or symbolic capital, is then established within the coterie, soon to be played out into the larger market for economic profit and recognition. Thus the mechanism of literary fame, an essential focus of this book, is apparent not only as a matter of how aggressively capitalistic each circle's leader was in promoting his authors, but in how socially functional their chosen method for doing literary business actually was. Lydia Child, for example, employed a far more functional approach toward the management of her authors to make her journal surpass that of Garrison's *Liberator* in subscriptions. Elizabeth Peabody, like Child, will not be remembered as a rabid capitalist, but one nonetheless who shared her unorthodox, even revolutionary, approach to literary business.

The coteries of this book simultaneously commented on and embodied antebellum commercial culture as reflected in their public profiles. Each circle promoted itself through its trademark image, from the rumpled rambling bachelor Diedrich Knickerbocker and repeated *Ledger* ads in New York to the lichen coat of arms of the arboreal noble family Thoreau imagines in the New England countryside. The lasting icons of coteries ranged from Peabody's bustling 10 West Street bookshop and Garrison's burning Constitution in the Boston streets to the stately white pillars of Fitzhugh's plantation fantasy of filial social harmony. Authors hotly contested the values of these trademark images in the literary market to promote their own careers and to repay their debts to the circles that supported them. Authorship continues to be a social business both within circles and across them, now complicated more than ever by the exigencies of their institutionalization in higher education's creative writing programs. Such programs now constitute an interconnected national network of patronage in which "the university," as Engle envisioned, "is the Greenwich Village of the 1920s diffused across the country, made more orderly, more efficient."[56] Literary circles, clannish and spiritually committed to a common aesthetic and political ideology, either struggled to routinize literary production into the market like the Concord clique, or mastered both method and promotion into the most efficient instrument for reaching the masses. Part ambassador and administrator, figures like Bonner, Peabody, and Garrison, Engle will be remembered more for their promotional agency than their own writings. Irving, Emerson, and Fitzhugh would attain their status initially through their writings (*The Sketch Book*, *Nature*, and *Cannibals All!*) and manage their cohorts in such a way that abetted the trajectory of their own careers. Irving's empire, the first of its sort in American literature, was a social force that built its Knickerbocker identity from his charismatic writings. The bachelor author became fashionable under Irving, whose generous and often aggressive patronage of his Lads built the circle into a dynasty whose reign would extend more than half a century.

As this literary history has revealed, a "delicate aggression," as Engle phrased it, was the most successful approach in advancing authorial careers. The leading figures of these circles engaged in a variety of forms of patronage and support, both financial and aesthetic, bearing a significant relation to the coterie identity. Irving, Bonner, Emerson, Peabody, Fitzhugh/DeBow, and Garrison all allocated resources and managed their circles in ways that anticipated Paul Engle's administrative style. Max Weber's formulation of charismatic leadership illuminates precisely how "The followers share in the use of the goods which the authoritarian leader receives as a donation, booty, or endowment, and which he distributes among them without accounting or contractual fixation," yet always with the expectation that the followers will use that capital according to the ethos of the clan.[57] Styles of patronage were not all authoritarian, as Peabody's horizontal democratic promotional practice stood in sharp contrast to Garrison's vertical autocratic rule. But more than merely relying on their leaders for their well-being, coterie members independently promoted themselves in the market in such a way that also perpetuated the influence of their circle. Weber's observation about Protestantism's development into capitalism is especially relevant to the historical trajectory of literary circles in nineteenth-century America. He writes, "The great majority of disciples and followers will in the long run 'make their living' out of their 'calling' in a material sense as well. Indeed, this must be the case if the movement will not disintegrate."[58] Active marketing was essential to the posterity—its influence and vitality—of the major nineteenth-century American literary circles. As Ellison and Mailer agreed, the development of mass media has enabled American authors to reach for increasingly broad audiences, regardless of how insular their coterie may appear. Coteries competed for prestige and capital by selling their attitudes—whether aesthetic or political, commercial or romantic—toward market conditions. The social construction of literary success continues to occur on the level of the literary circle with the author's coterie affiliation functioning as their stock in trade, the basis for their public identity and status in the industry. As the commercial condition of authorship moves into the twenty-first century, antimaterialistic aesthetics bear an increasingly problematic relation to global trade. The situation brings not only difficulty, but also opportunity, especially for authors associated with powerful literary circles. In antebellum America, as now, an author's coterie—particularly its relation to the market—determined their prestige in the publishing world in which, according to the N.P. Willis character of *Ruth Hall*, "It is a great thing for a young writer to be *literarily connected*."[59]

Notes

Introduction

1. J.D. Salinger, *The Catcher in the Rye* (New York: Little, Brown, 1951), 18.
2. Pierre Bourdieu's identification of the tendency among contemporary art historians to "stop at the apparent object, meaning the artist…instead of constructing and analyzing the field of production of which the artist, socially instituted as 'creator,' is the product" echoes Holden's naïve desire for access to a humanized author behind novels as an anonymous consumer, *The Rules of Art: Genesis and Structure of the Literary Field*, ed. Werner Hamacher and David E. Wellbery (Stanford, CA: Stanford University Press, 1992), 291. His boyish longing for friendship, for a literary kindred spirit, like old forms of literary history, overlooks the reality of the market condition that would prevent him from not only accessing, but also fully understanding, and thus demystifying, the authors of his favorite books. Indeed, "the ritual inquiry concerning the place and time of the appearance of the artist" overlooks the role of that artist more as socialized craftsman, engaged in commercial enterprise, and fully aware of his/her friends, potential patrons and publishers, sympathetic and hostile audiences, and competitors that comprise the social matrix of the literary marketplace, Bourdieu, *Rules of Art*, 291. The market conditions demanded such awareness; obliviousness to the social and economic nature of authorship, as scholars have fully demonstrated, was virtually unheard of.
3. Salinger, 18.
4. John S. Hart, *The Female Prose Writers of America: With Portraits, Biographical Notices, and Specimens of Their Writings* (Philadelphia: E.H. Butler, 1852), 7.
5. Ibid., 7.
6. Among other things, Chapter 91, "The *Pequod* meets the Rose Bud," of *Moby-Dick* is an inside joke about Hawthorne's baby daughter Rose's noxious smelling diapers, an apt figure for the equally paradoxical ambergris, a substance culled from the foulest depths of the whale's intestines refined into perfume and jewelry, like the baby, as beautiful and fragrant as a rose. Gordon V. Boudreau, "Herman Melville, Immortality, St. Paul, and Resurrection: From Rose-Bud to Billy Budd" *Christianity and Literature* 52.3 (2003), 343.

7. Lytle Shaw, *Frank O'Hara: The Poetics of Coterie* (Iowa City: University of Iowa Press, 2006), 6.
8. Ibid., 6.
9. For an interesting early study of Transcendentalism's connection to Marxism, see David Herreshoff, *American Disciples of Marx: From the Age of Jackson to the Progressive Era* (Detroit: Wayne State University Press, 1977), 11–52. Imaginative socialistic alternatives to free market enterprise should be understood in the context of how "Anti-capitalism has been a part of middle-class ideology ever since the mid-eighteenth century. The critique of modernization expressed itself in Rousseau, Adam Ferguson, the early Goethe, Herder, the Romantics, and others, as a critique of greed, self-interest, and *amour-propre*," reflected in a literature in which "villains are always after money, gold, wealth," as Jochen Schulte-Susse accurately observes in "Can the Disempowered Read Mass-Produced Narratives in their Own Voice?" *Cultural Critique* 10 (1988), 179. The "rise of capitalism," as intellectual historian Thomas L. Haskell notes, was concomitant with the origins of humanitarianism not just as a medium for the expression of class interest, but as a change in "*perception or cognitive style*" marked by a "change in the perception of causal connection and consequently a shift in the conventions of moral responsibility [at the heart of] the new constellation of attitudes and activities that we call humanitarianism," "Capitalism and the Origins of the Humanitarian Sensibility, Part 1" *American Historical Review* 90.2 (1985), 342. This new style of perception exposing the immoral behavior behind economic domination and its resultant social inequality, I argue, is particularly well suited to the history of literary circles. These circles entered the market from an alternative point of access given the morally freighted nature of their product compared to other nonliterary products. As such, coteries were not only allowed to, but in the antebellum era at the height of the market revolution, they were indeed expected to, comment on the materialistic tendencies in the culture, hence the outgrowth of humanitarianism and anticapitalism coteries represented as ideological positions toward the shifting economic terrain.
10. Henry David Thoreau, *Walden*, ed. J. Lyndon Shanley (Princeton: Princeton University Press), 1971, 118. For an especially insightful treatment of Thoreau's ambivalence toward the market, see Richard Teichgraeber's "'A Yankee Diogenes': Thoreau and the Market," *The Culture of the Market: Historical Essays*, ed. Thomas L. Haskell and Richard Teichgraeber (Cambridge: Cambridge University Press, 1996), 293–324.
11. The circle book is a very old species of literary history, consisting of single-author focused studies utilizing the "circle" as a kind of supporting cast for the canonical male star as evidenced by *Joseph Conrad and His Circle* (1935), *Michael Drayton and His Circle* (1941), *Dr. Johnson and His Circle* (1913), *Ruskin and His Circle* (1910),

Wordsworth and His Circle (1907), and *Hawthorne and His Circle* (1903). For a postmodern revision of this approach constructed around the absence of an actual circle, see William B. Dillingham's *Melville and His Circle: The Last Years* (Athens: University of Georgia Press, 2008), whose title is an ironic misnomer, since he views Melville's "circle" as disembodied authors whom he engaged in print only. A recent article-length feminist study of a major woman writer's exclusion from male dominated antebellum literary circles exposing their hegemonic gender politics is Charlene Avallone's "Catharine Sedgwick and the Circles of New York" *Legacy* 23.2 (2006), 115–31. My sense of the literary circle, by contrast, is less concerned with the circle's influence upon a single author, but instead sees it as a social matrix of literary production and promotion and thus an aesthetic point of reference for its authors (contributing to its group identity) and marketing tool.

12. Loughran, xviii.
13. Nathaniel Hawthorne, *The Blithedale Romance* (Mideola, NY: Dover, 2003), 7.
14. Ibid., 10.
15. George Ripley, qtd. in Philip F. Gura, *American Transcendentalism: A History* (New York: Hill and Wang, 2008), 156.
16. Older definitions of associationism acknowledge that informal groups combine in response to "economic pressures and necessities (urbanization) as well as to define an ideological position opposite that of individualism," as Robert Dean Lewis describes in "Individualism and Associationism in American Literature, 1830–1850" (Ph.D. Dissertation, St. John's University, 1970), 6. The link he makes to socialism is commonly understood as well, as both "describe a variety of enterprises involving combined human effort," Lewis, 6. Though he does not make it explicit, Lewis's lexical choice of "enterprise" would indicate at least an intuitive sense that while such socialistic patterns of group formation may have opposed individualism, they very much espoused an energized, emboldened form of capitalism based on humanized collectivism.
17. Qtd. in Charles C. Cole, Jr., *The Social Ideas of Northern Evangelists, 1826–1860* (New York: Columbia University Press, 1966), 102.
18. John Evelev, *Tolerable Entertainment: Herman Melville and Professionalism in Antebellum New York* (Amherst: University of Massachusetts Press, 2006), 67. Evelev's single author project differs from my emphasis on commercial strategies—both within and outside of the literary texts—each coterie used to enter the market, as well as its internal workings, economies of exchange, social capital building, and methods of "controlling the terms of its members' entrance into the marketplace," 67.
19. The 1840s saw a sharp rise in the "wave of association" in the United States, the source of which is traced by business economics historians Alexander M. Carr-Saunders and P.A. Wilson, *The Professions*

(New York: Frank Cass, 1964), 300. For details on the emergence of professional associations, see Burton J. Bledstein, *The Culture of Professionalism: The Middle Class and the Development of Higher Education in America* (New York: W.W. Norton, 1976), and *The Rise of Professionalism: A Sociological Analysis* (Berkeley: University of California Press, 1977). For the impact of the association movement on literary themes, see Robert Dean Lewis, *Individualism and Associationism in American Literature, 1830–1850* (New York: St. John's University Press, 1971).
20. Hawthorne, 11.
21. Lucy Larcom, qtd. in Ronald J. and Mary Saracino Zboray, *Literary Dollars and Social Sense: A People's History of the Mass Market Book* (New York: Routledge, 2005), 173.
22. Trish Loughran emphasizes in her superb history of the construction of American national identity that print culture was decentralized, and that there was "no 'nationalized' print public sphere…but rather a proliferating variety of local and regional reading publics scattered across a vast and diverse geographical space," *The Republic in Print: Print Culture in the Age of U.S. Nation Building, 1770–1870* (New York: Columbia University Press, 2007), xix. My book proceeds from precisely this assumption as applied to the literary movements and circles, each with its own internal and external economies of exchange and attendant codes of behavior governing them. I do not set them in mutually exclusive opposition, but show how there was a surprising confluence of methods for promotion of talent and exchange of borrowed, and even shared, ideas in the rhetoric of their works, particularly in their critiques of capitalism and material culture.
23. The romantic myth of the individual author depended on the elevated uniqueness of their products as distinct from other nondistinct and replaceable mass-produced products on the market. At this phase of capitalist development in America known as the market revolution, the proliferation of mass produced products encouraged authors and publishers alike to distance their merchandise and indeed elevate it in the market, which Pierre Bourdieu describes as "the methodical attempt to distinguish the artist and the intellectual from other commoners by positing the unique products of 'creative genius' against interchangeable products, utterly and completely reducible to their commodity value," "The Market of Symbolic Goods," *The Field of Cultural Production: Essays on Art and Literature* (New York: Columbia University Press, 1993), 114. My argument is that such distance and elevation of literature from other products, paradoxically, was accomplished through a distinctly commercial discourse and played out through the collective judgments of literary intermediaries circulating that literature throughout the market. For more on the history of cultural and literary criticism of paradoxical economic postures that attempt to transcend the market as much as they cater to it beginning with Marc Shell's studies of money in literature,

see Michael Hutter and C.D. Throsby's edited volume, *Beyond Price: Value in Culture, Economics, and the Arts* (Cambridge: Cambridge University Press, 2007), especially the preface, 1–22, and the chapter by Richard Teichgraeber, "'More than Luther in these Modern Days': The Construction of Emerson's Reputation in American Culture, 1882–1903," 159–78.

24. In *The Business of Letters: Authorial Economies in Antebellum America* (Stanford, CA: Stanford University Press, 2008), Leon Jackson argues that Duyckinck was exclusive and hegemonic in his rejection of commercial writers, a view he said was perpetuated by Charvat in the twentieth century. Jackson usefully describes an overly rigid paradigm in Charvat, yet its origins are not in Duyckinck, at least as evidenced by his *Cyclopedia*, which was actually not guilty of excluding "mass poets" in "a trend toward discounting purely commercial authors that has continued to the present and is typified by Charvat," 17. When one surveys its pages, one is struck by its deviance from the critical commonplace that Duyckinck was an elitist dandy, sneering at any sign of the commercial other than Irving or Cooper. Indeed, entries on EDEN Southworth, Susan Warner, Lydia H. Sigourney, Louisa Tuthill, and Harriet Beecher Stow, all wildly popular domestic novelists who might be assumed to have lived "off of" rather than "for" literature, all grace the pages of Duyckinck's magnum opus and ode to the literary world. Garish and lurid sensationalists like T.S. Arthur (described as being "engaged in the active career of authorship, which he has since pursued with popular favor") share space with Transcendentalists like Margaret Fuller and even perennial outsider Thoreau, complete with illustration of the Walden cabin and an excerpt from his "battle of the ants" section of the "Brute Neighbors" chapter from *Walden* as an example of his humorous writing, Evert A. and George L. Duyckinck, *Cyclopedia of American Literature*, vol. 2 (New York: Scribner, 1855), 601. Next to such representatives of what many at the time considered the outer fringe of an already eccentric coterie of Concord writers, Duyckinck included mass writers such as saccharine sentimentalist Donald G. Mitchell, whose narrative persona and pseudonym, Ik Marvel, became something of a latter day Geoffrey Crayon in the 1850s and his *Reveries of a Bachelor* a second generation *Sketch Book*. A closer look at Duyckinck's career indeed offers even better evidence of his own mass market ties, especially in his investment in establishing American literature by pitching it to as broad an audience as possible as the series editor of the Library of American Books (1846) under G.P. Putnam within a competitive market dominated by cheap British reprints, as Ezra Greenspan demonstrates in his fine biography, *George Palmer Putnam: Representative American Publisher* (State College, PA: Penn State University Press, 2000), 182. Duyckinck's optimism for reaching a mass market was evident in his hope that if "the American series goes well here...we shall want 200 at least of all the vols.—and I hope 500

for this market—indeed there ought to be one or two thousand sold here," qtd. in Greenspan, 182.
25. Bourdieu, "The Market," 135.
26. Leon Jackson, "The Social Construction of Thomas Carlyle's New England Reputation, 1834–36" *Proceedings of the American Antiquarian Society* 106.1 (1996), 186. The circulation of Carlyle's book throughout the Transcendental circle established his prominence among the group as rapidly as it was expunged. The example is telling of the importance of the group's collective reputation, which according to Jackson, came under direct threat when Carlyle's surprising sympathy with the South surfaced in his insistence on publishing proslavery articles, Jackson, "Carlyle," 186. For the cultural construction of Emerson and Thoreau's public reputations, see Richard Teichgraeber, *Sublime Thoughts/Penny Wisdom: Situating Emerson and Thoreau in the American Market* (Baltimore: Johns Hopkins University Press, 1995).
27. Bourdieu, "The Market," 136.
28. Lawrence Stone, "Prosopography" *Daedalus* 100 (Winter 1971), 57.
29. Alison Booth, *How to Make It as a Woman: Collective Biographical History from Victoria to the Present* (Chicago: University of Chicago Press, 2008), 13.
30. For more on the market revolution behind the professionalization of authorship, see Charles Sellers, *The Market Revolution: Jacksonian America, 1815–1846* (Oxford University Press, 1991). On the issue of professionalization of authorship during the antebellum period, Leon Jackson's *The Business of Letters* offers the finest, and to my knowledge only, challenge to William Charvat, *The Profession of Authorship in America* (Columbus: Ohio State University Press, 1968), the wildly influential pioneer of the study of literary economics. Jackson rejects his progressive, triumphalist historiography as well as his definition of authorship as full-time application to the craft, which he rightly claims, would eliminate Hawthorne and Irving from the category of "professional author," leaving very few qualifiers other than Cooper, 10–23. Jackson's assessment informs my understanding of authorship as a pursuit narrowly straddling amateurism and professionalism, which the Zborays have reinforced in *Literary Dollars and Social Sense*. On specialization and the formation of the cultural definition of artistic genius as a category both feared and revered, see Gustavus Stadler, *Troubling Minds: The Cultural Politics of Genius in the United States, 1840–1890* (Minneapolis: University of Minnesota Press, 2006). A fine history of the movement toward specialization is in Evelev, 51–78. I make use of all of these superb studies in my examination of coterie culture, which receives mention in each of these works, but not as a sustaining overarching concept. The Zborays' history is mainly author (and reader) driven, while Jackson emphasizes the multitude of economies of exchange that animated the literary market, particularly

the ethos and graft of gift exchange, with close attention to complementary books and their circulation as indices of a significant portion of an author's work extending beyond composition into tactics of extra-textual self-promotion. His theory is invaluable to this book, as it provides a useful framework for understanding the economic function, monetary and otherwise, of the coteries I explore.

31. Pierre Bourdieu, *Acts of Resistance: Against the Tyranny of the Market* (New York: New York Press, 1998), 7.
32. Ibid., 37.
33. A superb study of Garrison's own personal ambition to forge a career and an authorial presence in the literary market through the printed word is in R. Jackson Wilson's *Figures of Speech* (Baltimore: Johns Hopkins University Press, 1989). I cast Wilson's insight that Garrison "came to his radicalism in the course of his attempt to establish a career as a writer, and not the writing through his dedication to antislavery or any other cause" in the broader context of *The Liberator* circle and his relationships therein (especially with writers like Lydia Marie Child, who would eventually flee from his radical ethos) that dictated the course of the abolitionist agenda, 123.
34. Ibid., 96.
35. Henry James, Review of *Waiting for the Verdict*, by Rebecca Harding Davis *The Nation* 21 November 1867, rpt. in *Literary Criticism: Essays on Literature, American Writers, and English Writers*, ed. Leon Edel (New York: Library of America, 1984), 220.
36. Lytle Shaw describes coterie's association with impenetrable, exclusive language in his study of the mid-twentieth century New York poetry scene in *Frank O'Hara: The Poetics of Coterie* (2006). I argue, as he does for O'Hara's circle, that a sense of close-knit family and kinship permeated coterie culture to the extent that it worked its way into the very themes of the literature and "*thematized* the idea of a close-knit audience through the intimate, seemingly shared references," 3. Yet such gestures, as I find them in the antebellum literature, are pitched outward, inviting the reader into the circle. I extend Shaw to show how such themes signaled to readers the authorial persona's (and the author's by extension) allies, thereby illustrating at once an ideological stand as well as a fashionable, and thus commercially marketable, alternative lifestyle. Coterie studies, like Shaw's, focus on twentieth-century modernism or early British literature, and rarely treat multiple circles under one umbrella, as I do here.
37. Matthew Giordano, "Public Privacy: Melville's Coterie Authorship in *John Marr and Other Sailors*" *Leviathan: A Journal of Melville Studies* 9.3 (2007), 68. Arthur F. Marotti also defines coterie by its narrowly exclusive audience in *John Donne, Coterie Poet* (Madison: University of Wisconsin Press, 1986), but does not draw out the broader implications for the popular readership. Other scholarship on the English coteries ranges as far back as Sandra A. Burner's biography, *James Shirley: A*

Study of Literary Coteries and Patronage in Seventeenth-Century England (Lanham, MD: University Press of America, 1988), which, unlike Marotti's, does make inroads toward "a broad perception of the social and professional milieu of Caroline dramatists" despite missing echoes in Shirley's plays and poems of how "the patrons and his fellow playwrights, the political and literary circles to which writers belonged, the complex class structures that were open to Shirley and his colleagues provided the fictional subjects and the fashionable standards of taste to which seventeenth-century dramatists responded," xiv. In a critical analysis rooted in the market context, Jennifer Wicke argues that Virginia Woolf wrote *Mrs. Dalloway* mainly for her private circle of like-minded Modernists in "Coterie Consumption: Bloomsbury, Keynes, and Modernism as Marketing" *Marketing Modernisms: Self-Promotion, Canonization, Rereading*, ed. Ken J. H. Dettmar and Stephen Watt (Ann Arbor: University of Michigan Press, 1996), 109–32. Wicke also takes coterie as an insular characteristic with no mass market ambitions. Other scholarship on the English literary circles includes A.S. Collins, *The Profession of Letters: A Study of the Relation of Author to Patron, Publisher, and Public, 1780–1832* (New York: E.P. Dutton, 1929). Relevant to this study is his concern for book clubs, literary societies, coffee house and conversation clubs, all of which usefully draws out how such social capital building functioned not only as a networking opportunity, but as a forum for the judgment of literary works. These circles "both created and sent abroad a certain kind of public opinion, and in the matter of books and plays helped to build up the average criticism and to elevate or depress the sales," Collins, 71. Although caustic in his harsh dismissal of popular literature, Collins's early study nonetheless anticipates a Charvatian sensibility toward the shift in publishers' business practice toward increasing liberality in dispensing loans and gaudy salaries as the big houses accrued unprecedented power making them appear more like patrons of old.

38. David S. Shields, *Civil Tongues and Polite Letters in British America* (Charlottesville: University of North Carolina Press, 1997), xix.
39. Stephen Shapiro, *The Culture and Commerce of the Early American Novel: Reading the Atlantic World-System* (State College, PA: Penn State University Press, 2008), 172–73.
40. See also Brian Waterman's, *The Republic of Intellect: The Friendly Club of New York City and the Making of American Literature* (Baltimore: Johns Hopkins University Press, 2007). Waterman's study also shows the historical antecedents for the commercialization of nineteenth-century literary circles. He chronicles the rise of Charles Brockden Brown through his involvement in the club, which bonded over the death of one of its most influential members, Elihu Hubbard Smith. He focuses on the 1790s in particular, the decade in which Brown would achieve international success in what has been often described as America's first professional literary career. The crucial function of

the Friendly Club in the process of his career is particularly relevant to my approach toward the career triumphs and failures that stemmed directly from coteries ties, influences, and rivalries.
41. Deirdre N. McCloskey, *The Bourgeois Virtues: Ethics for an Age of Commerce* (Chicago: University of Chicago Press, 2006), 126.

1 "As Merchants on the 'Change": The Economy of Literary Circles, 1807–64

1. Andrew Delbanco, *Melville: His World and Work* (New York: Knopf, 2005), 96–97. Although I class Edward Widmer among those who artificially segregate Young America from the Knickerbockers, he deserves credit for having advanced a more complex and nuanced view of the political transformation of the two generations of Young America beyond Miller's picture of them as intellectuals led by a detached and bookish Duyckinck. Widmer usefully notes that Duyckinck's participation in politics thus has been drastically underestimated as that of "an effete snob who nearly ruined his disciple Melville with his prudery" (an image Hershel Parker forwards in his biography of Melville, particularly with respect to the editor's disapproval of Melville's antimissionary bent in his early novels of the 1840s). In more rare cases, Duyckinck is painted as the extreme opposite, a "raving locofoco hell bent on world revolution," *Young America: The Flowering of Democracy in New York City* (New York: Oxford University Press, 1999), 15. The picture is more complex than this, and the social linking between Knickerbockers and Young America was more prevalent than assumed, as I show in the next chapter.
2. Qtd. in Delbanco, 97.
3. Catharine Maria Sedgwick, qtd. in Hart, 303.
4. Evelev, 67–69.
5. For an excellent study of the salon culture of nineteenth-century American women writers in which Lynch forged her success, see Mary Loeffelholz, *From School to Salon: Reading Nineteenth-Century American Women's Poetry* (Princeton: Princeton University Press, 2004). For more on gender in poetry circles of the day, see Eliza Richard, *Gender and the Poetics of Reception in Poe's Circle* (Cambridge: Cambridge University Press, 2004). It is telling of her unusually powerful connections that Lynch managed to become such a central figure in poetry's publishing world, since it was so clearly dominated by men, unlike the market for fiction. Poe systematically competed with and excluded a number of women poets from his circle, for example. Poet Elizabeth Oakes Smith was bitter toward such exclusive male coterie culture on the occasion of Margaret Fuller's untimely death at the height of her powers. Such a genius as "Margaret had no fair chance," she observed, "no blessed opportunity to be what she might have been, such as the poorest masculine

dullard finds ready at hand, and crowds of approving on-lookers waiting to give him a godspeed," Oakes Smith, qtd. in Richard, 189.
6. Hart, 303.
7. George Foster, "The Literary Soirees" *New-York Tribune* (27 September 1848).
8. Barbara L. Packer, *The Transcendentalists* (Macon, GA: University of Georgia Press, 2007), 48.
9. Robert D. Putnam, *Bowling Alone: The Collapse and Revival of American Community* (New York: Touchstone, 2001), 22–24. More recent research supporting Putnam's claim that linking is a potent producer of profit can be found in David Halpern, *Social Capital* (Cambridge, UK: Polity Press, 2005), who notes that economic performance is most positively affected by bridging social capital, especially at the macro-level. While bonding within groups can be beneficial to health, too much of it at the expense of bridging capital can lead to suffering finances caused by corruption from excessive inner, rather than outer, dealings. The trend in social capital among nineteenth-century literary coteries is analogous to current nations, such as Sweden, in that their "growing individuality within a lifestyle maintains and enhances the connections between them." Halpern calls this "solidaristic individualism" as opposed to a splintered isolating individualism in which the group dissipates, a process that occurs in literary circles when authors depart to seek their own fortunes, 223. The uniqueness of the coterie identity, I argue, within the literary market encouraged authors to link their individual public profiles to their literary circles. For a clear definition of economic, cultural, social, and symbolic capital, see Pierre Bourdieu, "The Forms of Capital," *Handbook of Theory and Research for the Sociology of Education*, ed. J.G. Richardson (New York: Greenwood Press, 1986), 241–58. An excellent description of the four types of capital appears in Leon Jackson's antebellum biographical sketches, 32. Jackson explains bonding and bridging capital as the two forms of social capital vital to the function of antebellum periodicals, since "magazines required an immense amount of social capital [because] cooperation of many parties was required and collaboration (hence good will) was not only desirable but downright necessary," *The Business of Letters*, 126–27. I would add that literary clubs and societies were crucial sources of the bonding capital that sustained magazines, particularly Gaylord Taylor's *Knickerbocker Magazine* inspired by Irving's literary circle, discussed in chapter 2, and the *New York Ledger* in chapter three. Periodicals variously functioned as the hub of social capital building in the cases of the *Dial*, *DeBow's*, and *The National Anti-Slavery Standard*, as discussed respectively in chapters four, five, and six. I examine Elizabeth Peabody's short lived *Aesthetic Papers*, along with her work on *The Dial*, but only insofar as they supported her vital role as the owner of the Concord bookstore that would host a series of transcendental "conversations," and eventually become a locus of exchange for the circle essential to the careers of Hawthorne

and Fuller. Although this is not a magazine history per se, it certainly focuses on the operation of these journals as of one of several key methods supporting its primary emphasis on negotiations with booksellers and informal transactions with other associates and intermediaries in the book industry as methods by which literary circles engaged the market.
10. Halpern, 19.
11. Ibid., 25.
12. Jackson, 3.
13. Henry Brevoort, *The Letters of Henry Brevoort to Washington Irving*, ed. George S. Hellman (New York: Putnam, 1918), xx–xxi.
14. Though no works explicitly link sympathy with the function of authorial literary coteries of the antebellum United States, Hester Blum does mention in her stellar sociology of literary practice and folkways at sea that seamen at the time uniquely "formed their own literary coteries" in the close quarters of sea vessels, but mainly as readers of "the popular books of the day," or as individual writers rather than in groups as I treat them, *The View from the Masthead: Maritime Imagination and Antebellum Sea Narratives* (Chapel Hill: University of North Carolina Press, 2008), 20. The function of sympathy in antebellum literature and culture as an agent of social cohesion is described in Glenn Hendler's *Public Sentiments: Structures of Feeling in Nineteenth-Century American Literature* (Chapel Hill: University of North Carolina Press, 2001), and in Mary Louise Kete, *Sentimental Collaborations: Mourning and Middle-Class Identity in Nineteenth-Century America* (Durham: Duke University Press, 2000) as it occurs in poetry, which establishes the "ground for participation in a common cultural or intellectual project," xiv.
15. Bourdieu, *The Rules of Art*, 291.
16. Alexis De Tocqueville, *Democracy in America,* vol. 2 (New York: Vintage, 1990 [1830]), 254.
17. Henry David Thoreau, *Walden*, ed. J. Lyndon Shanley. (Princeton: Princeton University Press, 1971 [1854]), 50, 89.
18. Nicholas K. Bromell, *By the Sweat of the Brow: Literature and Labor in Antebellum America* (Chicago: University of Chicago Press, 1993). See particularly his introduction for a useful discussion of skepticism in antebellum culture toward intellectual work, "'Ain't That Work?'" 1–14.
19. Ann Douglass, *The Feminization of American Culture* (New York: Farrar, Strauss and Giroux, 1998), notes this pattern in "male sentimentalists" in general, 237. Evelev makes the connection to commercial culture explicit in terms of the broader trends toward professionalization in the literary marketplace, 55. A superb examination of the cultural status of bachelors at the time, particularly in the early Republic's backlash against them as threats to conventional separate spheres domesticity by way of celibacy, masturbation, and homosexuality, can be found in Bryce Traister, "The Wandering Bachelor: Irving, Masculinity, and

Authorship" *American Literature* 74.1 (2002), 111–37. Traister's focus is on the sexuality of the wandering bachelor as metaphor for political stances toward nationhood and methods of establishing an original national narrative voice—America and its literature as bachelor— designed to reconcile fraught relations with England. Sandra Tomc makes a more direct case for the marketability of the bachelor image, asserting that its packaging marked "the new entrepreneurial style of professionalism" attendant to the new commercialization of literature by the 1840s in "An Idle Industry: Nathaniel Parker Willis and the Workings of Literary Leisure" *American Quarterly* 49.4 (1997), 781. For a more recent, expanded examination of the commercial savvy of Willis, especially his skill at packaging and promoting sentimentality, and particularly controversy surrounding the wayward bachelor, see Thomas N. Baker, *Sentiment and Celebrity: Nathaniel Parker Willis and the Trial of Sentimentality* (Oxford: Oxford University Press, 1998), 68, 84, 88, 90, 163. Baker's account of Willis's adultery scandal involving famous actor Edwin Forrest, and the savage attack on him by his own sister, Fanny Fern, in her roman a clef, *Ruth Hall* (1855) is particularly telling of the bachelor as a cultural locus of attention, if not a lightning rod for controversy, 115–33.

20. John Paul Pritchard, *Literary Wise Men of New York: Criticism in New York, 1815–1860* (Baton Rouge: Louisiana State University Press, 1963), 9.
21. Thoreau, *Walden*, 323.
22. Pierre Bourdieu, *Distinction: A Social Critique of Judgment and Taste* (Cambridge, MA: Harvard University Press, 1987), 55.
23. Bourdieu, *The Rules of Art*, 56.
24. Ishmael Reed, *Conversations with Ishmael Reed* (Oxford: University of Mississippi Press, 1995), 25.
25. Jill R. Ehnenn, *Women's Literary Collaboration, Queerness, and Late Victorian Culture* (Aldershot: Ashgate, 2008), 2.
26. Gustav Flaubert, qtd. in Bourdieu, *The Rules of Art*, 82.
27. Ibid., 82.
28. Bourdieu, *The Rules of Art*, 83.
29. David S. Reynolds, *Beneath the American Renaissance: The Subversive Imagination in the Age of Emerson and Melville* (Cambridge, MA: Harvard University Press, 1988. Sheila Post-Lauria, *Correspondent Colorings: Melville in the Marketplace* (Boston: University of Massachusetts Press, 1996).
30. Bourdieu, *The Rules of Art*, 142.
31. Ibid., 142.
32. Colton, writing in 1844, is specifically complaining about the "policy of the Federal Administration from 1829 to 1841" that had removed what he felt were necessary protections for banks on investments, ruining the economy and "inoculating the poor with a mania against the rich, and the laborer with jealousy against the moneyed capitalist,"

blaming Jacksonian demagoguery, "the love of ONE MAN POWER [Andrew Jackson]...the chief malady that afflicted the nation," *The Juris Tracts, No. VII: Labor and Capital* (New York: Greeley and McElrath, 1844), 13.
33. Ibid., 249.
34. Meredith McGill, *American Literature and the Culture of Reprinting, 1834–1853* (Philadelphia: University of Pennsylvania Press, 2003), 14.
35. Ibid., 15.
36. Ibid., 283.

2 "An Instinct for Gold": Irving's Knickerbockers

1. Duyckinck's original had sequenced it thus: "When the war was ended the next year, sailing for Liverpool in the month of May, he passed over to Birmingham, in connection with the business with his house [to assist in his family's transatlantic import firm] which received such a shock from the commercial revulsions which followed, that he was thrown upon his resources as an author." Then, *after* committing to professional authorship, Duyckinck's narrative continues, Irving "settled at Birmingham in one of the finest regions of England [making] excursions in the neighbouring counties, studying English rural life and manners; materials which furnished some of the most attractive portions of the *Sketch Book*." Evert Duyckinck, qtd. in Andrew B. Myers, *The Worlds of Washington Irving, 1783–1859: From an Exhibition of Rare Book and Manuscript Materials in the Special Collections of the New York Public Library* (Tarrytown, NY: Sleepy Hollow Restorations), 33.
2. Ibid., 33.
3. Ibid., 33.
4. For two excellent studies of Young America see Perry Miller's foundational *The Raven and the Whale: The War of Words and Wits in the Era of Poe and Melville* (New York: Harcourt, Brace, and World, 1956), and the more recent Edward Widmer, *Young America: The Flowering of Democracy in New York City* (Oxford: Oxford University Press, 1999). Miller emphasizes the controversies between the developing factions within the New York literary circles, and Widmer takes on the political dimensions of Young America's literary project, rescuing them from critical typecasting as hidebound and conservative with a portrait that highlights their radical and diverse features. This chapter remedies the lack of such recent histories focusing specifically on the early Knickerbocker from their origins to 1830.
5. Quoted in Henry A. Pochman, "Washington Irving: Amateur or Professional?" *A Century of Commentary on the Works of Washington*

Irving, ed. Andrew B. Meyers (Tarrrytown, NY: Sleepy Hollow Restorations, 1976), 429.
6. Ben Harris McClary, "Washington Irving's Literary Pimpery" *American Notes and Queries* 10 (1972), 150–51. The pejorative diction of the title arises from McClary's discovery of Irving's proposal to aid a friend's career by attempting to place a manuscript, as if it were his friend's, with a publisher given to him several years prior by a Boston businessman. It is "quite good" he assured his friend, and would go far to launch his career. Prior to the findings in this research, McClary was not so damning about the ethics of Irving's business dealings, tracing his promotion of several authors through archival letters in an earlier study he entitled, "Washington Irving's Literary Midwifery: Five Unpublished Letters from the British Repository" *Philological Quarterly* 46 (1967): 277–83. McClary's finding, though provocative, is not typical of Irving's business practice that, however aggressive, was not so grossly unethical.
7. By 1848, Irving was well aware of the value of the Knickerbocker name in the literary market, and was careful to shape his own image of it for popular consumption in Putnam's Author's Revised Edition of *A History of New York*. He took special pride in the name's currency in commercial culture so that "when I find its very name become a 'household word,' and used to give the home stamp to everything recommended for popular acceptation, such as Knickerbocker societies, Knickerbocker insurance companies, Knickerbocker steamboats, Knickerbocker omnibuses, Knickerbocker bread, and Knickerbocker ice...I please myself with the persuasion that I have struck the right cord." Careful not to make his alliance with the market too obvious, Irving makes his signature self-effacing move to emphasize geniality and domesticity, hoping that the history, though it lacks "higher claims to learned acceptation" will "be thumbed and chuckled over by the family fireside," qtd. in *The Knickerbocker Tradition: Washington Irving's New York*, ed. Andrew B. Myers (New York: Sleepy Hollow Restorations, 1974), 9.
8. Much of Irving's legacy as a literary entrepreneur centers on *The Sketch Book*'s publication in England. The myriad narratives of it read like a compendium of competing mythologies of American commerce. William Cullen Bryant, memorializing Irving in reverent tones, praises him for his "enterprise" in persisting through an initial rejection of his manuscript, and defends him from the common charges of pandering to the English in the book, arguing that his friendly depiction of the English was "not to pay court" to them, but because it was his "instinct of mind to attach itself to the good and the beautiful," "Discourse on the Life, Character, and Genius of Washington Irving," *Washington Irving* (New York: G.P. Putnam, 1860), 14–15. Stanley T. Williams, Irving's first twentieth-century biographer responsible for tarnishing much of Irving's memory, accounts for *The Sketch Book*'s publication in England by saying it was all the work of Sir Walter Scott,

The Life of Washington Irving, vol. 1, 176. In fact, after initially being rejected by John Murray, Irving had craftily refused Scott's publisher, Archibald Constable, for a lesser one to hold out for Murray, Byron's publisher and the most fashionable in London at the time, who he eventually won over. Ralph M. Aderman does not mention Constable and concludes that Murray rejected *The Sketch Book* simply because "he could not secure the copyright," "Introduction," *Critical Essays on Washington Irving* (Boston: G.K. Hill, 1990), 4. Copyright concerns were not Murray's sole reason for rejecting him, as he later admitted to his biased underestimation of Irving's character: "I am convinced I did not half know you, and esteeming you highly as I did, certainly my esteem is doubled by my better knowledge of you," qtd. in Ben McClary, *Washington Irving and the House of Murray* (Knoxville, University of Tennessee Press, 1969), 18. Biographers like Mary Weatherspoon Bowden who are silent about Constable or Miller's roles in the process, *Washington Irving* (Boston: Twayne, 1981), echo Ben McClary's unproblematic rendition of the events that offers no reason why Irving refused Constable, merely stating, "nothing came of this," 19. Daniel Burstein takes Irving's revisionist history in the 1848 preface at its word, from Murray's humbling rejection, Irving's "gamely" contracting with Miller, and Scott's aid in securing Murray, all events rendered, the historian admits blithely in an aside, "(as Irving tells it)," *The Original Knickerbocker: The Life of Washington Irving* (New York: Basic Books, 2007), 150. William L. Hedges, *Washington Irving: An American Study, 1802–1832* (Baltimore: Johns Hopkins University Press, 1965) makes compelling comments about Irving's commercial inclinations, but none on the particulars of the publishing history of *The Sketch Book* in England; Robert Weisbuch eschews such publishing details to cast Irving as a British mimic in *Atlantic Double-Cross: American Literature and British Influence in the Age of Emerson* (Chicago: University of Chicago Press, 1986), 17; Pierre M. Irving, Washington's nephew and author of the "authorized" biography, suggests that Irving had already made up his mind to sign with Miller before receipt of Scott's letter offering Constable's services, but never speculates as to why he made such a decision, *The Life and Letters of Washington Irving*, vol. 4 (New York: G.P. Putnam and Sons, 1862–1864), 445. Irving's own rendition in the 1848 preface of the *Sketch Book* suggests naive haste and carelessness, part of his studied pose of amateurism, was behind it, yet that explanation willfully suppresses the significant delay between the rejection letter's arrival in early December 1819 and the closure of the Miller contact 9 January 1820, a time when Irving was amassing more numbers to qualify for English copyright, as David Pancost convincingly argues, "How Washington Irving Published *The Sketch Book* in England" *Studies in American Fiction* 14.1 (1986), 81.

9. Evert Ducykinck, *The Cyclopedia of American Literature*, vol. 2 (New York: Scribner, 1855), 2. For more on the Calliopean Society, see Eleanor

Scott, "Early Literary Clubs in New York City" *American Literature* 5.3 (1933), 3–16. One of the longest standing literary societies in American history, the Calliopeans met on occasion for more than a half century from 1788 to 1831. A branch of the Calliopeans, the Belles Lettres Club, included Irving's brother, John Treat Irving, who held office as secretary for a year and a half before entering a law practice. Recent graduates commonly joined such clubs for instruction in English composition, which was a deficiency in the college curriculum at the time, as Scott points out, 11. More than learning the art and science of the essay, the clubs functioned as a kind of finishing school in which future lawyers and businessmen could add literary and cultural taste to their professional acumen, knowledge deemed essential for serving elite clientele. Also related to the Calliopean Society was the Debating Society, which, according to New York Public Library manuscript records, met from April 1803 to April 1806, exactly the time leading up to *Salmagundi* (1807). Indeed, the society appears to have laid the groundwork for that collaborative effort, for in attendance were Irving, Paulding, and other members of the original Lads of Kilkenny. Its orations bore the unmistakable satirical stamp of *Salmagundi* with titles like, "Bobtail, One of the Brethren" by Peter Doodle and Simon Pure, as Scott notes, 12. The Addisonian wit and pen names of *Salmagundi* thus had their beginnings in the Debate Society.

10. Ibid., 2.
11. Ibid., 2.
12. Pierre M. Irving, *The Life and Letters of Washington Irving* (New York: G.P. Putnam, 1863), 179.
13. Ibid., 166.
14. Henry Brevoort, *Letters of Henry Brevoort to Washington Irving*, ed. George S. Hellman (New York: G.P. Putnam and Sons, 1918), xxi.
15. Pierre M. Irving, 169.
16. Ibid., 167.
17. Ibid., 167.
18. Since the early national period, bachelors had been subject to additional taxes because they were assumed to be a burden on society, associated with vagrancy, gambling, drunkenness, and homosexuality. By the mid-nineteenth century, boarding houses were 75 percent male in forty-five New York boarding houses according to one survey, Howard P. Chudacoff, *The Age of the Bachelor: Creating an American Subculture* (Princeton: Princeton University Press, 1999), 32. The Pennsylvania legislature resolved in 1824 "to lay a tax upon Bachelors above 25 years of age, the proceeds to be set apart as a fund for the support of Widows and Orphans of old soldiers," "Bachelor's Tax," *Albany Microscope*, 13 March 1824. Such taxes had been levied as early as 1656, as in the case of Hartford, Connecticut, where bachelors were required to pay twenty shillings per week as compensation for shirking their "family duties" and indulging in "the selfish

luxuries of solitary living," qtd. in Willystine Goodsell, *A History of Marriage and Family* (New York: Macmillan, 1934), 368.
19. "Tax on Old Bachelors" *New-England Galaxy*, 20 February 1824.
20. "Character of a Bachelor" *Saturday Evening Post*, 31 January 1824.
21. Donald G. Mitchell ("Ik Marvel") to Washington Irving, 13 June 1853, Washington Irving Papers, Manuscripts and Archives Division, New York Public Library.
22. Although its time period is the one just after Irving's, a particularly relevant study is by David Leverenz, *Manhood and the American Renaissance* (Ithaca: Cornell University Press, 1989).
23. Chudacoff, 8.
24. Washington Irving to Governeur Kemble, 1 July 1809, The Washington Irving Papers, Manuscripts and Archives Division, New York Public Library.
25. Ibid., 35.
26. John Bryant, *Melville and Repose: The Rhetoric of Humor in the American Renaissance* (Oxford: Oxford University Press, 1993), 54.
27. Pierre M. Irving, 177.
28. Bryce Traister, "The Wandering Bachelor: Irving, Masculinity and Authorship" *American Literature* 74.1 (2002), 111–37.
29. Pierre M. Irving, 167.
30. Washington Irving, *Salmagundi; or The Whim-whams and Opinions of Launcelot Langstaff, Esq. & Others*, ed. Bruce I. Granger and Martha Hartzog (Boston: Twayne, 1977), 239.
31. Pierre M. Irving, 171.
32. Ibid., I, 405.
33. Burstein, 118.
34. Ben Harris McClary, *Washington Irving and the House of Murray* (Knoxville: University of Tennessee Press, 1969), 14.
35. Washington Irving, *Letters I*, 654.
36. Qtd. in John W.M. Hallock, *The American Byron: Homosexuality and the Fall of Fitz-Greene Halleck* (Madison: University of Wisconsin Press, 2000), 114.
37. Halleck, qtd. in James Grant Wilson, *The Life and Letters of Fitz-Greene Halleck* (New York: D. Appleton, 1869), 272; 353.
38. Fitz-Greene Halleck, *Fanny* in Kendall B. Taft, *Minor Knickerbockers* (New York: American Book Company, 1947), 115.
39. Hallock posits that "readers were unsuccessful in their attempt to identify a real woman cloaked behind the name Fanny because Halleck's heroine caricatured a man, Drake," 75. The psychological truth of this forceful and striking claim can be augmented by my contextual reading of Halleck's use of Fanny as a target of excessive criticism of his own artistic and intellectual culture, and indeed his participation in it.
40. Wilson, 365.
41. Ibid., 368.
42. Halleck, *Fanny*, 108.

43. Ibid., 100.
44. Ibid., 116.
45. Washington Irving, *The Complete Works of Washington Irving: Letters, Vol. I, 1802–1823*, ed. Ralph M. Aderman (Boston: Twayne, 1978), 508. Brevoort married Laura Elizabeth Carlson on 20 September 1817. It should be mentioned that Irving does take on a humorous tone in the letter, as he poses as "poor me, left lonely & forlorn," 508. Yet his attempts to assure his friend that he is not jealous, his best wishes for the new marriage constantly are expressed in comparison to their own relationship, as he hopes this "unknown piece of perfection [who] has usurped my place...may prove as constant & faithful to you as I have been," 509.
46. Ibid., 2.
47. Ibid., 3.
48. Evert Duyckinck, "Preface," *Salmagundi; or, the Whimwhams and Opinions of Launcelot Langstaff, Esq. and Others*, ed. Evert Duyckinck (New York: G.P. Putnam's Sons, 1860), 11.
49. Pierre M. Irving, 178.
50. Qtd. in Ralph M. Alderman and Wyne R. Kime, *Advocate for America: The Life of James Kirke Paulding* (Selinsgrove, PA: Susquehanna University Press, 2003), 48.
51. Duyckinck, "Preface," 10.
52. Dr. Samuel Johnson, "Salmagundi," *Dictionary*, 1813; qtd. in Burstein, 49.
53. For more on this literary club that formed during Irving's absence in Europe, see Nelson F. Adkins, "James Fenimore Cooper and the Bread and Cheese Club" *Modern Language Notes* 47 (1932), 71–79. The club made Washington Irving and Washington Allston honorary members in 1826. For more precise dates based on Cooper's letters rather than anecdotal evidence, see Albert W. Marckwardt, "The Chronology and Personel of the Bread and Cheese Club" *American Literature* 6.4 (1935), 389–99. The club included roughly thirty-five prominent New Yorkers, including Bryant, Halleck, Sands, Verplank, Dunlap, Anthony Bleeker, and Henry Brevoort.
54. Qtd. in Duyckinck, *Cyclopaedia*, 110.
55. Strong qtd. in Miller, 29.
56. Cooper, qtd. in Miller, 29.
57. Bruce Redford, *The Society of Dilettanti: The Antic and the Antique in Eighteenth-Century England* (Los Angeles: J. Paul Getty Museum/Getty Research Institute, 2009), 34.
58. Washington Irving, *Letters I*, 90–91.
59. Washington Irving, *Knickerbocker* 13.206 (March 1839). In some ways Irving's sketch was the literary equivalent of standing at the fringes of a party, conspicuously detached from the strain and display of the central action. The cool, aloof option of sketching was indeed consonant with the fashionable code of the bachelor established by Lord Byron and Beau

Brummel, who opted for an understated and detached public presence compared to the aggressive self-promotional bravado of figures like P.T. Barnum and Robert Bonner, who is discussed in the next chapter. Leo Braudy aptly captures the Byron and Brummell sensibility that Irving pursued in his writings and popular bachelor image. This type of dandy was never flashy like the seventeenth-century "gaudy and feathered fop," and "sought to be noticed not for his lavish dress but for the intricate self-consciousness of his restraint. Like Byron going to parties and standing on the fringes and in the corners, Brummell's version of the dandy conveys a sense of separation and melancholy, as if he were in mourning for society itself with all its misdirected splendor," *The Frenzy of Renown: Fame and Its History* (New York: Oxford University Press, 1986), 404.

60. Washington Irving, *Letters I*, 90–91.

61. Critic Kristie Hamilton has produced the fullest and best study of the cultural conditions that gave rise to the literary sketch. In particular, she aptly observes that the increasing diversity and class mobility brought by sharp rises in immigration, along with a print culture that flooded American lives with more information than ever, literary sketches "presented such living as comprehensible," and indeed more manageable due to their lightness, and their classification into tropes and conventions mediated by the capitalist marketplace. The sketch compartmentalized the dizzying profusion of data inundating American culture into consumable, and pleasing vignettes so that "places became *scenes*," as Hamilton notes, "people were transformed into *characters*" (hence the sudden rise in popular biographies), and "events...were abstracted as *incidents*." The result was the domestication of otherwise unwieldy and potentially dangerous class conflicts and economic tension: "differences in regional and territorial cultures, ethnic histories, class positions, occupational identifications, and so on, were thus made comprehensible, even consumable, and what is more to the point, ordinary," *America's Sketchbook: The Cultural Life of a Nineteenth-Century Literary Genre* (Athens: Ohio University Press, 1998), 143. This usefully describes the politics behind Irving's aesthetic defense of the sketch as a literary genre preferable to the novel.

62. In *Moby-Dick*, Melville claims through the voice of his narrator, Ishmael, that we "rise and swell with [the] subject," just as his handwriting "unconsciously...expands into placard capitals." Subtle shading, and muted tones be damned, "Give me Vesuvius' crater for an inkstand! Friends, hold my arms!" for "so magnifying is the virtue of writing on a liberal theme! We expand to its bulk," he roars, noticing by chapter 104 the sheer immensity and concentration of his work thus far. "To produce a mighty book, you must choose a mighty theme," he reasons, in an attempt to explain his magnificent ambition. Herman Melville, *Moby-Dick* (Oxford: Oxford University Press, 1998 [1855]), 409.

63. McDonald Clarke, *The Elixir of Moonshine; Being a Collection of Prose and Poetry by the Mad Poet* [1822], qtd. in Taft, 400.
64. Wilson, 467.
65. Qtd. in Burstein, 71.
66. Brevoort, 63. On the economy of gift book exchanges and complementary copies distributed by authors with the intention of furthering their careers, see Leon Jackson, *The Business of Letters: Authorial Economies in Antebellum America* (Stanford: Stanford University Press, 2008), particularly chapter 3, "Authorship and Gift Exchange," 89–141. Jackson is especially compelling in his discussion of how complementary copies create a sense of debt in the recipient that is often paid by way of advocacy of the book throughout his or her social network. As I mention in the introduction, such a gesture typifies the sort of social capital building through bonding and linking described by social theorist Robert Putnam in *Bowling Alone: The Collapse and Revival of American Community* (New York: Simon and Schuster, 2000).
67. Brevoort, 77.
68. Ibid., 65.
69. Ibid., 83.
70. Ibid., 99.
71. Ibid., 172.
72. Halleck, qtd. in Wilson, 327.
73. Ibid., 330.
74. Duyckinck, "Preface," 9.
75. Wilson, 224.
76. Miller, 36.
77. Wilson, 234.
78. Ibid., 236.
79. Ibid., 232.
80. Ibid., 440.
81. Ibid., 237.
82. Ibid., 239.
83. Brevoort, ix.
84. Ibid., 254.
85. Qtd. in Myers, 70.
86. Ibid., 70.
87. Daniel Embury, a fellow clerk at Astor's mansion, tells the anecdote: "Halleck often used to joke Mr. Astor about his accumulating income, and perhaps rather rashly said, 'Mr. Astor, of what use is all this money to you? I would be content to live upon a couple hundred dollars a year for the rest of my life if I were only sure of it.' The old man remembered that and, with a bitter satire, reminded Halleck of it in his will," Wilson, 477.
88. Qtd. in Hallock, 128.
89. Halleck, "Alnwick Castle," qtd. in Taft, 117.
90. Ibid., 109.

3 Staff Bonds: Bonner's *New York Ledger*

1. "Robert Bonner Is Dead" *New York Times*, 7 July 1899, 1. (Hereafter, "Obituary").
2. Ralph Admari, "Bonner and the 'Ledger,'" *American Book Collector* 6 (1935), 90.
3. Bonner's relationship with Sylvanus Cobb only, and not the *Ledger* staff as a whole, is the subject of an older anecdotal narrative history by the adventure writer's relative, Stanwood Cobb in *The Magnificent Partnership* (New York: Vantage, 1954). The *Ledger* has not been discussed as a force in American literary history more recently, as the nineteenth-century periodical scene instead has been explored, for example, with respect to its early forms of feminist social activism by Aleta Feinsod Cane and Susan Alves, eds., *"The Only Efficient Instrument": American Women Writers and the Periodical, 1837–1916* (Iowa City: University of Iowa Press, 2001), and Ann Stephens's cautionary magazine novels warning against the function of fashion as a mask for predatory capitalist swindlers has been convincingly treated by Patricia Okker, *Social Stories: The Magazine Novel in Nineteenth-Century America* (Charlottesville, VA: University of Virginia Press, 2003), 55–78.
4. Studies such as Elizabethada Wright's "Pen-Ended Oratory: Fanny Fern's Use of the Periodical as a Rhetorical Platform" *American Journalism* 18.2 (2001), 64–82 typify this trend. Carole Moses, in "The Domestic Transcendentalism of Fanny Fern," has amassed the most extensive evidence of the overwhelming critical commonplace of treating Fern as a radical rebel feminist to the exclusion of her sentimentally driven writings, which she argues, refigure dominant tropes of Transcendentalism for ready application to the domestic sphere, *Texas Studies in Literature and Language* 50.1 (2008), 90. I would argue that Fern's tough minded individualism not only serves the seldom discussed domestic sentimentality of her fiction, but also serves as the basis for her business ethic and practice within the literary marketplace. Specifically, the code of sympathy and love within a market setting emerge in her close ties to Bonner (immortalized in his fictional counterpart's endearment to the protagonist of *Ruth Hall*) and *Ledger* colleague, James Parton, whom she married.
5. Joyce Warren, "Uncommon Discourse: Fanny Fern and the *New York Ledger*" in *Periodical Literature in Nineteenth-Century America* (Charlottesville: University of Virginia Press, 1995), 51–68.
6. P.T. Barnum to Robert Bonner, 5 February 1862, The Robert Bonner Papers, Manuscripts and Archives Division, New York Public Library (Hereafter "Bonner Papers," NYPL). This archive provides much of the evidence supporting the nature of his relationship with his staff and his management style discussed in this chapter.
7. *The Boston Daily Atlas* reported that "Mr. Robert Bonner set 25,500 ems in twenty hours, twenty-eight minutes, without a moment's rest," fueled in this test of speed and endurance by lemon pie. "This instance

of 'type sticking,'" they certified, "is the swiftest we have ever heard of." Not to miss an opportunity to hire new hands capable of surpassing this feat, the *Atlas* declared, "if more can be accomplished by any other printers in the U.S., we should like to be informed of it," *Boston Daily Atlas* 14.34 (1845), 2.
8. William Cullen Bryant to Robert Bonner, 5 October 1861, "Bonner Papers," NYPL.
9. N.P. Willis to Robert Bonner, 17 February 1871, "Bonner Papers," NYPL.
10. Longfellow's astronomical payday of $3000 for his *Ledger* poem "The Hanging of the Crane" was eclipsed by the humble Tennyson, who initially refused Bonner's extravagant offer of $5000 (roughly $125,000 in today's currency) for "England and America in 1782." But, like Fanny Fern, who demurred offers of twenty-five, fifty, and seventy-five dollars per column before finally accepting his outlandish $100 per column bid, and lecturer Edward Everett, who could not refuse Bonner's $10,000 donation to his Mount Vernon Project in exchange for his writing, the English poet eventually succumbed to the lucrative deal. Details about the Tennyson negotiation, and the ideological, aesthetic, and cultural tensions inherent in an English poet's alliance with the American mass commercial market are available in Kathryn Ledbetter's "Resistance and Commodification: Tennyson's 'Indecent Exposure' in the Periodicals" *Tennyson and Victorian Periodicals: Commodities in Context* (Surrey, UK: Ashgate, 2007), 45–100.
11. The New England literary elite skewered Bonner in the *Boston Transcript*, for example, in a barb reprinted in the *Vanity Fair*, an arbiter of taste for the affluent. The *Transcript*'s headline read, "Bonner A Critic," lampooning the editor's conflation of the language of literary criticism with that of advertising copy. They seized upon the bombast of his proclamation that Bancroft's "Battle of Lake Erie" "combines the accuracy of mathematics with the interest of romance," jibing that "one advantage" our American authors derive from publishing with the *Ledger* is "the profound criticism of their merits by the publisher." *Vanity Fair* issued a mock defense of Bonner claiming, "he is a tradesman and should not be blamed for trying to sell his wares." Then the assault begins, as they offer "characterizations of his writers who he has not yet described," eviscerating his staff: "The leaves of Fanny Fern join the pregnancy of the potato salad with the sharpness of the steel trap! The novels of Mrs. Southworth fuse the detail of the Flemish school with the indescribable horrors of the French Revolution!" "Ledger Demain," *Vanity Fair* 10 November 1860, 242. This response is representative of the outcry against the radical and aggressive literary capitalism the *Ledger* introduced to the market.
12. Frank Luther Mott's statistic here has been taken at face value for some time as it appears in *A History of American Magazines, vol. II, 1850–1865* (Cambridge, MA: Harvard University Press, 1938), 359.

Yet his estimate of 400,000 is based solely on Bonner's advertisement boast in the 7 January 1860 *Harper's Weekly*, which could very well have been exaggerated, especially given what we know about his aggressive and audacious advertising tactics. James Dabney McCabe estimated in 1871 that "the 'Ledger' now circulates over 300,000 copies per week and is growing in the public favor" according to his biographical sketch, "Robert Bonner," *Great Fortunes and How They Were Made* (New York: E. Hamaford, 1871), 415. Though the figure certainly reached 400,000, it is not likely to have done so as early as 1860. McCabe's estimate appears to be conservative in light of Stanford University Libraries data file on the *Ledger*, which lists a circulation of 377,000 in 1870, *Dime Novels and Penny Dreadfuls*, "*New York Ledger*: Description," Stanford University Libraries, 13 July 2009, suloas.stanford.edu/.

13. Kenneth Salzer discusses this pattern convincingly in "Call Her Ishmael: E.D.E.N. Southworth, Robert Bonner and the 'Experiment' of *Self-Made*," *Popular Nineteenth-Century American Women Writers and the Literary Marketplace*, ed. Earl Yarington and Mary DeJong (Newcastle upon Tyne, England: Cambridge Scholars, 2007), 215–35. Salzer usefully makes light of how Southworth models Worth after Bonner, which I expand to encompass a larger pattern among *Ledger* writers, particularly Cobb and Fern, who create fictional characters based on their beloved editor. Such characters in Southworth (Ishmael Worth), Cobb (Ruric Nevel), and Fern (Mr. Walter, Ruth's editor) are Bonneresque capitalist heroes, who embody the principles of Bonner's own business practice characterized by staunch advocacy, particularly the wise use of power, usually portrayed as professional skill, to bravely protect friends and loved ones from enemies. I treat Mr. Walter as an extension of Bonner in "Capital Sentiment: Fanny Fern's Transformation of the Gentleman Publisher's Code" in *Capital Letters: Authorship in the Antebellum Literary Market* (Iowa City: University of Iowa Press), 65–81.

14. After the *Ledger* offices burned down in 1860, Bonner promptly commissioned the construction of a large marble building to serve as the paper's headquarters on the corner of Spruce and William Streets in New York City. The operation remained there through Bonner's retirement in 1887, when he handed over the reins to his sons. Cobb's death that year and the new management signaled a sea change for the *Ledger*, which sharply declined in sales, as rival journals took advantage of mail order advertisements to defeat the once mighty magazine, Mott, 362–63.

15. Qtd. in Mott, 359.

16. Critical outrage at presumably improper, indecorous content in Southworth's tales is usefully outlined in Linda Narajo-Huebl's "The Road to Perdition: E.D.E.N. Southworth and the Critics" *American Periodicals* 16.2 (2006): 123–50.

17. Robert Bonner to Sylvanus Cobb, 4 April 1884, "Bonner Papers," NYPL.
18. Matthew Hale Smith, "Robert Bonner and the New York Ledger," *Sunshine and Shadow in New York* (Hartford: J.B. Burr, 1869), 621.
19. Henry Ward Beecher, *Norwood, or Village Life in New England* (New York: Scribner, 1868), v.
20. Mary Noel, *Villains Galore: The Heyday of the Popular Story Weekly* (New York: Macmillan, 1954), 91.
21. Smith, 610.
22. Beecher, 551.
23. "Editorial," *Freedom's Champion* 10.31 (12 September 1867), 4.
24. Beecher, vi.
25. Bonner's brassy, shrill advertisement announced that "'Fanny Fern' writes for the *Ledger*!" in the tone of a carnival barker, flashing the price of the author, "Read the thousand-dollar story in the *Ledger*!" in a kind of Barnumesque freakshow of literary commerce in which he enticed readers into glimpsing for themselves a story of such an unimaginable cost. Qtd. in Laura Carter Holloway, *Famous American Fortunes and the Men Who Made Them* (Philadelphia: Bradley, 1884), 486. The spectacular $1000 price tag for the story automatically made it something of a curiosity to be indulged by readers for a mere six cents, a seemingly insane economy of exchange grossly favoring the consumer.
26. Ibid., 522.
27. Henry Ward Beecher to Robert Bonner, 23 January 1872, "Bonner Papers," NYPL.
28. Mark Twain attended one of Beecher's wildly popular sermons at Plymouth Church in Brooklyn, which attracted thousands of listeners. He observed a flamboyant theatricality in Beecher's preaching style, which bore much in common with Bonner's interest in entertaining the masses. Indeed the two seemed naturally to gravitate toward each other, as Bonner's letters to him appear to be the most frequent and candid of his entire correspondence. From the evidence of the letters, Bonner appears to have been best friends with the man Twain described as a charismatic showman on stage at the height of his powers, "a remarkably handsome man when he is in the full tide of sermonizing and his face is lit up with animation, but he is as homely as a singed cat when he isn't doing anything." His antics in the pulpit were more carnival barker than preacher, "as he went marching up and down the stage, sawing his arms in the air, howling sarcasms this way and that, discharging rockets of poetry, and exploding mines of eloquence" in a pyrotechnic rhetorical display, "stopping now and then to stamp his foot three times in succession to emphasize a point." Acutely aware of Beecher's total control over his congregation, Twain observed a performance better suited to the theatre than to church, noting that "I could have started the audience with a single clap of the hands and brought down the house," qtd. in Debby Applegate, *The*

Most Famous Man in America: The Biography of Henry Ward Beecher (New York: Random House, 2007), 372–73.
29. Henry Ward Beecher to Robert Bonner, 9 March 1865, "Bonner Papers," NYPL.
30. Henry Ward Beecher to Robert Bonner, 20 August 1874, "Bonner Papers," NYPL.
31. Various types of community were envisioned in the larger theories of Robert Owen, Charles Fourier, and Karl Marx, who observed of the 1840s that "only in community has each individual the means of cultivating his gifts in all directions; only in the community…is personal freedom possible," *The Portable Karl Marx*, ed. Eugene Kamenka (New York: Penguin, 1983), 193.
32. Sylvanus Cobb to Robert Bonner, 12 January 1862, "Bonner Papers," NYPL.
33. Ralph Waldo Emerson, "Gifts," *Essays: Second Series* in *The Essential Writings of Ralph Waldo Emerson* (New York: Modern Library, 2000 [1844]), 363.
34. Sylvanus Cobb to Robert Bonner, 10 April 1864, "Bonner Papers," NYPL.
35. Sylvanus Cobb to Robert Bonner, 18 October 1864, "Bonner Papers," NYPL.
36. Sylvanus Cobb to Robert Bonner, 22 December 1864, "Bonner Papers," NYPL.
37. Sylvanus Cobb to Robert Bonner, 24 January 1874, "Bonner Papers," NYPL. For a sympathetic, if not excessively adoring, history of Cobb's relationship with Bonner, see *The Magnificent Partnership*, by Cobb's grandson, Stanwood (New York: Vantage, 1954).
38. Terry Novak, "Fanny Fern (Sara Willis Parton)," *Writers of the American Renaissance*, ed. Denise D. Knight (Westport, CT: Greenwood Press, 2003), 128.
39. I discuss Fern's depiction of Ruth's search for employment in the business streets and the gender dichotomy represented in the periodical press in *Capital Letters: Authorship in the Antebellum Literary Market* (Iowa City: University of Iowa Press, 2009), 75–81, and Melville's parody of gender politics in chapter 6, "Satirizing the Spheres: Refiguring Gender and Authorship in Melville," 127–44.
40. Critic Carole Moses links Fuller's understanding of gender fluidity to Fern's articles, "Look on this Picture, and Then on That" and "A Little Talk with 'The Other Sex'" in "The Domestic Transcendentalism of Fanny Fern," 108. The connection, I argue, has intriguing implications for the "gender" of the *New York Ledger*, and specifically, Fanny Fern's position at its heart that mediates the bifurcated genres of the magazine's content according to men's and women's reading.
41. Margaret Fuller, *Woman in the Nineteenth Century* in *The Essential Margaret Fuller*, ed. Jeffrey Steele (New Brunswick, NJ: Rutgers University Press, 1995), 245.

Notes

42. Joyce Warren, "Fanny Fern: Performative Incivilities and Rap" *Studies in American Humor* 3 (1999), 17.
43. Beecher, 552. For an excellent discussion of the family literary magazine as a genre engaged in the moral instructions of young women in both America and England, see Jennifer Phegley's *Educating the Proper Woman Reader: Victorian Family Literary Magazines and the Cultural Health of the Nation* (Columbus: Ohio State University Press, 2004). Although she does not discuss the *Ledger*, Phegley's stimulating coverage of *Belgravia Magazine*'s defense of the sensational novel supports my focus on Bonner's promotion of the *Ledger* as a family magazine to thwart negative associations with sensational novels through a broad staff of writers deliberately including moral instruction and the high profile minister, Beecher, 110–51.
44. Warren, "Uncommon Discourse," 58.
45. Mott, 360.
46. Beecher, 552.
47. Mott, 360.
48. Lydia Sigourney to Robert Bonner, n.d., "Bonner Papers," NYPL.
49. Fanny Fern, "House-Furnishings by Proxy" *Ruth Hall and Other Writings*, ed. Joyce W. Warren (Rutgers: Rutgers University Press, 1986), 315.
50. Fern, "Shall Women Vote?" 317.
51. "Literature," Classified Advertisements, *New York Herald* (7 April 1863), 10. Although he made no pretensions to the status of an exalted figure like Dickens, Cobb's celebrity often placed him in the role of dignified author of serious literature. He was frequently called to deliver orations, for example, such as one he described that was attended by "a huge crowd, a fine band of music, &c. and the people praised by effort much. Twice they stopped me during the delivery—once to give three cheers and once to give three times—thrice! The speakers in the afternoon had much to say about 'Cobb' and the 'N.Y. Ledger,'" Sylvanus Cobb to Robert Bonner, 6 July 1860, "Robert Bonner Papers," NYPL.
52. "Obituary," 1. Mott makes it clear that Everett's reputation cannot be overestimated, noting he "had inherited from the dead Webster the mantle of greatness which popular imagination had conferred upon the 'God-like' orator," 23. Such emphasis is crucial, as Everett has not been well preserved in the annals of history, whether popular political or literary, despite his prominent place in the culture.
53. Robert Bonner to George Bancroft, 20 January 1865, "Bonner Papers," NYPL.
54. *Vanity Fair*, 1.28 (1860).
55. "Obituary," 1.
56. This was a particularly telling moment in the history of the literary marketplace, as it was the first real forecast in America of the total domination of the romance genre over literary fiction that has come

to characterize the publishing industry today. The most recent findings, as reported by Lauren Collins, show "romance generated nearly $1.4 billion in sales in 2007 [which was] more than literary fiction (four hundred and sixty-six million). Of people who read books, one in five read a romance," Lauren Collins, "Real Romance: How Nora Roberts Became America's Most Popular Novelist" *The New Yorker* 85.18 (22 June 2009), 66.
57. "Literature," Classified Advertisements, *New York Herald* (7 April 1863), 10.
58. Holloway, 486.
59. Frederic Hudson, *Journalism in the United States from 1690 to 1872* (New York: Routledge, 2000 [1876]), 649.
60. Smith, 609.
61. Ibid., 609.
62. *New York Ledger* Advertisement, *The Farmer's Cabinet* [Amherst, NH] ,57.33 (1859), 1, 4.
63. Ledbetter, 188.
64. "Robert Bonner's Income" *New York Herald* 32.153 (2 June 1867), 3.
65. Sylvanus Cobb, "Ideas for *Ledger* Stories," n.d., "Bonner Papers," NYPL. *Gunmaker* was published in 1856 and republished in the *Ledger* three times and was not brought out as a book until 1888. According to standard Bonner protocol, Southworth's *Hidden Hand* was also published three times before appearing as a bound novel. This may appear exploitative since those serial republications do not bring the author any direct profits. Yet those republications, along with the audacious $20,000 advertising campaigns Bonner fronted for each work, rooted these tales deeply in print culture, making their titles and authors household names and thus securing a popular reception before introducing them into the high risk book trade.
66. Sylvanus Cobb, *The Gunmaker of Moscow* (New York: Robert Bonner's Sons, 1888), 29.
67. Ibid., 90–91.
68. Ibid., 99.
69. Ibid., 181.
70. For a full analysis of the extent to which Fern models Mr. Walter after Bonner, see David Dowling, *Capital Letters: Authorship in the Antebellum Literary Market* (Iowa City: University of Iowa, 2009), 65–77. Salzer's "Call Her Ishmael: E.D.E.N. Southworth, Robert Bonner and the 'Experiment' of *Self-Made*" links Southworth's protagonist, Ishmael Worth, to Bonner. No other published studies, however, have explained the extent to which Cobb's Ruric Nevel, his most famous protagonist, was patterned after Bonner.
71. M.M. Smith, *Kick Him Down Hill; or, Ups and Downs of Business "Gold Wins"* (New York: United States Publishing, 1875), 168.
72. Charles Tracy Bronson, "Robert Bonner" *New York Times* (23 May 1897), SM2.

73. Helen Papashvily, *All the Happy Endings: A Study of the Domestic Novel in America* (New York: Harper & Brothers, 1956), 125.
74. Mott, 25.
75. Charles Astor Bristed, *Blackwood's Magazine* 63.106 (January 1848).
76. Receipt of Payment to George W. Clarke, 26 Decemeber 1865, "Bonner Papers," NYPL.
77. Sylvanus Cobb to Robert Bonner, 10 February 1863, "Robert Bonner Papers," NYPL.
78. James Parton, *Noted Women of Europe and America* (Hartford: Phoenix, 1883), 3.
79. Milton Embick Fowler, *James Parton: The Father of Modern Biography* (New York: Greenwood Press, 1968).
80. John C. Abbott to Robert Bonner, 12 January 1863, "Bonner Papers," NYPL.
81. Qtd. in James Parton, *Fanny Fern: A Memorial Volume* (New York: G.W. Carlton, 1874), 65.
82. Leon Lewis to Robert Bonner, 23 June 1870, "Bonner Papers," NYPL.
83. Ibid. Lewis was fond of donning a carnival barker's rhetorical flourish in his letters to Bonner, braying out in one particularly ripe example, "I have got forty A.1 ideas here, but only *one extra best*, and that has come to me at the 11th hour." Selling the pieces to Bonner was Lewis's role, while his wife carried the weight of writing the stories almost entirely on her own. Lewis relished selling his wife's writing to the most notorious literary salesman in the world, urging him at one point that "you will find in our new story something that will *entirely please you*, whether for extra pushing in the way of advertising or in ordinary routine," Leon Lewis to Robert Bonner, 1862 (?) n.m, n.d., "Bonner Papers," NYPL.
84. Leon Lewis to Robert Bonner, 26 September 1878, "Bonner Papers," NYPL.
85. Harriet Lewis to Robert Bonner, 1 May 1878, "Bonner Papers," NYPL.
86. Leon Lewis to Robert Bonner, n.d., n.m., 1898, "Bonner Papers," NYPL.
87. Ibid., 89–90.
88. Gerald Fallon to Robert Bonner, 9 August 1882, "Bonner Papers," NYPL. It should be mentioned though that many authors in good standing with Bonner such as Cobb routinely asked for money, especially advanced payments, almost always citing some financial calamity. "I have a note to pay in Boston of $210," Cobb wrote in one letter requesting a total of three hundred dollars, "the last note on my lot of land in Fairmount, and I must send that on as soon as I can," Sylvanius Cobb to Robert Bonner, 30 July 1861, "Robert Bonner Papers," NYPL.

89. Addey Atwood to Robert Bonner, 20 April 1865, "Bonner Papers," NYPL.
90. Mary C. Ames to Robert Bonner, 29 January 1861, "Bonner Papers," NYPL.
91. Mary C. Ames to Robert Bonner, 17 January 1862, "Bonner Papers," NYPL.
92. Mary C. Ames to Robert Bonner, 18 March 1873, "Bonner Papers," NYPL.

4 "THE SECTION TO WHICH WE BELONG": EMERSON'S TRANSCENDENTALISTS

1. Cornelius Matthews, *The Career of Puffer Hopkins* (New York: Harper and Brothers, 1843), 183.
2. Ralph Waldo Emerson, *The Collected Works of Ralph Waldo Emerson: Nature, Addresses, and Lectures*, ed. Robert E. Spiller (Cambridge, MA: Belknap Press of Harvard University Press, 1970), 69.
3. Ralph Waldo Emerson, "Self-Reliance," *The Collected Works of Ralph Waldo Emerson: Essays, First Series*, ed. Robert E. Spiller (Cambridge, MA: Belknap Press of Harvard University Press, 1979), 28, 29.
4. For more on Emerson's management of his own professional career, particularly through his detailed account books that led him away from book publishing toward what for him was the more lucrative lecture circuit, see Joel Myerson, "Ralph Waldo Emerson's Income from His Books," *The Professions of Authorship: Essays in Honor of Matthew J. Ruccoli*, ed. Richard Layman and Joel Myerson (Columbia: University of South Carolina Press, 1996), 135–49, 136.
5. N.P. Willis, "Emerson" *Home Journal* (2 February 1850).
6. Duyckinck, *Cyclopaedia II*, 365.
7. Ibid., 655.
8. Several exceptions to this general pattern, of course, can be cited. Writing for the *Tribune Office*, transcendentalist and Brook Farm founder George Ripley, for example, bowed to Irving's lofty status in a letter apologizing for the "slight and inadequate notice of your *Biography of Goldsmith*," asked him forgiveness, and complimented him profusely. "Let me, at the same time express my gratitude for the delight which for many years I have received from your writings," he wrote in his laudatory salutation, signing off as "your obliged servant," George Ripley to Washington Irving, 6 September 1849, The Washington Irving Papers, Manuscripts and Archives Division, New York Public Library.
9. Ralph Waldo Emerson, *The Journals and Miscellaneous Notebooks of Ralph Waldo Emerson, vol. 7, 1838–1842*, ed. A.W. Plumstead and Harrison Hayford (Cambridge, MA: Harvard University Press, 1969), 394.

10. Anne C. Rose, *Voices of the Marketplace: American Thought and Culture, 1830–1860* (New York: Twayne, 1995), 99.
11. Margaret Fuller, *Summer on the Lakes* in *The Essential Margaret Fuller*, ed. Jeffrey Steele (New Brunswick, NJ: Rutgers University Press, 1995), 107.
12. Ibid., 88. Later in her career when she accepted employment for Horace Greeley's *New-York Tribune*, Fuller developed an affinity for New York City. Upon her departure for Europe, she reflected on her time there, "where twenty months have presented me with a richer and more varied exercise for thought and life than twenty years could in any other part of these United States." Not only did the city offer a living situation amenable to her independent spirit—"a person who is independent and knows what he wants, may lead his proper life here unimpeded by others"—she also appreciated New York's position "at the point where American and European interests converge," specifically as a locus of revolutionary thought and social change "on two great leadings—the superlative importance of promoting National Education by heightening and deepening the cultivation of individual minds, and the part which is assigned to Woman in the next stage of human progress in this country," Margaret Fuller, "Farewell," *New York Daily Tribune* (1 August 1846), qtd. in Steele, 403. No Transcendentalist thrived or spearheaded such progressive social change in New York as she did; her success there was uncommon, and thus she represents a significant voice in scrutinizing the shortcomings of the Concord coterie as a detached enclave of thinkers.
13. Ibid., 105.
14. Susan Cheever's chapter, "Emerson Pays for Everything," in *American Bloomsbury*, goes so far as to say that "Emerson wrote some wonderful lines, and some true biographical portraits, but it is as the sugar daddy of American literature that he really takes his place in the pantheon of Concord writers," 38. Were Cheever not writing a popular history, the assertion would be unforgivable, given the profound aesthetic debts so much of New England literature owes Emerson. Indeed, much of Fuller and Thoreau's writings directly respond to, elaborate on, and carefully illustrate with details from embodied lived experience (especially in *Summer on the Lakes* and *Walden*) many of Emerson's more compelling principles about self-reliance and nature. Yet short of sweepingly dismissing his aesthetic and philosophical influence, Cheever's claim is provocative and compelling. I follow through with the premise that he was the key intermediary in promoting Transcendental careers, but take it less as a blunt economic contribution to the circle—a series of handouts in the form of paid bills, free rent, and arranged employment—and more as an invitation to explore his management style, and how it reinforced, and in some cases clashed with his philosophical ideals that had little good to say about commercialism and the market. For within Emerson's

intermediary method lies the very ways in which Transcendentalism not only accommodated for but also embraced the market.
15. In his engaging narrative history, Samuel A. Schreiner, Jr., notes that Emerson's legal victory did not translate into instant wealth for the Concord sage. "Although Ellen's estate finally came through, bringing the total to twenty-three thousand dollars," the equivalent of nearly a half million dollars in today's currency, "which should yield an annual income of some twelve hundred dollars, much of it was in temporarily unyielding bank stock," *The Concord Quartet: Alcott, Emerson, Hawthorne, Thoreau, and the Friendship That Freed the American Mind* (Hoboken, NJ: John Wiley and Sons, 2006), 51. Emerson was also burdened with bailing out his brother William from a debt of sixty-five hundred dollars to secure his properties and investments because he could not find a lender in New York, even at a 20 percent interest rate. In the heart of the economic Panic of 1837, few were completely solvent, given the failure of the wheat crop, plunging price of cotton, and Andrew Jackson's dissolution of the central bank and mandate that all loans to the United States be paid in hard currency. Emerson did, however, gain control over his capital once the stock market recovered.
16. Mary Kupiec Cayton, *Emerson's Emergence: Self and Society in the Transformation of New England, 1800–1845* (Chapel Hill: North Carolina University Press, 1992), 202.
17. See Jeffrey Steele, "Transcendental Friendship: Emerson, Fuller, and Thoreau," *The Cambridge Companion to Ralph Waldo Emerson* (New York: Cambridge University Press, 1999), 121–36, for a revealing assessment of their relationship's strain under the individualistic terms of the transcendental theory of friendship. Robert Sattlemeyer, "'When He Became My Enemy': Emerson and Thoreau, 1848–49" *New England Quarterly* 62.2 (1989), 187–204, and Joel Porte, *Emerson and Thoreau: Transcendentalists in Conflict* (Middletown, CN: Wesleyan University Press, 1965) both divulge the sources of the Emerson-Thoreau rift in the late 1840s, the former tying it directly to Thoreau's passion that merged dangerously close to romantic love for Emerson's wife Lidian while Emerson was touring Europe. The latter investigates the philosophical divergence separating the two during the late 1840s and early 1850s, which Harmon Smith has updated with his fine narrative of their emotional lives together in *My Friend, My Friend: The Story of Thoreau's Relationship with Emerson* (Amherst: University of Massachusetts Press, 1999). The most recent treatment of the subject appears in *Emerson and Thoreau: Figures of Friendship*, ed. John T. Lysaker and William Rossi (Bloomington: University of Indiana Press, 2010).
18. Ralph Waldo Emerson, *Journals and Miscellaneous Notebooks of Ralph Waldo Emerson, Vol. VIII; Volumes 1841–1843*, ed. William H. Gilman and J.E. Parsons (Cambridge, MA: Belknap Press of Harvard University Press, 1970), 36.

19. Fuller, *Summer on the Lakes*, 118, 119.
20. Emerson, *Journals*, vol. 8, 36.
21. Clark Davis, *Hawthorne's Shyness: Ethics, Politics, and the Question of Engagement* (Baltimore: Johns Hopkins University Press, 2005).
22. Qtd. in Cayton, 203. For more on the Hedge Club's transformation into the Transcendentalist Club, see Barbara Packer, *The Transcendentalists* (Athens, GA: University of Georgia Press, 2007), 165. Packer carefully traces the diaspora of the Transcendentalist movement into smaller groups that dispersed throughout the nation. One of those groups, led by Elizabeth Palmer Peabody as the key literary intermediary of a Boston circle consisting of many Concord affiliates, is the subject of chapter 5 to follow.
23. Emerson, "The American Scholar," *Collected Works*, 69.
24. George Templeton Strong, *The Diary of George Templeton Strong*, ed. Allan Nevins and Milton Halsey Thomas (Seattle: University of Washington Press, 1988), 118. David S. Reynolds argues that critics have enjoyed making the claim that the Transcendentalists were murky and bewildering to listeners under the assumption that most popular public figures were, on the contrary, lucid and straightforward. Reynolds aptly points out that Emerson, in particular, was not only the most famous lecturer of the entire era, but his capacity to lose his audiences was tantamount to the trick of the trade employed by so many mesmerists and mystics who manned podiums and commanded huge profits in antebellum America, noting that "even the obscure moments of his lectures were not out of line with popular taste in an age when traveling trance lecturers, animal magnetists, and phrenologists palmed off their mystical pseudoknowledge to gaping audiences," "'A Chaos Deep Soil': Emerson, Thoreau, and Popular Literature," *Transient and Permanent: The Transcendentalist Movement and Its Contexts*, ed. Charles Capper and Conrad Edick Wright (Boston: Massachusetts Historical Society, 1999), 297. The success of such acts, as well as Emerson's lecturing career, extended well into the Gilded Age. For a revealing glimpse into the ethics of bewildering the masses for profit, a situation of which Emerson was well aware, see Mark Twain's story of the mesmerist in *Life on the Mississippi* (New York: Harper, 1917).
25. Emerson, "The Transcendentalist," *Collected Works*, 203–4.
26. Ibid., 207.
27. Ibid., 209.
28. See "Transcending Capital: Whitman's Poet Figure and the Marketing of *Leaves of Grass*" for more on Whitman's capacity to sell spirituality through his verse in David Dowling, *Capital Letters: Authorship in the Antebellum Literary Market* (Iowa City: University of Iowa Press, 2009), 82–106.
29. Ralph Waldo Emerson, "Circles," *The Collected Works of Ralph Waldo Emerson, Vol. 2, Essays: First Series*, ed. Alfred R. Ferguson

and Jean Ferguson Carr (Cambridge, MA: Belknap Press of Harvard University Press, 1980), 179.
30. Emerson, "The American Scholar," *Collected Works*, 52.
31. Ibid., 53.
32. Ralph Waldo Emerson, "Compensation," *Collected Works*, II, 56.
33. Qtd. in Ronald J. and Mary Saracino Zboray, *Literary Dollars and Social Sense: A People's History of the Mass Market Book* (New York: Routlege, 2005), 169.
34. Emerson, "The American Scholar," *Collected Works*, 73.
35. Thoreau, *Walden* (New York: Signet, 1960 [originally pub. 1854]), 75.
36. Emerson, "The American Scholar," *Collected Works*, 73.
37. Fuller, *Summer on the Lakes*, 119.
38. Ibid., 144.
39. Ibid., 148.
40. Ralph Waldo Emerson, *The Letters of Ralph Waldo Emerson*, vol. 2 (New York: Columbia University Press, 1939), 332.
41. Margaret Fuller, *Woman in the Nineteenth Century* in Jeffrey Steele, ed. *The Essential Margaret Fuller* (New Brunswick, NJ: Rutgers University Press, 1995), 296.
42. Fuller, *Summer on the Lakes*, 134–35.
43. Ibid., 148.
44. Jeffrey Steele, "Introduction," *The Essential Margaret Fuller* (New Brunswick, NJ: Rutgers University Press, 1995), xiv, xv.
45. Fuller, *Summer on the Lakes*, 157.
46. Ibid., 161.
47. Ibid., 163.
48. Ralph Waldo Emerson, "Heroism," *Collected Works*, II, 153.
49. See Charles R. Anderson, "Thoreau and the Dial: The Apprentice Years," *Essays Mostly on Periodical Publishing in America: A Collection in Honor of Clarence Gohdes*, ed. James Woodress (Durham, NC: Duke University Press, 1973), 97–102.
50. Margaret Fuller, "At Concord with the Emersons in 1842," *Emerson in His Own Time*, ed. Ronald A. Bosco and Joel Myerson (Iowa City: University of Iowa Press), 24. Also see Christina Zwarg, *Feminist Conversations: Fuller, Emerson, and the Play of Reading* (Ithaca, NY: Cornell University Press, 1995), for an excellent discussion of the passionate correspondence between Emerson and Fuller that rhetorically, if not physically, interlaced the erotic and intellectual components of their relationship, 40.
51. Judith Mattson Bean, "Texts From Conversation: Margaret Fuller's Influence on Emerson," *Studies in the American Renaissance 1994*, ed. Joel Myerson (Charlottesville: University of Virginia Press, 1994), 228.
52. Joel Myerson, *The New England Transcendentalists and the Dial* (Rutherford, NJ: Fairleigh Dickinson Press, 1980), 54–55.
53. Fuller, *Woman in the Nineteenth Century*, 308.

54. Qtd. in Anne C. Rose, *Transcendentalism as a Social Movement, 1830–1850* (New Haven: Yale University Press, 1981), 102.
55. Emerson's string of failed projects, all promising young New England authors, included Jones Very, Henry David Thoreau, William Ellery Channing II, Christopher Pearse Cranch, and Charles King Newcomb. As William Moss notes, "He discovered all five within four years, 1838–1842. Each has an air of the transcendental about him. Each initially inspired Emerson to enthusiasm, and each later brought disappointment," "'So Many Promising Youths': Emerson's Disappointing Discoveries of New England Poet-Seers" *New England Quarterly* 49.1 (1976), 47. Moss effectively surveys Emerson's projects with specific apprentices, and I add to it an understanding of his role as literary agent and promoter specifically of Thoreau and Fuller within the Transcendentalist circle.
56. Robert D. Richardson, Jr., "Emerson as Editor," *Emersonian Circles: Essays in Honor of Joel Myerson*, ed. Joel Myerson (Rochester, NY: University of Rochester Press, 1997), 109. Ronald J. and Mary Saracino Zboray also make light of Emerson's introduction of this "department of the *Dial* without print as an end," yet problematically note that the move "seems undermining of social authorship and at the same time respectful of it," 185. Social authorship appears encouraged and not at all undermined by Emerson's move, which, I would add, aimed to unify the increasingly divergent coterie. Aside from this qualification, the Zborays' suggestion that the solicitation was made for manuscripts "without print as an end" revealingly raises the paradox that Emerson was notorious for the editorial changes he demanded of Thoreau's poetry, which eventuated in a frustrating quagmire whereby the young apprentice could not please his mentor, and abandoned the genre, for the most part, for the remainder of his career.
57. Philip F. Gura similarly observes that Emerson struggled, not always successfully, to keep the "unruly" movement within the coterie integrated, *American Transcendentalism: A History* (New York: Hill and Wang, 2007), 14.
58. Ralph Waldo Emerson, *The Dial* 1.2 (October 1840), 220.
59. Ibid., 220.
60. Ibid., 220.
61. Ibid., 220.
62. Walt Whitman, "Song of Myself," *Leaves of Grass*, ed. Malcolm Cowley (New York: Penguin, 1988 (originally pub. 1855), 87.
63. Ralph Waldo Emerson, "The Transcendentalist," *The Essential Writings of Ralph Waldo Emerson*, ed. Brooks Atkinson (New York: Modern Library), 93.
64. Ralph Waldo Emerson, "Wealth," *Essential Writings*, 625–26.
65. John Patrick Diggins, "Transcendentalism and the Spirit of Capitalism," *Transient and Permanent: The Transcendentalist Movement and Its Contexts*, ed. Charles Capper and Conrad Edick

Wright (Boston: Boston Historical Society and Northeastern University Press, 1999), 235–36.
66. Emerson, *Letters, II,* 246.
67. Judith Mattson Bean, "Texts from Conversation: Margaret Fuller's Influence on Emerson," *Studies in the American Renaissance, 1994,* ed. Joel Myerson, (Charlottesville: University of Virginia Press, 1994), 227.
68. See Leon Jackson's meticulous tracking of Emerson's nonmonetary economy of exchange—which mainly took the form of the dissemination of free copies of *Sartor Resartus*—that spread Carlyle's reputation throughout Concord with alarming celerity. Jackson notes that Carlyle was summarily dropped from the coterie after his racist proslavery allegiances were embarrassingly revealed. "The Social Construction of Thomas Carlyle's New England Reputation" *Proceedings of the AAS* 103.2 (1993), 165–89.
69. Ralph Waldo Emerson, *The Dial* 1.2 (October 1840), 220.
70. Zboray and Zboray, 184.
71. Margaret Fuller, "Emerson's Essays," *The Essential Margaret Fuller,* ed. Jeffrey Steele (New Brunswick: Rutgers University Press, 1999), 382.
72. Larry J. Reynolds, "From *Dial* Essay to New York Book: The Making of *Woman in the Nineteenth Century,*" *Periodical Literature in Nineteenth-Century America,* ed. Kenneth W. Price and Susan Belasco Smith (Charlottesville: University Press of Virginia, 1995), 20.
73. Margaret Fuller, *Literature and Art* (New York: Fowlers and Wells, 1852), 137–38.
74. Margaret Fuller, *Letters,* vol. 2, ed. Robert N. Hudspeth (Ithaca: Cornell University Press, 1994), 131. For a stimulating study of the typology of authorship represented in Fuller's professional career, see Steven Fink, "Margaret Fuller: The Evolution of a Woman of Letters," *Reciprocal Influences: Literary Production, Distribution, and Consumption in America,* ed. Steven Fink and Susan S. Williams (Columbus: Ohio State University Press, 1999), 55–74.
75. Rose, *Voices in the Marketplace,* 108.
76. Kenneth Walter Cameron, *Transcendental Log: Fresh Discoveries in Newspapers Concerning Emerson, Thoreau, Alcott, and Others of the American Literary Renaissance* (Hartford: University of Connecticut Press, 1973), 148.
77. Ralph Waldo Emerson, *Emerson in His Journals,* ed. Joel Porte (Cambridge, MA: Harvard University Press, 1982), 301.
78. Henry David Thoreau, *Journal, Vol. 5: 1852–1853,* ed. Patrick F. O'Connell (Princeton: Princeton University Press, 1997), 459.
79. See Gura for thorough coverage of the process by which Emerson aided Carlyle's first American publications, 91.
80. Anticipating the successful reception of his lecture, "The American Scholar," Emerson invited the all-male Transcendental Club to his

home for dinner, and craftily used the ruse that Fuller's attendance might "gentilize their dinner with Mrs. Ripley if I can get her, and what can you not mould them into an hour!" qtd. in Schreiner, 53. More than gentilizing the men, Fuller and other women who became permanent fixtures at future club affairs went on to establish careers in their own right—especially Louisa May Alcott, and Elizabeth Palmer Peabody—and lent invaluable advice to colleagues. Thoreau credited Fuller's *Summer on the Lakes* as a major source of inspiration for *A Week on the Concord and Merrimack Rivers*. The two works are kindred Transcendental travel narratives in the experimental pastiche portfolio mixed genre form.
81. "Authors and Authorcraft," *Brother Jonathan* I.ii (12 March 1842), 296–97.
82. Zboray and Zboray, *Literary Dollars*, 204.

5 Boston and Beyond: Elizabeth Peabody's Promotional Practice

1. Elizabeth Palmer Peabody, *Letters of Elizabeth Palmer Peabody: American Renaissance Woman*, ed. Bruce A. Ronda (Middletown, CT: Wesleyan University Press, 1984), 55–56.
2. Charlene Avallone, "Elizabeth Peabody and the 'Art' of Conversation," *Reimagining the Peabody Sisters*, ed. Monica M. Elbert (Iowa City: University of Iowa Press, 2006), 23–44.
3. Avallone, 24.
4. Margaret Fuller, "Translator's Preface," *Conversations with Goethe* (Boston: James Munroe, 1839), viii.
5. Bruce Ronda, "Scandal and Seductive Language: Elizabeth Peabody Reads *Clarissa*" *ESQ* 44 (1988), 302.
6. Peabody, *Letters*, 53.
7. Elizabeth Palmer Peabody, *Reminiscences of Rev. Wm. Ellery Channing, D.D.* (Boston: Roberts Brothers, 1880), 408.
8. Peabody, *Reminiscences*, 408.
9. Ibid., 404.
10. Ibid., 402.
11. Bruce Ronda, *Elizabeth Palmer Peabody: A Reformer on Her Own Terms* (Cambridge, MA: Harvard University Press, 1999), 158.
12. Ibid., 406–7.
13. Ibid., 409.
14. Anne C. Rose, *New England Transcendentalism as a Social Movement, 1830–1850* (New Haven: Yale University Press, 1981), 103.
15. Nathaniel Hawthorne, *The House of the Seven Gables* (London: G. Routledge, 1852), 45.
16. Ronald J. Zboray, *A Fictive People: Antebellum Economic Development and the American Reading Public* (New York: Oxford University Press, 1993), 155.

17. Bruce Ronda, "Print and Pedagogy: The Career of Elizabeth Peabody," *A Living of Words: American Women in Print Culture*, ed. Susan Albertine (Knoxville: University of Tennessee Press, 1995), 41.
18. Shortly after the publication of her acclaimed biography, *The Peabody Sisters: Three Women Who Ignited American Romanticism* (Boston: Houghton Mifflin, 2005), Megan Marshall asserted that "there seems to have been a brief period during which he and Elizabeth shared an 'understanding' that they would marry—before Sophia had entered the picture," "Epilogue: The Peabody Sisters as Sisters," *Reinventing the Peabody Sisters*, ed. Monika M. Elbert (Iowa City: University of Iowa Press, 2006), 23–44.
19. Hawthorne, 45.
20. Qtd. in George Willis Cooke, *An Historical and Biographical Introduction to the "Dial,"* vol. 1 (New York: Russell and Russell, 1961 [originally pub. 1902]), 148.
21. Peabody, *Reminiscences*, 409.
22. Caroline Healey Dall, *Margaret and Her Friends; or, Ten Conversations with Margaret Fuller* (Boston: Roberts Brothers, 1895).
23. Charles Capper, "Margaret Fuller as Cultural Reformer: The Conversations in Boston" *American Quarterly* 39 (Winter 1987), 511, 523.
24. Ralph Waldo Emerson, *Memoirs of Margaret Fuller Ossoli*, vol. 1 (Boston: Roberts Brothers, 1884), 147.
25. Ronda, 42. Into the later part of the century, Transcendentalism's heroic era waned according to Perry Miller, ed. *The Transcendentalists* (Cambridge, MA: Harvard University Press, 1950) along with key figures like Peabody, who retreated into spinsterhood, yet maintained her characteristic overexuberance, 14.
26. Ralph Waldo Emerson, *The Journals and Miscellaneous Notebooks of Ralph Waldo Emerson*, ed. William Gilman (Cambridge, MA: Harvard University Press, 1960), 262.
27. Sarah Josepha Hale, *Ladies' Magazine* 3.1 (January 1830), 42–43.
28. Steven Fink, "Antebellum Lady Editors and the Language of Authority," *Blue Pencils and Hidden Hands: Women Editing Periodicals, 1830–1910*, ed. Sharon M. Harris and Ellen Gruber Garvey (Boston: Northeastern University Press, 2004), 206. A publicist-agent like Peabody who did not write for a living, it must be noted, also did not share precisely the same struggles with authorial identity. The socially imposed shame Mary Kelley argues most popular women writers suffered from in *Private Woman, Public Stage: Literary Domesticity in Nineteenth-Century America* (New York: Oxford University Press, 1984) did not apply to Peabody. Indeed, her comfort in business dealings and courtship of the market is more consonant with Susan Coultrap-McQuin's assertion that many bestselling female authors like Harriet Beecher Stowe happily took to their roles as literary professionals, as they embraced the

role of domestic lady creative counterpart to the public gentleman businessman, *Doing Literary Business: American Women Writers in the Nineteenth Century* (Chapel Hill: University of North Carolina Press, 1990). Peabody is so revolutionary that she explodes even Coultrap-McQuin's progressive refiguring of Kelley's old theory by proving that she could very well thrive in the gentleman's role of publisher to Hawthorne and Channing's lady writers, as it were, in a full inversion of such gender roles seemingly so neatly inscribed in the code of business ethics and practice of the literary market.

29. Qtd. in Schreiner, 79.
30. Charles H. Foster, "Elizabeth Palmer Peabody," *Notable American Women*, ed. Edward T. James (Cambridge, MA: Belknap, Harvard University Press, 1971), 34.
31. Ralph Waldo Emerson, *Letters of Ralph Waldo Emerson*, ed. Ralph Rusk and Eleanor Tilton (New York: Columbia University Press, 1939), 46.
32. Rose, 101.
33. Peabody, *Letters*, 199–200.
34. Elizabeth Palmer Peabody, "Review of *Twice Told Tales*" *The New-Yorker* 5 (24 March 1838), 1–2. Peabody, *Letters*, 223.
35. Peabody, *Letters*, 199.
36. Ronda, "Print and Pedagogy," 35.
37. Katharine Rodier, "Authorizing Sarah Winnemucca?: Elizabeth Peabody and Mary Peabody Mann," *Reinventing the Peabody Sisters*, ed. Monika M. Elbert (Iowa City: University of Iowa Press, 2006), 108.
38. My point here on the significance of Peabody's understanding of Christ as a key to her own understanding of her role as coterie intermediary builds on Bruce Ronda's provocative observation that "she saw in the person of Jesus the most perfectly socialized being, one who was simultaneously in touch with his own inner worth and power and in perfect social relations with his disciples," "Elizabeth Peabody and the Fate of Transcendentalism," *Reinventing the Peabody Sisters*, ed. Monika M. Elbert (Iowa City: University of Iowa Press, 2006), 241.
39. Ralph Waldo Emerson, "Wealth," *The Conduct of Life* in *The Essential Writings of Ralph Waldo Emerson*, ed. Brooks Atkinson (New York: Modern Library, 2000), 629.
40. Peabody, *Letters*, 405.
41. Ibid., 406.
42. Ibid., 406–7. See also Ronda, *Elizabeth Palmer Peabody: A Reformer on Her Own Terms*, 151–53, and Robert D. Richardson, *Emerson: The Mind on Fire* (Berkeley: University of California Press, 1995), 301–6, for fine renditions of this strange chapter in Transcendentalist history.
43. Elizabeth Palmer Peabody, "Language," *The Aesthetic Papers*, ed. Elizabeth P. Peabody (Boston: The Editor, 13 West Street; New York: G.P. Putnam, 1849), 221.

Notes

44. William Ellery Channing, *Slavery* (Boston: James Munroe, 1835), 9.
45. Ronda, "Elizabeth Peabody and the Fate of Transcendentalism," 242. "The gospel of wealth" finds its most famous expression later in the century through Andrew Carnegie's assertion that the public is best served not through socialism, high taxation, or larger government, but through massive accumulations of wealth that can then be doled out as needed and at the discretion of the wealthy for the greater good. In this sense, "the gospel of wealth provided an ideological antidote to socialist, anarchist, Communist, agrarian, single-tax, and labor protests against the unequal distribution of wealth," David Nasaw, *Andrew Carnegie* (New York: Penguin, 2007), 351.
46. Peabody, *Reminiscences*, 412.
47. *The Sixth Annual Report of the Committee of the American Anti-Slavery Society* (New York: William S. Dorr, 1839), 51.
48. Ralph Waldo Emerson, "Wealth," *The Conduct of Life* in *The Essential Writings of Ralph Waldo Emerson*, ed. Brooks Atkinson (New York: Modern Library, 2000), 632, 631.
49. Ralph Waldo Emerson, "Self-Reliance," *Essays: First Series* in *The Essential Writings of Ralph Waldo Emerson*, ed. Brooks Atkinson (New York: Modern Library, 2000), 147.
50. Peabody, *Letters*, 261.
51. Elizabeth Palmer Peabody, "Prospectus," *The Aesthetic Papers*, ed. Elizabeth P. Peabody (Boston: The Editor, 13 West Street; New York: G.P. Putnam, 1849), iv.
52. Henry David Thoreau, *Walden* (New York: Signet, 1960 [originally pub. 1854]), 75.
53. Elizabeth Palmer Peabody, Holograph Journal, Thursday, 15 April 1836. The Elizabeth Palmer Peabody Collection of Papers, 1832–38. The Berg Collection of English and American Literature, New York Public Library.
54. Peabody, "Prospectus," iii.
55. Ibid., iii.
56. Advertisement for *First Nursery Reading Book*, *The Aesthetic Papers*, ed. Elizabeth P. Peabody (Boston: The Editor, 13 West Street; New York: G.P. Putnam, 1849), back matter.
57. Elizabeth Palmer Peabody, Holograph Journal, Thursday, 15 April 1836. The Elizabeth Palmer Peabody Collection of Papers, 1832–38. The Berg Collection of English and American Literature, New York Public Library.
58. Ibid.
59. Ibid.
60. Ibid.
61. Margaret Fuller, *Woman in the Nineteenth Century* in *The Essential Margaret Fuller*, ed. Jeffrey Steele (New Brunswick, NJ: Rutgers University Press, 1995), 306.
62. Peabody, "Language," 218.

63. Fuller, *Woman in the Nineteenth Century*, 311.
64. Joel Myerson, *Fuller in Her Own Time: A Biographical Chronicle of Her Life, Drawn From Recollections, Interviews, and Memoirs by Family, Friends, and Associates*, ed. Joel Myerson (Iowa City: University of Iowa Press, 2008), 37.
65. Elizabeth Palmer Peabody, Holograph Journal, 29 December 1834. The Elizabeth Palmer Peabody Collection of Papers, 1832–38. The Berg Collection of English and American Literature, New York Public Library.
66. Rose, 102.
67. Peabody, *Letters*, 181.
68. Ibid.
69. Gloria Steinem, qtd. in Nancy Levit, *The Gender Line: Men, Women, and the Law* (New York: New York University Press, 2000), 145.
70. Marshall, *The Peabody Sisters*, 443.
71. Marshall, "The Peabody Sisters as Sisters," 254. (Emphasis mine).
72. Peabody qtd. Marshall, "The Peabody Sisters as Sisters," 256.
73. Helen R. Deese, "A New England Women's Network: Elizabeth Palmer Peabody, Caroline Healey Dall, and Delia S. Bacon" *Legacy* 8.2 (1991), 89.

6 Print Warriors: Garrison's Abolitionists

1. Reynolds identifies two major branches of the reform movement before the Civil War, "the rationalists and the evangelicals, who often shared similar goals...but who battled bitterly over ideology and tactics," emphasizing that "every reform—temperance, antislavery, labor reform, antiprostitution, and so forth—had both" types of supporters, *Beneath the American Renaissance: The Subversive Imagination in the Age of Emerson and Melville* (Cambridge, MA: Harvard University Press, 1989), 57. Rationalists, including Unitarians, free thinkers, and Quakers, promoted education and steady, rational self-improvement and were appalled by radicals who called for immediate abolition through disunion as the Garrisonians had. Reynolds observes that "William Lloyd Garrison ushered in an extraordinarily harsh rhetoric that threatened to overwhelm moral statement and even to subvert the very meaning of vice and virtue," 57, a tendency visible in the antiprostitution reform writings of John McDowall, and even more notably, Rebecca Harding Davis's "Margaret Howth: A Story of To-Day," about a child forced into the trade in order to avoid starvation.
2. William Lloyd Garrison, "The National Anti-Slavery Standard" *Liberator* (17 June 1842), 94–95. Headlines quoted in Reynolds, 74.
3. Qtd. in Wendell P. and Francis J. Garrison, *William Lloyd Garrison, 1805–1879: The Story of His Life*, *I* (New York: 1885), 224.
4. Ibid.

NOTES

5. William Lloyd Garrison, "Editor's Table," *Liberator* (3 October 1845), 158.
6. Ibid., 199.
7. Lawrence J. Friedman notes that Garrison's circle was "fragmented by friendship pairings and periodical flare-ups between its members" and thus "had to arrive at a consensus on the degree to which deviations in ideology, tactics, and personal behavior could be tolerated. Unless its members could define and enforce certain limits on behavior, further fragmentation would ensue and the group would never be more than a center for bickering and ineffective action" Lawrence J. Friedman, *Gregarious Saints: Self and Community in American Abolitionism, 1830–1870* (New York: Cambridge University Press, 1982), 62. Friedman's useful analysis and copious history of the tension and struggles within Garrison's circle surprisingly leaves out Child's defection to the *Standard*. Child's precarious place among the *Liberator* staff, I argue, offers a telling glimpse into the management and leadership style of Garrison, which became especially pronounced when she revolutionized the role of abolitionist editor.
8. Augusta Rohrbach has recently noted that Garrison's innovative use of typeface and layout began when he worked as assistant editor on Benjamin Lundy's *Genius of Universal Emancipation*. During his six-month tenure that began in 1829, Garrison brought the paper a distinctly radical form and content. Upon his departure in 1830, the paper was restored to its original look, Augusta Rohrbach, "'Truth Stronger and Stranger than Fiction': Reexamining William Lloyd Garrison's *Liberator*" 73.4 (2001), 755. This depiction of Garrison as a print entrepreneur adept at manipulating the mechanisms of production for sale in the marketplace resonates with my portrayal of Robert Bonner's revolutionary protopostmodern use of print to call attention to the process of production to advance the sale of his *New-York Ledger*.
9. William Lloyd Garrison, *An Address before the Free People of Color* (Boston: 1831), 9.
10. William Lloyd Garrison, *Liberator* (1 January 1832).
11. For more on the rise of the abolitionist press, see Ford Risley, *Abolition and the Press: The Moral Struggle against Slavery* (Evanston, IL: Northwestern University Press, 2008), 33, 41–42.
12. When Garrison "went to Boston, benevolent organizations and 'societies' were being formed in the city at a fantastic rate," R. Jackson Wilson notes. "The organizing mania dated back to the Revolution, but it was at a very high pitch when Garrison began his adult career," R. Jackson Wilson, *Figures of Speech: American Writers and the Literary Marketplace from Benjamin Franklin to Emily Dickinson* (Baltimore: Johns Hopkins University Press, 1989), 148. Indeed, Garrison would find his first editorial position in Boston's boarding houses where he lived with dozens of self-styled "city missionaries" and other reformers.

It was there that the founder of the *National Philanthropist* offered him the job of editing the magazine in the late 1820s.
13. Ralph Waldo Emerson, "The Transcendentalist," *The Essential Writings of Ralph Waldo Emerson* (New York: Modern Library), 90.
14. Frank Luther Mott, *A History of American Magazines, 1741–1850* (Cambridge, MA: Harvard University Press, 1938), 456.
15. William Lloyd Garrison, "Editor's Table" *Liberator* 30 (6 January 1860), 2.
16. William Lloyd Garrison, "A Brief Sketch of the Trial of William Lloyd Garrison for an Alleged Libel on Francis Todd," *Slave Rebels, Abolitionists, and Southern Courts: The Pamphlet Literature*, vol. 1, *Slavery, Race, and the American Legal System, 1700–1872*, Series 4, ed. Paul Finkelman (New York: Garland, 1988), 205.
17. Robert Fanuzzi, *Abolition's Public Sphere* (Minneapolis: University of Minnesota Press, 2003), 14.
18. Garrison, "A Brief Sketch," 205.
19. Rohrbach, 740.
20. See, for example, "Tract No. 515: Novel-Reading" and "Tract No. 493: Beware of Bad Books" for representative antebellum vilifications of prose fiction as a social evil in *Popular American Literature of the Nineteenth Century*, ed. Paul Gutjahr (Oxford: Oxford University Press, 2001), 71–74, 59–61.
21. Ibid., 740.
22. Charles Sellers, *The Market Revolution: Jacksonian America, 1815–1846* (New York: Oxford University Press, 1991), 404.
23. Qtd. in Sellers, 404–5.
24. Qtd. in Wilson, 155.
25. William Lloyd Garrison, "Repeal of the Union" *Liberator* (6 May 1842), 71.
26. Wilson convincingly argues that Garrison essentially made a career choice when he decided to become an antislavery writer, because the movement "could do for him what no other reform movement could do so well: provide him with a cause over which there could be no compromise at all, propel him into fame (and infamy), threaten his life, and send him into jail cells in Baltimore and Boston," 150. "The most important fact of William Lloyd Garrison's experience was that he came to his radicalism in the course of his attempt to establish a career as a writer, and not to writing through his dedication to antislavery or any other cause," 122. Wilson should not be misconstrued as implying that Garrison insincerely pursued antislavery; instead, Wilson argues that Garrison was writing himself into a persona he desperately wanted to acquire, and eventually did.

Reynolds similarly details the showmanship and promotional tactics while also allowing that, paradoxically, "the sincerity of Garrison's antislavery views was indisputable," 74. Strikingly, there is no evidence that Garrison had any moving personal experience that may have affected him to crusade against slavery with such zeal. "Garrison had had almost no direct contact with slavery. He had never seen a plantation. He had seen very few slaves," and the one black woman who cared for his mother during her final days in Baltimore was already free, so the racial implications of her position had little impact on him, Wilson 150. Wilson's thesis aptly supports my contention here that Garrison was embroiled in controversy with fellow abolitionists as an extension of the self-promoting professionalism Wilson describes. Indeed, Garrison's management style reflects not just a reformist's evangelical zeal, but also a proto-corporate capitalist's competitive jockeying for position in the local market.

27. Douglass's break from Garrison has received extensive coverage in John R. McKivigan's "The Frederick Douglass-Gerrit Smith Friendship and Political Abolitionism in the 1850s," *Frederick Douglass: New Literary and Historical Essays*, ed. Eric J. Sundquist (Cambridge: Cambridge University Press, 1990), 205–32. Child's biographer, Carolyn Karcher, details her split from Garrison in the chapter, "*The National Anti-Slavery Standard*: Family Newspaper or Factional Organ?" *The First Woman in the Republic: A Cultural Biography of Lydia Maria Child* (Durham, NC: Duke University Press, 1994), 267–94.

28. Friedman, 5–7. See also, David S. Ericson, *The Debate over Slavery: Antislavery and Proslavery Liberalism in Antebellum America* (New York University Press, 2000), 12–13.

29. Qtd. in Wendell P. and Francis J. Garrison, *William Lloyd Garrison, 1805–1879: The Story of His Life*, I (New York: 1885), 224.

30. William Lloyd Garrison, *Liberator* (2 November 1855).

31. Harvey Wish, *George Fitzhugh, Propagandist of the Old South* (Baton Rouge: University of Louisiana Press, 1943), 199.

32. William Lloyd Garrison, *Liberator* (15 August 1835).

33. Qtd. in Henry Mayer, *All on Fire: William Lloyd Garrison and the Abolition of Slavery* (New York: St. Martin's Press, 1998), 118–19.

34. Rohrbach aptly weaves Franklin and Barnum's significance into Garrison's biography, 728–29, and provides a stimulating discussion of Garrison's self-promotional features as directly impacting the onset of literary realism, 745. Her book, Augusta Rohrbach, *Truth Stranger than Fiction: Race, Realism, and the U.S. Literary Marketplace* (New York: Palgrave Macmillan, 2002), casts these ideas in the broader context of literary capitalism and the publishing industry. I add to her sense of Garrison as entrepreneur by exploring the commercial group dynamics of his *Liberator* circle.

35. George Fitzhugh, *Cannibals All! or Slaves without Masters*, ed. C. Vann Woodward (Cambridge, MA: Belknap Press of Harvard University Press, 1968 [originally pub. 1857]), 95.

36. Qtd. in Karcher, 254.

37. Patricia Okker, *Our Sister Editors: Sarah J. Hale and the Tradition of Nineteenth-Century American Women Editors* (Athens, GA: University of Georgia Press, 1995), 26.
38. For more on preaching as persuasion, a combination of "hot passion and cold logic" in Finney, see Charles E. Hambrick Stowe, *Charles G. Finney and the Spirit of American Evangelicalism* (Grand Rapids, MI: Wm. B. Eerdmans, 1996), 35.
39. Ibid., 9
40. Ibid., 4.
41. Garrison and Garrison, III, 125–26.
42. James C. Jackson, "National Anti-Slavery Standard" *National Anti-Slavery Standard* (11 June 1840), 2.
43. Garrison and Garrison, II, 137–38.
44. Qtd. in Friedman, 61.
45. Russel B. Nye, *William Lloyd Garrison and the Humanitarian Reformers* (New York: Little, Brown, 1955), 140.
46. Edward Pessen, *Riches, Class, and Power Before the Civil War* (Lexington, MA: D.C. Heath, 1978), 39.
47. Nathaniel P. Rogers, "The National Anti-Slavery Standard" *The National Anti-Slavery Standard* (6 May 1841), 191.
48. William Lloyd Garrison, "MRS. CHILD" *The Genius of Universal Emancipation* (20 Nov. 1829), 85.
49. Lydia Maria Child, *An Appeal in Favor of That Class of Americans Called Africans* (Boston: Allen and Ticknor, 1833), 222.
50. Lydia Maria Child, *Lydia Maria Child: Selected Letters, 1817–1880*, ed. Milton Meltzer (Amherst: University of Massachusetts Press, 1982), 107.
51. Ibid., 114.
52. Lydia Maria and David Child, *Liberator* (8 February 1839).
53. Qtd. in Karcher, 268.
54. Lydia Maria Child, "PROSPECTUS of the Anti-Slavery Standard for 1841–42" *Anti-Slavery Standard* (20 May 1841), 199.
55. Ibid.
56. Lydia Maria Child, "A, B, C, of Abolition" *National Anti-Slavery Standard* (31 August 1841), 34. For more on the didactic function of pedagogical rhetoric in abolitionist almanacs, see Teresa A. Goddu, "The Antislavey Almanac and the Discourse of Numeracy" *Book History* 12 (2009), 129–55. Goddu argues that the *American Anti-Slavery Almanac* prior to 1830 was saturated with statistical data to "produce abstract knowledge out of a mass of particulars" to "indoctrinate [readers] into the visual literacy of market culture," 136. She aptly and provocatively claims that the almanac simultaneously sought to convert readers to abolitionism while teaching the "values and habits of market society... by including multiplication tables, a mathematical question, or tables that calculated simple interest as well as maxims on economy and thrift," for enhanced "economic skills and

market concepts" demanded by "the new industrial order," Goddu, 133. However, her characterization of the almanac's transformation into a narrative organ, especially a key vehicle for the slave narrative in the post-1830s era, notes only that its unevenness and incoherence were due to a rise of diverse narrative forms without mention of the public disputes between abolitionist parties that dominated its pages.

57. Lydia Maria Child, "The Press" *National Anti-Slavery Standard* (24 March 1842), 166–67; "A, B, C, of Abolition," 34.
58. Qtd. in Karcher, 278.
59. "Address to the Slaves of the United States, by the Convention of the 'Liberty Party' Abolitionists, held in Peterboro, N.Y. January 19th, 1842" *National Anti-Slavery Standard* (24 February 1842), 149.
60. Lydia Maria Child, "Gerrit Smith's Address to the Slaves" *National Anti-Slavery Standard* (24 February 1842), 150.
61. Karcher, 282.
62. William Lloyd Garrison, "The Annual Meeting at New-York" *Liberator* (22 April 1842), 63.
63. Qtd. in Karcher, 285.
64. "Abolitionism. Treason to the Union" *Morning Courier and New-York Enquirer* (27 April 1842), 2.
65. A good representative of the disclaimer that circulated to all the New York newspapers is the editorial notice, "CORRECTION" *Morning Courier and New-York Enquirer* (3 May 1842). Noting that the circular promised to keep "peace of the city," the editors of the *Enquirer* were "gratified to perceive by it that Garrison's authority to bring the subject of a dissolution of the Union before the approaching session of the Abolition Society in this city, is distinctly disclaimed," n.p.
66. My connections between Ahab and Garrison throughout this chapter are not without critical precedence. Reynolds notes that the *Pequod*'s captain in Melville's *Moby-Dick* not only "has been variously associated with the radical abolitionist William Lloyd Garrison," but also "with Garrison's archopponent John C. Calhoun, and with the moderate politician Daniel Webster!" 156. I invoke Ahab not to suggest that Melville modeled him exclusively upon Garrison, but as a fictional analogue of Garrison's intensity and monomaniacal leanings especially in contrast to Child's Starbuck-like moderation. Child, like Starbuck, possessed the most cogent integrated ethos for the mutiny of Garrison. The parallels are not delimiting, since Melville's characters represent "subversive reform *energy* and *rhetoric*, rather than reform *message*." Indeed, Ahab's carefully constructed messianic public persona reflected the "suprapolitical, powerfully human volatility that linked Garrison, Calhoun, and many other clamorous reform orators," Reynolds, 157.
67. Qtd. in Karcher, 286.
68. Ibid., 289.
69. Qtd. in Karcher, 290.
70. Ibid., 289.

71. Fanuzzi, 104.
72. Frederick Douglass, *My Bondage and My Freedom* (New York: Miller, Orton, and Company, 1857), 354.
73. Ibid., 358.
74. Ibid., 361.
75. Ibid., iii.
76. Ibid., 459.

7 Proslavery and the Pen: Fitzhugh's Apologists

1. R.G.B., "The Late J. D. B. De Bow" *DeBow's Review* 4.2 (1867), 3.
2. For an excellent explication of the transformation of the *Almanac* from statistical to narrative based political polemics, see Teresa A. Goddu, "The Antislavery Almanac and the Discourse of Numeracy" *Book History* 12 (2009): 129–55. Frank Luther Mott describes a similar shift in focus in *DeBow's* from statistically driven commercial ledger to vehicle for political propaganda in *A History of American Magazines, 1850–1865* (Cambridge, MA: Harvard University Press, 1938), 340.
3. Two distinct camps have emerged with divergent interpretations of the antebellum South's economy. Eugene Genovese, whose most recent work is *The Political Economy of Slavery: Studies in the Economy and Society of the Slave South*, 2nd ed. (Westport, CT: Wesleyan University Press, 1989), leads the tradition of viewing the pre–Civil War South in opposition to Northern wage-labor industrial capitalism. Averse to risk in the free market, Southerners, Genovese argues along with Raimondo Luraghi, *The Rise and Fall of the Plantation South* (New York: New Viewpoints, 1978), constructed their economy in opposition to the narrow interests of free market individualism, and instead cast themselves in a quasi socialism that was reactionary more than revolutionary, a retrograde feudalistic Medieval fantasy. Robert Fogel, *Time on the Cross: The Economics of American Negro Slavery* (Boston: Little, Brown, 1974), and Stanley Engerman have led the contrary position that the South was actively profit seeking and laissez-faire in its economics, liberal and progressive even in its pursuit of capital. The argument, as Tom Downey, *Planting a Capitalist South: Masters, Merchants, and Manufacturers in the Southern Interior, 1790–1860* (Baton Rouge: Louisiana State University Press, 2006), has usefully pointed out, has led to a stalemate with both sides offering some concessions to the other. Genovese himself admitted in his early research that a strong strain of capitalism characterized the Old South. My concern here is to move beyond this binary and place the antebellum South in the context of bourgeoning capitalistic development that, as in the North, was characterized by a strong romantic backlash against industrialization and acquisitive culture. The socialistic leanings of the South, as I discuss in this chapter, overlapped significantly with

Northern writers like Orestes Brownson intent on exposing the limitations of individualism in the free market. The effort of Southerners, much like Brownson's, was to deride what they perceived as the worst face of emergent capitalism—its unequal distribution of wealth, rampant poverty, urban blight, and culture corrosive to the moral value of sympathy as a kind of social glue—and offer a humanized collectivist alternative. The socialist thought, therefore, of Brownson's labor advocacy resonates with Fitzhugh's emphasis on the protection of slaves and even anticipates postbellum writings like that of Edward Bellamy's Christian socialism. The ascendance of capitalism during the antebellum period, known as the market revolution, necessarily brought its critics and reformers. The kinship crossed surprising lines indeed. My larger argument is that however much these circles advocated a socialistic economy, theirs was more a brand of cooperative capitalism that actively sought profit and wealth, but worked in coordinated, collaborative ways to achieve it. Thus, while I bring emphasis to the socialist leanings of the *DeBow's* circle, it should be admitted that its function kept the protocorporate and ostensibly competitive edge of laissez-faire capitalism. Proslavery could, therefore, espouse protection at home, indeed, domestically, while waging war with the pen across regions.
4. Mott, 339.
5. James D.B. DeBow, "Position of the *Commercial Review*" *DeBow's Review* 6 (October–November 1848), 378.
6. "Pioneers of the Southwest: Maunsel White of Louisiana" *DeBow's Review* 25.4 (1858), 481.
7. Ibid., 482.
8. Clement Eaton, "Maunsel White," *The Mind of the Old South* (Baton Rouge, LA: Louisiana State University Press, 1964), 51.
9. Charles Gayarre, "James Dunwoody Brownson De Bow," *After the War Series, III* (June 1867), 500.
10. Mott, 342.
11. George Frederick Holmes, "Review of *Sociology for the South*," *Richmond Examiner* (January 1855), qtd. in Wish, 115.
12. I use the phrase "cooperative capitalism" to denote what the Genoveses describe as "a defense of property rights into a doctrine that included both free-market economics and a social corporatism appropriate to a slave society," Eugene D. Genovese and Elizabeth Fox Genovese, *Slavery in White and Black: Class and Race in the Southern Slaveholders' New World Order* (New York: Cambridge University Press, 2008), 166.
13. George F. Holmes, "Observations on a Passage in the Politics of Aristotle Relative to Slavery" *Southern Literary Messenger* 16 (1850), 193.
14. Qtd. in Wish, 116.
15. The first to present Fitzhugh as a fringe radical rather than a central figure was George Frederickson, *The Black Image in the White Mind: The Debate on Afro-American Character and Destiny, 1817–1914* (Hanover,

NH: Wesleyan University Press, 1987). Frederickson argues that there were two camps of proslavery thinkers, one he calls the Herrenvolk democrats in the southwest, and the other the costal conservative elite, consisting of Simms, Tucker, Ruffin, Hammond, and Holmes. The outlier rejected by both camps was Fitzhugh. This bifurcation was never so crisply dualistic, however, as the Holmes-Fitzhugh relationship was instrumental to the development of Fitzhugh's influence over the entire region, and the democratic media of *DeBow's*. Drew Gilpin Faust's group biography of the coastal conservatives brings even more emphasis to Frederickson's position, arguing that "Fitzhugh was in fact both personally and intellectually isolated from the society of most Southern defenders of the peculiar institution," *A Sacred Circle: The Dilemma of the Intellectual in the Old South, 1840–1860* (Baltimore: Johns Hopkins University Press, 1977), 127. Faust finds his support in Holmes's letters describing Fitzhugh's "want of moderation" and "idiosyncrasy" in his "too broadly and incautiously asserted" theories evoking an "utter recklessness of both statement and expression," qtd. in Gilpin, 127. Yet Gilpin misses that Fitzhugh even describes himself as such in the letters, as both he and Holmes readily acknowledged as a kind of in-joke that these characteristics comprised his public persona designed to appeal to the mass readership. Gilpin instead is bent on diminishing the significance of Fitzhugh to a literary side-show and a great egotist who had little interest in "the works of the mind," and thus not worthy of the historical attention of other "true intellects" like Simms, Tucker, Ruffin, Hammond, and Holmes.

To measure Fitzhugh so inappropriately, and perhaps inadvertently, brings an aesthetic assessment to defenders of one of the most appalling social institutions in history. The poetics of proslavery are beside the point, and in fact impose an elitist standard by which to distance the most audacious promoter of proslavery on the mass market, whose significance instead should be measured by his status as Garrison and Lincoln's biggest target. Gilpin's argument that Fitzhugh was "atypical and even antithetical to the moral-philosophical mainstream of proslavery thought" is nothing short of historical revisionism, 128. Fitzhugh, as this chapter demonstrates, set the standard for the mainstream of proslavery thought and shaped others' visions, such as DeBow's. To argue that Fitzhugh was a "mutant strain within" proslavery because his "polemical tone and his anti-intellectualism profaned the ideals of the men of mind from Dew onward" committed to "sober and cautious reflection" posits a high-low brow split, Gilpin, 129. That binary frighteningly admires as sacred the "men of mind" he sets in contrast to Fitzhugh's role of tawdry villain of mass manipulation. In fact, the "men of mind" were every bit as engaged in the production of propaganda and could hardly be viewed as "sacred" in light of their ardent defenses of slavery. Faust clearly scapegoats

Fitzhugh in an attempt to polish the memory of Simms, Tucker, Ruffin, Hammond, and Holmes.
16. George Fitzhugh, "Editorial" *Richmond Examiner* (June 1856), qtd. in Wish, 127.
17. Genovese and Genovese, 163.
18. George Fitzhugh, "Commercial Importance and Future of the South" *DeBow's Review* 31.1–2 (1862), 124.
19. Fitzhugh, *Cannibals*, 247.
20. Ibid., 94.
21. Qtd. in Robert E. Bonner, *Mastering America: Southern Slaveholders and the Crisis of American Nationhood* (Cambridge: Cambridge University Press, 2009), 5.
22. C. Vann Woodward, "George Fitzhugh, *Sui Generis*," George Fitzhugh, *Cannibals All!, or Slaves without Masters*, ed. C. Vann Woodward (Cambridge, MA: Harvard Belknap Press, 1960 [originally pub. 1857]), 40. xvii.
23. Fitzhugh, *Cannibals*, 96.
24. Ibid., 85.
25. Ibid., 93.
26. George Frederick Holmes, "The Nineteenth Century" *The Southern Literary Messenger* 17 (1851), 457. Also see Holmes, "Greeley on Reforms" *Southern Literary Messenger* 17 (1851): 257–80.
27. George Fitzhugh, *Sociology for the South, or the Failure of Free Society* (Richmond, VA: A. Morris, 1854), 228, 233.
28. Genovese and Genovese, 160.
29. For more the proslavery resonance of Wilson's antimarket rhetoric, see David Dowling, "'Other and More Terrible Evils': Anticapitalist Rhetoric in Harriet Wilson's *Our Nig* and Proslavery Propaganda," *Capital Letters: Authorship in the Antebellum Literary Market* (Iowa City: University of Iowa Press, 2009), 27–43.
30. Orestes Brownson, "The Laboring Classes, Pt. 2" *Boston Quarterly Review* 3 (1840), 471.
31. Ibid., 467. For more on the socialist legacy of American writers, see David Herreshoff, *American Disciples of Marx: From the Age of Jackson to the Progressive Era* (Detroit: Wayne State University Press, 1967), and David Anthony Harris, *Socialist Origins in the United States, American Forerunners of Marx, 1817–1832* (Assen, The Netherlands: Van Gorcum, 1966).
32. Fitzhugh, *Cannibals*, 96.
33. James D.B. DeBow, "Uniform Postage, Railroads, Telegraphs, Fashions, etc." *DeBow's Review* 26 (1859), 657.
34. "The Macon Cotton Planter's Convention" *DeBow's Review* 12.2 (1852), 124.
35. Ibid., 123.
36. Mott, 342.
37. Fitzhugh, *Sociology*, 144.

38. Vann Woodward, xxx, xxix.
39. "Mobile and Dog River Factory" *DeBow's Review* 22.1 (1857), 11–12.
40. Downey, 122.
41. Qtd. in Wish, 200.
42. George Fitzhugh, *Cannibals All! or Slaves without Masters*, ed. C. Vann Woodward (Cambridge, MA: Harvard Belknap Press, 1960 [originally pub. 1857]), 40.
43. Genovese and Genovese, 163.
44. Jeffrey Sklansky, *The Soul's Economy: Market Society and Selfhood in American Thought, 1820–1920* (Chapel Hill: University of North Carolina Press, 2002), 95.
45. Qtd. in Mott, 339. Fitzhugh "has been referred to as the American Carlyle" for his "attack on mammonism, Manchester economics, and the idea of a free society" and he borrowed liberally from Carlyle's *Latter-Day Pamphlets*, and *The Present Time* for a significant portion of *Cannibals All!* as noted by Jules Paul Seigel in *Thomas Carlyle: The Critical Heritage* (New York: Routledge, 1996), 369.
46. James D.B. DeBow, *The Industrial Resources of the Southern and Western States* (New Orleans: Office of *DeBow's Review*, 1853), 332, 337–88.
47. Qtd. in Harvey Wish, *George Fitzhugh, Propagandist of the Old South* (Baton Rouge: Louisiana State University Press, 1943), 111.
48. Fitzhugh, *Cannibals*, 239.
49. H.C. Nixon, "J.D.B. De Bow, Publicist" *Southwest Review* 20 (1935), 217.
50. Hughes, 175.
51. Genovese and Genovese, 167.
52. Ibid., 167.
53. Ibid., 264.
54. Fitzhugh, *Cannibals*, 192.
55. Ibid., 191.
56. Ibid., 196, 198.
57. Appalled at the un-Christian behaviors slavery encouraged, the deeply religious Mary Chestnut would describe extremism in South Carolina in 1860 as satanic: "Nobody could live in this state unless they were a fire-eater," qtd. in Fox Butterfield, *All God's Children: The Bosket Family and the American Tradition of Violence* (New York: Knopf, 1995), 33.
58. Genovese and Genovese, 175.
59. James D.B. DeBow, Editorial Note to "Slavery and the Bible" *DeBow's Review* 9 (September 1850), 281.
60. George Fitzhugh, *Slavery Justified—Liberty and Equality—Socialism—Young England—Domestic Slavery* in "Appendix," *Sociology for the South* (Richmond, VA: A. Morris, 1854), 226.
61. See David S. Ericson's, *The Debate Over Slavery: Antislavery and Proslavery Liberalism in Antebellum America* (New York: New York

University Press, 2000), for a convincing demonstration of how Fitzhugh in *Cannibals All!* courts the "possibility of white slavery, asking 'how can we contend that white slavery is wrong, whilst all the great body of free laborers are starving; and slaves, white or black, throughout the world, are enjoying comfort?' He soon answers his own query and completes his retreat from white slavery by invoking racial inequality to justify the wholesale enslavement of the black, as opposed to the white, race [arguing that] 'the peculiarity of the race [means that] almost all negroes require masters,'" 115. Carlyle would also entertain the possibility of white slavery, much to the horror of Emerson, suggesting to "*Blacklead* those 2 million idle beggars" of indigent Irish "and sell them to Brazil as Niggers" in order to "moderate the windpipe of eloquence one hears on that subject," Thomas Carlyle, *The Correspondence of Thomas Carlyle and Ralph Waldo Emerson, 1834–1872*, vol. 2, ed. Charles Eliot Norton (Boston: Houghton Mifflin, 1896), 214.
62. James D.B. DeBow, "The Origins, Progress, and Prospects of Slavery" 9 (July 1850), 19.
63. Ibid., 9.
64. Ibid., 10.
65. H.C. Hornady, qtd. in Harrison Berry, *Slavery and Abolition, As Viewed by a Georgia Slave* (Atlanta: M. Lynch, 1860), 2.
66. Ibid., 10.
67. Ibid., v.
68. Ibid., iii.
69. Ibid., vi.
70. E.N. Elliott, "Introduction," *Cotton Is King, and Pro-Slavery Arguments Comprising the Writings of Hammond, Harper, Christy, Stringfellow, Hodge, Bledsoe, and Cartwright*, ed. E.N. Elliott (New York: Negro Universities Press, 1969 [originally pub. 1860]), xiii.
71. S.A. Cartwright, "Slavery in the Light of Ethnology," *Cotton Is King, and Pro-Slavery Arguments Comprising the Writings of Hammond, Harper, Christy, Stringfellow, Hodge, Bledsoe, and Cartwright*, ed. E.N. Elliott (New York: Negro Universities Press, 1969 [originally pub. 1860]), 715–16.
72. Ibid., 715.
73. Charles Sellers has claimed that "the religious defense of slavery as a great missionary institution for the conversion and uplift of blacks implied an ultimate change in their status," and forwarded an argument too liberal and empowering for blacks to prevail as the dominant proslavery defense, *The Market Revolution: Jacksonian America, 1815–1846* (New York: Oxford University Press, 1991), 409. This argument was not thrown out altogether, however, as Berry's narrative shows. Berry is upwardly mobile, but clearly not so much that he presents a threat through his change in status precisely because he continues to subserve the system that oppresses him in his rise

from the fields into the ranks of middle management. Proslavery's support of elevating the status of slaves (without granting them real power) was prompted by Fitzhugh's humanitarian portrait of slavery that warned against evils of hating blacks and advocated loving them. "The Southerner is the negro's friend," he assured, "his only friend. Let no intermeddling abolitionist, no refined philosophy dissolve this friendship," qtd. in Wish, 110.

74. Catherine Beecher, *An Essay on Slavery and Abolitionism, with Reference to the Duty of American Females* (Philadelphia: Henry Perkins, 1837), 128–29. See Bonner (Robert E.) for more on this backlash against female involvement in abolition, 186–205.

75. *Cannibals All!* posits that every society is built around the dependence of individuals in lesser power and status upon those who are in power. Like Berry, Fitzhugh urges that slavery is merely another form of the compulsory labor demanded of every civilization. His examples range from Feudalism, Fitzhugh, 79–80, to churches, families, soldiers, sailors, prisoners, and governments. The British Colonies, he observes, were built with Chinese labor, Fitzhugh, 232–33.

76. Chancellor Harper, "Slavery in the Light of Social Ethics," *Cotton Is King, and Pro-Slavery Arguments Comprising the Writings of Hammond, Harper, Christy, Stringfellow, Hodge, Bledsoe, and Cartwright*, ed. E.N. Elliott (New York: Negro Universities Press, 1969 [originally pub. 1860]), 570.

77. Although Fitzhugh posits that cannibalistic behavior reigns in a laissez-faire social climate in *Cannibals All!*, he should not be misconstrued as adhering to a Hobbesian view of human nature as Ericson has in his recent study, *The Debate over Slavery*, 109. Quite the contrary, Fitzhugh understood the benevolent purpose of slavery would draw out humanity's natural inclination toward sympathy rather than competition. The free market only makes their interests more antagonistic, while the institution of slavery not only protects the "weak" from the "strong," but nurtures their mutual trust and cooperation in a shared vision of domestic harmony. In *The Soul's Economy*, Sklansky more accurately explains that Fitzhugh understood "Human nature was rather passionately social, manifested in the loyalty of slaves and the benevolence of masters, in the love of men and women, and devotion of parents and children, and the honor of southern society," 98. Fitzhugh firmly believed that slavery cultivated humanity's natural inclination toward social cohesion, and even love, while the Northern free market encouraged the development of unnatural divisive hostility and self-interest. "The institution of slavery gives full development and full play to the affections," he asserted, whereas "free society chills, stints and eradicates them...Love for others is the organic law of our society, as self-love is of theirs," Fitzhugh, *Sociology*, 248.

78. Harper, 607.

79. James D.B. DeBow, Editorial Note to "Memoir on Slavery" by Chancellor Harper, *DeBow's Commercial Review* 2.3 (March 1850), 232.
80. John R. Thompson, "Editor's Table" *Southern Literary Messenger* 26 (May 1858), 392.
81. John R. Thompson, "Editor's Table" *Southern Literary Messenger* 33 (September 1861), 261.
82. John R. Thompson, "Editor's Table" *Southern Literary Messenger* 33 (November 1861), 395.
83. Michael O'Brien, "On the Mind of the Old South and Its Accessibility," *Rethinking the South: Essays in Intellectual History* (Baltimore: Johns Hopkins University Press, 1988), 33–35. See also Amy M. Thomas, "Literacies, Readers, and Cultures of Print in the South," *A History of the Book in America: The Industrial Book, 1840–1880*, vol. 3, ed. Scott E. Casper (Chapel Hill: University of North Carolina Press, 2007), 383–85.
84. Genovese and Genovese, 207.
85. Ibid., 183.

Conclusion: The Boston Bellamy Club, Rand's Objectivists, and Iowa Writers' Workshop

1. Eric Hoffer, *The True Believer: Thoughts on the Nature of Mass Movements* (New York: Harper, 2002 [originally pub. 1951]), 89.
2. Ralph Waldo Emerson, "Self-Reliance," *The Essential Writings of Ralph Waldo Emerson*, ed. Brooks Atkinson (New York: Modern Library), 135.
3. Martha Schoolman, "Emerson's Doctrine of Hatred" *Arizona Quarterly* 63.2 (2007), 1.
4. Emerson, "Self-Reliance," 137.
5. My insight that competing coteries engaged the mechanism of the literary market with their own unique brand of sympathy extends Cindy Weinstein's claim in *Family Kinship, and Sympathy in Nineteenth-Century American Literature* (Cambridge: Cambridge University Press, 2004) that "sympathy was a litmus test for a text's politics." I would argue that sympathy was also a litmus test for the prestige and status of the literary circle, and thus its position in the hierarchy of the publishing industry. Weinstein rightly says that sympathy was "the very test that many antebellum Americans applied to their daily activities and the principles around which their lives were organized. Mothers read advice manuals in order to learn to be more sympathetic; the south was sympathetic, it insisted, because it cared for slaves; the north claimed that it was sympathetic because it opposed slavery and had a system of free labor; the law aimed to be sympathetic," which was a particularly vexing issue in Melville's *Billy Budd*, 1–2. This issue was not just pervasive, it was indeed a bargaining chip bearing the unique emblem of each cultural faction vying

for America's ever expanding mass readership. See also Elizabeth Barnes, *States of Sympathy: Seduction and Democracy in the American Novel* (New York: Columbia University Press, 1997).
6. Many other examples of this rhetoric abound throughout the literature of the era. Whitman's *Franklin Evans*, his first and last novel, a lurid temperance tale, even engages in the politics of coterie representation. Saluting the increasingly popular Washingtonian temperance society in a self-promotional intertextual commercial advertisement of the sort he became notorious for in his many editions of *Leaves of Grass*, Whitman climbed onto their growing bandwagon. "They call themselves 'WASHINGTONIANS,'" he sang out, celebrating them and thus himself as "upright and noble spirits, determined never to turn back from the work, or to discredit the name they bear, and the Society to which they belong!" Walt Whitman, *Franklin Evans*, ed. Christopher Castiglia and Glen Hendler (Durham: Duke University Press, 2007 [originally pub. 1842]), 112. Significantly, Washingtonians prided themselves on revising the prior generation's clergy-led temperance that vilified, rather than sympathized with, the drunkard. In his only true antebellum bestseller, *Typee* (1846), Melville also alludes to the essential role of sympathy in the social politics of production with clear implications for coterie function. The natives worked in such a way that is utterly cohesive, "everything was done in concert and good-fellowship," he writes, remarking that "while employed in erecting a tenement, [they] reminded me of a colony of beavers at work," only not in silence, but with such "a perfect tumult of hilarity [which] seemed actuated by an instinct of friendliness, that it was truly beautiful to behold," Herman Melville, *Typee* (New York: Signet, 1979 [originally pub. 1846]), 229.
7. Ibid., 137.
8. Paul Avrich, *The Haymarket Tragedy* (Princeton: Princeton University Press, 1984), xiii.
9. J.A. Hobson qtd. in Matthew Beaumont, "William Reeves and Late Victorian Radical Publishing: Unpacking the Bellamy Library" *History Workshop Journal* 55 (2003), 93.
10. Loren Glass notes that the Workshop "became the model, and initially the key personnel resource, for the remarkably rapid proliferation of writing programs across the country in the fifties and sixties. Indeed, it is impossible to think of a reputable postwar novelist, and neigh impossible to come up with a postwar poet, who did not spend some time, if not an entire career, affiliated with an MFA program, usually one started by an Iowa graduate; and, of course, a visit to Iowa City has become a standard line of any writer of any literary standing anywhere in the world," "Middle Man: Paul Engle and the Iowa Writers' Workshop" *Minnesota Review* 71–72 (2009) http://www.theminnesotareview.org/journal/ns7172/glass.shtml.

11. Thomas Wentworth Higginson, "Step by Step" *Nationalist* 1 (September 1889), 145.
12. Qtd. in Bowman, 114.
13. Cyrus Willard, "Declaration of Principles" *Nationalist* 1 (May 1889), 16.
14. William Morris, *The Manifesto of the Socialist League*, in E.P. Thompson, *William Morris: Romantic to Revolutionary* (New York: Pantheon, 1976), 737.
15. For more on the formation of the "Collective," see the chapters, "The Cult While the Guru Lived," and "Entrails: The Anatomy of the Cult," in Jeff Walker's *The Ayn Rand Cult* (Chicago: Open Court, 1999), 11–74.
16. Barbara Branden and Nathaniel Branden, *Who Is Ayn Rand?* (New York: Paperback Library, 1964).
17. Barbara Branden, *The Passion of Ayn Rand: A Biography* (New York: Doubleday, 1986), 391.
18. Qtd. in ibid., 255.
19. Ibid., 227.
20. Anne C. Heller, *Ayn Rand and the World She Made* (New York: Nan A. Talese, 2009), 419.
21. Nathaniel Branden, *My Years with Ayn Rand* (San Francisco: Jossey-Bass, 1999), 298.
22. In 1954, Jewel Limar Prestage was the first African American woman to earn a doctoral degree in political science from a university in the United States. Also noteworthy in this progressive tradition at the University of Iowa is its status as the first university in America to award a law degree to a woman, Mary B. Hickey Wilkinson, in 1873. The University of Iowa, "Graduate Admissions: A Proud Tradition" 24 December 2009, http://www.uiowa.edu/admissions/graduate/diversity.
23. Edward J. Delaney, "Where Great Writers Are Made" *Atlantic Monthly* (16 July 2007) http://www.theatlantic.com/magazine/archive/2007/08/where-great-writers-are-made/6032/.
24. David Haven Blake, "Reading Whitman, Growing Up Rock and Roll" *Virginia Quarterly Review* 81 (2005), 34. Creative writing faculty Charles Johnson is among many who have responded to the lack of rigor in creative writing courses by steeping them in literature, history, and philosophy. He similarly asked "how long would Kafka, Emerson, Melville, or Dostoyevski have lasted in a soft-at-the center...highly subjective, 'touchy-feely' course asking twenty-somethings to 'write what they know' [which becomes] the same underwhelming story, usually of their first sexual experience," "A Boot Camp for Creative Writing" *Chronicle of Higher Education* 50.10 (31 October 2003), B7.
25. Paul Engle, "The Writer and the Place," *Midland, An Antholgy of Poetry and Prose*, ed. Paul Engle (New York: Random House, 1961), iv.

26. Harmon Smith, *My Friend, My Friend: The Story of Thoreau's Relationship with Emerson* (Amherst: University of Massachusetts Press, 2001), 108.
27. Stanwood Cobb, *Discovering the Genius within You* (Cleveland: World, 1933), 18.
28. Mark McGurl, *The Program Era: Postwar Fiction and the Rise of Creative Writing* (Cambridge, MA: Harvard University Press, 2009), 128.
29. Ibid., 128.
30. Ibid., 114.
31. I limit my claims to the first three decades of the program under Engle during the postwar years. After Engle's era, especially in creative writing programs of the 1980s and 1990s, authors became complacent within the protective institutional enclaves of universities, and thus productivity suffered dramatically. Such declining productivity has been documented by Shirley Lim, who outlines how critics have noted that "creative writing programs have composed a system of patronage between universities and writers that has resulted in a mediocre literary culture and intellectual dereliction for creative writing students and faculty," "The Strangeness of Creative Writing: An Institutional History" *Pedagogy* 3.2 (2003), 157. "The professional success rates for graduates in creative writing [based on the success rate for publication] is about one percent (compared with 90 percent for graduates of medical school)," according to D.G. Meyers, *The Elephants Teach: Creative Writing since 1880* (Englewood Cliffs, NJ: Prentice Hall, 1996), 2. August Kleinzahler has correlated the sharp "decline in the quality of contemporary poetry with the spread of creative writing programs," qtd. in Ron McFarland, "An Apologia for Creative Writing" *College English* 55 (1993), 28. Dana Gioia also noted a correlation between the rise of creative writing programs and poetry's disappearance from "public view" in his editorial introduction to *Can Poetry Matter?: Essays on Poetry and American Culture* (St. Paul, MN: Gray Wolf, 1992), 2. He has since advocated for more aggressive commercial engagement on the part of poets, actively supporting *Poetry* editor John Barr's attempts to commercialize the vocation through a kind of economic stimulus package funded by a windfall two hundred million dollar donation from a pharmaceutical heiress. (See Dana Goodyear's "The Moneyed Muse" *New Yorker* [19 February 2007] http://www.newyorker.com/reporting/ for a skeptical approach toward the enterprise). Lauding the comparative quality and quantity of American verse that attended authorship prior to the university's shelter from the free market, Gioia laments the passing of the era when financial pressure to produce "delivered the collective cultural benefit of frightening away all but committed artists." Ironically enough Engle's founding vision was to

maintain that pressure through stressing publication among faculty and students in the Workshop, 13.
32. For more on Engle's dabbling in the greeting card trade, see Michael Chasar's "Remembering Paul Engle" *Writer's Chronicle* 41.2 (October/November 2008), 56–68.
33. Stephen Wilbers, *The Iowa Writers' Workshop: Origins, Emergence, and Growth* (Iowa City: University of Iowa Press, 1980), 91.
34. Engle's letter defending himself from HUAC witch-hunters alludes to the patriotism evident in his published poetry, much of which sung the praises of the prairie with Whitmanian nationalism. "My devotion to this country has been proved in book after book celebrating the American way—some titles are, AMERICAN SONG, AMERICAN CHILD, CORN, WEST OF MIDNIGHT," he insisted in defense of his use of taxpayer dollars to host Communist speakers (Paul Engle to Curtis Baxter, 15 November 1952, Papers of Paul Engle, University of Iowa Libraries, Iowa City, Iowa).
35. Paul Engle, ed. *On Creative Writing* (New York: E.P. Dutton, 1964), vii.
36. All quotations in the paragraph are from Kiyohiro Miura, "'I'll Make Your Career,'" *A Community of Writers: Paul Engle and the Iowa Writers' Workshop*, ed. Robert Dana (Iowa City: University of Iowa Press, 1999), 57, 59.
37. Paul Engle to "Former Workshop Students" 14 December 1956, Papers of Paul Engle, University of Iowa Libraries, Iowa City, Iowa.
38. Engle's income for his books, *Poet's Choice*, and *On Creative Writing*, was $1593.09 from E.P. Dutton and Company for a five-month period ending in April 1965. *An Old Fashioned Christmas* garnered steady royalty checks, yet scant earnings for *Poems in Praise* are on record, with many checks like one for *American Child* from the Dial Press dated 30 June 1959 worth as little as $11.09. Engle sold 29,268 Valentine cards for Hallmark Inc. in February 1967 (receipt dated 31 March 1967) securing a tidy $7,317 for his efforts; Hallmark had established a lucrative relationship with him several years prior, with a steady stream of checks coming during the 1960s of over $500. Christmas cards were his cash cow, as indicated by his first Hallmark payday of $184.50 on 20 January 1961. Engle's creative writing fed greeting card and television industries. *The Golden Child* aired on television, was published in *Guideposts* (a white middle-class protestant general interest magazine), and rehashed into a greeting card by that journal. A 14 October 1960 letter from Glenn D. Kittler of *Guideposts* indicates a business relationship with Engle. Engle also dabbled in popular sports poetry, netting a nifty $2000 advance for a poem on the Kentucky Derby for *Sports Illustrated* as revealed in a letter from Percy Knauth dated 23 April 1961. Though considerable time and effort went into them, none of these publications is mentioned in Wilbers or Clarence A. Andrews, *A Literary History*

of Iowa (Iowa City: University of Iowa Press, 1973). It is also worth noting that his Random House Receipts are miniscule in comparison to those of these mass market productions. *Poems in Praise,* for example, earned him $20.16 in royalties on 4 August 1961 (as indicated in a letter from Jane Wilson of William Morris and Company, his agent). Papers of Paul Engle, University of Iowa Libraries, Iowa City, Iowa.

39. The student in question was Charles Embree, who attended the Workshop sporadically from 1946 to 1952, Wilbers, 89.
40. Ibid., 88.
41. Ibid., 94, 104. "I work hard on these trips [to New York City] as well as do the obvious theatre in the evening, and see countless publishers, editors, people of usefulness," he wrote to the chair of the English department, in a letter that points to the intensity of promotional efforts. "If the University does get a Ford grant of real size (I'm aiming at a million), it would be because, like getting the Rockefeller $40K, I came here on my own, paying my own expenses, by lecturing." Paul Engle to Baldwin Maxwell, 10 February 1956. Papers of Paul Engle, University of Iowa Libraries, Iowa City, Iowa.
42. Paul Engle, Lecture Notes, 24 August 1954, Papers of Paul Engle, University of Iowa Libraries, Iowa City, Iowa.
43. Promotional Brochure for Paul Engle by W. Colston Leigh, 16 May 1951, Papers of Paul Engle, University of Iowa Libraries, Iowa City, Iowa.
44. Transcript of the *Esquire* Symposium on "The Writer in a Mass Culture," 4 December 1959, Iowa City, 9, 15. Papers of Paul Engle, University of Iowa Libraries, Iowa City, Iowa.
45. Ellison's point here has been underscored by recent theorists commenting on literature deliberately written for the masses, such as the serial fiction of the *New York Ledger*. Michael Denning's suggestion that "questions about the sincerity of [popular literature's] purported beliefs or the adequacy of their political proposals are less interesting than questions about the narrative embodiment of their political ideologies," a point that, I would argue, equally applies to self-conscious attempts at serious literature for the elite market, *Mechanic Accents: Dime Novels and Working Class Culture in America* (New York: Verso, 1987), 103.
46. Ibid., 18, 23.
47. Engle, "Writer and the Place," xv–xxvi.
48. Engle wrote Sinclair Lewis to convince him to join the faculty because the teaching salary allows the freedom to engage the literary market at will rather than necessity. It is not so much that he portrays teaching as a paradise sheltered from the rigors of the literary market. Rather, he asserts that the teaching salary frees literary production from economic necessity to ebb and flow with creative interests and fecundity. Faculty positions thus afford professional authors an advantageous

position from which to access the market. "One reason writers teach at universities is very close to my own," he offered. "I couldn't make a living by writing poetry alone, but my reputation as a poet helps get me a job teaching. Further, I am independent because I earn my living with the teaching job and can write as much or as little as I please, and of any kind, without having to shape my talent, perhaps unconsciously, toward a market. I don't have that financial dependence toward magazine editors and on publishers which the writer out bucking the market always has. In that sense, the university is a release, not a hindrance." In an effort to win over Lewis, Engle was overstating the case here. With or without the financial cushion of a teaching position, there of course always already was pressure for authors (with any legitimate claim to the title) to shape their talent toward the market. In fact the work of the faculty writer could be measurably better than that of an independent author, according to his logic, precisely because it was more precisely attuned to the market, rather than desperately so. Calculated pitches rather than wild rushes at publishers could be made, as Engle's own steady stream of Random House and Hallmark card poetry attests. For Engle, the option of turning away from the market entirely was inconceivable, and when it occurred among his colleagues, he regarded it as nothing less than a heretical abomination, a form or treason against the code of ethics governing the community of university authors. Paul Engle to Sinclair Lewis, February 27, 1951. Papers of Paul Engle, University of Iowa Libraries, Iowa City, Iowa.

49. Jane Smiley recalls a system in 1974 Iowa City by which such "pets" would angle for social status with hopes of being tapped by the next publisher to make his rounds through the Workshop. Pets, Smiley writes, "were able to contemplate using the teachers and the editors in a way that reciprocated the use that the teachers and the editors thought of putting them to. They knew that being a pet was not a one-way street, that the teachers and the editors needed a little flattery. They didn't wait until the day the teachers and editors introduced themselves to bone up on the work of that person. The pets were knowing," "Iowa City, 1974," *Mentors, Muses, and Monsters: 30 Writers on the People Who Changed Their Lives*, ed. Elizabeth Benedict (New York: Free Press, 2009), 262.

50. Leon Jackson, *The Business of Letters: Authorial Economy in Antebellum America* (Stanford, CA: Stanford University Press, 2008), 237.

51. Qtd. in Wilbers, 132. Students who had written manuscripts discussed at workshops were routinely asked to remain silent while hearing critical feedback and made powerless to respond to it. Frank Conroy, Workshop faculty, had allowed that "some observers find surprising" this practice that leaves authors prostrate before their audience. But the benefits are inherent in forcing the author to face

"what the text, standing alone, appears to be doing to the readers" because it provides "a tension the writer should face," Frank Conroy, "The Writers' Workshop," *Dogs Bark, But the Caravan Rolls On: Observations Then and Now* (Boston: Houghton Mifflin, 2002), 99.
52. Ibid., 133.
53. This point augments Loren Glass's accurate assertion that the university insulated authors from direct dependence on the literary marketplace in exchange for the use of their charisma as a marketing tool advancing the status of the institution at large. The University of Iowa has anointed itself "The Writing University" to this end. Notwithstanding this reciprocally beneficial arrangement for the author and the university, I would argue that the early years of the Workshop provided writers more than just a protective shield from market forces, as it also conditioned and prepared them for professional careers. The testimony cited in this section underscores how crucial publication was in establishing the social hierarchy within the program. Insulation—both geographical, due to the remote rural setting in Iowa, and economic, due to the institutional security provided by the University—from the mass culture and the market thus should not obscure the very real standard for publication to which Engle held both his students and faculty. His mantra, "Produce or get out," hardly insulated his cohort from the realities of the market, but instead actively drove them to it, Paul Engle, Response to draft chapter, "Engle Workshop," Papers of Paul Engle, University of Iowa Libraries, Iowa City, Iowa.
54. Pierre Bourdieu, *In Other Words: Essays Towards a Reflexive Sociology* (Stanford, CA: Stanford University Press, 1990), 143.
55. Pierre Bourdieu, *The Field of Cultural Production: Essays on Art and Literature*, ed. Randal Johnson (New York: Columbia University Press, 1993), 7.
56. Paul Engle to Sinclair Lewis, 27 February 1951, Papers of Paul Engle, University of Iowa Libraries, Iowa City, Iowa.
57. Max Weber, *Economy and Society: An Outline of Interpretive Sociology*, ed. Guenther Roth and Claus Wittich (Berkeley: University of California Press, 1968), 243.
58. Ibid., 249.
59. Fanny Fern, *Ruth Hall* (New Brunswick, NJ: Rutgers University Press, 1986 [originally pub. 1855]), 177.

Index

abolitionism, 9, 203
　and commercialism, 157
　identity, 22, 148, 165–72
　and moral reform, 153, 155–6, 159, 163
　and Peabody, 133, 144, 147
　see also Garrison, William Lloyd
active interlocution, 119
advertising
　and Bonner, 16, 24, 63, 66, 72, 76–9, 80, 84
　and Garrison, 149, 153, 157
　and Peabody, 139
Aesthetic Papers, 131, 135–7, 139, 182
African Americans, 132, 149, 166, 195, 216
　see also free blacks
agent, *see* intermediary
Alcott, Bronson, 96–7, 99, 120, 137–40, 143
Allston, Washington, 43, 95, 123, 127
American Anti-Slavery Society, 150, 156, 159, 163, 168
American Tract Society, 150, 153
Analectic, 34, 56
anticommercialism, 22, 24, 119, 203, 206
　and Transcendentalists, 92–4, 102–3, 110, 116
　see also commercialism
antimaterialism, 14, 24, 27, 29, 51, 80, 97, 101, 111, 121, 206
　and Transcendentalists, 92
　see also anticommercialism
antislavery, *see* abolitionism
apologists, 149, 194, 202
　identity, 22, 174, 188, 203
　see also Fitzhugh, George
associationism, 5–7
　and Bellamy, 210
　and South, 174, 192
　and Transcendentalism, 97, 137, 182
　see also collectivism; literary circle benefits
association movement, 6
　see also Brook Farm; Hawthorne, Nathaniel; Melville, Herman
Astor, John Jacob, 59, 60

Atlas Shrugged, 210, 217
audience, *see* coteries: audience; readership
authorship, 3, 5
　belligerent, 152
　commercial, 62, 179, 222, 228
　competitive, 9, 24, 27, 92, 225
　coterie, 2, 45, 49, 51–2, 98, 116, 203
　professional, 1, 5, 7, 13–14, 23, 35, 84, 92, 138–9, 148, 207, 213, 217–18, 222
　radical, 218
　romantic, myth of, 4, 7, 17, 128–9, 131, 206
　social, 4, 7, 8, 24, 112, 225, 227
　see also individualism; Iowa style
bachelor aesthetic, 40–4, 52, 224
　and homosexuality, 43–4
Barnum, P.T., 63, 123, 157, 172
Beecher, Catharine, 65, 73, 129, 198
Beecher, Henry Ward, 64–8, 74
Bellamy, Edward, 12, 130, 183, 205–6
　economic philosophy, 208–10
　see also Boston Bellamy Club
benevolent paternalism, 3, 9, 11, 25, 174, 176, 181, 189, 192–4, 205
　see also Fitzhugh, George; proslavery
bohemia, 25, 27, 207
Bonner, Robert, 7, 66, 68, 70, 75, 82–3, 88, 205, 211, 227
　advertising tactics, 16, 24, 63, 66, 72, 76–80, 84
　and Beecher, 66–8
　ethos, 68–70, 75, 80, 84, 154, 206
　and Fern, 85–6
Boston Bellamy Club, 206–8, 210
　see also Bellamy, Edward
Boston Female Anti-Slavery Association, 156, 159
Bourdieu, Pierre, 7, 9, 22, 24–5, 27–9, 225–6
　see also individualism; intermediary
Branden, Barbara (aka Barbara Weidman), 210–15
　see also Objectivists

Index

Branden, Nathaniel (aka Nathan Blumenthal), 210–15
  see also NBI; Objectivists
branding of writers, 1, 68
  literary brand name, 5, 6, 23, 25
Bread and Cheese Club, 15, 26, 49, 56
Brevoort, Henry, 21, 37, 47, 53–5, 57–8, 60
Bronte, Charlotte, 217–18
Brook Farm, 4–6, 24, 97, 103, 118, 120, 123, 132, 182
Brownson, Orestes, 68, 97, 154, 174, 184, 205
Bryant, William Cullen, 17, 24, 26, 56–7, 63, 72
business sponsorships, *see* literary partnerships

Calhoun, John C., 174–5, 182, 185
Calliopean Society, 35, 56
Cannibals All!, or, Slaves Without Masters, 157, 186, 189, 193
capital building
  cultural, 20, 226
  economic, 2, 11, 18, 20, 28, 226
  social, 2, 3, 6, 12, 18, 20–2, 64, 130, 136, 205
  symbolic, 20, 28, 225–8
Capital Coteries, 3, 8
capitalism, 3, 4, 36, 39, 41, 45, 61, 63, 67–9, 92, 100, 120, 132, 182, 184, 193, 198–9, 205–6
  cooperative, 149, 176–8, 180–1, 185–6, 189, 202
  laissez-faire, 95, 149, 154, 180, 188–9, 191, 209, 213
  radical, 207–8, 210, 212
  see also commercialism; free market; market
Carlyle, Thomas, 7, 8, 48, 112, 115, 181, 190
  and Emerson, 2
Catcher in the Rye, 1
  Holden Caulfield (narrator), 1, 8, 18
Channing, Ellery, 112, 115
Channing, Rev. Dr. William Ellery, 119–21, 123, 130, 132, 143–4, 155, 165
Child, Lydia Maria, 18, 72, 148–9, 151–2, 155–7, 159–60, 162–70, 204, 226
clubs, 6, 13, 40, 56, 115, 117, 144, 206, 217
  see also coteries; literary circles
Cobb, Sylvanus, 61–2, 65, 68–70, 73, 81, 83–4, 147, 211
collaboration, *see* collectivism
Collective, The, 211–13, 215
collective biography, 8
collectivism
  authors' responses to, 9
  and Bellamy, 206–8, 210
  and Fitzhugh's apologists, 149, 172, 174–5, 178–81, 186–9, 191, 199, 201
  and Garrisonians, 160
  and Transcendentalism, 3, 103–4, 106, 112
commercialism, 2, 203, 220–8
  of authorship, 24
  of clubs and circles, 13, 22, 62–3
  history, 4, 5
  and North, 150–1, 157
  see also anticommercialism; capitalism; free market
common enterprise, *see* collectivism
communal living, *see* Brook Farm
competition, *see* individualism
Comte, August, 155, 189–90, 192, 201
Concord circle, 10–11, 19, 29, 91, 104, 112–14, 116, 227
  see also Emerson, Ralph Waldo; Hawthorne, Nathaniel; Peabody, Elizabeth Palmer; Transcendentalism
conformity, 39, 100, 103
constructivism, 140–1
conversation
  as art, 117–19, 127, 140, 224
  democratic, 121, 125–6, 136–7, 139–42
Cooper, James Fennimore, 34, 42, 49–50, 56, 93, 95
cooperation, *see* collectivism
corporate sponsorships, *see* literary partnerships; protocorporate entrepreneurial enterprise
coteries, 1, 2
  audience, 2
  culture, 26, 102, 204, 227–8
  functions, 17–25, 111, 205, 225
  identity, 2, 20–2, 24–5
  intellectual, 5, 22, 102, 111, 113
  literary, 5, 6, 8, 11, 12, 23, 68, 101, 105, 130
  and literary circles, 3–5, 12
  as marketing vehicles, 3, 23–5, 28–9, 53, 100, 223
  as method of political entrenchment, 4
  as models of association, 3, 9, 21, 26–7, 39, 96, 102, 110
  organizational models, 3, 6, 9, 40
  see also literary circles
Croakers, 45–6, 57
Cyclopedia of American Literature, 7, 33–5, 41, 93

INDEX

DeBow, James D.B., 173–7, 188, 190, 192–5
DeBow's Review, 173–81, 188, 191, 202, 205
  business practices, 178, 186, 188
  commercial and agricultural roots, 173–5
  politics, 175, 180, 192, 200, 202
  readership, 177
  threat to Garrisonians, 174
Dial, The, 96, 107–9, 112–13, 115–16, 134–5
Dickens, Charles, 22, 30, 57, 64
disunion of U.S.
  and Fitzhugh, 182
  and Garrison, 151, 154, 158, 161, 164, 166–9
Diverting History of John Bull and Brother Jonathan, The, 42, 47–8
Douglass, Frederick, 148–9, 151, 155–6, 170–2, 192, 196
Drake, Joseph Rodman, 45, 57
Durand, Asher B., 18, 24
Duyckinck, Evert, 7, 15, 18, 21, 27, 33, 93–4
  and Paulding, 35, 48–9

economic philosophies, *see* Bellamy, Edward; Rand, Ayn; slavery
egoism, 211
  see also Objectivists
elite salon system, *see* salon system
Ellison, Ralph, 222–4, 228
Emancipator, 159, 169
Emerson, Ralph Waldo, 6, 7, 11, 93–4, 106, 110, 113–15, 227
  and antimaterialism, 27, 92, 96, 101–2
  Bush, 18, 96
  and capitalism, 96, 100–1, 116, 203–4
  and Carlyle, 2, 115
  and Fuller, 102–9, 114–15
  and Peabody, 134–5
  and reform, 151
  and social groups, 97–8, 100–2
  and Thoreau, 10, 21, 114, 226
  see also Transcendentalism
Engle, Paul, 215, 217, 219–28
  see also Iowa Writers' Workshop
entrepreneurial economy, *see* capitalism; commercialism
Evening Post, 53, 55
Everett, Edward, 74–6
Examiner, 178–80
exchange economy, 17–18, 20, 22, 25, 30, 54, 79, 95, 97

family
  and business, 21–2
  and Fitzhugh, 175, 181, 190, 192–5, 198
  and Knickerbockers, 40, 42, 55
  and *Ledger*, 62, 64–70, 73–4, 80, 88
  and Transcendentalists, 101, 103
Fanny, 45–7, 57
Fanuzzi, Robert, 152, 170
Fern, Fanny, 21, 61–2, 67, 70–6, 82–5, 121, 132, 211
Fitzhugh, George, 11, 21–2, 68, 178, 200, 202
  ethos, 182–6, 189–93
  and Garrison, 149, 157–8
  and Holmes, 178–81, 183, 190
  literary circle, 149, 175, 203
  style, 180, 191, 201, 227
  see also apologists; benevolent paternalism; proslavery
Foster, George, 16, 19
Fountainhead, 210–11
  children of, 213, 218
Fourier, Charles, 5, 104, 182
  see also Brook Farm
free blacks, 149, 153–4, 170, 184, 194
  see also Wilson, Harriet
free enterprise, *see* capitalism; free market; literary market
free market, 1–4, 14, 68, 121, 154, 176, 181, 189, 193, 225
  and Bellamy, 208
  and Rand, 210
  see also capitalism
Fuller, Margaret, 16, 18, 71, 96, 98–9, 159, 170, 205
  and Greeley, 18, 113–15
  and Knickerbockers, 94–5
  and nature, 95
  and Peabody, 118, 120, 126, 128
  and Transcendentalism, 18, 92, 102–9, 112–16

Garrison, William Lloyd, 11, 147–72
  and Child, 166–9
  ethos, 151–4, 161
  and Fitzhugh, 149, 157–8, 186
  and free speech, 151–2, 154, 160, 163
  literary circle, 148–9, 152, 155–6, 162, 203–4
  style, 148, 152, 155–7, 168, 171, 227–8
  war room, 18
  see also abolitionism
gender discrimination, 132–4

Index

gender ideology, 8, 71–4, 109, 119, 120, 126, 129, 158–9, 198
 see also separate spheres of gender; women
Genovese, Eugene D. and Elizabeth Fox, 180, 183, 189, 191–2, 201
Ginsberg, Allen
 Beat Generation, 10, 207, 215, 223
Godey's Ladies Book, 74, 79, 200
Greeley, Horace, 66–7, 83, 113–15, 117, 183
Greenspan, Alan, 211–12
Grimke, Angelina and Sarah, 5, 158–9, 164, 198
group identity, 5, 10, 14
 see also abolitionists; apologists; authorship; branding of writers; coteries; Knickerbockers; *Ledger, New York*; literary circles; Transcendentalism

Halleck, Fitz-Greene, 17–18, 26–7, 43–4, 46, 50, 52–3, 55–6, 58–60, 93
 and Bonner, 63
 and Irving, 44–5, 57–8
Hallock, John W.M., 43, 45
Harper, Chancellor, 198–9
Harper's Weekly, 76–7, 200
Hart, John S., 1, 8
Hawthorne, Nathaniel, 96, 98
 Blithedale Romance, 6
 on Brook Farm, 4, 6, 103
 House of the Seven Gables, 22, 122, 124
 and Peabody, 117, 124, 128–9, 142–3
Hedge, Frederic Henry, 19, 97–9, 113, 127
Hedge Club, 19, 96–8, 139
Hemingway, Ernest, 10, 218
Hidden Hand, 64, 73
History of New York, 40, 42, 54
Holden Caulfield, see *Catcher in the Rye*
Holmes, George Frederick, 178, 202
 and Fitzhugh, 178–81, 183, 190
homosexuality, 39, 43–4
Hughes, Henry, 179–80, 189, 191–2, 202

individualism
 for Bourdieu, 9
 and Garrison abolitionists, 148, 150, 154, 160–1, 167, 172, 174
 and Knickerbockers, 39, 41
 limitations of, 3
 and Rand, 210
 and Transcendentalists, 92, 95, 98, 100, 103, 105–6, 112, 114, 174, 204

intermediary, 4
 and Bourdieu, 7
 and Brevoort, 54–5, 58
 and DeBow, 177
 and Emerson, 114–15, 117
 functions, 7
 and Peabody, 119, 121–3, 126–9, 132–3, 137, 140, 142, 144, 205
Iowa style, see Iowa Writers' Workshop: style
Iowa Writers' Workshop, 206–7, 215–16
 authors in, 216, 218, 220, 224–5
 and business ties, 220–3, 225
 competition in, 220, 224–6
 finances, 219–20, 224
 literary capitalism, 221–2
 style, 217–19, 224–5
 see also Engle, Paul
Irving, Peter, 37–8, 42, 47, 56
Irving, Pierre M., 37, 60
Irving, Washington, 6, 25, 37, 41, 43–4, 47, 50, 56
 and Duyckinck, 33
 and Geoffrey Crayon, 34, 38, 44, 47–9, 57
 and Halleck, 44–5, 57–8
 image, 34–5, 39, 41, 51, 53
 and Knickerbockers, 33, 35–6, 53, 57, 59, 61, 70, 96, 226
 and marketing, 53–4, 58, 60
 and Melville, 41, 52
 and Paulding, 35–6, 45, 48–9
 and writing, 51–2, 55
 see also Irving, William; Lads of Kilkenny; Knickerbockers; *Salmagundi*
Irving, William, 35, 37, 56
 see also Irving, Washington; *Salmagundi*

Jackson, James C., 160, 162, 165
Jackson, Leon, 4, 7, 20, 224
Jackson, Lydia, 96, 127–8
journals, private, 98, 109–12, 115, 140–1, 201
 see also *Aesthetic Papers*; *DeBow's Review*; *Dial, The*; Knickerbockers; *Ledger, New York*; *Liberator*; Objectivists; *Standard, National Anti-Slavery*

Kemble, Francis Anne, 18, 45–7
Kemble, Gouverneur, 21, 37, 39–40, 42, 47, 54, 56
Kerouac, Jack, 215, 223
Knickerbocker (journal), 51, 57–8

INDEX

Knickerbocker, Diedrich, 40, 53, 227
Knickerbockers
  authors in, 18, 26, 35, 47, 52–3, 63, 94
  coterie, 59–60, 116, 150
  definition, 15–16, 53
  ethos, 24, 34–5, 39–40, 51–3, 55, 62
  and homosexuality, 39
  identity, 9, 21–2, 24, 26, 34–6, 38–42, 46, 50, 58, 98, 205, 227
  and *Ledger*, 64, 70–2, 88
  and Transcendentalists, 91, 93–6, 102, 116
  see also Irving, Washington; Lads of Kilkenny; Young America
knot of dreamers, 4, 6, 95–8
  see also Brook Farm; Transcendentalism

labor
  in antebellum America, 17, 23–4, 26, 39–40, 154, 161–2, 184, 205
  and apologists, 154, 183–4, 189–91, 197–9
  cooperative, 103
  and Garrison, 12, 154, 161
  see also labor unions; slavery
labor unions, 5, 160–2
  see also labor
Lads of Kilkenny, 15, 21, 29, 35–44, 47, 50–2, 60–1, 96, 179, 216
  see also Knickerbockers
Larcom, Lucy, 6, 102
Ledger, New York, 5, 7, 11, 200, 205
  commercial ethos of, 62–3, 65, 68–9, 74–6, 79, 88, 206
  and Garrison, 147, 155
  identity, 22, 62, 64, 70, 72–4, 76, 79–80, 86, 227
  and Knickerbocker style, 64, 70–2, 88
  moral code, 64–6, 68, 72–3, 75
  and politics, 75
  staff, 24, 61–2, 64–5, 72, 74–5, 83, 207, 211
Lewis, Harriet and Leon, 61, 68, 72, 86–7
liberalism, 149, 152, 154, 192, 196
Liberator, 18, 147–51, 153–4, 156–8, 169–70
  and Child, 163, 165–7
  staff, 148, 154, 160, 162, 169, 207
Lincoln, Abraham, 151, 186
literary biography, 8
  see also women: as writers
literary business practices, *see* capitalism; commercialism; coteries; literary circles; literary circles, business of

literary circle benefits, 3
  association, 5, 9, 22, 26–7, 30, 220, 227
  brand name, 5–6, 23, 25
  collaboration, 2, 4, 5, 16, 25–6
  collective identity, 2
  economic capital, 17–23, 50, 63
  innovation, 25, 28
  professional support, 18, 25
  promotion of authors, 19, 23, 25
  social capital, 17–23, 25
  see also associationism; collectivism; coteries; literary circles; literary circles, business of
literary circles, 1–2
  audience, 2, 12
  clubs, 13, 206
  competition, 16, 204
  and coteries, 3–5, 12
  definition, 12
  economics of, 3–4, 9, 17, 22–3, 28, 30, 50, 92
  history, 9, 13
  purpose of, 9, 24, 227
  see also coteries; intermediary; literary circle benefits; literary circles, business of
literary circles, business of, 3, 9–14, 26–30, 50, 223–8
  Fitzhugh, 149
  Garrison, 149
  see also literary circle benefits; literary circles
literary coteries, *see* coteries
literary culture
  English vs. American, 41, 46–50
  see also patronage; salon system
literary market, *see* capitalism; commercialism; market
literary partnerships, 4, 57, 220–1
  see also Iowa Writers' Workshop: business ties; patronage; protocorporate entrepreneurial enterprises
literature as trade, *see* capitalism; commercialism; literary culture
Longfellow, Henry Wadsworth, 63–4
Looking Backward, 183, 206–7, 209
  see also socialism
Lost Heiress, 24, 73, 82
Lynch, Anne, 16–20

magazines, *see* periodicals
Mailer, Norman, 222–4, 228
Mann, Horace, 128–9, 142–3

market
  conditions, 24, 96, 228
  and literature, 1, 2, 8, 28, 54, 223–4, 228
  research, 4, 6
  see also capitalism; commercialism; free market
market competition, see capitalism; free market
market culture, 2, 24, 26–30, 100
marketing, 3, 23–30, 93
  and Bonner, 77
  and Engle, 220–3
  and Fitzhugh, 178–9
  and Garrison, 152–4, 157
  see also advertising; commercialism; promotion of authors
market revolution, 5, 9, 11
marriage
  and Knickerbockers, 43, 47
Marshall, Megan, 11, 142–3
Marvel, Ik (Donald Grant Mitchell), 24, 38
Marx, Karl, 22, 104, 183, 190, 206
mass media, 78, 221–4, 228
  and religion, 67
mass readership, 2, 12, 67, 70, 74, 76–7, 88, 141, 204, 224
Matthews, Cornelius, 4, 17, 91, 150
McGurl, Mark, 218–20
Melville, Herman, 6, 27, 52, 227
  Knickerbocker roots, 15, 20, 41, 52
  and Transcendentalists, 91, 95, 203
Merchant's Ledger, 61, 79
Messenger, Southern Literary, 173–4, 178–9, 200
Miller, Perry, 11, 15–16, 50, 57
Mitchell, Donald Grant, see Marvel, Ik
Miura, Kiyohiro, 220–1
Moby-Dick, 6, 44, 71, 148
moralism, see religion
Munroe, James (publisher), 114–15, 122, 135

National Anti-Slavery Standard, see *Standard, National Anti-Slavery*
Nationalist, 208–9
NBI (Nathaniel Branden Institute), 211–12, 215
New England connection, 18–19, 174
new organization, 160–2, 165–6, 169, 204
  see also *Emancipator*; Tappan, Arthur and Lewis
New York Ledger, see *Ledger, New York*

Northern ideology, 172, 174, 179, 181–4, 188, 192–3, 198
  see also abolitionism; Child, Lydia Maria; Garrison, William Lloyd; sectarianism

Objectivist (magazine), 212, 214–15
Objectivists, 206, 210–13, 215, 218
  see also Rand, Ayn
Our Nig, or Sketches in the Life of a Free Black, 153, 184

Parton, James, 73, 84–5
patronage, 4, 27–8
  in Europe, 12, 17
  in U.S., 129, 150, 154, 175, 224, 226–8
  see also literary partnerships; salon system
Paulding, James K., 29–30, 35–7, 42, 45–9, 53, 56–7, 59
  see also *Salmagundi*
Peabody, Elizabeth Palmer, 11, 93, 117–44, 170, 227–8
  as editor, 135–7, 144, 159, 205
  and Emerson, 117, 134–5, 143
  and Hawthorne, 117, 124, 128–9, 142–3
  and Transcendentalism, 120–2, 125, 128
  West Street, 121–5, 135, 227
  see also Concord circle; conversation: as art
Peabody Sisters, 11, 142
peculiar institution, 48, 153, 167, 191, 194, 197
  see also slavery
peer criticism, 217–18, 224–5
  see also Iowa Writers' Workshop: style
periodicals
  market, 13, 61, 72, 77, 93, 109, 123, 136, 151, 166, 180, 200–1, 204–5, 209, 222
  writing, 51, 137, 159
  see also *DeBow's Review*; *Ledger, New York*
Phillips, Wendell, 154, 161, 165
Pierre, 9, 15, 27
professionalism of authors, see authorship: professional
professional societies, see societies
profit, 6, 9
  see also commercialism; free market
promotion of authors, 2, 7, 23, 101
  see also free market; marketing
proslavery
  socialism, 182
  writing, 48, 173, 176, 179, 181, 190, 192–7, 200

INDEX

see also apologists; benevolent paternalism; *DeBow's Review*; Fitzhugh, George; peculiar institution; slavery
prosopography, *see* collective biography
protocorporate entrepreneurial enterprises, 2, 24, 40, 110
see also literary partnerships
publishing industry, 2, 6, 7, 9, 23, 50, 187, 221
pulp fiction, see *Ledger, New York*

Quincy, Edmund, 160, 169

racism, 160, 162, 166
Rand, Ayn, 12, 206–7, 211–15, 217
   economic philosophy, 210, 214
   see also Objectivists
Randolph, J.W., 201–2
Raven and the Whale, 15–16
readership
   groups, 8
   isolation from writers, 1, 7
   South, 173–4, 186
   West, 173–4
   see also mass readership
religion
   and Christian socialism, 127, 129–30, 132
   and clergy, 158–60, 163–4
   and moral reform, 153–4
   see also spirituality
Ripley, George, 97, 120–1, 123, 125
Rogers, Nathaniel P., 148–9, 160–2, 169
Ronda, Bruce, 123, 129–30, 132
Rose, Anne C., 94, 114, 122, 128
Ruth Hall, 21, 61, 70–1, 82, 85, 121, 132, 211, 228

Salmagundi, 10, 34–8, 40–3, 45, 47–9, 51, 56–7, 60
   see also Irving, Washington; Irving, William; Paulding, James K.
salon system, 12, 17
   vs. American, 12–13, 17, 95, 223–4
   see also patronage
Saxe, John G., 72, 74, 86
Scott, Sir Walter, 50, 54, 60
sectarianism
   and Child, 165–9
   and North, 148–9, 151, 155, 162–3
   and South, 175, 181–8
   see also DeBow, James D.B.; Fitzhugh, George; Garrison, William Lloyd; Northern ideology; Southern ideology
Self-Made, 64, 81

self-made man, 81, 83, 157
   see also Bonner, Robert; Garrison, William Lloyd
self-promotion, *see* marketing; promotion of authors
self-reliance, *see* individualism
separate spheres of gender, 71, 121, 127, 158–9
   see also gender ideology
Shaw, Lytle, 2, 3
Sigourney, Lydia, 61, 72–3
Sketch Book, 10, 34, 36, 38, 40–1, 47, 49, 53–5, 93
slave narratives, 153
slavery
   and Aristotle, 180
   as domestic institution, 193
   economics, 174–5, 177, 183, 195
   and miscegenation, 192
   and morality, 174, 184, 193–5
   see also abolitionism; benevolent paternalism; family: and Fitzhugh; peculiar institution
Smith, Adam, 188–90
Smith, Gerrit, 156, 166, 172
social capital, *see* capital building: social
socialism
   and Bellamy, 206–10
   in literary circles, 3, 4
   and Northern view, 183–4, 205
   and Southern view, 174, 181–5, 188–90, 199, 202, 205
social networking, *see* authorship: coteries; capital building: social; literary circle benefits; literary circles
social reform, *see* abolitionism; socialism
societies, 6, 13, 25, 132–3, 144, 150–1, 159–60
Society of Dilettanti, 50–1
socioliterary attitude, 8
Sociology for the South, 178–9, 186, 188, 192
Southern ideology, 172, 174, 179–96, 198–202
   see also apologists; Fitzhugh, George; proslavery; sectarianism
Southern Literary Messenger, see *Messenger, Southern Literary*
Southworth, E.D.E.N., 19, 24, 27, 61–2, 64–5, 68, 70, 72–3, 82–4, 147, 211
spirituality, 105, 111, 132, 161
   see also religion
Standard, National Anti-Slavery, 18, 152, 159–70

Stephens, Anne, 24, 159
Stowe, Harriet Beecher, 65, 201–2
Stringfellow, Thornton, 179, 188, 202
Strong, George Templeton, 50, 99, 100
Summer on the Lakes, 10, 29, 92–5, 98, 103, 105–6, 114, 139
sympathy, 1, 4, 198, 204–5, 210, 224–5

Tappan, Arthur and Lewis, 150–2, 156–7, 165, 169–70
Temple School, 119, 127, 140–1
Tennyson, Alfred Lord, 63–4
Theosophists, 208
Thompson, John R., 179, 200
Thoreau, Henry David
　critics, 94
　and Emerson, 10, 15, 21, 96, 114–15, 217, 226
　and government, 182
　lifestyle, 25, 27, 94, 98, 102, 212
　and periodicals, 136
　and Transcendentalism, 4, 20, 116
　and work, 23
Transcendental Club, 117, 127
Transcendentalism
　authors associated with, 11, 16, 19, 68, 96, 112, 115
　criticism of, 91, 93–4, 105, 138
　ethos, 24, 92, 95–8, 102, 111, 116, 151, 203, 206
　identity, 22, 95, 99–100, 103–4, 107, 111, 182
　and Knickerbockers, 91, 93–4, 96, 102, 116
　and *Ledger*, 93–4, 101–2
　as literary circle, 8–9, 19, 96–7, 99, 112, 204
travel writing, 29
　see also Fuller, Margaret
Tribune, 16
　see also Greeley, Horace

Uncle Tom's Cabin, 29, 201
Unitarian Church, 96–7

Van Winkle, Rip, 35–6, 38–41, 52
Verplank, Gulian C., 26, 59
Very, Jones, 130–1

Walden Pond, 27, 93–5
Warren, Joyce, 62, 72
Week on the Concord and Merrimack Rivers, 10, 19, 92, 114, 217
Weinstein, Cindy, 4, 21
White, Maunsel, 175–8, 181, 190
Whitman, Walt, 101, 110, 148, 224
Willis, N.P., 16, 24, 58, 63, 70–1, 93
Wilson, Harriet, 153, 184
women
　as entrepreneurs, 119–20, 123, 125–7, 129, 132, 205
　as hosts, 17–19, 117–18
　as moral instructors, 159, 163, 198
　as writers, 8, 17–18, 28, 62, 65, 72–3, 85, 103–4, 108, 115, 121, 158–9, 202
work ethic
　and Irving, 37
　and Thoreau, 23
works in progress, 109–12
Wright, Henry, 148–9, 160–1
writers, *see* authorship; branding of writers; women: as writers
writing, 8, 27
　see also authorship

Young America, 4, 7, 9–10, 15, 27, 33–4, 59, 150
　identity, 50
　see also Duyckinck, Evert; Melville, Herman

Zboray, Ronald J. and Mary Saracino, 112, 116, 123